IT Auditing, Second Edition Reviews

"This guidance will enable an auditor to properly determine the scope of the control environment and residual risks. The authors present the information in an easy-to-consume but comprehensive format that generates both thought and action."

—Kurt Roemer, Chief Security Strategist
Citrix

"*IT Auditing,* Second Edition is a must-have resource for auditors in today's complex computing world. This book is filled with the essential how-to guidance necessary to effectively audit today's technology."

—Shawn Irving, Sr Manager IT Security Standards & Compliance
Southwest Airlines – Information Technology

"Traditional IT audits have focused on enterprise systems using enterprise-based tools. As enterprise systems move to outsourced and cloud-based services, new cloud-based tools are needed to audit these distributed systems. Either enterprise vendors will rewrite their tools to address cloud-based systems or new and existing cloud-based tools will be used to assist auditors with these distributed systems. The book gives good insights on how to address these new challenges and provides recommendations on auditing cloud-based services."

—Matthew R. Alderman, CISSP, Director, Product Management
Qualys, Inc.

"An essential contribution to the security of Information Systems in the dawn of a wide-spread virtualized computing environment. This book is crucial reading for anyone responsible for auditing information systems."

—Peter Bassill CISSP, CITP
ISACA Security Advisory Group and CISO of Gala Coral Group

"We used the first edition in the graduate IT Audit and Risk Management class during the past year, and it was an outstanding resource for students with diverse backgrounds. I am excited about the second edition as it covers new areas like cloud computing and virtualized environments, along with updates to reflect emerging issues. The authors have done a great job at capturing the essence of IT risk management for individuals with all levels of IT knowledge."

—Mark Salamasick, Director of Center for Internal Auditing Excellence
University of Texas at Dallas School of Management

"This book is indispensible. It is comprehensive, well laid out, and easy to follow, with clear explanations and excellent advice for the auditor. This new edition is timely and will be particularly useful for those encountering the latest developments of the industry as it continues to evolve."

—Mark Vincent, CISSP
ISO for Gala Coral Group

IT Auditing: Using Controls to Protect Information Assets

Second Edition

Chris Davis
Mike Schiller

with Kevin Wheeler

New York • Chicago • San Francisco • Lisbon
London • Madrid • Mexico City • Milan • New Delhi
San Juan • Seoul • Singapore • Sydney • Toronto

The McGraw·Hill Companies

Library of Congress Cataloging-in-Publication Data

Davis, Chris (Christopher Michael)
  IT auditing : using controls to protect information assets / Chris Davis, Mike Schiller ; with Kevin Wheeler. — 2nd ed.
  Includes bibliographical references and index.
  ISBN-13: 978-0-07-174238-2
  ISBN-10: 0-07-174238-7
  1. Electronic data processing—Auditing.   2. Information auditing.   3. Computer security.   4. Computer networks—
Security measures.   I. Schiller, Mike.   II. Wheeler, Kevin.   III. Title.
  QA76.9.A93D38 2011
  005.8—dc22

2011000207

IT Auditing: Using Controls to Protect Information Assets, Second Edition

4567890 QFR QFR 10987654

ISBN: 978-0-07-174238-2
MHID: 0-07-174238-7

Sponsoring Editor Megg Morin	**Proofreader** Martin V. Benes
Editorial Supervisor Jody McKenzie	**Indexer** Karin Arrigoni
Project Editor LeeAnn Pickrell	**Production Supervisor** James Kussow
Acquisitions Coordinator Joya Anthony	**Composition** Apollo Publishing Sevice
Technical Editors Michael Cox, Michael Curry, and Vishal Mehra	**Illustration** Apollo Publishing, Lyssa Wald
Copy Editor Lisa Theobald	**Art Director, Cover** Jeff Weeks

To *my Sarah* and our wonderful children Joshua, Caleb, and Kelsea.
This project is the culmination of far too many hours away from you.
Thank you for your incredible love and support. I love you!

—Chris

To Steph, Grant, and Kate—this book was possible
only because of your love, patience, and support.
I'm amazed every day by how lucky I am
and by the joy you bring to my life.

—Mike

ABOUT THE AUTHORS

Chris Davis, MBA, CISA, CISSP, CCNP, has trained and presented in information security, forensic analysis, hardware security design, auditing, and certification curriculum for government, corporate, and university requirements. He was part of the writing teams responsible for *Hacking Exposed Computer Forensics* (McGraw-Hill Professional, 2009, 2004), *Anti-Hacker Toolkit* (McGraw-Hill Professional, 2006, 2003), and the first edition of *IT Auditing* (McGraw-Hill Professional, 2006). He also contributed to other titles, such as *Digital Crime and Forensic Science in Cyberspace* (Idea Group Publishing, 2006) and *Computer Security Handbook*, 5th Edition (Wiley, 2009). His contributions include projects and presentations for PCI-SSC Virtualization Special Interest Group, ISACA, Spice World, SANS, Gartner, Harvard, Black Hat, CEIC, and 3GSM. He is an adjunct professor for Southern Methodist University and has enjoyed positions at Accudata Systems, ForeScout, and Texas Instruments. Chris holds a bachelor's degree in nuclear engineering technologies from Thomas Edison State College and a master's in business from the University of Texas at Austin, where he specialized in information security. Chris served eight years in the U.S. Naval Submarine Fleet onboard the "special projects" submarine NR-1 and the ballistic missile submarine USS Nebraska, where delivery was guaranteed in 30 minutes or less.

Mike Schiller, CISA, has more than 15 years of experience in the IT audit field, including positions as the worldwide IT audit manager at Texas Instruments (TI) and as the IT audit manager at The Sabre Group. He is an active speaker on IT auditing, including conferences such as CACS, InfoSec World, and ASUG (Americas' SAP Users' Group), and has been an instructor of IT audit curriculum at Southern Methodist University. Mike is currently a leader of IT operations at Texas Instruments, with responsibility for the company's server, database, and storage infrastructure organization. He also has led departments such as the company's data center operations, IT asset management, central help desk, web application support, and PC support functions. In addition to his years of experience in corporate management, Mike is also involved in leadership at his church, Richardson East Church of Christ. He has a bachelor's degree in business analysis from Texas A&M University. Mike enjoys watching baseball in his spare time and has attended games in every major league stadium. His baseball allegiance is to the Texas Rangers and Cincinnati Reds. Mike's son, Grant, is a well-known baseball blogger (see http://texasrangerstrades.blogspot.com) and was named 2005 Texas Rangers Fan of the Year. Mike's daughter, Kate, is a soon-to-be-famous artist.

About the Contributing Authors

Stacey Hamaker, CIA, CISA, is the president of Shamrock Technologies, which provides enterprise-class IT consulting to Fortune 500 companies, midsized firms, and the public sector. Stacey has been heavily involved in regulatory compliance initiatives since the inception of the Sarbanes-Oxley Act of 2002. She serves on the board of the North Texas chapter of ISACA (formerly Information Systems Audit and Control Association) and is active in the Institute of Internal Auditors (IIA). Her numerous articles on Enterprise and IT Governance have been published in such industry publications as the *IS Control Journal*. Stacey's speaking engagements span local, national, and international venues. She received her MBA in MIS from the University of Texas at Arlington and her undergraduate degree in accounting from Marietta College in Ohio.

Aaron Newman is the founder and chief technology officer of Application Security, Inc. (AppSecInc). Widely regarded as one of the world's foremost database security experts, Aaron coauthored the *Oracle Security Handbook* for Oracle Press and holds patents in database encryption and monitoring. Prior to founding AppSecInc, Aaron founded several other companies in the technology area, including DbSecure, the pioneers in database security vulnerability assessment, and ACN Software Systems, a database security consulting firm. Aaron has spent the last decade managing and designing database security solutions, researching database vulnerabilities, and pioneering new markets in database security. Aaron has held several other positions in technology consulting with Price Waterhouse, Internet Security Systems, Intrusion Detection Inc., and Banker's Trust.

Kevin Wheeler, CISA, CISSP, NSA IAM/IEM, is the founder and CEO of InfoDefense, an information security consultancy. Kevin's project and employment portfolio includes organizations such as Bank of America, EDS, McAfee, Southern Methodist University, and the State of Texas. He has performed information security audits and assessments as well as information security design, computer incident response, business continuity planning, and IT security training for both government and commercial entities in the financial services, healthcare, and IT services industries. He holds a bachelor of business administration degree from Baylor University and is an active member of ISSA, ISACA, Infragard, the North Texas Electronic Crimes Task Force, and Greater Dallas Chamber of Commerce.

About the Second Edition Technical Reviewers

Michael Cox currently works as a network security engineer for Texas Instruments, where he has also worked as an IT auditor developing numerous audit programs and automated audit tools. Prior to this, he worked as a network engineer for Nortel, and he enjoys doing Linux sysadmin work whenever he can get it. Michael holds the CISSP certification and has a bachelor of arts degree in history from Abilene Christian University. Michael also served as a technical reviewer for the first edition of this book.

Mike Curry, CISA, has more than 15 years of service at Texas Instruments, the last 12 of which have been spent performing internal audits. Working as a Senior IT Auditor, he is responsible for leading audits evaluating internal controls and security over operating systems, database management systems, networks, system applications and related processes, and assessing compliance with relevant standards and regulations.

Vishal Mehra is currently responsible for the engineering and strategy of server, storage, security, and database infrastructure at Texas Instruments and holds the title of senior member of technical staff. He has worked at the company for more than 10 years and has held numerous positions ranging from web application development, to complex application/infrastructure architectures, to global infrastructure operations. As part of his current role, Vishal is also heavily involved in operating system, computing, storage, virtualization, and data protection strategies for Texas Instruments. Vishal has an MS in computer science from University of Houston, Clear Lake.

About the First Edition Technical Reviewers

Barbara Anderson, CCSP, CISSP, CCNP, CCDP, has worked in the information technology industry as a network and server security professional for more than 12 years. During that time, she has acted as a senior network security engineer, providing consulting and support for all aspects of network and security design. Barbara comes from a strong network security background and has extensive experience in enterprise design, implementation, and lifecycle management. Barbara proudly served her country for four years in the United States Air Force and has enjoyed successful positions at EDS, SMU Fujitsu, ACS, and Fishnet Security. These experiences and interactions have allowed her to become an expert in enterprise security, product deployment, and product training.

Tim Breeding, CISA, CGEIT, currently serves as senior director of U.S. Transformation Systems at Wal-Mart Stores, Inc., where his responsibilities include ensuring U.S. business user engagement in the software development lifecycle and user readiness to receive major transformational systems. Previously, Tim served as the director of information systems audit at Wal-Mart Stores, Inc. His responsibilities included oversight of project teams that assess information technology risks and mitigation strategies from both an audit and consulting capacity. Prior to joining Wal-Mart, Tim served Southwest Airlines as systems audit manager for more than 6 years. At Southwest Airlines, Tim presided over substantial growth of the IS audit function. Before joining Southwest Airlines, Tim served more than 13 years in several capacities at Texas Instruments. His responsibilities included computer operations, software development, software quality assurance, and IS audit.

Subesh Ghose has worked for Texas Instruments for the past 13 years in various IT roles. Starting in IT audit, he led audits reviewing the internal controls of various data centers, ERP implementations, and infrastructure environments. As part of his role, he was responsible for designing and implementing audit methodologies for various technical platforms and performing project reviews to provide internal control guidance early in the project development lifecycle. Since then, he has managed functions in IT security and security infrastructure, where he oversaw the architecture/process development for securing external collaborative engagements, development of security controls in enterprise projects, and operations supporting Texas Instruments' enterprise identity management systems. Currently, Subesh manages the infrastructure supporting Texas Instruments' global manufacturing operations. Subesh has an MS in computer science from Southern University.

Keith Loyd, CISSP, CISA, worked for 7 years in the banking industry, where he developed technology solutions for stringent legislative business requirements. He was responsible for implementing and testing networking solutions, applications, hardened external-facing platforms, databases, and layered mechanisms for detecting intrusion. After moving to Texas Instruments, Keith primarily dealt with vulnerability and quality testing new applications and projects, worldwide incident response, and civil investigations. He earned a BS in information technology from Cappella University and an MS in information assurance from Norwich University. Keith passed away after the first edition of this book was published and is greatly missed.

CONTENTS AT A GLANCE

CONTENTS

FOREWORD

As I reviewed this book, which has been effectively updated to cover new and emerging audit topics, I couldn't help but reflect on the history of our great profession.

The word "audit" can be traced back in history to the Latin word *auditio,* meaning a hearing, and the French word *auditre,* meaning audible. The concept of an audit as a means of informing others about the health of businesses didn't take hold until the 1700s, with the advent of large trading "partnerships" such as the East India Company and the Hudson's Bay Company. Absentee owners and financiers wanted assurance on the safety of their investment.

The 1800s saw the invention of the steam engine, and huge industries arose with the advent of railroads and easy shipment of goods over land. But all was not well, and many railways in England failed. Investors wanted to know what caused this collapse and what happened to their money. In the mid 1800s, William Welch Deloitte, who specialized in railway bankruptcies, started the firm that, following a number of mergers and acquisitions, today bears only his name.

All the while, handwritten, double-entry bookkeeping—the key to modern accounting—was being dealt with in much the same manner for almost 500 years. But change was on the horizon. Inventor Herman Hollerith devised a system of encoding data on cards through a series of punched holes. This system proved useful in statistical work and was used in the 1890 U.S. census. Hollerith also designed a means to "read" the cards by passing them through electrical contacts. Closed circuits, which indicated hole positions, could then be selected and counted. His Tabulating Machine Company, incorporated in 1896, was a predecessor to the International Business Machines Corporation—today's IBM.

Throughout the first few decades of the 1900s and up to the 1980s, punched cards remained a widely used method to input data. Accounting machines were invented that could read and accumulate numeric information using counter wheels to add and subtract numbers. This ability to electronically "read" data paved the way for computing in the 1940s. It applied the idea of machines that could read and record numbers to the field of scientific calculation previously dominated by logarithms and other tables of functions and hand-operated machines for adding, subtracting, multiplying, and dividing numbers.

The information age was born, some say, with the invention of the digital computer ENIAC 1 in 1944. Although there is little evidence to support the alleged 1943 statement by Thomas J. Watson Jr., "I think there is a world market for maybe five computers," IBM archives indicate that in a 1953 presentation to stockholders, his son, Thomas J. Watson, Jr., then president of IBM, spoke about the new IBM 701 Electronic Data Processing Machine and indicated that the company had identified "some 20 concerns that we thought could use such a machine."

More than half a century later, we have seen unprecedented changes in the way business is conducted. We quickly evolved from the pen-and-pencil world to machine accounting, computers, the wired world, and now a wireless world. To perform meaningful audit work, the accounting profession quickly embraced computer technology—first with new techniques such as flowcharting to assess and document computer application processes and controls and shortly thereafter with the development of generalized auditing software, such as the Haskins & Sells Auditape system in 1968 to interrogate client computer files directly.

In the 1960s, auditors, through The Institute of Internal Auditors and the newly formed EDP Auditors Association (now ISACA), further pushed the information technology audit envelope. At that time, there were only a few articles and three recognized books on IT auditing, or as it was known in those days, electronic data processing (EDP) auditing: *Electronic Data Processing and Auditing* by Felix Kaufman, Ph.D, CPA, published in 1961; *Auditing with the Computer* by Wayne S. Boutell, Ph.D., CPA, published in 1965; and *Auditing and EDP* by Gordon Davis, Ph.D., published in 1968. I have all three in my library! It is not often that one can read a number of articles and three books and have absorbed the documented collective wisdom on a subject. That was the way it was with EDP auditing at that time.

From the heady days of the 1960s when I joined the auditing profession, IT auditing has had to keep pace with the advent of new technologies, new risks, and new threats. The profession of IT audit and control has grown to include many related activities and disciplines, such as risk management and security and value-based assessments, to mention a few. Yet, their roots still go back to IT auditing, and that is where *IT Auditing: Using Controls to Protect Information Assets*, Second Edition, excels.

The challenges facing IT auditors today revolve around change—in technology, the business environment, business risks, the legislative and regulatory environment, and the knowledge and skills required to audit effectively in this evolving environment.

Today's auditing environment involves cloud computing, virtualization, and, on the horizon, the parallel universe and multicore processing. The role of the IT auditor must change to match these new requirements and associated risks, and the IT auditor must understand the business and the business risks to audit the business and its supporting applications effectively. Knowledge requirements are expanding, as are the skills required to perform in the new environments.

Social networks, bring-your-own-technology, and portable media only serve to increase the risks facing business today. Social networks introduce risks of entities' information being posted, blogs created, or inappropriate photos and other information circulating in the public arena. Increasingly entities are requiring, encouraging, or permitting employees to use their own technology for business purposes. Mobile phones, smart phones, tablets, netbooks, and other technologies are all finding their way into the office environment. However, since they are personally owned, the entity has little control over their content or use. Similarly risky are portable media, memory sticks, camera cards that can be used to store data, and other devices expose the entity to potential loss of information and data.

IT Auditing: Using Controls to Protect Information Assets, Second Edition, meets the challenge of capturing both the roots of IT auditing and the emerging technologies and issues with which today's auditors must familiarize themselves. The book provides IT audit and assurance professionals with superb information on the profession of IT auditing. Its scope provides information for novice IT auditors as well as more seasoned professionals. It covers areas frequently missed by providing a clear definition of IT audit and the roles it can play, explaining what an appropriate mandate is and clarifying when IT audit should become involved.

The book starts out by explaining why to perform an IT audit, how to organize an IT audit function and develop its mandate, and how to recruit skilled resources. Too many books skip or gloss over these important topics. From beginning to end, the information in *IT Auditing*, Second Edition is presented in a clear and concise manner. The notes provide useful information to clarify comments or provide insight into performing audit work, furthering one's career, or understanding the politics of business environments. The audit checklists provide good "memory joggers" at the management level to help ensure that the planning is appropriate and that the audit progresses as planned. The "how" sections provide good detailed instruction on conducting specific IT audit work.

IT Auditing: Using Controls to Protect Information Assets, Second Edition covers a lot of ground that is essential to the IT audit and assurance professional. It is an excellent resource to help readers understand our rapidly changing profession.

Robert G. Parker, MBA, FCA, CA*CISA, CMC
Past International President, ISACA
November 20, 2010

Robert G. Parker, MBA, FCA, CA*CISA, CMC, is a retired Enterprise Risk Management partner from Deloitte & Touche, where he had responsibility for its privacy and business continuity practices as well as internal risk management for the Canadian ERS practice. A frequent author and presenter, he was international president of ISACA from 1986 to 1987 and continues to serve on various ISACA committees. He is the principal architect of ISACA's Information Technology Assurance Framework, a member of the CICA's Information Technology Advisory Committee, a member of the Board of the University of Waterloo's Centre for Information Systems Integrity and Assurance (UW-CISA), and a member of the AICPA-CICA Privacy Task Force.

ACKNOWLEDGMENTS

We simply could not have done this without the help of many, many people. It was an amazing challenge coordinating the necessary depth of corporate, legal, and technical expertise across so many subjects. Many old and new friends; organizations such as ISACA, NIST, and OWASP; and many others donated knowledge, time, techniques, tools, and much more to make this project a success.

Writing this book required tireless hours of writing, research, and corroboration among the authors, contributing authors, technical editors, industry peers, copy editors, layout team, and publisher leadership team while our loved ones took the brunt of our efforts. It is only appropriate that we thank and acknowledge those that supported and carried us despite ourselves. We are truly grateful to each of you.

The wonderful and overworked team at McGraw-Hill is simply outstanding. We sincerely appreciate your dedication, coaching, and long hours during the course of this project. Megg Morin, this book is a result of your tireless dedication to the completion of this project and your extreme patience. We look forward to working with you again in the future. We would also like to extend a big round of thanks to Joya Anthony, our acquisitions coordinator, for her coordination and work with the technical editors. Thank you so much for being a part of this. We also would like to thank the wonderful efforts of project editor LeeAnn Pickrell; copy editor Lisa Theobald; proofreader Martin Benes; indexer Karin Arrigoni; editorial supervisor Jody McKenzie; production supervisor James Kussow; art director, cover, Jeff Weeks; and compositor and illustrator, Apollo Publishing and Lyssa Wald.

A special thank you goes to Michael Cox, Mike Curry, and Vishal Mehra for their deep technical reviews for the second edition. Your involvement truly made the difference. Your reviews were wonderful, detailed, and significant in providing a useful product for the readers. Additionally, thank you Robert G. Parker for taking the time to deliver an incredible introduction to this work and to Michael Cangemi for the foreword to the first edition. Your words are thoughtful, kind, and relevant, and they illustrate the experience you have in this industry.

We also want to acknowledge and extend our thanks to the many people who were involved with editing, reviewing, and publishing the first edition. Without your work on the first edition, there would be no second edition. Thank you to our first edition technical reviewers: Barbara Anderson, Tim Breeding, Michael Cox (who signed on for a second tour of duty with this edition), Subesh Ghose, and Keith Loyd (we miss you, Keith). And thank you to the fine folks at McGraw-Hill who played critical roles in the first edition: Jane Brownlow, Jennifer Housh, Madhu Bhardwaj, Jim Madru, Ragini Pandey, Kevin Broccoli, Janet Walden, George Anderson, and Jeff Weeks. Last but not least, thank you to the contributing authors from the first edition: Stacey Hamaker, Aaron Newman, and Kevin Wheeler.

We are truly grateful to four organizations that allowed us to borrow content. We would like to thank the people at ISACA for bringing a cohesive knowledge set to the auditing field and the CISA certification. There is still much work to be done, and we as a team would like to encourage our peers to contribute to this wonderful knowledge base. Likewise, thank you Jeff Williams and Mark Curphey for founding and contributing to OWASP. Your selfless investments are helping thousands of professionals worldwide, and many more that would never know where to start securing their websites. Thank you. And thank you to NIST, specifically Peter Mell, for supporting this book and allowing us to leverage some of your work in Chapter 14. The work you're doing to bring consistency and understanding to the subject of cloud computing and its security are a benefit to all of us in the IT security and audit professions. And thank you Craig Isaacs of the Unified Compliance Framework for allowing us to use your materials in our book and a recent class at Southern Methodist University.

Finally, thank you to everyone who bought, read, used, and supported the first edition of this book. Special thanks to the folks at ISACA for recognizing our work by carrying it in your bookstore and to all of the professors (such as Mark Salamasick of the University of Texas at Dallas) for selecting our book to supplement your courses. We have been extremely honored and humbled by the response we received to the first edition and inspired to improve on our work with this second edition.

—Chris and Mike

Thank you, Sarah. This book would not exist without you. I'm thankful and blessed to have you as my wife and look forward to the many wonderful years we have left. I love you! Little Joshua, Caleb, and Kelsea: your mother and I love you so much. Not a day goes by that we don't think about sharing, teaching, and helping you to grow and mature into your own. Thanks to our Lord and Savior for the many opportunities and blessings you've so generously given us.

I also want to thank Mike Schiller. I always appreciate the opportunity to work with you and learn from you. Your input greatly impacted the quality of the book, and your selfless friendship and leadership has impacted me personally and professionally. I'm grateful to have you as part of this project.

Through all of this project's challenges, between the authors, contributors, reviewers, editors, layout team, and project managers, we pulled it off. I also want to thank Anton Abaya, David Vance, and Stephen Lengel for their helpful insights. Thank each of you for your generous time and reviews. Many of you balanced active work and home lives to fit this into your schedule. Thank you for your tremendous help. The crew at McGraw-Hill is a wonderful group to work with. I am grateful for your outstanding guidance and continual support.

And finally, a special thank you goes to my father for passing along his interest in how everything works and patiently answering my endless barrage of questions as a child. Now that I have my own...I understand.

—Chris

I would like to thank my good friends Tim Breeding, Michael Cox, Mike Curry, Subesh Ghose, and Vishal Mehra for helping with this book and making it better than we could have made it on our own. You're each not only outstanding technical professionals but also outstanding friends.

I would also like to thank Chris Davis for his excellent work and for being my valued partner in this endeavor. I'm grateful for your friendship and always value the opportunity to work with and learn from you.

Thanks also to Megg Morin and Joya Anthony of McGraw-Hill for their support of this project and dedication to making it happen. And I would like to express appreciation to Edward Dorsey, whose Unix auditing class (via the MIS Training Institute and Automated Design Enterprises, Inc.) way back in 1997 was very influential to me and inspired a lot of the content in Chapter 7.

To Shawn Irving, thank you for your continued friendship throughout the years and for serving as an unofficial advisor for the second edition. The insights you provided resulted in significant improvements to this edition.

I would also like to thank the many people who have worked on audit teams that I managed. It was an honor to work with you, and there's a piece of each of you in this book. Thanks to Jon Mays and Nancy Jones, for putting up with me in my first management position; to Sally West and Andrea Khan, for enhancing my knowledge of project auditing; to Chris Speegle, Steve Holt, Kylonnie Jackson, Dottie Vo, Dean Irwin, Gus Coronado, Hans Baartmans, Prabha Nandakumar, and all the others who worked with me on the TI teams I managed—it was a pleasure and I learned from you all.

Thanks to Kirk Tryon and Jay Blanchard, for being my friends and peers for so many years. It was fun. A lot of our discussions are reflected in this book. Extra thanks to Kirk for letting me pick your brain and helping me improve Chapter 1 for this edition. Thanks also to Richard Hudson and Geoff Sloma for giving me the chance to learn and grow as a manager.

Of course, thanks go to God and Jesus Christ for my salvation and for the many blessings in my life.

Most of all, thanks to my family. To Mom and Dad, the perfect parents, for all your love and guidance throughout my life. To David, for not only being a great brother, but one of my best friends. To Kate, for all the energy and happiness you bring to my life. Now that I'm done, I promise to play some extra Littlest Pet Shop with you. And I'll take you to Disney World, too. To Grant, my pal, for being patient about this book (even when it was hard), for how proud you make me, and for how much fun we have together. I know it was frustrating to deal with all the time I was locked away in my office yet again for this edition. Now that it's over, I'll play hockey or football in the game room with you every day for two weeks. And the absolute biggest thanks go to my wonderful wife, Stephanie, for believing in me and supporting me, for being my proofreader, and for being my best friend. Every year, I'm more amazed by how lucky I am to have you as my partner in life. I couldn't have done this without you. To show my appreciation, I promise not to sign up for any extracurricular activities for at least six months.

—Mike

INTRODUCTION

When we began writing this book, we had a fundamental tenet: Write a clear handbook for creating the organization's IT audit function and for performing their IT audits. We wanted this book to provide more than checklists and textbook theories but instead to provide real-life practical guidance from people who have performed IT audit work day in and day out in real corporations. If we've been successful, reading this book will accomplish three objectives for the reader, above and beyond what can be obtained from most IT auditing books and classes:

Guide the reader in how to perform the IT audit function in such a way that the auditors maximize the value they provide to the company.

Part I of this book is dedicated to providing practical guidance on how to perform the IT audit function in such a way that it will be considered an essential and respected element of the company's IT environment. This guidance is pulled from years of experience and best practices, and even the most experienced of IT auditors will find a plethora of useful tools and techniques in those chapters.

Enable the reader to perform thorough audits of common IT topics, processes, and technologies.

Part II of this book is dedicated to guiding the reader with practical, detailed advice on not only what to do but also *why* and *how* to do it. Too many IT audit resources provide bullet-oriented checklists without empowering the auditor with enough information to understand why they're performing that task or how exactly to accomplish the step. Our goal is to fill that gap for the reader.

Give the reader exposure to IT audit standards and frameworks as well as the regulations that are currently driving the IT audit profession.

Part III focuses on standards and frameworks such as COBIT, ITIL, and ISO 17799 as well as regulations such as Sarbanes-Oxley, HIPAA, and PCI. Another goal of this section is to demystify risk assessment and management, which is required by most regulations.

A wealth of knowledge and resources for hardening systems and performing detailed penetration tests are available in other texts. That is not the focus of this book. In our experience as auditors, we have been called on more often to judge the quality of internal controls from an insider's standpoint. Therefore, the majority of audit steps in this book are written with the assumption that the auditor has full access to all configuration files, documentation, and information. This is not a hackers' guidebook but is instead a guidebook on how an auditor can assess and judge the internal controls and security of the IT systems and processes at his or her company.

How This Book Is Organized

This book is organized into three parts. Part I, "Audit Overview," helps you understand the IT audit process, how to build and maintain an effective IT audit team, and how to maximize the value of the IT audit function. Part II, "Auditing Techniques," then helps you understand what specific components or audit steps might be necessary for an audit of a specific system or process. Finally, Part III, "Frameworks, Standards, and Regulations," covers the frameworks, standards, regulations, and risks that govern the scope of the audit function.

Audit Technique Chapters

Part II contains a series of suggested audit programs or techniques for commonly audited systems and processes. The chapters in this section are structured to help you quickly digest the information that's most useful to you.

Background

This part of the chapter contains information about the topic's history or background information that helps you acclimate to the subject matter.

Auditing Essentials

For chapters dealing with a specific technology, this part of the chapter describes getting around within the technology and introduces you to basic concepts, commands, and tools.

Test Steps

This is the meat of the chapters in Part II and provides details about what the auditor should look for, why they should do so (that is, what risk is being addressed), and how the step can be performed.

This is the audit step that should be performed The text immediately following the step states why this step is important. This section states the reason why, such as the risk and business need, the step should be performed.

How

This describes how to perform the step. We commonly use design elements such as tables and code listings to help you navigate the content.

```
This is an example code listing.
```

Tools and Technology

This section lists the tools used in the test steps and other tools not covered but mentioned as popular for more closely examining the technology. The purpose of this is to provide in a shortened format some of the tools readers might want to consider as they look further into the technology.

Knowledge Base

This section provides a list of websites and books where readers can find more information about the topics covered in the chapter. We can't discuss everything, but we can point to other places where others discuss more than you could possibly want to know.

Master Checklist(s)

This check-boxed table summarizes the steps listed in the chapter. Similar to other checklists, you may need to customize this checklist according to what makes sense to you and what you consider to be your own high priorities.

A Final Word to Our Readers

Thank you for taking the time to read this book. Technology continues to evolve and audit techniques need to evolve as well. In the years since the first edition of this book was released in 2006, areas such as virtualization and cloud computing have matured and entered the mainstream. In this second edition, you will find all-new chapters providing guidance on auditing cloud computing and outsourced operations, virtualization, and storage. In addition, all other chapters have been updated and enhanced to reflect recent trends and advances.

We have put countless hours and enormous effort into creating something we hope will be useful for you. Read this book all the way through, and then, when you are done using it as a tutorial, you can keep it around as a reference. Auditing is a detail-oriented job, and it is easy to get overwhelmed and overlook something. In addition, it is easy to get in over your head. This book is a great place to start, learn, and expand on what you know. We hope you enjoy reading this book as much as we enjoyed writing it. Good luck in all your audits.

PART I

Audit Overview

Building an Effective Internal IT Audit Function

In this chapter we'll discuss the purpose of internal audit departments and how they can best be leveraged to provide a benefit to the company. We will discuss

- The audit department's real mission
- The concept of independence and how to avoid misusing it
- How to add value beyond formal audits via consulting and early involvement
- How to enhance effectiveness by building relationships
- The role of the information technology (IT) audit and how to choose the correct focus
- How to build and maintain an effective IT audit team

The philosophies and guidance provided in this chapter form a foundation on which the rest of the book is built. Although this first chapter is written from an internal auditor's perspective, the concepts and philosophies presented here can be adapted to guide the external audit function as well. The rest of this book (certainly Part II) is essentially internal/external auditor neutral.

Why Are We Here? (The Internal Audit Department's Mission)

Before you can develop an effective internal audit department, you must first come to an understanding of the department's purpose. Why does the internal audit department exist? What's the end goal?

Is your purpose to issue reports? To raise issues? To make people look bad? To show how smart you are and how dishonest, incompetent, and corrupt the rest of the company is? To flex your muscles and show that you can do anything and tell on anyone because you report to the board of directors? Hopefully, it's obvious that none of these is an appropriate answer. Sadly, though, you will find that many (perhaps most) internal audit departments function as if the answer is indeed one or more of the preceding examples. Many audit departments spend their existence in adversarial relationships with the rest of the company, keeping themselves comfortably removed from, and "independent" of, everyone else. Unfortunately, such departments are missing the point by failing to realize the potential benefits that they could be providing to their companies.

Most audit departments were formed by the company's audit committee (a subset of the board of directors) to provide the committee with independent assurance that *internal controls* are in place and functioning effectively. In other words, the audit committee wants an objective group that will tell it what's "really going on" in the company. The committee wants someone it can trust to reveal all the evildoers who refuse to implement internal controls. Internal audit departments usually report directly to the chairman of the audit committee, so they feel protected from the repercussions that could result from blowing the whistle on the hordes of dishonest managers within the company.

Despite the levity in the preceding paragraph, it is absolutely essential that the audit committee have an internal audit function that can serve as their eyes and ears within the company. This is critical for the committee to function and serve the company's shareholders. In addition, most companies' audit departments also report to an executive within the company, such as the chief executive officer (CEO) or the chief financial officer (CFO). Later in this chapter, we'll discuss this reporting relationship; for now, you should know that senior management, just like the audit committee, is interested in the state of the company's internal controls. From an IT perspective, the audit committee and senior management want honest answers to such questions as, "Are our firewalls really secure?" and "Is our plan to collaborate and share networks with our biggest rival going to expose us to any security concerns?" This is certainly an important role for the audit department to play. However, this is not the whole picture.

Merely reporting issues accomplishes nothing, except to make people look bad, get them fired, and create hatred of auditors. The real value comes when issues are addressed and problems are solved. In other words, reporting the issues is a means to an end. In this context, the end result improves the state of internal controls at the company. Reporting them provides a mechanism by which the issues are brought to light and can therefore receive the resources and attention needed to fix them. If I tell senior management that I discovered a hole in the wall of our most important data center, it may help in my goal of making myself look good at the expense of others, but the hole is still there, and the company is still at risk. It's when the hole is patched that I've actually done something that adds value to the company (and that's true only if the company wasn't already aware of and planning to fix the hole prior to my audit).

Therefore, the real mission of the internal audit department is to help improve the state of internal controls at the company. Admittedly, this is accomplished by performing audits and reporting the results, but these acts provide no value in and of themselves. They provide value only when the internal control issues are resolved. This is an important distinction to remember as you develop your approach to auditing and, most important, to dealing with the people who are the "targets" of your audits.

 NOTE The internal audit department's goal should be to promote internal controls and to help the company develop cost-effective solutions for addressing issues. This requires a shift in focus from "reporting" to "improving." Like any other department, the audit department exists in order to add value to the company via its specific area of expertise—in this case, its knowledge of internal controls and how to evaluate them.

In summary, the internal audit department's mission is twofold:

- To provide independent assurance to the audit committee (and senior management) that internal controls are in place at the company and are functioning effectively.
- To improve the state of internal controls at the company by promoting internal controls and by helping the company identify control weaknesses and develop cost-effective solutions for addressing those weaknesses.

The rest of this chapter will discuss how this mission can be accomplished most effectively, specifically for the IT audit function.

 NOTE   The term *internal controls* is used frequently throughout this chapter. Stated in the simplest terms, internal controls are mechanisms that ensure the proper functioning of processes within the company. Every system and process exists for some specific business purpose. The auditor must look for risks that could impact the accomplishment of those purposes and then ensure that internal controls are in place to mitigate those risks. Chapter 2 delves further into the meaning of this term.

Independence: The Great Myth

Independence is one of the cornerstone principles of an audit department. It is also one of the biggest excuses used by audit departments to avoid adding value. Almost all audit departments point to their independence as one of the keys to their success and the reason that the audit committee can rely on them.

But what is independence really? According to *Webster's Universal College Dictionary*, *independence* is "the quality or state of being independent." Since this is not very helpful, let's look at the word *independent*, which Webster describes as "not influenced or controlled by others; thinking or acting for oneself." This definition fits with the concept that's flaunted by most audit departments. Since they, at least partially, report to the chairman of the audit committee, they believe that they are therefore not influenced or controlled by others. But this isn't really true; let's examine this a little closer.

Although the audit department reports to a member of the board of directors, in almost every company, the audit director also reports to the company's CFO or CEO (Figure 1-1). The budget for the audit department is usually controlled by this executive, and so is the compensation paid to members of the audit department. It is hard to see how a person can feel that he or she is not being influenced by these individuals. In addition, the internal auditors generally work in the same building as their fellow employees, inevitably forming relationships outside the audit department. The auditors have 401k plans just like all other employees, usually consisting largely of company stock. Therefore, the success of the company is of prime interest to the auditors.

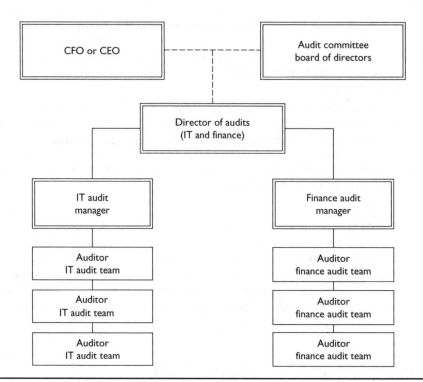

Figure 1-1 Audit team reporting structure

More important, as will be discussed later in this chapter, most successful audit departments include some people who have joined the department from other areas in the company and/or plan to rotate out of the audit department and into another area of the company at some point. You can talk all you want about independence, but these auditors know that if they tick off a lot of people, they're going to have a tough time finding another job in the company. If an IT auditor plans to move into the IT organization, it's probably best if the chief information officer (CIO) doesn't think that the auditor is an arrogant, know-nothing idiot.

It should be apparent by now that internal audit departments are not truly independent. Nevertheless, the core concept behind the independent auditor role is valid and important. An auditor must not feel undue pressure to bury issues and must believe that he or she will be allowed to "do the right thing." This is where the relationship with the board of directors comes into play. On those rare occasions when company management truly refuses to do the right thing, the audit department must have the ability to go to the board with some expectation of protection from management's wrath. This should be a tool used only as a last resort. Ultimately it is not healthy if the auditors constantly have to go over management's head.

NOTE The bottom line is this: As an auditor, you work for the company and report to its management; therefore, you are *not* independent.

It seems that *objective* is perhaps a more appropriate word than *independent* when describing an internal auditor's behavior. Objectivity requires that the auditor be unbiased and that he or she not be influenced by personal feelings or prejudice. Although the internal auditor, by definition, is not really independent, it is fair to expect him or her to be objective. Good auditors are able and willing to put their personal feelings aside during an audit and view circumstances in an unbiased fashion.

To maximize their effectiveness, internal auditors should capitalize on their lack of independence. In other words, instead of doing their best to sit in an ivory tower and pretend that they're not part of the everyday business, they should leverage their knowledge of the business. No external audit firm can bring the depth of knowledge of the company's operations to bear during audits that a properly constructed internal audit group can. If you refuse to get involved and be a part of what's going on in the company, and if you refuse to hire auditors with prior knowledge of the company's business and operations, all you're doing is making it easy for management to outsource the audit function.

 NOTE As an auditor, you need to show the board and senior management that they could never hire an outside firm that would have the knowledge of and relationships within the company that you do. You need to prove that using your internal auditors offers the company a competitive advantage. Otherwise, you're just a bottom-line cost, and if management can perform the function for a lower cost with another provider, that is what they'll do.

Consulting and Early Involvement

There's more to being an auditor than auditing. Although performing formal audits is a critical and necessary function of the audit department, the cost of correcting issues and adding controls post-implementation is significantly higher than the cost of doing it right the first time. In terms of independence, there is no difference between providing an assessment of a system or solution prior to implementation and providing an assessment after implementation. There is a difference, however, in how much value the auditor is adding to the company.

NOTE Just like quality, internal controls need to be built in up front.

Unfortunately, many auditors use independence as an excuse not to add value and not to provide opinions. You can be independent and still work side-by-side with your fellow employees to help them as they develop a solution to an internal control problem. Being independent doesn't mean that you can't provide an assessment of controls within a system prior to deployment. Time and time again, you'll see internal audit departments that refuse to provide guidance and input to teams that are developing new systems or processes. They say that they can't provide input on the controls within the system because to do so means that they'll no longer be independent. They say, "How can you audit something if you've already signed off on the controls?" This is a great way to avoid work, but it is utter nonsense.

Many auditors are terrified when they are asked for a pre-implementation opinion. What if they give bad advice? Then they are as responsible for the control failure as the IT folks who implemented the system. Surely it's better to say nothing and let the IT people "sink or swim" on developing controls, right? The auditors always can audit them later and tell them where they screwed up. This is a ridiculous scenario, but, unfortunately, it happens all the time. It's wrong for the company, and it's wrong for the auditor. Auditors need to be willing to step up to the plate and provide input. Whether you provide an opinion before implementation or after, you still should be providing essentially the same input. How does providing such input this week damage your independence, whereas providing it next week (after implementation) doesn't do the same? There's no logic to it.

Is there a chance that you might miss something or give bad advice with such upfront involvement? Of course. Just as there's a chance during any traditional audit that you might miss something or offer bad advice. There's always a risk, but you need to get over it and do your best.

 NOTE A key question relates to the future independence (or objectivity) of the auditor who performed the upfront consulting work. Can the auditor be allowed to audit the system in the future? Or is this person compromised by the fact that he or she signed off on the controls and won't want to look bad by admitting that something was missed? This is worth considering, but we all need to reserve the right to "get smarter" and not apologize if a post-implementation audit results in an issue being raised that we didn't consider pre-implementation. The auditor who was involved before implementation is going to be your most knowledgeable resource for a post-implementation audit. It seems a shame not to use this resource. Who is better suited to perform a detailed audit than the person who was involved with the project team in the first place? If the auditor's objectivity is questionable, you might consider making him or her a team member but not the team leader. This will provide an extra layer of review over the auditor's work to ensure that the person is not being unduly influenced by prior work.

When it comes to working with teams before implementation, some lines shouldn't be crossed. The auditor generally should be involved with the team in an advisory capacity, which can and should include being involved in detailed discussions regarding how the internal controls are going to be designed. The auditor should not be afraid to brainstorm with the team about how the controls should work. However, this should not include actually executing the control, writing the code for implementing it, or configuring the system. You can't both own the control and audit it, but you should feel comfortable providing as much input as possible regarding what the control should look like. To do less is just limiting your ability to do what you are paid to do, which is to improve the quality of the company's internal controls.

Four Methods for Consulting and Early Involvement

Now that we've established that it's okay to speak to your fellow employees about internal controls even when you're not auditing them, let's talk about some of the best ways to do this. We will discuss four methods for promoting internal controls at the company outside of your formal audits:

- Early involvement
- Informal audits
- Knowledge sharing
- Self-assessments

Early Involvement

Any manufacturing firm will tell you that it's cheaper to build quality into a product than to try to add it after the fact. Internal controls are the same way: Once you've created a system, tested it, and implemented it, it is much more expensive to go back and change it than if you had done it right the first time. As an auditor, you're also much more likely to encounter resistance after implementation. Everyone has moved on to other projects, and none of them are motivated to go back and make changes to a completed project. On the other hand, if you can provide the internal control requirements early in the process, they become just another part of the project scope to the implementers, and they don't mind it so much (provided that the control requirements are reasonable).

How you accomplish this differs by company, but every company should have some sort of project approval or review process. (If your company doesn't, you've got an issue right there that needs to be addressed.) Try to shoehorn yourself into this process. Does the project review group meet weekly or monthly? Try to get yourself invited to it. Even better, if the company has a group of people or an organization that has to sign off at various stages of a project before it can be implemented, ask to be part of the sign-off group. Be bold about it. Forget about all that "independent auditor" stuff and be willing to sign your name to something and take some ownership in the company. Just make it clear that your role is to provide input on the internal controls of the system or technology and nothing else. There is, of course, the possibility that you will make a mistake and sign off on the project; even though the system has internal control weaknesses, but that's a chance you have to take. All the other approvers are putting their names on the line, and you need to be willing to do the same, unless you are satisfied with the ivory tower model of audit departments that minimizes their value.

You may run into some resistance as you try to take on this additional role. The IT groups may not want you at their meetings, and they may not want to have to deal with you during project implementation. This is especially true if you're working for an audit department that has a history of adversarial relationships and/or hasn't been successful at displaying its value in the past. They may see you as someone to be avoided, not someone to be invited to the table as a participant. You may need to begin by developing good relationships. Be sure to let the IT groups know that your motive isn't to slow anything down or stop anything; instead, you are expressing a willingness to step up to the plate and help out. You shouldn't suggest that you think they need your approval, but let them know that you'd like to be part of the solution, not part of the problem. Let them know that you might be auditing them some day and that you want to help them build their system so that it will pass an audit when the time comes. Point out that the company pays you to be an expert on internal controls and that you would like to share that expertise with them during their project implementation so that you can help them to build in the controls up front.

> **NOTE** Nowhere can you add more value to the company than by early involvement.

Early involvement is infinitely more cost-effective and efficient than after-the-fact audits. If you can work your way into being involved in projects before implementation, and if you can prove the value of your involvement, you will find yourself getting more requests than you ever imagined. It will be tempting to turn down some projects, saying that they're not important enough or don't have any internal control impact, but that would be a mistake. You don't want to chase away people who are looking to be educated on internal controls. If you are successful at your attempts to be invited to the table, you will need to dedicate appropriate resources to make it work.

So what does it really mean to be involved in projects pre-implementation? Does it mean that you have to perform a full audit on each and every project? Not at all. This obviously would be impossible from a resource standpoint. Many auditors are confused about what they need to do when asked to provide input on a project. It seems like a daunting task, and it is important to simplify it. From a conceptual standpoint, it's no different from planning a traditional audit. When you're getting ready to execute an audit, what do you do? You spend time understanding the system, technology, or process that you'll be auditing. You then think through the risks involved and determine what sorts of controls you expect to see to mitigate those risks.

This is exactly what you do with early involvement. It's just like planning an audit. You need to spend time understanding the system, technology, or process being implemented. You need to think through the potential risks that might affect its security, integrity, or reliability. You then can provide input to the teams regarding what controls you would be looking for if you were auditing the implementation after the fact. Basically, you're planning the audit and sharing the key points of your audit plan with the auditee as the system is being developed (The chapters in Part II of this book will serve as an excellent guide in performing this planning). From your standpoint, you are sharing your audit plan. From their standpoint, you are giving them a set of internal control requirements. If this is all you can do, you've already provided an excellent service.

However, if you're in a position to get the project team to confirm with you how it has implemented those control requirements so that you can ensure the controls appropriately mitigate the risks, then you've really arrived.

Is the auditor actually required to perform independent testing and validation to ensure that the controls are working as described? In other words, does the auditor really have to perform an audit of the system before implementation before signing off on it? This is probably a good idea for major enterprise application implementations and other implementations of that magnitude, but from a resource standpoint this is not realistic for every project that comes along. It is perfectly acceptable to make it clear to all that your sign-off is based on the assumption that the information that you've been given is accurate. If you audit the system later and it turns out that the controls weren't implemented as described, it's not a failure on your part.

You should also understand that not all of these early involvement opportunities will be time-consuming. Some projects have a significant internal control impact. For example, implementation of new tools that provide the ability for external business partners to access the internal network needs to be scrutinized heavily and will take some time. On the other hand, implementation of a new conference room scheduling system has almost no internal control impact and should be quickly dispositioned by the auditor. You should not indicate that internal controls are not applicable to the system and refuse to participate; instead, you can provide some high-level guidance and be done with the project for all intents and purposes. There's a big difference image-wise between saying that a system doesn't matter to you and saying that you want to provide sign-off as usual but that you don't have many concerns: one is a negative message, and the other is positive.

 NOTE Remember that for every project with which you're involved, no matter how insignificant it is from an audit standpoint, you have a unique opportunity to educate your fellow employees on internal controls and their importance.

Informal Audits

One of the issues facing almost every department in almost every company is resource constraints. There's never enough time to do all the things you want to do, and most departments don't have time to address all the risks out there. There are always requests for audits that you can't fulfill. Realize that if your audits are to be thorough, you'll have time to audit only a handful of areas every year. In fact, if your audit scheduling process is purely risk-based (as opposed to having everything on a set rotation), some areas will never make the cut. You'll likely never go to the audit committee and report that one of the top fifteen risks that you need to review for the year is a tiny data center in a remote location supporting a small handful of people performing a less-than-critical business process. But does this mean that you should never work with those employees to help them understand the state of their internal controls? Does this mean that you should never understand the risks at that site? There has to be some way to perform reviews of such areas without turning them into unnecessarily large efforts. The *informal audit* is the mechanism to use.

Chapter 2 discusses potential processes for forming your audit plan (that is, the list of audits you plan to perform). For now, let's take it as a given that you have some sort of risk evaluation process that helps you form your audit plan each year. Even with a plan, you'll notice two major gaps in what you'll be able to cover:

- If the process is risk-based, you'll never get to some areas.

- Sometimes management requests an audit (once you've developed the right sort of relationship with them), but that audit just doesn't make the cut after you perform a risk ranking.

It is important that formal audits be performed in a disciplined and thorough manner. The audit process is discussed in Chapter 2; for now, just accept the fact that, to do audits right, they need to be thoroughly documented and tested, including taking representative samples of data before arriving at conclusions. Although all of this is important and necessary, it is also time-consuming.

But what if you had the flexibility to perform some audits in a more on-the-fly manner? If you've built a strong IT audit team, with good depth of knowledge and experience, you should be able to let them loose to perform a "quick and dirty" review of a system, site, or technology. Remove the constraints of documenting their work in detailed work papers. Forget about taking large representative samples. Let the auditors act as consultants. Give an auditor a couple of weeks to review the controls of the area, and tell him or her that all he or she needs to produce at the end of the project is a memo summarizing the results. You'll be amazed both at the quality of the results and the appreciation shown by the people you audited. You'll also be amazed at how much the auditors are able to accomplish in a short time when released from the shackles of the normal audit process (which are important for formal audits).

Of course, it's also important that you add caveats to the work and the results. Make sure that the people you are informally auditing understand that this will not be as thorough as a formal audit, that you are not claiming that you will find all the issues, and that you are not testing statistical samples. Even though auditors tend to shy away from the word *consultant,* you should make it clear that this is exactly what you are in this case. You are loaning them your control expertise. If you are of a particularly paranoid nature, you might even want to state these caveats in your final memo so that the review doesn't come back to haunt you later if more issues are found.

A common question with these sorts of informal reviews is whether the auditors are required to track the issues to completion. There is no right answer to this question, but, in general, "No" is the best answer. This is an informal audit, and the issues have not been substantiated as thoroughly as in a formal audit. Therefore, you are on a little shakier ground when it comes to turning around and *requiring* that the issues you raised be fixed. Also, since this was an area that wasn't risky enough to make the formal audit plan, it's likely that the risks are relatively minor from a company perspective. Forcing and tracking their mitigation may be unnecessary overhead. Also, it may make others less likely to request your services in the future. If they invite you in as a consultant and then you turn around and beat them up and tell them they need to fix all the issues or be reported to the audit committee, they're not likely to ask for your help again.

But what if you uncover a major issue that is creating a significant risk for the company? Clearly, in such a case, you have an obligation to make the appropriate level of management aware of the issue and ensure that the risks are mitigated. Therefore, a happy medium for these engagements is to tell the people you're auditing that you don't intend to track the issues coming out of the review but that if you find a major issue, you'll have to make an exception. Most people will be understanding and accepting of this obligation.

What does the audit process look like for an informal audit? It should be simple and straightforward, consisting of the following basic steps:

1. The audit department should agree on the timing and scope of the informal review with the people who are to be audited.

2. The auditor who will be performing the review should create a basic checklist of areas that will be under review. (The checklists throughout this book provide a good starting point.)

3. The auditor executes those steps, keeping notes as needed but not creating work papers for review. The notes do not need to be kept after the audit is completed. Remember that speed is of the essence, and this is a consulting engagement, not a formal audit review. If you can't get comfortable with this, you'll get bogged down with documentation and process, losing the flexibility to perform this sort of review effectively.

4. At the end of the project, the auditor compiles all concerns from the review.

5. The auditor has a debriefing meeting with the people who were audited to discuss the issues and consult about how serious the issues are and potential means for addressing them.

6. The auditor documents the final list of concerns, along with relevant thoughts on resolving them, in a memo. This memo does not need to include due dates and can include the caveats mentioned earlier (for example, this is not a formal audit, we will not be tracking issues, and so on). The memo also should indicate the auditor's willingness to continue consulting with the team as it addresses these items.

7. The auditor issues the memo and archives it electronically for future reference.

This list of steps may seem overly simplistic, and this is intentional. You need to avoid over-engineering the process. The idea is that you're the department with internal control expertise, and you're consulting with other departments in this regard. Send knowledgeable, experienced auditors in, and let them "do their thing." Informal consulting engagements are another tool in your toolkit that you can use to promote internal controls at your company. They are yet another way that you can add value to your company.

 NOTE You have the internal control expertise, and you need to use it in every way imaginable. Quick, informal audits greatly increase your coverage of the company's risks and improve your ability to accomplish your mission of promoting internal controls.

Knowledge Sharing

As an internal auditor, you have a unique blend of knowledge of the company and expertise in internal controls. The internal audit department must be creative in finding new ways to share its unique knowledge with the rest of the company. Of course, much of the knowledge sharing should occur as you perform audits, as you perform consulting reviews, and as you provide input as part of your early involvement activities. However, this still leaves some gaps. In this section, we'll discuss how to close some of the remaining gaps.

One of the easiest communication vehicles should be the company's intranet. The internal audit department should have its own website. Unfortunately, for many companies, this website simply contains the audit department's organization chart, a description of its mission and processes, and its audit schedule. While these are certainly useful elements for a website, they don't offer much in the way of communication. Following are three key opportunities for obtaining additional value from the audit department's website.

Control Guidelines

As you prepare for audits, one of the most frequent questions you'll hear is, "What do you people look for?" Wouldn't it be nice if you could just tell them to go to your website for the answer?

Obviously, for some one-time audits, if you've never reviewed the area before and it will be years before you review it again, this wouldn't be practical. For common technologies and topics, though, it can be extremely helpful to provide control guidelines describing the sorts of things that you usually review during audits. The areas covered in Part II of this book are good candidates for this. Why not let people know what you look for when auditing Unix, for example? Why not let them know the basic sorts of controls you look for when auditing an application? This will not only help people prepare for your audits, but it will also provide excellent information for anyone else at the company who may be interested but whom you have no plans to audit.

If you have checklists of things you look for in an audit, it's trivial to turn those checklists into control guidelines that can be posted on the intranet and used throughout the company. For example, perhaps you have a Unix test step that says, "Ensure that a shadow password file is used to prevent users from viewing the encrypted passwords." The control guideline could say this: "A shadow password file should be used to prevent users from viewing the encrypted passwords." Turn your audit programs into control guidelines, put them on your website, and you've helped reach your goal of open communication and promotion of controls. It's important, however, to note that your control guidelines are not policy, and make sure that they supplement and support the company's formal policies.

 NOTE Posting control guidelines on your website empowers groups expecting an audit. Some groups actually will spend time up front finding weaknesses and implementing appropriate controls. This effort benefits the company and the group being audited.

Some may say that by giving your audit customers the details of what you plan to look for during an audit, they will clean up their environment prior to the audit and you therefore will not capture a true picture of the control environment. But remember that your goal is to help improve the state of internal controls at your company, not to generate issues for the audit report. Therefore, whether controls are implemented before the audit or after the audit, you've achieved your goal. If the group you will be auditing wants to prepare for the audit by performing a self-assessment and strengthening controls prior to your arrival, you should encourage and enable them. You should also partner with them during the audit to understand their processes for monitoring and maintaining those controls on an ongoing basis.

Common Issues, Best Practices, and Innovative Solutions

Auditors are in a unique position in that they are able to review the processes and technologies that exist all across the company, allowing them to note trends and to compare and contrast various organizations. Unfortunately, they rarely take time to consider how the results of an audit might be useful to other similar organizations at the company.

Many audit results are not applicable to any other organization. On the other hand, in most companies, some functions are performed by multiple decentralized organizations. For example, perhaps Unix administration is performed at each company site by the site IT folks. In such a case, the results of a Unix security audit at one site could be very useful if shared with the Unix administrators at all other sites. These results could help them to analyze their own controls to ensure that they don't have the same problems. In this way, your one audit can have an impact on other organizations months or years before you actually get around to auditing them.

It's usually not healthy to air an organization's "dirty laundry" unnecessarily, but results usually can be "sanitized" so that they do not directly indicate the organization that was audited. Even better, if an area such as Unix security is going to be audited at multiple sites, wait until you have three or four of the audits under your belt, and then compile the results to determine what issues are surfacing commonly. This can be the basis of a common issues communication sent to all personnel with similar responsibilities. This sort of message should be communicated both on your website and also as an e-mail that is sent to all relevant personnel. This provides both a push and a pull delivery mechanism for your message.

Use the auditor's company-wide perspective to compile best practices and innovative solutions from past audits. As you perform your audits, you may find that a group has implemented a control particularly well, or a group may have developed an innovative solution for an issue found commonly in other sites or groups. This information also should be compiled and shared via the website and e-mail. This will help others to improve their controls and resolve issues that they may have in their own environments.

Tools

Do you have audit tools that you use in performing your audits? Why not make those tools available to others in the company so that they can assess themselves if desired? For example, if you use a vulnerability scanning tool for reviewing the security of various devices at the company, consider making that tool available via your website, along with some basic "how-to" documentation. Of course, licensing issues must be considered, but this is worth investigating. This is another way that you can promote internal controls, allowing people to assess themselves. If you're using open-source tools, consider providing links to the websites where those tools can be retrieved. It's all part of sharing your knowledge and expertise.

NOTE Sharing the tools auditors use with others enables groups to self-assess their controls. It is important that you carefully package the tools inside a strong policy stating who can use the tools, on what systems, at what times, and with whose permission. Other things to consider are controlled areas of the audit website open only to the IT organization and how to regulate the use of hacking tools such as password crackers and spoofing utilities. Inappropriate use of these tools can compromise personal information or violate the integrity of critical data.

You may know of instances where a group has developed an innovative solution to a common problem. If the solution involved developing a tool, ask the group if you can have a copy and post it on your website for others to use. For example, if a group has developed a script to enforce password aging in a Unix NIS (Network Information Service) environment, get a copy of it and place it on your website. In this way, other organizations running NIS can access the tool and improve their control environments too.

If you use the website for this purpose, it will be important to place a caveat on your site stating that you don't provide support for the tools. You don't want to get in a position where people are calling you at all hours expecting you to help them debug problems. Of course, you should be willing to help where you're able, but you don't want to set an expectation that turns you into a software support organization. Also, you should check with your IT security organization prior to making these tools available on your website to ensure that distribution and use outside of the IT security and IT audit teams is not a violation of company policy. Finally, you should include a disclaimer stating that there are no guarantees regarding the compatibility of the tools with any specific system and suggesting that they first be executed in a test environment. There is always the risk that a tool will interact oddly with "buggy" software, and you don't want to be held responsible should something unfortunate occur.

Self-Assessments

Another concept for promoting controls outside a formal audit is the self-assessment. Entire books have been written on this concept, and it is up to each audit department to determine whether it wants to implement a control self-assessment (CSA) model formally. We will not get into the details of this process here. However, conceptually, facilitating an organization in assessing itself is another potential tool for your toolkit. This could be as simple as walking through your control guidelines (described earlier in this chapter) and asking the organization whether or not it has implemented each control. This can lead to healthy dialogue regarding the purpose of each control and what level of mitigation is truly necessary.

Earlier in this chapter, you learned about the informal audit, which is something less than a formal audit but provides an organization with good input on the state of their internal controls. The self-assessment exercise is something less than an informal audit, in that it provides absolutely no independent validation of the controls in the environment, but it also can be a useful vehicle for promoting controls. Once again, a knowledgeable and experienced auditor is critical for making this tool work.

Final Thoughts

There are many methods of reviewing and promoting internal controls at a company in addition to formal audits. Of course, one of your challenges will be getting company management and the audit committee to approve use of your resources in this way. They may be resistant to using resources for anything except formal audits. Your best bet is to get the focus away from counting how many audit reports are issued and toward looking at how the department is helping to improve internal controls at the company. If you convince management to let you try it, even on a test basis, the results will speak for themselves. You may need to put some extra reporting in place, at least at first, so you can report on how you're using your audit resources (for example, the number of projects on which you've consulted, how your involvement resulted in strengthened controls, and so on). Vocal support from the IT organization also helps. If IT is supportive of and is making adjustments based on your work and if they are willing to communicate that fact to senior management, you'll have an easier time building a sustainable program.

 NOTE If the audit department focuses solely on formal audits, it severely limits its coverage and ability to fulfill its mission successfully.

Relationship Building: Partnering vs. Policing

If your mission is to promote and improve the state of internal controls at the company, then the more informed you are about what's going on, the more effective you'll be as an auditor. Unfortunately, too many companies take the approach of doing "drive-by" audits. They decide what they want to audit with little input from management. They decide when they want to perform the audit and inform those who will be audited, sometimes with very little advance notice. They then swoop in, perform the audit, throw the issues over the wall to be fixed, tell senior management how screwed up the area is, and disappear. They are seen again only when they are beating people up for not addressing the issues by the due dates (which are often dictated by the auditors).

Audits conducted in this way are painful and unpleasant experiences; people just want to get it over with. They're likely to take the "just answer their questions and don't volunteer any information" approach. After the auditors leave, the people they have been auditing laugh about all the big, gaping internal control holes that the auditor missed. Was that audit effective? Absolutely not. It was an adversarial exercise in which the auditors had to fight their way through to the end, usually missing important issues.

NOTE An effective internal audit department considers the audit to be a partnership with fellow employees and not a policing function. An effective audit department is involved year-round with key functions and does not just swoop in and out when performing audits. The audit should be an occasional event in an ongoing relationship.

By combining your internal controls expertise with the auditee's expertise in their business and day-to-day operations, together you can best determine what risks need to be addressed. When you are successful in this area, the people you are auditing begin volunteering information about potential audit issues. They go beyond just answering the questions you've posed and brainstorm with you regarding potential exposures. You have credibility, and when you raise potential issues, their first reaction is not to fight you on them but instead to accept them and try to understand the reasons behind your concern.

At the end of an audit, the people you've been auditing should look back and realize that it was a helpful experience and was not unpleasant. Of course, exceptions will occur. On rare occasions, auditees will be uninterested and unwilling to implement the internal controls necessary for their area. Conflicts should be rare if the auditors know what they're doing and bring a customer-oriented approach to the job.

Advocating positive relationships does not abdicate the auditor of his or her responsibility to be objective. The auditors must bring healthy skepticism to the job, and this can be done in a negative or positive way. You can imply that you don't trust the auditee and make him or her verify everything, setting up the relationship as a defensive one. Or you can bring an attitude to the table that implies trust: "I believe what you're saying, but the standards of my profession require me to validate it independently—can you help me get access to the information I need to do so?" Very few people will be offended or defensive about the latter approach (unless, of course, they're among the small percentage of truly dishonest employees).

NOTE Relationships will make or break the audit department's ability to add value to the company. Adversarial relationships get in the way of the core objective of the audit department. It is the responsibility of the audit department to do everything it can to minimize those negative relationships and foster positive ones. If you don't have good relationships, you won't have credibility and you won't be effective.

Learning to Build Partnerships

To arrive at these results, the relationship between the IT auditors and the IT organization must be a cooperative, collaborative one. The auditors must have credibility and trust within the IT organization. This requires an investment of time and some patience as the relationship develops. Following are some basic steps that you can take to start the journey:

- Be intentional about regular updates and meetings with IT management.
- Establish formal audit liaisons with different IT organizations.

- Get yourself invited to key meetings.
- Cultivate an attitude of collaboration and cooperation.
- Implement job swaps with the IT organization.
- Involve the IT organization in IT audit hiring decisions.

Be Intentional About Regular Updates and Meetings with IT Management

Select the IT managers for key areas and get on their calendars. During meetings, get an understanding of upcoming activities in their area, and look for opportunities to help and consult on internal control needs for those activities. This information will help you identify the early-involvement opportunities discussed earlier in this chapter. Get their input on the audits they want you to perform; these will be used as input into your formal audit planning. Be sure to include the CIO and his or her direct reports in this process, as these meetings are an excellent opportunity to talk about issues, upcoming projects, and their areas of concerns on a regular basis, which helps ensure that you're staying in alignment with senior IT management.

Establish Formal Audit Liaisons with Different IT Organizations

Assign an auditor (or the IT audit manager) to be the relationship manager for each significant IT organization. These relationship managers will be responsible for maintaining contact and relations with the management and key contributors of their assigned organization. This could involve regular (such as monthly, bimonthly, or quarterly) meetings with those contacts to keep up with their activities and understand their concerns. It could involve attending department meetings. It could also involve getting their input as each year's audit plan is developed to obtain their recommendations for formal or informal audit activities. Use the meetings not only to develop relationships but to "sell" the audit department and the value it offers. Each member of the audit team should be able to articulate a clear vision and compelling story as to the value of IT audit and why working with the audit team is helpful and in the best interests of the company.

Get Yourself Invited to Key Meetings

Get yourself invited to key meetings, such as project reviews, strategy sessions, and IT communications meetings. They are a great way to keep up with what's going on and are also excellent networking opportunities. As people grow accustomed to seeing you as part of their normal routine, they become more comfortable with you and much more likely to call you when they have internal control concerns or questions. Maintain a presence in the IT community. Some IT groups support the network and some support business applications. You're the IT group that provides internal control assurance. You're part of the overall team and have a unique and important function, just like they do. When you're invited to key meetings, don't take the "fly on the wall" approach that many auditors do. Instead, be vocal, join in the discussion, and provide your perspective as an auditor to the proceedings. This is a more value-added approach than merely observing. Similarly, look for opportunities to present at staff and department meetings on relevant internal control concepts. This is an excellent vehicle for spreading the word.

Cultivate an Attitude of Collaboration and Cooperation

Do not allow IT audit team members to take the old-fashioned, heavy-handed approach to auditing, where the audit department is the police department coming in to beat people into submission for not following the rules. Small things such as calling people *customers* instead of *auditees* can do wonders for altering the mindset of team members and fostering the right attitude. The audit team should avoid "gotcha" tactics and language in its communications, instead presenting its concerns in an open way that shows respect and fosters discussion. Building and sustaining trust with IT should be a priority for the audit team. The ability to work well with customers should be a part of each auditor's performance evaluation.

Implement Job Swaps with the IT Organization

Work with key IT organizations to "trade" staff members occasionally on a short-term basis. This could, for example, involve bringing in a guest auditor from IT operations to perform an audit or two, while sending a member of the audit team to the operations group for a few weeks. Or you might bring in a member of your database administration team to help you perform an audit that involves auditing a database (as long as that person wouldn't be auditing his or her own team and environment, of course). At the same time, perhaps a member of your audit staff who specializes in database auditing might join the database administration team for a few weeks. At the end of the assignment, each employee would return to his or her normal jobs.

This practice provides a number of benefits:

- It enhances knowledge and understanding of internal controls within operations, as the guest auditor will return to his or her work group with practical experience in auditing. This will lead to better understanding of the controls that should be implemented within the individual's environment.

- It increases the audit staff's knowledge; the auditor who spends a few weeks in database operations will gain an in-depth understanding of the area, from both a technical standpoint and in understanding the day-to-day issues and pressures faced by the operations group. This will help enhance your ability to audit the area.

- It promotes better overall understanding and partnership between the audit and operations teams.

- It provides insight into potential career opportunities, both for the operations personnel and the audit team members.

Involve the IT Organization in IT Audit Hiring Decisions

When hiring new IT auditors, you should include one or more members of the IT operations organization in the interview process. This will give you additional expert input into the evaluation of the candidate. Who better to evaluate a candidate's technical skills than a technical expert who works in the field every day? For example, if you're interviewing someone who lists SAP (Systems Applications and Products) as a strength, arrange for a member of the SAP support team to interview the candidate.

Arranging for members of the IT Security team to assist in interviews is also a good practice, given the natural partnership between the audit and security teams. Another benefit of this practice is that it gives the operations team enhanced ownership and understanding of the audit function in general and sends the message that you consider them to be partners. It also enhances the credibility of the audit team, as members of the operations organizations can vouch for people they had a hand in hiring. For the same reasons, the CIO should be involved in the hiring of the IT audit manager or director. If the CIO and the leader of the IT audit function don't get along and don't share a vision regarding the value of the function, it is difficult for the audit function to be effective.

The Role of the IT Audit Team

So isn't this a book about IT auditing? So far, most of what you've read in this chapter is pretty much applicable to any sort of auditing. The concepts discussed thus far are foundational to building an effective internal audit team, whether it's focused on IT auditing or another sort.

So what is IT auditing? The obvious answer is that it's the auditing of information technology, computer systems, and the like. If you're reading this book, you probably understand the basic difference between an IT auditor and a financial or operational auditor, so let's not belabor the point by coming up with a technical definition of IT auditing. However, a number of variations and interpretations exist regarding the role of an IT audit group within the overall audit function. We'll look at a few models:

- Application auditors
- Data extraction and analysis specialists
- IT auditors

Before exploring what these mean, consider a greatly simplified basic stack of potential technical subject areas that an IT audit group might be called on to review (Figure 1-2).

- **Data center facilities**   This, quite simply, is the physical building and data center housing the computer equipment on which the system in question resides.
- **Networks**   This allows other systems and users to communicate with the system in question when they do not have physical access to it. This layer includes basic networking devices such as firewalls, switches, and routers.
- **System platform**   This provides the basic operating environment on which the higher level application runs. Examples are operating systems such as Unix, Linux, and Windows.
- **Databases**   This tool organizes and provides access to the data being run by the end application.

Figure 1-2
Potential auditing
subject areas

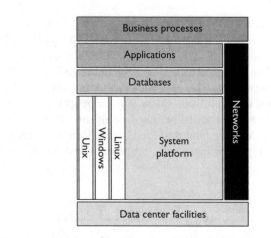

- **Applications**   This is the end application, which actually is seen and accessed by the end user. This could be an enterprise resource planning (ERP) application providing basic business functions, an e-mail application, or a system that allows conference rooms to be scheduled.

All these technical subject areas exist, of course, to support and enable one or more business processes.

NOTE   This is not intended to be an exhaustive list of potential subject areas and technologies that could be reviewed by an IT auditor. It is instead intended to illustrate some of the more common layers that might be reviewed during an audit. The stack of potential auditing subject areas could be made significantly more complex and granular if desired, spiking out topics such as storage, middleware, and web servers. However, this simplified version will help illustrate the following discussion regarding types of IT auditors.

Some element of all these technical subject areas generally will be relevant to all systems reviewed. The majority of this book is dedicated to detailing exactly how to audit these areas (and others), so we won't spend time on that here. However, it is important that you understand that these layers work together and that each forms a foundation for the next layer.

With this as a background, let's look again at those models of IT auditing mentioned earlier that describe the role of an IT audit group within the overall audit function.

Application Auditors

An amazing number of IT audit groups really aren't IT audit groups at all. These groups generally contain no true IT auditors but instead comprise business or financial folks who know how to use business application systems. These audit teams focus almost solely on the application layer. They do a very thorough job of ensuring that access is properly controlled and that segregation of duties issues do not exist. They likely will do a good job of ensuring that unauthorized changes to the application cannot occur and that good controls are in place to ensure the integrity of data being entered into the system.

However, they miss most or all of the other layers, meaning that they are seeing only part of the picture. They are not reviewing the foundational controls on which all systems rely, such as the security of the network and of the operating system environment. If those areas are not controlled properly, it's like locking the door but leaving the windows open. People can exploit security weaknesses at those other layers in many ways and disrupt the integrity, reliability, and security of the application systems. IT audit groups usually take this approach when they have not hired people with the appropriate technical skill sets that would allow them to understand and review the other layers of the stack. They focus on the application layer because that is all they understand.

Data Extraction and Analysis Specialists

Still other IT audit groups spend the majority of their time pulling data and analyzing it. They are likely to be experts at data extraction and analysis tools, such as Audit Command Language (ACL), but are not truly auditors in the traditional sense of the word.

Some of these teams will receive requirements primarily from the financial auditors and then execute those requirements. For example, the financial audit team may be reviewing an accounts receivable process, and might ask the data specialists to pull a list of all invoices greater than 90 days past due. However, merely serving as data deliverers is not the most effective and value-added implementation of this model.

The most effective implementation of this model involves developing analytics that allow for continuous monitoring for evidence of fraud, internal control violations, policy noncompliance, and other abuses. For example, monitoring might be set up to look for evidence of duplicate payments to vendors, split payments to vendors (to circumvent spending approval limits), employees who are set up as vendors, duplicate direct deposit numbers (which may indicate a ghost employee), duplicate travel and expense claims for the same time period, and so on. The specific items to be monitored will vary by company. When the analytics indicate a possible exception, the data specialists will investigate those potential issues. This could lead to a formal fraud investigation (which should then be turned over to the appropriate organization within the company), or it could lead to the identification of an internal control issue (which should then be formed into a traditional audit issue, with assigned responsibility, solution, and due date). The data specialists might also provide support to audits, helping the audit team to obtain and analyze relevant data, but that is not their primary focus.

This is an extremely difficult function to establish effectively, but it is one that can be an extremely powerful complement to your traditional audits if done correctly. It allows for 100 percent testing of data instead of relying on sampling. However, if you're serious about establishing this sort of function, you will need to invest in dedicated resources with a focus on data extraction and analysis. Attempting to train all auditors in the necessary tools and skills is usually not effective. Those auditors get pulled in too many directions and have too many other priorities. Staffing this team effectively requires finding people who understand both data and auditing, which is a unique skill set.

Even once you find the people with that unique skill set and form your dedicated team, they will need to invest significant time in identifying the most important things to monitor at your company, determining where the applicable data is located, getting access to that data, understanding its format, and porting it into your analytics tool (such as ACL). Time will be spent on trial and error as you and the team sort through the false positives and tune your analytics.

It's important to arrange for ongoing access to the database(s) that contains the golden copy of whatever data you need for your monitoring. This allows you to perform your tests on demand, as opposed to having to ask for the data each time or rely on data feeds, both of which present the possibility of the data being altered before you receive it. Those methods also make the timing of your testing predictable, therefore making it easier for people to cover their tracks. IT organizations will often be resistant to providing you with ongoing access to their data, so it's important to have knowledgeable IT personnel on the data analysis team who can assist with this negotiation.

These types of auditors can be a valuable part of an audit department, but if they constitute your entire IT audit function, you're missing a lot of the risk.

IT Auditors

Other departments have IT auditors that spend the majority of their time focusing on areas beneath the application layer in the stack. They ensure that the core infrastructure supporting the company's systems has the proper security and controls. These audit teams generally consist of IT professionals, as opposed to business folks who understand how to use application systems. The database layer and below constitute the domain of these IT auditors, and application audits are driven by the financial auditors with support provided by the IT auditors as needed. For example, the IT auditors might look at the database layer and below as they apply to that specific application (assuming that those items haven't been covered previously in larger scale audits of the IT environment). In addition, the IT auditors might help to review some of the general application controls, such as change controls and overall system access administration. However, the financial auditors should have the knowledge and be in a better position to understand what sorts of data integrity controls and segregation of duties are necessary for that particular business application.

 NOTE The third model (IT auditors) is critical for performing thorough and effective IT auditing because it ensures that all layers are being covered and that they are being covered by the people with the highest level of subject matter knowledge.

All three of these scenarios can exist in the same audit department and be very successful. Companies need some IT auditing that goes beyond the application layer to perform the function successfully.

Forming and Maintaining an Effective IT Audit Team

In this chapter we have discussed the real purpose of auditing, ways to add value outside of formal audits, how to build relationships, and what the IT audit function should do. However, none of these things is possible without an effective team in place to execute them. In this section, we'll discuss how to build and maintain an effective IT audit team.

In the preceding section we discussed different models of the function of the IT audit team. The model you choose will greatly influence how you build your team. As mentioned in that section, some companies really look for their IT audit team to focus their efforts at the application layer. In such cases, people with knowledge of the company's principal applications and the business functions that those applications support are critical. Likewise, if the intent is for the IT audit team to spend its time pulling data, it will be critical to hire IT auditors with detailed knowledge of data extraction and analysis tools.

However, let's assume that the intent is for the IT audit team to perform comprehensive IT auditing, performing work at all layers of the stack but relying on the financial auditors to be involved in reviewing the finer points of the business application controls. How should this team be staffed? Let's look at the two basic profiles of IT auditors and the pros and cons of each. After this discussion, we'll also look at the option of cosourcing the IT audit function.

Career IT Auditors

These are the people whose entire background basically consists of performing IT audit work at various companies. They generally will have Certified Information Systems Auditor (CISA) and/or Certified Information Systems Security Professional (CISSP) certifications and lots of experience at performing general controls reviews and Sarbanes-Oxley compliance reviews.

It is essential that some career IT auditors are on your team, because they are well versed in audit theory and in internal controls at a conceptual level. They understand how the audit process works and the important concepts of testing and substantiation. However, an entire team shouldn't be made up of career IT auditors. They tend to understand IT in theory, but most have never been responsible for day-to-day operations of an IT environment. Their depth of technical understanding is therefore often fairly light and would limit the team's ability to perform in-depth technical reviews.

These auditors often stay at the surface general controls review level when performing reviews. Their lack of operations experience can lead to credibility problems with your audit customers, because they sometimes can be fooled and often don't have the ability to keep up with their customers during in-depth conversations about issues. When the customers state that implementing a control is technically impossible, these auditors often won't have the knowledge to refute or validate the claim and won't know of potential alternative mitigating technical controls to suggest. This sometimes leads to customer complaints, because they have to spend too much time training the auditor on the basics of the environment.

These are obviously generalities, and plenty of career IT auditors have extreme technical knowledge. But even these auditors are prone to live in a fantasy world, where they believe that every control must be fully mitigated, without consideration for the operational impact and the need to perform cost/benefit analyses. Again, it is critical that some career IT auditors be on your team, because they form your foundation. However, creating an entire team of these types of auditors would likely lead to the team having a reputation of not really understanding how things work. Also, make sure that the career auditors you hire fit the culture and share the audit vision you're trying to create. If they don't, they can be an impediment to your success.

Sources for Career IT Auditors

Except in rare cases, these auditors will come from outside your company. (It's highly unlikely that you'll find someone with audit experience already working in your IT organization.) There are three basic sources for these auditors: those with internal IT audit experience at other companies, those with experience at external IT audit firms, and direct college hires.

People with Internal IT Audit Experience at Other Companies These people are the most likely to come on board and quickly contribute. Ensure that their IT audit shops had the same focus as yours. (That is, if you plan to be a comprehensive IT audit shop, you might not want to bring in someone from an IT audit shop that reviewed things only at the application layer.) They are the most likely to have performed in-depth technical reviews and understand the importance of positive relationships with audit customers.

People with External IT Audit Experience These people can provide a valuable asset to the team, bringing a deep understanding of audit theory. Unfortunately, many of the auditors at "Big 4" external auditing companies do not perform in-depth technical reviews. During their IT audits, they tend to skim the surface and focus on generic general controls. It is often difficult to find someone from an external audit firm that really understands the technology he or she is reviewing. These folks are the most likely to hurt your credibility with your audit customers and give you a reputation of not really understanding how things work. They are also the most likely to push for all controls to be 100 percent mitigated instead of bringing some perspective to the table that not all issues are created equal. Again, these are generalities and there are some extremely talented and technical auditors working at external audit firms. The key is to vet this out during the interview process.

College Hires Some universities offer good IT audit programs. You can hire people from these programs who have a good theoretical understanding of auditing and also have played around with lots of different technologies. The key is to find the truly technical folks who enjoy learning new things and have an aptitude for the auditing process. Obviously, college hires will require more guidance, and you wouldn't want to build a whole team around them, but they can provide a lot of energy to your team and can bring knowledge of the latest technologies.

IT Professionals

IT professionals are subject matter experts on technology but have no experience with auditing. These auditors can bring incredible maturity of understanding to your team in their specific field of expertise, allowing you to enhance your audit approach and audit tools for reviewing those technologies. However, it is tough to find the right personality fit. If you use IT professionals on your team, you need to be aware of some common pitfalls.

NOTE These auditors can do wonders for your ability to perform in-depth value-added audits and they speak the language of your customers. They bring credibility to your organization because they've done what your customers have done.

Many IT professionals get their job satisfaction from touching and supporting the technology day-to-day. When they join an IT audit team, it is a shock to their system, and they find that they've lost the part of their job that they enjoy the most. Although they are working with technology, they are not responsible for operations and are instead looking at other people's environments. When recruiting IT professionals, you should be up front with them about this aspect of the job so that they are joining your team with their eyes open.

It is also important that you find someone who has shown that he or she can learn new things quickly. Maybe in their old job, an IT professional supported Unix exclusively. In the auditing job, that professional will be expected to audit not only Unix but also every other significant technology that exists at the company. You want people on the team who are quick learners and also enjoy learning new things.

Another downfall of these sorts of auditors is that sometimes IT professionals never really "get it." They never develop the ability to perform complex risk assessment, especially when it comes to examining processes (as opposed to looking at technical settings within a technology). They need to be able to examine a beginning-to-end process and determine where the holes are, and this skill often does not come easily to people who have been supporting a specific technology only. During the interview process, you'll need to gauge the potential auditor's ability to "think like an auditor" by posing some scenarios and examining how his or her mind works.

It is also important that you find technical professionals with the appropriate communication skills, both oral and written. They must be able to explain technical concepts and issues at all levels. They must be able to explain their concerns in a way that convinces the most technical person and also in a way that will allow senior management to understand the concern to the extent that they can understand the need for action. During the interview process, ask prospective auditors to explain a technical concept to you to determine whether they possess good communication skills.

Documentation skills can also be weak. They're not used to the process of documenting their work in the orderly fashion required for audit work papers. You'll have to spend time coaching them on how to get what's in their head onto paper.

Sources for IT Professionals as Auditors

These auditors also generally come from three sources: within the company, outside the company, and from college graduates.

Technical Professionals from Within Your Company   This profile is the ideal. Not only can such auditors have detailed knowledge of the technology they've been supporting, but they also understand how the company's specific processes work. In addition, they're likely to have established relationships throughout the company and will bring instant credibility to the IT audit team. This name recognition can be invaluable. Of course, you'll need to be careful not to assign them to audit the area where they worked before joining your team—at least for a while.

Another benefit of hiring from within is that it increases the integration, from a career development standpoint, of the IT audit team with the rest of IT. It is encouraging for the IT audit team to see movement back and forth between IT audit and the rest of IT. Although it is possible that an IT professional could rotate to IT audit and decide to make a career of it, it is more likely that he or she will rotate back to IT after a while. This helps in your company's goal of retaining top talent, because members of the IT audit team become more likely to look within the company when they are ready to move. As you move people in and out of the IT audit department, the transition becomes more and more natural, and the IT audit team becomes an area that people in IT consider while planning their careers.

Technical Professionals from Outside Your Company   These people can bring excellent depth of technical understanding with them, along with some knowledge of how other companies have implemented internal controls. However, you will have to teach them how your company's IT environment works, along with teaching them how to audit.

College Hires   It will be rare to find someone who obtained a non-audit technical degree but wants his or her first job to be in auditing. However, it can happen, and there can be some benefits to bringing in the right people who fit this profile. Look for someone who will bring fresh energy to the team, along with "book knowledge" of the latest technologies.

Career IT Auditors vs. IT Professionals: Final Thoughts

Of course, it is possible for people to move back and forth between these two categories. You may bring someone in from IT, and this person may decide to become a career auditor. Or you may have a career auditor who, after joining your company, decides that he or she wants to move into IT. You should be supportive of people making these transitions. The most successful IT audit shops have a mixture of these types of auditors and provide flexibility to people in managing their careers.

Some companies have a forced rotation, where the audit department is basically a training ground for the rest of the company. In these companies, people are forced to leave the audit department after a set amount of time (usually two or three years). While this is a good way to train people on the company's processes and technologies, it is not the way to build an effective IT audit team. If the team is experiencing constant turnover, it harms the ability of the department to form a mature foundation to provide for continuous improvement in how the team's mission is accomplished. The team instead is always focused on bringing the new folks up to speed. A great alternative is to have a mix of career and rotational auditors so that you maintain a firm foundation of long-term auditors and also are providing movement back and forth with IT.

Key Traits of a Successful IT Auditor

As you begin your search to build out your audit team, consider the following key traits of a successful IT auditor:

- *Ability to dig into technical details without getting lost in the details.*
- *Analytical skills.* It is critical for the auditor not only to understand technologies but also to be able to use that knowledge to uncover risk to the business and apply judgment regarding degrees of risk. You need people who can think through a process or technology and frame up the risk to the company. This requires the auditor to take a "big picture" perspective when evaluating risk and determining the significance of potential issues.
- *Communication skills (both written and oral).* An auditor must be able to help all levels (from the most detailed technical person to the highest level of management) understand exactly why something is of concern. This means that the auditor must be able to lay it out logically in layperson's terms for management but also explain all the technical details of a concern to the people who work in the area.
- *Ability to learn the key concepts of new technologies quickly and identify key risk points within those technologies.*
- *Willingness not to be touching a specific technology daily.* It's important for auditors to understand that although performing audit analyses requires a lot of hands-on work, they won't be acting as the administrator of a production Unix box, managing routers, and so on.
- *Relationship building skills.* Auditors must be able to build solid trust-based relationships with their customers. This includes the ability to feel empathy for their customers and consider the world from their side of the table.

Selling Points for Recruiting IT Professionals into IT Audit

As you attempt to recruit people out of your company's IT organization, keep in mind the following benefits of the job as selling points:

- *Exposure to a wide variety of technologies.* The audit department will perform hands-on audit work with just about any technology used at the company.

- *Opportunity to work with many levels of management.* Auditors get a chance to work with and present to all levels of IT management in all IT organizations.

- *Broad view of the company and other IT groups.* Very few jobs provide an opportunity to work with so many different IT groups. The IT audit job provides an unparalleled opportunity to network and build your career via the development of relationships across the company's IT landscape.

- *Opportunity to lead projects.* Most IT audit groups rotate project leader assignments (after a period of training, of course), giving everyone a chance to direct resources, set project milestones, work closely with management of areas being audited, and perform similar tasks.

Cosourcing

Some companies *cosource* the audit function, bringing in auditors from external companies as supplemental labor. This is a fine thing to do if you need extra resources to meet your audit plan, but it is best not to rely heavily on this approach. The rapport your internally sourced auditor has with the customer creates trust. The ability to build relationships and credibility in the IT organization depends on your internal employees performing the IT audit function and on those employees staying around long enough to build a reputation. Having different contractors and consultants constantly moving in and out is not conducive to the relationship-building goal.

However, it does have its place and can be useful in a pinch. It also can be useful when you are auditing technologies that your team doesn't know well and that you don't plan to audit very often. For example, if you plan to audit a mainframe operating system once every few years, it may not make sense to spend time getting the IT audit team trained on the technology. It may be more effective to bring in someone who has that expertise to help you out. On the other hand, if you're auditing a technology that's core to the company and that you'll be evaluating over and over again, it's worth the investment to get your own team up to speed rather than bringing in someone from outside (or you might look into bringing in someone from the outside once with the understanding that part of his or her assignment will be to provide training and develop repeatable audit steps). If you do bring in cosourcing partners, it is critical that you emphasize to them your customer-oriented approach to performing audits so that they don't mess up the hard work you've put into building positive relationships.

Maintaining Expertise

If you want to have an effective IT audit team, you must invest time and money in keeping their skill sets up-to-date. Training is essential for IT auditors because technologies and techniques change constantly. Your auditors won't be supporting the technologies day to day (which necessitates keeping up with changes), so if you're not intentional about maintaining your expertise, your team's knowledge will quickly become outdated. It's never fun when you take your department's expert to a meeting and you find out that he or she has become a "dinosaur" who lacks knowledge of the latest developments.

Sources of Learning

Fortunately for the auditor, a wealth of training exists to help keep skills sharp and current. The time away from formal audits and the cost involved in the training pay dividends in building a knowledgeable and effective team of auditors. Consider the following as sources for keeping the team's expertise current.

Formal Training

Each auditor should be given the opportunity to attend one or two outside training classes or conferences each year. If chosen wisely, these can be a great way for the auditor to concentrate on learning something new. Common vendors in this space include SysAdmin, Audit, Network, Security (SANS), the MIS Training Institute, and the Information Systems Audit and Control Association (ISACA).

Choose the training classes wisely. Look for technical training classes that provide hands-on activities, because they are much more likely to be teaching real technical skills. Too many technical training classes are focused at a high level and consist solely of looking at slides. Short 1- to 2-hour sessions are unlikely to provide enough information to allow an auditor to audit a technical area adequately. It's difficult to learn a technical skill without touching the technology.

Shy away from classes that are purely theoretical in nature or focus solely on soft skills unless they meet one of your specific objectives. Look instead for classes that deal with how to audit and secure specific technologies and that provide hands-on illustrations of how to do so. Also look for training classes related to technologies that you actually will be auditing in the near future. Training that is not used quickly is quickly lost.

Even though training classes are an important component of maintaining expertise, it is unrealistic to think that they are the only source for gaining knowledge. It is simply cost prohibitive to send someone to a class every time he or she needs to learn something new. The following options are at least as important as formal training classes and conferences.

Research Time

Consider providing dedicated time for your IT auditors for research and learning activities. Offer them a week here and there to perform self-study activities. Make sure that they have the leeway they need to purchase books to aid in this effort. This time can also be used to create or enhance standard audit programs/tools for auditing common technologies at the company.

Specialization

Closely related to research time, you might consider having one or two auditors specialize in each of the core technologies that the IT audit team will be auditing. These people become your resident experts, and they will be responsible for keeping up with the technologies and maintaining the department's tools related to auditing those technologies (using dedicated research time). They also would be responsible for providing assistance to other IT auditors who are performing audits dealing with those technologies. These specialists would be the primary points of contact for others within the company who might have questions regarding controls in those areas. They are also your top candidates for establishing liaison relationships (as discussed earlier in this chapter) with management of teams supporting those technologies.

Consider creating a mentoring relationship with one of the technical people in IT who works in the area. (For example, if you're developing a Unix specialist, try to set up a mentoring relationship between the Unix specialist and a member of the Unix administration team.) Benefits of this sort of relationship include establishing a practical connection for the technical knowledge and also reinforcing relationships with the technical organization. Also, attempt to get access to a development area or test lab so that the specialist can play around with the technology.

Knowledge Sharing After Training

We talked about training earlier. Training is a high-dollar method of maintaining expertise, and you need to make sure that you fully leverage that investment. Too often, people come back from training, stick their training books on the shelf, and never think about the class again. People should be held accountable for making full use of the knowledge they receive at a training class.

Consider implementing a requirement that each person must do some sort of knowledge sharing upon returning from a class. The method of delivery should be flexible. Potential delivery methods include holding a short training session for members of the auditing department, creating or enhancing a standard audit approach for the topic, creating or enhancing tools to automate and/or analyze the technology, and creating a knowledge-sharing document that highlights key learning from the training. There should be an expectation and accountability that the auditor will bring something back to the department once training is complete.

Certifications

A number of certifications are relevant to the IT audit profession, the most prevalent of these being the CISA. Another one that is becoming more popular among auditors is the CISSP. Certifications are a good way to ensure that auditors have a basic level of understanding, and they enhance the pedigree of the department. (Lots of audit directors like to brag to the audit committee about how many certifications the audit department staff has.) There's wisdom in encouraging auditors to receive these certifications, because undoubtedly they will enhance their knowledge in the process of examination preparation.

Job Swaps with the IT Organization

This concept was described earlier in this chapter under "Relationship Building: Partnering vs. Policing." In addition to the relationship-building benefits of this exercise, however, the auditor obtains practical knowledge of and experience with performing a specific technical operation.

Combining Options and Maintaining Skills

As you can see, there are a number of options for ensuring that the IT audit team has the appropriate level of knowledge or expertise. In an ideal world, it is best to implement a combination of all these things, creating a development process that includes formal instruction, self-paced research, knowledge sharing, and practical execution.

The important thing, however, is to be deliberate about establishing the methods that will be used. If you take your eye off the ball on these, you'll find that the world quickly passes you by and you lose the expertise and credibility necessary to accomplish your mission of effectively promoting internal controls at the company. Consider developing a skills matrix for the IT audit team, specifying the technical skills that are important for auditing the IT environment at your company. Rate each person on the team for each skill. This will allow you to determine whether you have adequate coverage in each area and identify development needs.

In addition to maintaining technical skills, it is critical for auditors to develop and maintain key soft skills such as communication, relationship building, presentation, and writing skills. While dedicated training classes often can be useful in strengthening these skills, they are not always necessary. However, it is important for audit management and team leaders to emphasize the importance of these skills constantly and coach the audit team in identifying opportunities to strengthen them.

Relationship with External Auditors

Finally, as we wrap up this chapter about building an effective internal IT audit function, we'll briefly discuss external auditors and their impact on the internal audit team. Your company's external auditors also will have a need to review IT controls, especially as they relate to Sarbanes-Oxley compliance. They will need to review the audit team's work and also perform their own independent testing in certain areas.

This may be viewed as an intrusion and an annoyance. No one likes having his or her work reviewed and questioned, even though the external auditors are just giving the internal auditors a taste of their own medicine. We must accept the fact, however, that the external auditors are a legitimate need. A healthy working relationship between the internal and external auditors, where information is shared freely, is the best environment to create and provides the most value to your company.

It's also important for each group to keep the other informed of their activities. This will allow you to notify your audit customers about situations in which it may appear that they are being asked duplicate questions. Do your best to smooth over those situations so that the customers at least understand the reasons for them. Also, you should encourage the external auditors to review the internal auditors' work prior to speaking with your customers. This at least will give them a baseline of knowledge and minimize the amount of time the customer has to spend explaining the basics of the environment. Again, the external auditors are there for a reason, so do your best to work together and minimize the impact for your customers.

Summary

This chapter covered the following:

- The real mission of the internal audit department is to help improve the state of internal controls at the company.
- Internal auditors are not truly independent, but they should be objective.
- It is important to find ways to accomplish the department's mission outside of formal audits. Early involvement, informal audits, knowledge sharing, and self-assessments are four important tools in this regard.
- Building and maintaining good relationships with the IT organization are critical elements of the IT audit team's success.
- The most effective IT audit teams ensure that every layer of the stack is covered, not just the application layer.
- Successful IT audit teams generally will consist of a combination of career auditors and IT professionals.
- It is critical to develop methods for maintaining the technical expertise of the IT audit team.
- A healthy relationship should be developed with external IT auditors.

 NOTE   If you're interested in more information on the overall management of the audit function, an excellent resource is *Managing the Audit Function: A Corporate Audit Department Procedures Guide,* by Michael P. Cangemi and Tommie Singleton (John Wiley & Sons, 2003).

The Audit Process

In this chapter, we'll discuss the basic stages of the audit process, how to conduct each one effectively, and the following:

- The different types of internal controls
- How you should choose what to audit
- How to conduct the basic stages of the audit
- Planning
- Fieldwork and documentation
- Issue discovery and issue validation
- Solution development
- Report drafting and issuance
- Issue tracking

This chapter is not intended to be an "Auditing 101" course, because entire volumes have already been written on that topic. Nor is it intended to be a recitation of auditing standards and guidelines, which also are subjects of other books. This chapter will, however, provide some guidance on how best to execute the audit process to ensure that your IT audit team is as effective as possible.

This chapter will conclude our overview discussions so that we can move on to Part II, where we will discuss the specifics on how to audit various technologies and processes.

Internal Controls

Before we embark on a discussion of the auditing process, you need to understand one of the most basic concepts of auditing: internal controls. The concept of internal controls is absolutely fundamental to the auditing profession. In Chapter 1, you learned that the real mission of the internal audit department is to help improve the state of internal controls at the company. But what are internal controls? If you don't know the answer to this question, you'll find it difficult to accomplish the department's mission. We won't spend too much time on this, for fear of turning this book into the aforementioned Auditing 101 course, but the topic does warrant a few paragraphs.

Internal controls, stated in the simplest terms, are mechanisms that ensure proper functioning of processes within the company. Every system and process within a company exists for some specific business purpose. The auditor must look for the existence of risks to those purposes and then ensure that internal controls are in place to mitigate those risks.

Types of Internal Controls

Controls can be preventive, detective, or reactive, and they can have administrative, technical, and physical implementations. Examples of administrative implementations include items such as policies and processes. Technical implementations are the tools and software that logically enforce controls (such as passwords). Physical implementations include controls such as security personnel and locked doors (Figure 2-1).

Preventive Controls

Preventive controls stop a bad event from happening. For example, requiring a user ID and password for access to a system is a preventive control. It prevents (theoretically) unauthorized people from accessing the system. From a theoretical standpoint, preventive controls are always preferred, for obvious reasons. However, when you're performing audits, remember that preventive controls are not always the most cost-effective solution, and another type of control may make more sense from a cost/benefit standpoint.

Detective Controls

Detective controls record a bad event after it has happened. For example, logging all activities performed on a system will allow you to review the logs to look for inappropriate activities after the event.

Reactive Controls (aka Corrective Controls)

Reactive controls fall between preventive and detective controls. They do not prevent a bad event from occurring, but they provide a systematic way to detect when those bad events have happened and correct the situation, which is why they are sometimes called *corrective controls*. For example, you might have a central antivirus system that detects

Figure 2-1
Types of internal controls and their implementation

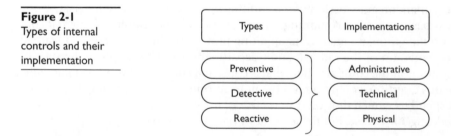

whether each user's PC has the latest signature files installed. Ideally, you could disallow network access to any machine that is not in compliance. However, this might not be practical from a business standpoint. Therefore, an alternative might be to log PCs that are not in compliance and perform some regimented follow-up activities to get the PC in compliance or remove its ability to access the network.

Internal Control Examples

Let's say that you're reviewing your company's accounts receivable system. That system exists for the purpose of ensuring that you're tracking who owes your company money so that you can nag the deadbeats who don't pay you, and so that you properly record payments from those who do. The financial auditors will worry about risks within the accounts receivable process itself, but the IT auditors need to think about the risks to the system accomplishing its business purpose.

Following are a few rudimentary examples that are intended to illustrate the concept of internal controls. The auditor must understand the business purpose of what he or she is auditing, think through the risks to that purpose being accomplished, and then identify any existing internal controls that mitigate those risks. The chapters in Part II of this book provide detailed guidance on what to look for when evaluating internal controls with regard to various topic areas.

Software Change Controls

If changes to the system code itself are not approved and tested properly, you might find that the logic being executed by the code is erroneous. This might mean that you lose your confidence in the integrity of the data within the system, resulting in an inability to know for sure who has paid your company and who hasn't. So what are some internal controls that would mitigate this risk?

- Do not allow programmers logical access to update the production code.
- People who do have logical access to update the production code may not do so without evidence of testing and approval.

Access Controls

If access to the system is provided to people who do not have a need for that access, system data might be changed, added, or deleted inappropriately. What are some internal controls that would mitigate this risk?

- Require a user ID and password to access the system.
- Have a limited number of application security administrators who control the ability to add new user accounts to the system.
- Ensure that the application security administrators are knowledgeable individuals who know which users actually need access to the system.

Backups and Disaster-Recovery Plans

If the system or its data were lost, system functionality would be unavailable, resulting in a loss of your ability to track outstanding receivables or post new payments. What are some internal controls that would mitigate this risk?

- Back up the system and its data periodically.
- Ship backup tapes offsite.
- Document a disaster recovery plan.

Determining What to Audit

One of the most important tasks of the internal audit department is determining what to audit. Chapter 1 discussed early involvement, informal audits, and self-assessments. In this section, we're focusing on traditional, formal audits—the kind of audits that have teams of auditors working on them, producing work papers, audit reports, lists of issues, and action plans for resolving those issues.

Your audit plan must focus your auditors on the areas with the most risk and on areas where you can add the most value. You must be efficient and effective in how you use your limited resources by spending your IT audit hours looking at the areas of most importance. This should not be done by arbitrarily pulling potential audits out of the air; instead, it should be a logical and methodical process that ensures that all potential audits have been considered.

Creating the Audit Universe

One of the first steps in ensuring an effective planning process is to create your IT audit universe. You must be aware of what audits you potentially might perform before you can rank them. You can slice the IT universe in many ways, and none is particularly right or wrong. What is important is to figure out a way to slice the environment so that you can perform the most effective audits.

Centralized IT Functions

First, determine what IT functions are centralized, and place each of the centralized functions on your list of potential IT audits (see Table 2-1). For example, if a central function manages your Unix and Linux server environment, one of your potential audits might be a review of the management of that environment. This could include administrative processes such as account management, change management, problem management, patch management, security monitoring, and other such processes that would apply to the whole environment.

Another example could include a review of the baseline security used by the centralized Unix and Linux function for deploying new servers. This audit could cover all those processes that apply to the whole Unix and Linux server environment. Then, if the financial auditors' plan calls for an audit of a particular financial application that resides on a Unix server, your participation in that audit could consist solely of auditing the security of that specific server without having to spend time understanding the processes for managing that server (which were covered already in your centralized audit).

Of course, each company will centralize these sorts of core IT functions to differing degrees. You must understand the environment well enough to determine what functions are centralized and add those functions into your audit universe. Audits of those sorts of functions form a baseline that will speed up the rest of your audits. As you perform other audits, you can remove those centralized functions that have already been audited from the audit scope.

For example, suppose you perform audits of the IT environment at each site, but the network configuration and support are centralized. It would be inefficient to talk to the network group about their processes during each and every site audit. Instead, you should perform one audit covering their processes, and then scope that area out of your site audits.

Decentralized IT Functions

After creating a list of all the company's centralized IT processes, you can determine the rest of your audit universe. Perhaps you can create one potential audit per company site. These audits could consist of reviewing the decentralized IT controls that are owned by each site, such as data center physical security and environmental controls. Server and PC support also may be decentralized at your company. The key would be to understand what IT controls are owned at the site level and review those. It may be necessary to get more granular than this and have numerous potential audits at each site. It all depends on the complexity of the environment, the hierarchy of the organization, and your staffing levels. You will have to determine what is most effective in your environment.

 NOTE   Understanding the potential audits in your universe is critical to your being an effective auditor. Perhaps the best way to scope the breadth of possible audits is to meet with the company's IT managers to help you understand how IT responsibilities are allocated and to determine what IT functions are centralized and decentralized.

Unix and Linux server administration	Central help desk
Windows server administration	Database management
Wireless network security	Telephony and voice-over IP
Internal router and switch management	Mobile services
Firewall/DMZ management	IT security policy
	Mainframe operations

Table 2-1   Potential Opportunities for Auditing Centralized Activities

Business Applications

You also might create a potential audit for each business application. You'll need to determine whether it is more effective to conduct these audits in the IT audit universe or in the financial audit universe. In many ways, it makes the most sense to have these audits be driven by the financial auditors, who are probably in the best position to determine when it is time to perform an audit of the procurement process. If they do make that decision, they can ask you to determine the relevant system aspects that should be included in the procurement audit (such as a review of the server on which the procurement application resides, the system's software change controls, the system's disaster recovery plan, and so on).

Regulatory Compliance

Depending on the services or goods your business provides, you might be responsible for ensuring compliance with certain regulations. Common examples include auditing compliance with Sarbanes-Oxley, Health Insurance Portability and Accountability Act (HIPPA), and Payment Card Industry (PCI) regulations and standards. You might have a separate audit in your audit universe for testing compliance with each relevant regulation.

NOTE A good source for ensuring that you have considered all significant areas of IT governance is to reference the *control objectives for information and related technology (COBIT)* framework, which defines the high-level control objectives for IT. Although your planning should always be tailored to the specifics of your company's environment, COBIT can be a good reference in creating your audit universe. COBIT is discussed in more detail in Chapter 16, and you can learn more about COBIT online at www.isaca.org.

Ranking the Audit Universe

Once you've created your IT audit universe, you must develop a methodology for ranking those potential audits (Figure 2-2) to determine your plan for the year (or quarter, month, and so on). You can include all kinds of factors in this methodology, but the following are some of the essential ones:

- **Known issues in the area**   If you know problems exist in the area, you should be more likely to perform an audit of that area.

- **Inherent risk in the area**   You may not be aware of specific problems in the area, but your experience tells you that this area is prone to problems, so you should consider performing an audit. For example, perhaps you consistently find significant issues when auditing site-level IT controls supporting a particular manufacturing activity. This experience would indicate a higher inherent risk in that area, steering you to perform similar audits at other sites, even if you're not aware of any specific problems at those sites.

- **Benefits of performing an audit in the area** Consider the benefits of performing an audit in the area, focusing particularly on whether an audit would add value to the company. This provides an offset of sorts to the first item in this list. For example, you might know of existing issues, but management is already aware of them and is addressing them. In this case, your telling management about all the problems they're already in the process of fixing adds no value. Instead of auditing it, consider serving as part of the team that is developing solutions to fix the problem (as discussed in Chapter 1). You should also consider the importance of an area to the company. For example, you may know that problems exist with the system used to order meals for internal meetings. Your ranking model needs to consider the fact that this system isn't really very important to the overall success of the company.

- **Management input** Chapter 1 discussed the importance of developing and maintaining good relationships with IT management. When those relationships are healthy, the input of IT management should be a large factor in your decisions regarding what to audit. If the chief information officer (CIO) and/or key members of the IT leadership team are concerned about an area and want you to audit it, then that input should weigh heavily in your decision process. In fact, if those relationships are healthy and you're doing a good job of maintaining contact throughout the year, your audit plan should almost create itself. You'll be aware of major changes in the environment and of significant concerns, so that your planning process can be a confirmation of the discussions you've been having throughout the year. Note that this factor might influence others as well. For example, if management is encouraging you to perform an audit, they probably know of problems in the area, which might lead you to increase your rating of the first factor (known issues in the area). It also might lead you to believe that you can add value by performing the audit, so that you can potentially increase your rating of the third factor (benefit of performing an audit in the area).

IT audit ranking table

Potential audit	Audit ranking	Total points	Known issues	Inherent risk	Benefit	Mgmt input
UNIX server administration	1	32	8	7	8	9
Corporate firewalls	2	29	7	8	6	8
Site 1 data center	3	26	7	6	7	6
Accounts receivable system	4	20	4	5	6	5
Central help desk	5	15	4	6	3	2

Figure 2-2 Example audit ranking table

Other factors can be included in an audit ranking model, but the preceding four are absolutely essential. Other factors can be added based on the environment at your company (for example, having a factor that measures the quantity of assets represented by the area or a factor that reflects the results of previous audits of the area).

In addition, the environment at your company may lead you to weight some of those factors more heavily than others. As an example of how the ranking model would work, you might decide to rank each factor from 1 to 10. If the CIO and the entire leadership team are encouraging you to perform an audit, the management input factor might get a 10. However, if you don't see much inherent risk in that area, you might give that factor a 5. And this goes on until you have assigned a point value to each factor for each potential audit in your audit universe. You also might decide that, for example, the "known issues" factor needs a higher weighting than the others, so you might count that factor double. The key is to have your universe of potential audits defined and then create some process that helps you rank the relative importance of performing each of those potential audits.

NOTE   See Chapter 18 for information covering detailed risk analysis techniques.

Some companies place a large emphasis on rotating audits, where each audit is performed on a specific schedule. This can be a valid way to ensure that all critical systems and sites are audited regularly; however, rotation schedules should be a guideline and not a firm rule. You should consider what is the most important area for you to audit *today* based on factors such as those just mentioned. A rotation schedule should not be an excuse for you to ignore known problems and the input of IT management. It is critical that you reserve the right to ignore the rotation schedule to ensure that you are hitting the areas where you can add the most value to the company. If rotations are a big part of how your audits are scheduled, you might consider adding rotation schedule as a factor in your audit ranking model. In this way, if an audit is due in the rotation (or past due), it is more likely to make the plan.

Of course, you may be required to perform some audits on an annual basis per regulatory requirements (such as Sarbanes-Oxley compliance). Such audits obviously do not need to be ranked.

Determining What to Audit: Final Thoughts

Once you have performed your ranking, you will need to estimate the resource requirements for each potential audit to determine the cut line for your audit plan (since you should already know what resources are available to you). It also will allow you to show management which audits you will *not* have time to get to, which can lead to healthy discussions about the appropriateness of audit staffing levels and/or the need to consider cosourcing options.

In summary, before you can feel comfortable that you're auditing the right things, you must determine your universe of potential audits and then develop a methodology for ranking those audits. Once you have determined what you will be auditing, you can

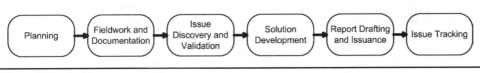

Figure 2-3   Audit process overview

execute each audit in the plan. The remainder of this chapter is devoted to discussing the methodologies for doing so.

The Stages of an Audit

Now that you understand the process of selecting what to audit, let's discuss the various stages for performing each of the audits in the audit plan. We'll discuss the following six major audit phases (Figure 2-3):

1. Planning

2. Fieldwork and documentation

3. Issue discovery and validation

4. Solution development

5. Report drafting and issuance

6. Issue tracking

You'll learn how to perform each of these stages most effectively.

Planning

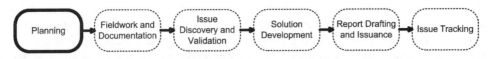

Before you begin work on any audit, you must determine what you plan to review. If the planning process is executed effectively, it will set up the audit team for success. Conversely, if it is performed poorly and work begins without a plan and without clear direction, the audit team's efforts could result in a failure.

The goal of the planning process is to determine the objectives and scope of the audit. You need to determine just what it is you're trying to accomplish with the review. As part of this process, you should develop a series of steps to be executed in order to accomplish the audit's objectives. This planning process will require careful research, thought, and consideration for each audit. Following are some basic sources that should be referenced as part of each audit's planning process:

- Hand-off from the audit manager

- Preliminary survey

- Customer requests
- Standard checklists
- Research

Hand-off from the Audit Manager   If the audit is included in the audit plan, there must be some reason. The audit manager should relay to the audit team the information that led to the audit being scheduled. This might include comments from IT management and/or known concerns in the area. The factors that led to the audit being scheduled need to be encompassed in the audit plan. In addition, the audit manager should be able to provide the audit team with the key contacts for the audit.

Preliminary Survey   The audit team should spend some time before each audit performing a preliminary survey of the area to be audited to understand what the audit will entail. This likely will include interviews with the audit customers to understand the function of the system or processes being reviewed, as well as review of any pertinent documentation. The goal is to obtain a basic background and understanding of the area to be reviewed. This is needed to perform the preliminary assessment of risks in the area.

Customer Requests   Chapter 1 discussed the importance of making the audit a collaborative, cooperative process. As part of accomplishing this goal, the audit customers should feel that they have some ownership in the audit. The audit team should ask the customers what areas they think should be reviewed and what areas are of concern. This input should be meshed with the results of the auditors' objective risk assessment to determine the scope of the audit. Of course, at times the auditors won't use the customers' input. For example, sometimes the audit customers will be concerned about areas that are more operational in nature and have no internal control impact. In such cases, it is perfectly legitimate for the audit team to keep those areas out of the audit's scope, with an explanation to the customer as to why the audit team is not positioned to execute that request. It is also important not to allow the customer to steer the auditors away from reviewing important areas. The auditors must ultimately apply their best judgment. However, obtaining the customers' input and incorporating it into the audit plan where possible will make the customers feel ownership in the audit project and optimize open and honest communication.

Standard Checklists   Standard audit checklists for the area being reviewed are often available. The checklists in Part II of this book can serve as an excellent starting point for many audits. In addition, the audit department might have its own checklists for standard systems and processes at the company. Having standard, repeatable audit checklists for common areas can provide a useful head start for many audits. Those checklists, however, should be evaluated and altered as necessary for each specific audit. Having a standard checklist does not remove the requirement for the auditor to perform risk assessment prior to each audit.

Research   Finally, the Internet, books, and training materials should be referenced and used as appropriate for each audit to obtain additional information about the area being audited.

Assessment

Once these resources have been referenced, the auditor must perform an assessment of the risks in the area being reviewed to identify the steps that must be accomplished during the audit. This concept is illustrated in the "Internal Controls" section earlier in this chapter. As mentioned, the auditor must understand the business purpose of the area to be audited, consider the risks to that purpose being accomplished, and then identify any existing internal controls that mitigate those risks. If a process is being reviewed, the auditor needs to lay out that process end to end and think about where it could break down. If a system or technology is being reviewed, the auditor needs to think through the risks to that system or technology functioning as intended.

The result of the preceding exercise should be a determination of the scope of the audit, including specifically determining and communicating what is out of scope and compiling a list of steps to be performed to accomplish that scope. These steps should be documented with sufficient detail to enable the auditors performing the audit to understand the risk being addressed by each step. This helps to avoid "checklist" auditing, where the audit team is mechanically executing a list of audit steps, and instead puts the focus on ensuring that the risks are being addressed, with the audit steps merely serving as guidelines. It is also important that you document the audit steps so that they are repeatable and easy to use by the next person performing a similar audit, thereby serving as a training tool and allowing for more efficient execution of repeat audits.

One way to accomplish these goals is to supplement each audit step with documented details regarding why that audit step is being performed (that is, the risk being addressed) along with how it can be performed. The audit steps in Part II of this book follow this format and can be used as a guideline.

Scheduling

An important element of the planning process is scheduling the audit (that is, determining when the audit will take place). Rather than dictating when the audit will occur based purely on the convenience of the audit team, audit scheduling should be performed in cooperation with the audit customers. This will allow the audit team to consider personnel absences and times of high activity, during which the audit team may not be able to get appropriate time and attention from the organization they're auditing. Scheduling audits in cooperation with the audit customers not only allows for a more effective audit, but it also starts the audit off on the right foot, establishing an atmosphere of flexibility and cooperation. Audit customers will appreciate the fact that their constraints and schedules were considered and will have a sense of mutual ownership regarding the schedule.

Kick-off Meeting

Near the end of the planning process, a kickoff meeting should occur with the audit customers so that you can communicate what is in and out of scope for the audit project and also receive their final input. During this meeting, you should continue to be open to the customers' input and flexible regarding making changes to the audit scope. Again, if the customers feel ownership in the audit, they are much more likely to cooperate fully when working with the auditors. The kick-off meeting is also a great time to solicit primary points of contact for each audit step and to determine a schedule and methodology (such as meetings or e-mails) for keeping the customers informed of the audit's status.

Once the kick-off meeting is completed, the audit's steps should be allocated among the audit team members, and the next stage of the audit can begin.

Fieldwork and Documentation

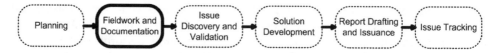

The bulk of the audit occurs during this phase, when the audit steps created during the preceding stage are executed by the audit team. Now, the team is acquiring data and performing interviews that will help team members to analyze the potential risks and determine which risks have not been mitigated appropriately.

Part II of this book provides detailed guidance for performing fieldwork for standard topics and technologies. In addition, Chapter 18 provides detailed guidance on performing risk analysis. Therefore, we will not spend much time on this topic here. It is important, however, that you understand the value of healthy skepticism. Wherever possible, the auditors should look for ways to validate independently the information provided and the effectiveness of the control environment. Even though this may not always be possible, the auditor should always think of creative ways to test things. For example, if the audit customer describes a process for approving new user account requests, the auditor should attempt to pull a sample of recently added users to see if they did indeed receive the proper approval. This will provide much more compelling evidence that a process is being followed than an interview.

Documentation is also an important part of fieldwork. The auditors must do an adequate job of documenting their work so that conclusions can be substantiated. The goal should be to document the work in enough detail so that a reasonably informed person can understand what was done and arrive at the same conclusions as the auditor. The auditor basically should be telling a story: "Here's what I did. Here's what I found. Here's my conclusion. Here's why I reached that conclusion." If a process was reviewed, the process should be described, and the key control points within that process should be highlighted. If a system or technology was reviewed, the specific settings and data reviewed should be described (along with how that information was obtained) and interpreted.

The documentation process may seem tedious, but it is important. First, it is needed to meet the standards of the profession. Second, it is possible that in the future the findings of the audit may be questioned or challenged, and the auditor who performed the work may no longer be employed by the company or department by that time (or may have just forgotten the details of the audit). It will be critical that documentation exists to explain and the auditing process and substantiate the conclusions. Third, if the audit is performed again someday, retaining detailed documentation will allow the next audit team to learn from the experience of the previous audit team, thereby allowing for continuous improvement and efficiency.

One final note on fieldwork: During the planning phase, you will develop checklists as to what you plan to review during the audit. Make sure those checklists don't result in audit team members turning off their good judgment. The team needs to remain flexible during the audit and be prepared to explore avenues that were not considered during the planning phase. Team members always need to keep in mind the overall objective of the audit and not just become automatons following a canned script. It is also critical that each team member understand the purpose behind the assigned audit steps. These steps should serve as a guideline for accomplishing a purpose, and each auditor needs to remain creative in how the step is carried out. If the step is performed, but it didn't really address the risk being investigated, the auditor has failed.

NOTE The purpose of the audit is not to execute the audit steps, but to evaluate the state of internal controls in the area being reviewed.

Issue Discovery and Validation

While executing fieldwork, auditors will develop a list of potential concerns. This is obviously one of the more important phases of the audit, and the auditor must take care to scrub the list of potential issues to ensure that all the issues are valid and relevant. In the spirit of collaboration, auditors should discuss potential issues with the customers as soon as possible. Nobody enjoys waiting for the auditors to complete an audit and then having to endure a laundry list of issues. Not only is this unpleasant for your customers, but it also can be unpleasant for you, because you may find that not all your information is accurate and not all your issues are valid. Instead of making a federal case out of each potential issue, take a more informal approach: "Hey, I think I uncovered something of concern. Can I discuss it with you to be sure I have my facts straight and am understanding the risk properly?" This allows the customer to work with you in validating the issue and also encourages the customer to take ownership of the issue.

In addition to validating that you have your facts straight, you need to validate that the risk presented by the issue is significant enough to be worth reporting and addressing. Don't raise issues for the sake of raising issues. Instead, raised issues should present significant risk to the company. Consider mitigating controls, and understand the whole picture before determining whether you have an issue worthy of being reported.

Except in businesses that are highly regulated, take the same approach with compliance with internal policies. While it is obviously important for IT auditors to review systems for compliance with the company's internal IT security policies, the approach still should be risk-based. There are times when a system is technically in violation of policy, but that violation represents no real risk owing either to mitigating controls or the nature of that particular system. In such cases, what is the value of raising an issue? Likewise, in many cases, the auditors should raise concerns that have nothing to do with policy but instead involve risks to the specific environment being reviewed. Do not allow your audit team to become the policy compliance team. You should instead consider policies as well as all other relevant factors in evaluating the true risks to the environment being reviewed.

 NOTE If you work with your customers throughout the audit to validate issues and come to agreement on the risks represented by those issues, the conclusion of the audit will go much more smoothly and quickly. Instead of debating all the issues at the end, you can focus on addressing the issues that you've been discussing throughout the audit.

Solution Development

After you have identified the potential issues in the area you're auditing and have validated the facts and risks, you can work with your customers to develop an action plan for addressing each issue. Obviously, just raising the issues does the company no good unless those issues are actually addressed. Three common approaches are used for developing and assigning action items for addressing audit issues:

- The recommendation approach
- The management-response approach
- The solution approach

The Recommendation Approach

Using this common approach, auditors raise issues and provide recommendations for addressing them. They then ask the customers whether they agree to the recommendations and, if so, when they'll get them done.

The following is a common scenario for this approach. The audit team discovers no process is in place to ensure that users have the latest security patches on their PCs prior to connecting to the network. They present the issue to the customers, along with a recommendation that says, "We recommend that a process for ensuring that users have the latest security patches on their PCs be in place prior to their being allowed to connect to the network," or something equally brilliant and useful. The auditors then ask the customers when the process can be finished. The customers throw out a date to get the auditors off their backs, generally without thinking through what the job really entails. The auditors go away happy because their recommendation was accepted, and they have a due date. Who cares that the customers have no ownership in the action plan and that they'll probably blow the due date? We'll worry about that in a few months when the job is due, right?

This example obviously is a bit exaggerated, but, unfortunately, it is not all that far from the truth. The recommendation approach can work if handled well by a knowledgeable audit team. However, it generally results in the customers feeling a lack of ownership in the action plan, because they're just doing what the auditors told them to do. In addition, the customers being audited are bound to have more detailed knowledge of the area being audited than the auditors, meaning that they're in the best position to develop a solution to the problem. By sticking a recommendation in front of them and asking if they accept it, customers are much less likely to think through the problem and develop a workable and realistic action plan. Instead, they may tend to "accept" the recommendation to get the auditors out of the way, only to discover the inevitable roadblocks and complexities down the line when the audit point is almost due and the auditors are following up. This leads to the audit point going overdue and/ or being extended. It is not an efficient process.

If this is the approach used by your company, it is important to engage the customers in brainstorming how to fix the problem prior to documenting your recommendation. Then the recommendation just becomes documentation of what has already been agreed to by all involved parties. This doesn't mean that the auditors can't bring ideas to the table. They can, and they should. However, the customers ultimately need to feel ownership of the action plan.

The Management-Response Approach

With the management-response approach, the auditors develop a list of issues and then throw them to the customers for their response and action plans. Sometimes the auditors send their recommendation for resolution along with the issue, and sometimes they just send the issue with no recommendation. Either way, the customers are supposed to send back their response, which is included in the audit report. This lends itself to polite finger-pointing and name-calling. The auditor writes, "There's a problem. We recommend that they fix it." Management then writes back, "We think this is stupid, but we'll go ahead and implement a half-baked solution that we believe adds no value to get the auditors off our backs." Or even worse, management's response may be more like this: "We think this is stupid and are going to do nothing about it. The auditors can go jump in a lake." In such cases, the auditors may include their counter-response, saying something like this: "Can you believe these people? They obviously don't care about controls. We're going to tell the CEO and get them in trouble."

Again, this is an exaggerated example, but it's not far off the mark. The management-response approach does not lend itself to reaching consensus but basically allows the auditors to wash their hands of the responsibility of getting buy-in on the issues and their resolutions. Instead of developing a mutually agreed-upon solution, they just say what they want and then allow the audit customers to say what they want, with the auditors then getting the last word in the report.

If this is the approach used by your company, try to get it changed. If you can't change it, try to work around the system. Prior to sending the issues and your recommendations to the customers, work out a solution that feels comfortable to everyone involved. Your recommendation then can reflect what you've already agreed on, allowing the management response to be something like, "We agree and will implement it by the end of the year." The management-response approach doesn't prevent you from going ahead and collaborating with your customers on mutually acceptable solutions.

The Solution Approach

Using this approach, the auditors work with the customers to develop a solution that represents a mutually developed and agreed-upon action plan for addressing the issues raised during the audit. It is a combination of the two preceding approaches, bringing in the best of each. As with the recommendation approach, the auditors are providing ideas for resolution based on their control knowledge. As with the management-response approach, the customers are providing ideas for resolutions based on their real-life operational knowledge. The result is a solution that the customers "own" and that is satisfying to the auditors. Because they have ownership of the issues, the customers are much more likely actually to follow through.

Under this approach, the audit report subtly reflects the shift in ownership. With the recommendation approach, the auditors might write something like this: "We recommend that audit logs be enabled" or "Audit logs should be enabled." These statements emphasize the auditors' wishes and often are interpreted by customers as heavy handed and bossy (and often clueless). With the solution approach, the auditors instead would write this: "The support team will enable audit logs." This statement is a crisp, clean statement of the customers' intentions and reflects something they have developed and agreed to with the auditors' help.

In this approach, the development of the solution must be truly collaborative. Although the auditors should try to allow the customers to develop some initial ideas, they should have some potential solutions ready in their "back pockets" in case the customers cannot come up with acceptable answers. In addition, the auditors should have some sort of idea as to the minimum amount of mitigation with which they will be comfortable. They need to be prepared to let the customers know if the solutions proposed do not meet the minimum risk mitigation needs.

Guidance on Solution Development

Regardless of the approach you use, you need to establish who is responsible for executing the action plans and the due dates by which they will be completed. This provides accountability and a basis for the auditors' follow-up. As these action plans are addressed, the auditors should be flexible regarding how finalized the action plan must be in the audit report.

Some issues lend themselves to straightforward solutions, such as changing a system setting or locking down file permissions. In these instances, you would expect the customers to be able to say exactly when the solution will be implemented. However, other issues require complex solutions and will involve engaging multiple organizations and developing complex processes or acquiring new technology. In these instances, it is not realistic to expect the audit customers to know immediately what they will do and when they will do it. Instead, an evaluation period occurs, in which the alternatives are examined and a detailed timeline is developed. Instead of pushing the customers to provide information when it is not realistic to expect them to do so, you can set an interim date by which they will have chosen a solution and developed a timeline. Once that date is reached, if they have indeed developed a detailed action plan, you can establish a new due date based on that plan.

NOTE When developing solutions, the auditor should keep in mind that it is not always practical for 100 percent of the risk to be mitigated. Sometimes mitigating 100 percent of the risk would be cost-prohibitive, but 80 percent of the risk may be mitigated for a reasonable cost. This is called the "Pareto concept," in which the first 80 percent of the risk can be addressed for 20 percent of the cost. If the auditor digs in his or her heels and insists on a 100 percent solution, the auditor's credibility and relationship with the customer is damaged, and the customers may do nothing toward mitigating the risk. Having 80 percent of the risk addressed is better than having 0 percent of the risk addressed. The auditor must remember that he or she is an employee of the company and should be pushing for solutions that are reasonable and cost-beneficial. Of course, the auditor must be objective and ensure that the unmitigated risk is not unreasonable. However, auditors who always insist on 100 percent solutions become auditors who are avoided and who are viewed as having no business sense.

It's also important that you work with audit customers to be flexible when setting due dates for issue resolution. Remember that much of the activity within the customer's organization has nothing to do with internal audit. Put the audit issues in context with the IT group's other pressures and priorities. Sometimes your audit points won't be the top priority, and that's OK. Setting realistic due dates with which the audit customers are comfortable will promote mutual buy-in, making it more likely the issues will be closed on schedule and helping you to avoid rescheduling and escalations.

As discussed earlier, the auditors should work diligently to reach agreement with the customers on the issues and solutions from the audit. Agreement may not always be achievable, and inevitably you and a customer won't see eye to eye. These cases should be few and far between, but they do happen. In addition, sometimes the customers agree with you but do not think they have the resources to address the issue. So how do you resolve such situations? Do you get in a yelling and screaming match? Do you threaten your customers, reminding them that you report to the audit committee and that you can get them in trouble for not addressing the issue? Absolutely not! These situations can be handled respectfully and cooperatively.

Remember that the concept of *audit requirements* is a misnomer. The audit department is not a requirements-setting body and therefore should not be in the business of trying to force action. Instead, the auditor's job is to identify risks and to ensure that the appropriate level of management is made aware of those risks so that decisions can be made as to whether or not to mitigate them. Accepting a risk is a legitimate option for management. The auditor must use his or her judgment to determine what level of management needs to be informed of the risk. Some audit issues represent only a small amount of risk. In such cases, if a lower level manager indicates that he or she understands and accepts the risk, the auditor can document this and move on. In some cases, the risk is more severe, and the auditor believes that the CIO should be made aware of the problem. However, if the CIO understands the risk and decides to accept it, once again, the auditor has done his or her job and no further action is necessary. Still other issues represent such a severe risk that the auditor will be comfortable only with sign-off by the CEO or even the audit committee.

NOTE There is always some level of management that can sign-off on accepting the risk for any given issue. The auditors must use their judgment to determine what that level is.

Even if you believe that you must go above someone's head to make the appropriate level of management aware of a given risk, this need not be an adversarial event. You can calmly explain to your audit customers that you understand their reasons for declining to address the issue and that your job requires you to inform higher levels of management about the risk to ensure that they are also comfortable with accepting it. You can even invite the customer to participate in any meetings to discuss the risk and/ or keep them copied on any e-mail traffic. This should not turn into a "he said/she said" match but instead can remain open and respectful, with the auditors explaining the customers' viewpoint as well as their own during management communications.

Escalating an issue often will result in a positive outcome for the customers, such as additional resources being allocated to allow for the issue to be addressed, so the escalation process does not have to be a contentious one. And sometimes the customers want the auditors to escalate an issue to provide additional backing to address a known issue that perhaps has not received proper attention prior to the audit.

When escalating issues to management, make sure to move up the chain of command so that no one feels he or she is being blindsided. For example, if you think that an issue ultimately needs to be escalated all the way to the CIO, talk with each level of management between the audit customer and the CIO, in order. This again helps avoid contentiousness in the escalation process.

Report Drafting and Issuance

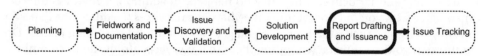

Once you've discovered the issues in the environment being audited, validated them with the customers, and developed solutions for addressing them, you can draft the audit report. The audit report is the vehicle by which you document the results of the audit. It serves two main functions:

- For you and the audit customers, it serves as a record of the audit, its results, and the resulting action plans.
- For senior management and the audit committee, it serves as a "report card" on the area that was audited.

Essential Elements of an Audit Report

There are as many audit report formats as there are internal audit departments. However, following are the essential elements of an audit report:

- Statement of the audit scope
- Executive summary
- List of issues, along with action plans for resolving them

Statement of the Audit Scope   Make it clear in the report what was included in the audit and, if necessary, what was not included in the audit. If an area or topic was specifically scoped out of the audit, it is important to state as much in the report to avoid misunderstandings.

Executive Summary   In addition to listing all the detailed issues and action plans, you need to write an executive summary so that someone who does not have the time or inclination to read all the details can understand the overall state of controls in the environment. This summary should be able to stand alone as an informative document, even if it were removed from the rest of the report. It should not list or discuss every issue, but only the most significant ones. It should not be a tedious listing of the results of each area reviewed. Instead, it should reflect relevant information about the results of the audit, assuming that the reader reads no other part of the report. It should not include platitudes and vague statements. Don't just say, "The area generally was well controlled, but there are opportunities for improvement." What does that mean? Be bold, and actually state an opinion. Say this instead:

> Strong controls were in place over account administration, but a number of control concerns were found related to software change controls. The most significant of these issues is the fact that developers have direct access to update production code. This means that these programmers can alter production code functionality without going through proper testing and approval. The development team has developed an action plan for addressing this concern, which will result in their access being removed from the production environment. Further details are found in the "Issues" section below.

This is obviously just an example, and most of your executive summary sections should be longer than this. The point is that you need to provide enough actual information so that management can understand the most important and relevant facts.

List of Issues and Action Plans   This is the meat of the report because it provides details on all the significant issues uncovered during the audit and what is going to be done to fix them. Quality and clarity of writing are essential, because each issue must be documented in such a way that multiple levels of readers can understand it. People who deal with the area day to day should be able to understand your issues and plans, and senior management should also be able to understand the risk and why it needs to be mitigated.

Explain concepts in layperson's terms and spell out each risk. For example, if you have a concern about the default umask setting on a server, you could write an issue that says, "The default umask on the server is set to 000." Although the Unix administrators will understand your concern immediately, this statement is completely meaningless to anyone else who reads it. Alternatively, you could write the issue this way: "File permissions on the server need improving." The lay reader will understand this, but the Unix administrator could interpret this in many ways and needs more detail about exactly what aspect of file permissions you're referring to. Instead, you might write the issue like this:

> The default umask on the server is set to 000. This means that, by default, when a new file is created, its file permissions are set such that anyone with access to the server will be able to read and write to the file. As this server contains critical financial data files, this could result in inappropriate access to data and/or unauthorized changes to the data.

All levels can understand this third example. The technical person understands exactly the system setting to which you're referring, and the layperson can understand the business risk being addressed.

NOTE   If you frequently audit certain systems or subject areas, you can develop a database (which could be as simple as a spreadsheet) of standard wording for common issues that are often raised during your audits. This prevents each audit team from spending time struggling with how to document the issue when writing the report and also provides consistency among audit reports. For example, if you frequently audit Unix security at various company sites, you could document standard wording for common issues such as the absence of password aging, easily guessed passwords, poor file security, and so on. Of course, the audit team should alter these as necessary to fit the circumstances of the specific audit, but the standard wording would provide an excellent starting point.

Many audit departments use a rating system in their audit reports that can provide an overall rating for the audit, such as rating each audited area as "unsatisfactory," "needs improvement," or "adequate," or could provide a number rating, with, for example, a 1 being worst and a 10 being best. The rating system also could involve rating the severity of each specific audit issue. Although your company's environment may require this sort of system, it is best to avoid it if possible. Rating systems lead to lots of wasted time and energy spent on debating with the customers what the exact rating should be. Instead of spending energy on debating whether the report should be a 5 or a 6, spend that time reaching agreement on the need to do something and on developing an action plan. The end goal is to improve the controls in the environment. Debating over a rating does not contribute to this goal.

Following is a simplified example of an audit report, using the elements described in the preceding section.

AUDIT SCOPE

During this audit, we reviewed the internal controls within the corporate accounts receivable (AR) system. This included a review of controls within the application and its related database and operating system. Physical security of the AR system server was not included in the scope of the review because those controls were tested during a recent audit of the data center.

EXECUTIVE SUMMARY

Strong controls were in place over account administration, but a number of control concerns were found related to software change controls. The most significant of these issues is the fact that developers have direct access to production code. This means that these programmers can alter production code functionality without going through proper testing and approval. The development team has developed an action plan for addressing this concern, which will result in their access being removed from the production environment. Further details are found in the "Issues" section below.

AUDIT ISSUES

1. Developers have direct access to update production code.

No technical or procedural controls are in place to prevent application support personnel from making unauthorized changes to the system.

Risk: Without proper software change controls, changes could be made to the application, either unintentionally or maliciously, that have not been approved and/or that have not been tested properly. These code changes could result in inaccurate system processing, the ability of an employee to execute fraudulent transactions, or system unavailability.

Solution: The AR system team will implement a baseline tool for protecting the production code. The ability to check new code into this tool will be limited to the group's manager and a backup, neither of whom has responsibility for performing code changes. Once this tool is implemented, the team will document procedures requiring approval and testing prior to submitting new production code for check-in.

Responsible: Clark Kent

Completion Date: *xx/xx/xx*

2. **The default umask on the server is set to 000.**
Risk: This means that, by default, when a new file is created, its file permissions are set so that anyone with access to the server will be able to read and write to the file. Since this server contains critical financial data files, this could result in inappropriate access and/or unauthorized changes to the data.
Solution: Nolan Ryan from the Unix infrastructure team will reset the default umask to 027 on the affected servers in the environment. Additionally, the Unix baseline documentation will be updated to include checking the default umask value prior to placing new systems into production.
Responsible: Nolan Ryan
Completion Date: *xx/xx/xx*

Additional Elements of an Audit Report

In addition to the three basic sections just mentioned, you might consider adding a few other elements to your reports.

Key Controls   In addition to the problems you found, you undoubtedly noticed some good things that were already being done. Some important controls were already in place that you relied on during your assessment. If these controls were not in place or were changed, it would change your overall assessment of the environment. Isn't it as important for your customers to know what they're doing right as it is for them to know what they need to improve? If you don't tell them that you considered a particular control to be important, they could make a decision to stop performing that control. For example, if you relied on the fact that they disabled all unnecessary network services on their servers and that they regularly run Tripwire to detect changes in the environment, you should state as much in the audit report. In this way, they'll know that they should not make changes to those controls.

Closed Items   If your audit customers resolve issues during the course of the audit, give them credit for it. List the issues that have already been resolved in a separate section. This keeps closed items from clogging up the "Issues" section, gives your customers credit for being proactive, and also ensures that the audit report reflects a complete picture of the problems in place at the time of the review.

Minor Issues   Sometimes you find minor issues during the project that do not represent a great risk. You have no interest in tracking their resolution because whether the customers address them or not is not important. Yet you would like to make the customers aware of your observations so that they can take action if they want. Minor issues can be listed in their own section, where you make it clear that they are being communicated purely for informational purposes and that you won't be requiring action plans or tracking resolution.

Distributing the Audit Report

Once you have drafted the report, you should let your customers review it and comment on it before it is issued. Be willing to make minor wording changes as long as they don't change the message of what you're saying. The goal should be for the customers to be comfortable with and in agreement with what's in the report.

After the report has been drafted and reviewed by the customers, it is time to issue it. Most audit departments issue all audit reports to senior management (including the CIO, CFO, and CEO) and sometimes even to the audit committee. This certainly fits with the department's goal of providing senior management with independent assurance on the state of internal controls at the company. However, it can damage your goal of partnering with management to assess and improve the state of internal controls.

 NOTE   If people know that everything you find is going to be sent all the way up the management chain, they'll likely be much less willing to share information and will be doing all they can to minimize what's in the report.

Consider seeking permission from senior management to allow you to issue reports only to the lower level management of the group being audited. Senior managers might be concerned that this will result in significant issues going unaddressed without their knowledge. You can compensate for this concern with a few additions to the process:

- Send the executive summary section of each audit to senior management. This could be compiled and sent on a quarterly basis. In this way, senior management stays in the loop and knows what's being audited and the overall results without being sent every detailed issue and action plan.

- Assure senior managers that if any issue is not resolved in a timely manner, you will escalate it to them. In this way, they will be notified only of the issues that are not being addressed.

- Assure senior managers that you will let them know about any particularly material or pervasive issues. If you find these sorts of issues on an audit, you can consider sending just those issues to senior management in an abbreviated audit report.

As you consider how to document and distribute your reports, keep in mind that your objective is to see the issues addressed, the risks mitigated, and the controls improved. Your objective is not to report things for the sake of reporting them or to show off all the things you found. Tailor your reporting process in such a way that it maximizes your chance of achieving your true objective.

Issue Tracking

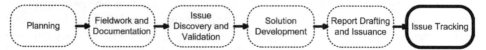

It is common for auditors to feel like the audit is "done" once the audit report has been issued. However, as discussed earlier in the book, issuing an audit report adds no value to the company unless it results in action being taken. The audit is not truly complete until the issues raised in the audit are resolved, either by being fixed (the preferred resolution) or by being accepted by the appropriate level of management. The audit department must develop a process whereby its members are able to track and follow up on issues until they are resolved. This likely will involve maintaining a database containing all audit points and their due dates, along with a mechanism for marking them as closed, overdue, and so on.

It is usually wise for the auditor who performed or led an audit to be responsible for following up on the points from that audit with the responsible customers as the due date for each point approaches. The auditor shouldn't wait until the point is due or past due before contacting the customer, but instead should be in regular contact regarding the status of the issue. This serves a number of purposes. First, it allows the auditor to consult with the customers as decisions are being made. Second, it allows the auditor to be alerted early if the solution being implemented isn't matching expectations. In this way, the auditor can try to redirect activities before things are finalized. Third, if the issue is not being resolved, it allows the audit department to try to address the problem prior to the point becoming overdue.

If it turns out that an issue is not being addressed as agreed, the auditors are responsible for initiating escalation procedures where needed. You know that not every issue has to be escalated to the audit committee if it's not being worked. The auditors must determine how important the risk is and make a decision as to what level of management needs to be aware of that risk and make a decision about whether to mitigate it. An issue should be escalated to this level of management if necessary. Every little issue does not need to be escalated to the audit committee, because the risks associated with some issues just don't warrant it. You don't need to tell the audit committee about a user having a bad password, for example.

Escalation should be a last resort and should not be a mechanical process. Judgment should be retained during the issue-tracking process. If a point is overdue, the first step should be to spend time with the responsible customers in understanding why. If they are working on the issue, but other priorities have gotten in the way, resulting in a delay, or if it has turned out that implementing the solution is more complicated than initially expected, the point need not be escalated. Instead, consider extending the due date while setting an expectation that you cannot extend it endlessly. Escalation should occur only in cases when work is truly not progressing on addressing the issue either because the customers are choosing not to take action or because the customers do not have the resources or authority to make it happen.

NOTE The escalation process should be a tool to enable the fulfillment of the audit department's goal of improving internal controls, not a mechanical process devoid of common sense.

Finally, a decision needs to be made regarding the validation of solutions implemented to address audit issues. How much emphasis needs to be placed on retesting the area to ensure that the new controls are working effectively? Although it would be nice to retest everything, it's probably not practical from a resource standpoint. In some cases, it would require a complete re-audit of the area to validate the solution. The practical answer is usually to perform a "best effort" attempt to validate that the control was indeed implemented. If the solution was to modify a system setting, for example, the auditor certainly can check the setting. If the solution was to create a disaster recovery plan, the auditor certainly can view the plan. However, sometimes the practical answer is to get the customer to explain and walk through the process or system that has been implemented without really testing its effectiveness. This is another area where the auditor's judgment and common sense need to be applied.

Standards

Standards exist for the audit profession and they should be adhered to as each company develops its audit process. On the website for the Institute for Internal Auditors (IIA), www.theiia.org, you can find the International Standards for the Professional Practice of Internal Auditing. These standards should be reviewed and incorporated into your audit process. In addition, on the same website you will find the Code of Ethics for the auditing profession, which explains the requirements for integrity, objectivity, confidentiality, and competency as they apply to auditing.

Summary

This chapter covered the following:

- Internal controls, stated in the simplest terms, are mechanisms that ensure the proper functioning of processes within a company. Controls can be preventive, detective, or reactive and have administrative, technical, and physical implementations.

- Your audit plan must focus your auditors on the areas that have the most risk and where you can add the most value. A comprehensive audit universe and effective ranking model are important elements to achieving this goal.

- An audit has six key stages: planning, fieldwork and documentation, issue discovery and validation, solution development, report drafting and issuance, and issue tracking.

- Some basic sources that should be referenced as part of each audit's planning process include handoff from the audit manager, preliminary survey, customer requests, standard checklists, and research.

- During fieldwork and documentation, wherever possible, the auditors should look for ways to validate independently the information given to them and the effectiveness of the control environment.

- If you work with your customers throughout the audit to validate issues and come to agreement on the risks those issues represent, the conclusion of the audit will go much more smoothly and quickly.

- Three common approaches are used for developing and assigning action items for addressing audit issues: the recommendation approach, the management-response approach, and the solution approach.

- The essential elements of an audit report are the statement of the audit scope, list of issues along with action plans for resolving them, and the executive summary.

- The audit is not truly complete until the issues raised in the audit are resolved.

In these first two chapters we have formed the foundation that will allow us to move on to Part II, which will provide details on how to audit specific processes and technologies.

PART II

Auditing Techniques

Guidance for Executing Test Steps

When reading the test steps provided in Part II, the reader should keep in mind some important guidelines.

One System vs. the Environment

With the exception of Chapters 3 and 4, these steps are written from the standpoint that a single system (such as a server, database, or application) is being audited. When multiple systems are being audited as part of one audit, most of these steps should be performed on each system. However, some steps, particularly those involving the review of processes (as opposed to system configuration), can likely be audited once for the whole environment, without being repeated for each system. This assumes, of course, that the same processes are being applied throughout the environment. When auditing multiple systems at once, the auditor should use judgment and adjust accordingly.

Exercising Judgment

The auditor should also use good judgment in assessing the true risk associated with these steps, based on the environment and on the overall security posture of the system. For example, in Chapter 7, "Auditing Unix and Linux Operating Systems," the controls referenced in the "Network Security and Controls" and "Account Management and Password Controls" sections tend to be some of the most important, as they deal with controls that prevent someone from accessing the system when they're not authorized to do so. Other controls, such as those mentioned in the "File Security and Controls" section, deal with controls used to prevent someone who's already on the system from accessing things they shouldn't and/or escalating their privileges. If you have a system sitting on your internal network, with network services locked down and with user accounts existing only for a small number of system administration personnel, the risk represented by some of the steps in that section is minimal. For example, file permissions become less important in that case, as you're confident that the only people accessing the system are those responsible for administering that system. It would still be good to keep everything locked down as part of a defense-in-depth strategy, but you might decide not to push as hard for some of the lesser controls.

On the other hand, systems in your DMZ usually need to be completely hardened and locked down, with even the smallest of holes closed. Likewise, systems housing critical data need to be locked down more than systems used for trivial purposes. The point is that the auditor should not use the audit steps in this section as a mindless checklist, raising an audit issue every time there is an instance of noncompliance.

Leveraging Scripts

In many of the steps discussed in this part of the book, you'll see commands that will generate the needed output. In some cases, these will simply be shown as they would be entered from the command line. In other cases, the code is written as it would appear in a shell script. It can be highly advantageous and efficient to create an audit script that you can give to the system administrator to collect needed information. This script should usually be run with the privileges of an elevated account (such as root for Unix and Linux), and can both list the information you need to see to complete the audit steps and, in some cases, actually evaluate that information for you.

Protecting Audit Data

Take care to protect the data generated by the audit, which may contain sensitive items such as account information. Encrypting this data in transit is always a good idea, using GnuPG for e-mail, for example, or other tools.

Auditing Entity-Level Controls

In this chapter we will discuss how to audit entity-level controls, which are pervasive across an organization. We will be discussing the auditing of *information technology* (IT) areas such as

- Strategic planning and technology roadmaps
- Performance indicators and metrics
- Project approval and monitoring processes
- Policies, standards, and procedures
- Employee management
- Asset and capacity management
- System configuration change management

Background

Because entity-level controls are pervasive across an organization, you can audit them once and feel confident that you have covered the topic for the whole company. This chapter discusses areas that the auditor should expect to see centralized in an organization. If the topics covered in this chapter are not centralized, or at least centrally coordinated, at your company, questions as to their overall effectiveness should arise. Most of these topics set the overall "tone at the top" for the IT organization and provide governance of the entire IT environment. If they are not centralized and/or standardized, the auditor should question the ability of the overall IT environment to be well controlled.

What is and is not considered an entity-level control is not always consistently defined and will vary by organization, depending on how the IT environment is defined. An area that is an entity-level process at one company will not necessarily be an entity-level process at another company. However, there's really no mystery to it—it all comes down to what is centralized and pervasive at your company. If a critical IT process is centralized, it is a good candidate for an entity-level controls review.

For example, Chapter 4 covers the topic of auditing data centers and areas such as physical security, environmental controls, system monitoring, and so on. Many companies have multiple decentralized data centers, meaning that these controls are not centralized for those companies. However, some companies have one data center and one set of processes for executing these areas, so physical security, environmental controls, and system monitoring would qualify as entity-level controls because they are centralized and pervasive. (However, such areas are not covered in this chapter as they are covered in Chapter 4.) Auditors must use good judgment and knowledge of the company to determine what is and is not an entity-level control.

As mentioned earlier, the topics covered in this chapter should be centralized to a large degree, because they provide for the core principles of IT governance. If these areas have no central coordination, the auditor should dig deep before signing off as to their effectiveness. Put another way, the areas covered in this chapter should be considered the minimum for an entity-level controls review. Other areas (such as data center operations) might be added based on the environment at your company.

NOTE   Strong IT entity-level controls form a foundation for the IT control environment within a company. They demonstrate that IT management is serious about internal controls, risk management, and governance. A strong overall control environment and attitude that originates from the top tends to trickle down throughout the organization and leads to strong controls over decentralized processes and functions. Conversely, weak entity-level controls increase the likelihood that controls will be weak throughout the organization, because upper management has not demonstrated and communicated to the organization that internal controls are valued. This often leads to inconsistency at the lower levels, because the personalities and values of lower-level managers will be the sole determining factors in how seriously internal controls are taken within the organization.

It is critical for upper management to communicate and set the tone that internal controls, risk management, and governance are valued and will be rewarded. Without this message, departments are more likely to focus on cutting costs, managing their budgets, and meeting their schedules, with no consideration given to internal controls.

Test Steps for Auditing Entity-Level Controls

1. Review the overall IT organization structure to ensure that it provides for clear assignment of authority and responsibility over IT operations and that it provides for adequate segregation of duties.

A poorly defined IT organization structure can lead to confusion regarding responsibilities, causing IT support functions to be performed inefficiently or ineffectively. For example, critical functions may be either neglected or performed redundantly.

Also, if lines of authority are not clearly established, it can lead to disagreement as to who has the ultimate ability to make a final decision. Finally, if IT duties are not segregated appropriately, it could lead to fraudulent activities and affect the integrity of the company's information and processes.

How

A "one size fits all" model for an IT organization doesn't exist, and you can't mechanically use a checklist to determine whether your company's IT organization is adequate. Instead, you must view the overall organization and apply judgment in determining whether it adequately addresses the most essential elements. With this in mind, the following discussion covers some key areas to consider during this review.

Review IT organization charts and ensure that they clearly indicate reporting structures. The organization charts should provide an indication as to where in the company the various IT organizations meet. For example, in most companies, all IT organizations eventually report to the chief information officer (CIO) so that one ultimate authority is able to set rules for the overall IT environment. Ensure that your company has IT organization reporting structures that eventually report to a single source that is "close enough" to day-to-day IT operations to allow for effective governance and direction setting. If the IT organizations report to multiple CIOs or consolidate only to a high-level executive such as the chief executive officer (CEO), additional processes will likely be needed to develop an effective method for establishing overall policies, priorities, and governance for IT at the company. Otherwise, it is likely that "fiefdoms" will exist within IT, preventing the establishment of true entity-level IT controls.

Review IT organization charts and charters and ensure that they clearly delineate areas of responsibility. Determine whether it is clear how responsibilities are divided between organizations, or evaluate whether there is significant opportunity for confusion and overlap. In addition to reviewing documented organization charts and charters, consider interviewing a sample of IT employees and customers to determine whether there is a consistent understanding of the division of responsibility.

Evaluate the division of responsibilities within the IT organization to ensure that duties are segregated appropriately. You also should consider criticality in making judgments. It is more important that separation of duties be in place over critical financial systems than over systems providing support for minor convenience functions (such as the company's internal training system).

 NOTE The specifics of which duties should be segregated from others will vary by company; however, the general idea is that the responsibilities for initiating, authorizing, inputting, processing, and checking data should be segregated so that one person does not have the ability to create a fraudulent transaction, authorize it, and hide the evidence. In other words, you're attempting to prevent one person from being able to subvert a critical process.

Following are some basic general guidelines that can be considered during the review. Again, this should not be used as a mechanical checklist, and the auditor should review for compensating controls when investigating potential exceptions.

- *IT personnel should not perform data entry.* Keep in mind that IT organizations differ in their composition across companies, so some data-entry personnel may be classified as IT in their companies. In this case, we're referring to IT personnel who are performing true systems support.

- *Programmers and those performing run/maintain support for systems should not directly be able to modify production code, production data, or the job-scheduling structure.* As with all these statements, when a segregation-of-duties issue seems apparent, the auditor should look for compensating controls before determining whether it is a true issue. Access to production data and code may not be a large risk if strict accountability and change-control procedures are in support of that access.

- *Programmers and those performing run/maintain support for systems should be separate from those performing IT operations support (such as support for networks, data centers, operating systems, and so on).*

- *An IT security organization should be responsible for setting policies and monitoring for compliance with those policies.* This IT security organization should have no operational responsibilities outside those related to IT security.

2. Review the IT strategic planning process and ensure that it aligns with business strategies. Evaluate the IT organization's processes for monitoring progress against the strategic plan.

To provide for long-term effectiveness, the IT organization must have some sort of strategy regarding where it plans to go, as opposed to being in reactive mode constantly, where day-to-day issues and crises are the only considerations. The IT organization must be aware of upcoming business needs and changes in the environment so that it can plan and react accordingly. It is important that IT priorities align with business priorities. Too many IT organizations lose sight of the fact that their only reason for existence is to support the company in meeting its business objectives. Instead, these IT organizations focus on becoming a "world-class IT shop," even when this goal doesn't directly support the overall company objectives. It is critical for IT organizations to stay grounded by tying their objectives to the company's objectives.

How

Look for evidence of a strategic planning process within IT, and understand how that planning is performed. Determine how company strategies and priorities were used in developing the IT strategies and priorities. Review documented short- and long-term IT priorities. Evaluate processes in place for periodically monitoring for progress against those priorities and for reevaluating and updating those priorities.

3. Determine whether technology and application strategies and roadmaps exist, and evaluate processes for long-range technical planning.

IT is a rapidly changing environment, and it is important that IT organizations understand and plan for change. Otherwise, the company's IT environment runs the risk of becoming obsolete and/or not fully leveraging technology to benefit the company.

How

Look for evidence that long-term technical planning is being performed. For purchased applications and technologies, determine whether IT understands the vendor's support roadmap for those products. The IT organization should understand when their versions of the products will cease to be supported and create plans for either upgrading or replacing the products. Determine whether processes are in place to monitor for changes in relevant technologies, consider how those changes will impact the company, and look for opportunities to use new technologies to help the company.

4. Review performance indicators and measurements for IT. Ensure that processes and metrics are in place (and approved by key stakeholders) for measuring performance of day-to-day activities and for tracking performance against service-level agreements, budgets, and other operational requirements.

The IT organization exists to support the business and its day-to-day operations. If minimum standards of performance are not established and measured, it is difficult for the business to determine whether the IT organization's services are being performed at an acceptable level.

How

Obtain a copy of any metrics being captured for the IT organization's routine activities (such as system uptime and response time). Determine the goals for those metrics, and ensure that the appropriate stakeholders have approved those goals. If actual performance is significantly inferior to goals, determine whether root-cause analyses have been performed to understand the problem and whether plans are in place to solve the problem.

Review any SLAs that have been established for supporting IT's key stakeholders. Ensure that processes are in place for measuring actual performance against the requirements of the SLA and for correcting any deviations.

Ensure that processes are in place for establishing budgets and for holding the IT organization accountable for meeting its budget. Obtain copies of the IT budget for the current and preceding years, as well as copies of any "budget versus actual" analyses. Determine how any significant variances were reported and resolved.

5. Review the IT organization's process for approving and prioritizing new projects. Determine whether this process is adequate for ensuring that system acquisition and development projects cannot commence without approval. Ensure that management and key stakeholders review project status, schedule, and budget periodically throughout the life of significant projects.

Without a structured process for approving and prioritizing new IT projects, IT resources probably will not be deployed efficiently. Instead, they will be assigned on an ad hoc basis to whatever potential project comes up next. Also, IT projects may commence that do not meet the needs of the business and/or that are not as important as other potential projects to which those resources could be deployed. Without a structured process whereby management and key stakeholders periodically review the project's progress, it is more likely that the project will get off track and fail to meet key goals and milestones.

How

Review any available documentation regarding the project proposal and approval process. Evaluate the process for potential holes that might allow a project to commence without approval. Look for evidence that proposed projects have been prioritized prior to approval and that some discipline and commonality exists within this approval process. Consider selecting a sample of active IT projects and obtaining evidence that those projects went through an appropriate process of proposal, prioritization, and approval. Review evidence that management and key stakeholders are periodically reviewing the status, schedule, and budget for active IT projects. Ensure that the project approval process calls for a thorough cost analysis before project commencement so that management can make an informed decision regarding expected return on investment (ROI) for the project. These cost analyses should consider not only the project start-up costs but also ongoing costs, such as software maintenance, hardware maintenance, support (labor) costs, power, and cooling requirements for system hardware, and so on. This element is often omitted erroneously, leading to misinformed decisions. Start-up costs are only a fraction of the total ongoing costs for implementing a new system. A multi-year (five years is often a good target) total cost model should be developed as part of the initial project analysis.

6. Evaluate standards for governing the execution of IT projects and for ensuring the quality of products developed or acquired by the IT organization. Determine how these standards are communicated and enforced.

If standards are not in place and enforced in the IT environment, projects probably will be executed in an undisciplined fashion, quality issues will exist in developed or purchased products, and the IT environment will be unnecessarily diverse (leading to increased support costs and potential interface issues).

How

Determine whether documented standards govern areas such as the following. If so, review those standards and ensure that they are adequate.

- **Project management** See Chapter 15 for guidelines regarding key elements that should exist within project management standards.

- **Software development** Standards should exist governing the development of code, including standards for naming, revision history, comments, and calls to other programs. Without such standards, the time and effort required for one person to support and troubleshoot another person's code increase significantly. Note that depending on the size of the IT organization, it may be acceptable for programming standards to be decentralized to a degree.

However, each significant development organization should have a set of standards. See Chapter 15 for guidelines regarding key elements that should exist within these standards.

- **System configuration** This would include standard configuration for laptops, desktops, servers, and common user software packages. Common configuration will help to ensure that the systems are supportable and that they have the appropriate security settings.

- **Hardware and software** Standards should exist governing the hardware and software that is approved and supported for use in the company. This should include the specific versions that are supported. Otherwise, the IT environment likely will consist of a multitude of products performing similar functions, driving up IT support costs and leading to problems with the ability of the various products to interface with each other.

- **Quality assurance standards** Standards should exist that ensure that the development process includes the evaluation of security risks and internal control requirements.

Look for evidence that these standards are communicated to all relevant IT employees, and determine how these standards are enforced.

 NOTE Consider reviewing a sample of recent and active IT projects for evidence that the standards were followed. Consider reviewing a sample of systems for deviations from configuration, hardware, and software standards.

7. Ensure that IT security policies exist and provide adequate requirements for the security of the environment. Determine how those policies are communicated and how compliance is monitored and enforced.

IT security policy sets a baseline of expectations for employees of the company. If policies don't exist or provide adequate coverage, employees are forced to make up their own rules regarding security-related issues. The same concept extends to computer systems, which require a standard by which system security can be evaluated. If IT security policies are too lenient, they will not provide adequate protection of the company's information assets. If they are too strict, they either will be ignored or will place unnecessary overhead and costs on the business.

If the IT security policies aren't communicated to employees, they won't be followed. Additionally, if compliance with those policies is not monitored and enforced, employees will learn quickly that the policies can be ignored with no consequences, causing the policies to become "suggestions" rather than requirements.

How

Verify Adequate Policy Coverage   Obtain a copy of your company's IT security policies. Ensure that they adequately cover your company's IT environment. At a minimum, the policies should include coverage of the following areas:

- Acceptable usage of the company's information assets by employees (for example, whether employees can use their computers, the Internet, and e-mail for personal reasons)
- Data classification, retention, and destruction
- Remote connectivity (for example, overall network security and security requirements for virtual private network (VPN), dial-up, and other forms of connection to external parties)
- Passwords
- Server security (such as security requirements for Unix and Windows servers)
- Client security (such as security requirements for desktops and laptops)
- Logical access (such as requirements for obtaining and granting access to systems)

Review the policies for adequacy based on industry standards and the specific needs of your company. The audit steps in the other chapters of Part II can be used as guidelines.

Specifically review the company's password policy. It should provide adequate guidelines dictating requirements for the composition of company passwords (for example, minimum of eight characters, combination of letters and numbers, difficult to guess, and so on), for aging company passwords (such as requiring that they be changed every 90 days), for locking accounts after a certain number of unsuccessful logon attempts, for timing out login sessions after a period of inactivity, and for retaining a password history so that previous passwords cannot be reused for a certain period of time.

Specifically review the company's logical access policy. It should provide adequate guidelines dictating requirements for every user to have a unique ID, for accounts to be suspended upon employee termination or job change, and for users to be granted the minimum access necessary to perform their jobs.

Verify Stakeholder Buy-in   Ensure that key stakeholders were included during policy creation. Obtain a list of employees involved in the creation and approval of the IT security policies, such as IT organizations that are expected to comply with the policy. If IT security policies are created in a vacuum by the IT security organization without involving others, they are likely to be viewed as unrealistic and will be ignored. Involvement from those who provide the day-to-day support of the IT environment will bring an important perspective to the policies and also will ensure buy-in from those who need to enforce and comply with the policies. Ensure that the IT security policies were approved by an executive, such as the CIO or CEO. This will provide the IT organization with the authority and backing necessary to enforce the policies.

Verify Processes Around the Policies Review processes for periodically reviewing and updating the policies to ensure that they keep up with the ever-changing IT environment. Look for evidence that these processes have been executed.

Review processes for periodically evaluating changes in the environment that might necessitate the development of new policies. Look for evidence that these processes have been executed.

Ensure that provisions have been made for obtaining approved exemptions from the policy. There inevitably will be occasions when people do not think that they can comply with the policy. A defined process should be in place whereby those people can formally request an exemption from the policy. They should be required to state why they need an exemption and define the compensating controls that will be put in place. The IT security organization should facilitate the exception process, including providing a recommendation and an opinion on the risk presented by the request, but they usually should avoid making the final decision as to whether or not to accept the risk. Instead, it should be a business decision. Review the escalation policy for the exemption process and ensure that business (as opposed to IT) management is involved at some point, at least for the acceptance of significant risks. Ensure that the final decisions are documented and retained.

 NOTE Look for evidence that the IT security policies are communicated adequately to all company employees. Potential vectors include referencing the policies during new-hire orientation and/or having all employees periodically sign a statement that they have read and agree to the policies.

Review processes implemented by IT security and other IT organizations for monitoring compliance with the policies. Ensure that enforcement and escalation processes are in place that result in the correction of noncompliant situations. Review a sample of recent applicable compliance-monitoring reports, and ensure that significant issues were tracked to resolution.

Ensure that a mechanism exists for employees to report security incidents or concerns and that those reports are followed up on and tracked to resolution. Review a sample of recently reported incidents, and determine whether they were resolved adequately.

8. Review and evaluate risk-assessment processes in place for the IT organization.

Without these processes, the IT organization will be unaware of risks to the achievement of its objectives and therefore will not have the ability to make conscious decisions regarding whether to accept or mitigate those risks.

How

Some overlap exists between this step and some of the other steps mentioned in this chapter, many of which are designed to determine how the IT organization is evaluating its own risks. You might consider this step to be adequately covered without explicitly performing it. However, you should look for evidence that the IT organization is periodically considering the risks to the IT environment and making conscious decisions as to whether to accept, mitigate, or avoid those risks. Risk-assessment mechanisms could include the following:

- Monitoring internal controls in the IT environment, including internal audits and self-assessments

- Performing formal threat and risk assessments of critical data centers and systems

- Performing periodic reviews of the strategic IT plans and technical roadmaps and assessing risks to the achievement of those plans

- Monitoring compliance with IT security policies and other relevant IT policies

9. Review and evaluate processes for ensuring that IT employees at the company have the skills and knowledge necessary for performing their jobs.

If employees in the IT organization are not qualified to perform their jobs, the quality of IT services will be poor. If mechanisms are not in place for maintaining and enhancing the knowledge and skills of IT employees, their knowledge can become outdated and obsolete.

How

Review human resources (HR) policies and processes as they relate to IT employees. Look for mechanisms that ensure that qualified people are hired and that provide for continuous enhancements of employee skills and knowledge. Review evidence that these policies and processes are followed. Here are some examples:

- Ensure that job descriptions exist for all IT positions and that the job descriptions specifically state the knowledge and skills required for each job. Review evidence that these job descriptions are referenced during the hiring process. Review processes for keeping the job descriptions up to date.

- Review the IT organization's training policies and ensure that they provide the opportunity for employees to attend training classes and seminars for enhancing and updating their skills and knowledge. Look for evidence that IT employees have taken training over the past year.

- Review performance-review processes. Look for evidence that IT employees are receiving regular feedback on their performance. Ensure that processes exist for identifying poor performers, coaching them, and moving them out of the organization if performance does not improve. Conversely, ensure that processes exist for identifying top performers, rewarding them, and providing them with incentives to remain at the company.

10. Review and evaluate policies and processes for assigning ownership of company data, classifying the data, protecting the data in accordance with their classification, and defining the data's life cycle.

Although IT is responsible for providing the technology and mechanisms for protecting company data, a framework must be in place for making decisions as to what level of protection is necessary for any given data element (based on the criticality of the data). Without such a framework, there will be inconsistency in how data are protected, likely resulting in some data being underprotected (thereby placing critical information assets at risk) or overprotected (leading to unnecessary costs). If the life cycle of data is not defined, it will lead to data being retained longer than necessary (resulting in additional storage costs and possible legal liabilities) or being destroyed prematurely (leading to potential operational, legal, or tax issues).

How

Review the company's data classification policy. It should have provisions for identifying owners for all critical company data. It also should provide a framework for classifying that data based on its criticality (for example, confidential, internal data, public data). This framework should provide specific definitions of each classification level, along with specific requirements for how data at each level should be protected (for example, encryption).

Review evidence that the data classification policy has been implemented. Look for a list of data owners and documentation indicating that those owners have classified their data. For a sample of this data, review evidence that protection has been implemented in alignment with the classification.

Determine whether life-cycle information has been created for company data. For a sample of major data elements, review documentation of the data's life-cycle requirements, including retention, archive, and destruction requirements. Ideally, requirements will be identified for how long the data should be active (online, easily accessible, modifiable if appropriate, and backed up periodically), when and for how long they should be archived (possibly offline, not necessarily easy to access, no longer modifiable, and no longer backed up periodically), and when they should be destroyed.

Review evidence that life-cycle requirements have been implemented.

11. Ensure that effective processes exist for complying with applicable laws and regulations that affect IT and for maintaining awareness of changes in the regulatory environment.

If your company is found to be in violation of applicable laws and regulations (such as Health Insurance Portability and Accountability Act [HIPAA] and Sarbanes-Oxley), it could face stiff penalties and fines, a damaged reputation, lawsuits, and possibly cessation of the company. If a robust process is not in place for monitoring the regulatory environment, the company may be unaware of new laws and regulations, resulting in noncompliance.

PART II

How

Look for a single point of contact that is responsible for monitoring the regulatory environment and its impact on IT. This person or organization should be responsible for identifying laws and regulations that apply to the company's IT environment, ensuring that the responsibility for complying with those rules has been explicitly assigned to the appropriate organization(s), and monitoring the regulatory environment for additions and changes that will affect the company. If no single person or organization is responsible for this (or a small subset of people, each with a specific regulatory domain to cover), it likely will be done on an ad hoc basis, providing no assurance of full coverage. Review the processes used to monitor the regulatory environment, and evaluate their effectiveness. Obtain a list of IT-applicable regulations that have been identified, and look for evidence that responsibility for compliance with those regulations has been assigned and is being monitored. See Chapter 17 for more information on laws and regulations that may be applicable to your company.

12. Review and evaluate processes for ensuring that end users of the IT environment can report problems, are appropriately involved in IT decisions, and are satisfied with the services provided by IT.

Because the IT environment exists to support the company's employees in performing their jobs, it is critical that processes exist whereby those employees can provide input into the quality of service they are receiving. Otherwise, the IT organization may be misaligned with its users and not be aware of it.

How

Ensure that a help desk function provides end users with the ability to report problems. Review and evaluate processes for capturing problems and ensuring that they are tracked to resolution. Obtain a list of recent tickets, and select a sample, ensuring that all tickets were resolved and that no tickets were closed without the consent of the user who entered the ticket.

Ensure that a process exists for obtaining end-user feedback after tickets are closed. Look for evidence that user-satisfaction metrics are kept and that management follows up on end-user feedback.

To ensure that the help desk does not seek customer satisfaction at the expense of security, review policies and processes for obtaining proper approvals prior to responding to user requests for having passwords reset and for obtaining system access. Review a sample of these sorts of tickets, and ensure that proper processes were followed and approvals obtained.

Look for the existence of customer steering teams to provide input and prioritization of IT projects and enhancements. For significant areas of the business, key stakeholders should be identified to provide guidance to the IT organization regarding projects and decisions that affect them. Otherwise, the IT organization will be making decisions in a vacuum and likely will work on projects or enhancements that do not provide the greatest value for the business.

Review any SLAs that have been established for supporting IT's key stakeholders. Ensure that processes are in place for measuring actual performance against the requirements of the SLA and for correcting any deviations.

13. Review and evaluate processes for managing third-party services, ensuring that their roles and responsibilities are clearly defined and monitoring their performance.

Many companies outsource some or all of their IT support processes, including areas such as PC support, web server hosting, system support, programming, and so on. If these vendors are not managed appropriately, it can lead to poor service and unacceptable quality in the IT environment. Depending on what portion of the IT environment has been outsourced, these problems could significantly impact the company's operations.

How

Review the process for selecting vendors. Ensure that the process requires soliciting multiple competitive bids, the comparison of each vendor against predefined criteria, involvement of knowledgeable procurement personnel to help negotiate the contract, evaluation of the vendor's technical support capabilities and experience providing support for companies of similar size and industries as yours, performance of a thorough cost analysis, and investigation of each vendor's qualifications and financial health. For a sample of recent vendor selections, review evidence that the process was followed.

Ensure that contracts with third-party service providers specifically define the roles and responsibilities of the vendor and include defined SLAs. Review a sample of contracts for evidence that expectations have been specifically defined.

Ensure that contracts include nondisclosure clauses, preventing the vendor from disclosing company information. Also ensure that contracts include right-to-audit clauses that allow you to audit vendor activities that are critical to your company. Review a sample of contracts for evidence that these clauses are in place where applicable.

Review processes for monitoring the performance and providing oversight of existing third-party service providers. For a sample of existing vendors, look for evidence that they are being monitored for compliance with SLAs and that they are performing the responsibilities defined in the contract.

See Chapter 14 for more details on auditing outsourced operations.

14. Review and evaluate processes for controlling nonemployee logical access.

Most companies employ some level of outsourcing and contract labor to supplement their internal workforce. Also, some companies allow third-party vendors a degree of logical access to purchased systems for troubleshooting and support purposes. Because these personnel are not employees of the company, they are less likely to have a personal investment in the company's success or an awareness of the company's policies and culture. If their access to company information assets is not governed, and if expectations regarding their use of that access are not communicated, it is more likely that company information assets will be exposed unnecessarily or misused.

How

Ensure that policies require approval and sponsorship from an employee prior to a nonemployee obtaining logical access to company systems. If feasible, obtain a sample of nonemployee accounts, and validate that they have appropriate approval and sponsorship.

Review and evaluate processes for communicating company policies (including IT security policies) to nonemployees prior to granting them system access. Look for evidence that this communication has taken place. For example, if all nonemployees are required to sign a statement that they have read and agree to the policies, pull a sample of nonemployees and obtain copies of these agreements.

Review and evaluate processes for removing logical access from nonemployees when they have ceased to work with your company or otherwise no longer need access. Consider obtaining a sample of current nonemployee accounts and validating that those nonemployees are still working with your company and still have a need for their current level of access.

Ensure that nondisclosure agreements (NDAs) are signed by nonemployees to legally protect your company from inappropriate use of company data. Pull a sample of nonemployee accounts, and obtain a copy of the NDAs for those accounts.

Ensure that consideration has been given to identifying data that should not be accessed by nonemployees and activities that should not be performed by nonemployees. For example, your company may decide that access to certain levels of financial data should never be granted to nonemployees. Or it may decide that nonemployees should never be granted system administration duties. The answer will depend on your company's industry and philosophies; however, an evaluation process should take place, and the results of that evaluation should be documented in company policy and enforced. This evaluation should be part of the data classification effort described in Step 10 and should drive the restrictions on nonemployee logical access.

15. Review and evaluate processes for ensuring that the company is in compliance with applicable software licenses.

Using software illegally can lead to penalties, fines, and lawsuits. It is increasingly easy for company employees to download software from the Internet. If companies do not develop processes for preventing or tracking such activity (as well as tracking the use of company licenses for purchased software), they can find themselves subject to software vendor audits without the ability to account properly for the company's use of the vendor's software.

How

Look for evidence that the company maintains a list of enterprise software licenses (such as for Microsoft Office, ERP application accounts, and so on) and has developed a process for monitoring use of those licenses and complying with the terms of agreement. Determine how decentralized (non-enterprise) licenses are monitored and tracked. This would include software purchased by employees and placed on their company computers, as well as software downloaded from the Internet. Truly comprehensive software asset management requires a centralized database that contains information on exactly what software the company has the right to use (licenses purchased) and on exactly what software is being used in the environment (licenses used) and can compare the two. Test the effectiveness of the method used at your company either by performing your own scans on a sample of computers or by reviewing evidence from the company's processes.

16. Review and evaluate controls over remote access into the company's network (such as dial-up, VPN, dedicated external connections).

Allowing remote access to a network basically results in that network being extended beyond its normal confines, bypassing normal perimeter controls such as firewalls. A lack of strong controls regarding this access can result in inappropriate access to the network and a compromised network.

How

Ensure that a user ID and strong password are required for remote access and that these credentials are transmitted over secure (such as encrypted) communication channels.

Determine whether approval processes are in place for granting remote access, especially for nonemployees. Pull a sample of users with remote access, and look for evidence of approval. Also evaluate processes for removing dial-up and VPN remote access accounts when employees leave the company. Pull a sample of users with remote access, and ensure that they are still active employees.

Evaluate controls for ensuring that dedicated external connections to business partners are removed when no longer needed. Pull a sample of current connections, and by means of interviews and documentation review, determine whether they are still legitimately necessary.

Evaluate controls for ensuring that unauthorized connections cannot be made to the network and/or for detecting them if they are. Evaluate controls for ensuring that unauthorized modems or VPN connection points cannot be placed on the network and/or for detecting them if they are.

Ensure that policies provide minimum security requirements that should be met by all machines accessing the network remotely. This should include requirements for operating system patch level and antivirus protection. Look for preventive or detective controls that enforce these requirements.

Ensure that machines that are remotely accessing the network are not permitted to be dual-homed, which would bridge networks. This should be enforced technically where possible and by explicit agreement otherwise.

17. Ensure that hiring and termination procedures are clear and comprehensive.

Hiring procedures ensure that employees are submitted to drug screens and background checks, where local laws permit, prior to beginning work within an organization. Termination procedures ensure that access to company systems and facilities is revoked before a disgruntled employee can cause damage and that company property is returned. Inadequate hiring or termination procedures would expose the company to sabotage or abuse of privileges that could result in an information security compromise.

How

Review HR policies and procedures for the hiring and termination of employees. Ensure that hiring procedures include background checks, drug screens, and confidentiality agreements. Ensure that termination procedures include physical and logical access revocation, return of company-owned equipment, and, where appropriate, supervision while the former employee collects his or her belongings.

18. Review and evaluate policies and procedures for controlling the procurement and movement of hardware.

Asset management is the controlling, tracking, and reporting of organizational assets to facilitate accounting for the assets. Without effective asset management, the company will be subject to the increased expense of duplicate equipment in situations where equipment is available but unaccounted for. The company will also be subject to unnecessary lease expenses if leased equipment is not adequately tracked and returned on time. Similarly, without adequate asset management, end-of-life equipment conditions may not be noted, resulting in increased risk of hardware failure. Additionally, theft of equipment that is not tracked likely would go unnoticed. In the context of this step, the assets being referred to are computer hardware, such as desktops, laptops, servers, and so on.

How

Review and evaluate the company's asset management policies and procedures, and ensure that they encompass the following:

- **Asset procurement process**   Ensure that this process requires appropriate approvals prior to the purchase of hardware.
- **Asset tracking**   Ensure that the company is using asset tags and has an asset management database.
- **Current inventory of all equipment**   Ensure that an inventory contains the asset number and location of all hardware, along with information about the equipment's warranty status, lease expiration, and overall lifecycle (that is, when it is no longer eligible for vendor support). Ensure that an effective mechanism is in place for keeping this inventory up to date. A sample of asset tags also should be inspected visibly and tied back to the inventory.
- **Asset move and disposal procedures**   Ensure that unused equipment is stored in a secure manner. Also ensure that data are erased properly from equipment prior to its disposal.

19. Ensure that system configurations are controlled with change management to avoid unnecessary system outages.

Configuration change management ensures that system changes are controlled and tracked to reduce the risk of system outages. It includes planning, scheduling, applying, and tracking changes to systems for the purpose of reducing the risk of those changes to the environment.

How

Change activities can affect two areas: hardware and software (including operating-system–level changes). Ensure that the configuration-management procedures include processes for the following:

- Requesting changes (including processes for end users to request changes)
- Determining the specifics of what should change
- Prioritizing and approving proposed changes
- Scheduling approved changes
- Testing and approving changes prior to implementation
- Communicating planned changes prior to implementation
- Implementing changes
- Rolling back (removing) changes that don't work as expected after implementation

Also review change-control documentation to verify that changes are fully documented, approved, and tracked. Approvals should incorporate a risk assessment and typically are granted by a committee made up of stakeholders. You should be able to obtain a sample of change-control requests, as well as other configuration management documentation, from IT management.

20. Ensure that media transportation, storage, reuse, and disposal are addressed adequately by company-wide policies and procedures.

Media controls ensure that information stored on data-storage media remains confidential and is protected from premature deterioration or destruction. Inadequate media transportation, storage, reuse, and disposal policies and procedures expose organizations to possible unauthorized disclosure or destruction of critical information. One increasingly common type of security incident is the loss of backup media in transit by third-party carriers. A number of high-profile companies have fallen victim to this threat in recent years, having incurred losses owing to legal actions, reputation damage, and incident response costs.

How

Computer media, including, but not limited to, backup tapes, CDs and DVDs, hard disks, USB jump drives, and floppy disks, must be strictly controlled to ensure data privacy. Since backup operators, computer technicians, system administrators, third-party carriers, and even end users handle storage media, media policies and procedures should address these disparate roles. When auditing media control policies and procedures, look for the following:

- Requirements for sensitive information to be encrypted prior to transporting it through a third-party carrier
- Requirements for magnetic media to be digitally shredded or degaussed prior to reuse or disposal
- Requirements for optical and paper media to be physically shredded prior to disposal
- Requirements for users to be trained adequately on how to store and dispose of computer media, including jump drives
- Requirements for computer media to be stored in a physically secure, temperature-controlled, and dry location to prevent damage to the media

You can obtain this information through the review of IT policies, procedures, and security awareness training documents, as well as user interviews.

21. Verify that capacity monitoring and planning are addressed adequately by company policies and procedures.

Anticipating and monitoring the capacity of data center facilities, computer systems, and applications are critical parts of ensuring system availability. When companies neglect these controls, they often experience system outages and data loss.

How

Review for the following:

- Selected architecture documents to ensure that systems and facilities are designed to anticipated capacity requirements
- Systems monitoring procedures, paying particular attention to capacity thresholds
- System monitoring logs to determine the percentage of systems that are approaching or exceeding capacity thresholds
- System availability reports to ensure that system capacity issues are not causing undue downtime

Since capacity management is addressed most often by the groups responsible for data centers, applications, or system management, specific procedures should be addressed within these areas.

22. Based on the structure of your company's IT organization and processes, identify and audit other entity-level IT processes.

By identifying those baseline IT controls, you should be able to reduce testing during other audits and avoid repetition. For example, if your company has only one production data center, you can test the physical security and environmental controls of that data center once. Then, as you perform audits of individual systems that are housed in that data center, instead of auditing the physical security and environmental controls for each of those systems (which would be very repetitive because they're all in the same place), you can just reference your entity-level audit of those topics and move on. Also, by performing audits of centralized processes, you will have an understanding of potential compensating controls in the overall IT environment that may mitigate concerns you have with lower-level controls.

 NOTE   If a critical IT process at your company is centralized, it is a good candidate for being reviewed during an entity-level controls audit. By auditing it once at the company level, you will be able to rely on the results of that audit when performing audits of other IT systems and processes.

How

Review the topics covered in the other chapters in Part II of this book, and consider whether any of those areas are centralized at your company. Those topics are candidates for an entity-level controls review. Here are some likely candidates:

- Data center physical security and environmental controls (see Chapter 4)
- System monitoring (such as performance and availability) and incident reporting (see Chapter 4)
- Disaster recovery planning (see Chapter 4)
- Backup processes (see Chapter 4)
- Network security and management (see Chapter 5)
- Windows system administration processes (such as account management, security monitoring) (see Chapter 6)
- Security of baselines used for deployment of new Windows systems (see Chapter 6)
- Virus protection (such as antivirus, patching, compliance checking) (see Chapter 6)
- Unix/Linux system administration processes (such as account management, security monitoring, security patching) (see Chapter 7)
- Security of baselines used for deployment of new Unix and Linux systems (see Chapter 7)
- Software change controls for internally developed code (see Chapter 13)
- Enterprise password and account management practices (see Step 7 in this chapter for guidance)

Knowledge Base

As mentioned throughout this chapter, the specifics of entity-level controls will vary from company to company. However, the best general sources of information on IT-specific entity-level controls can be found on the Information Systems Audit and Control Association (ISACA) website (www.isaca.org), where details on the control objectives for information and related technology (COBIT) framework and guidelines for Sarbanes-Oxley IT compliance testing are available. In addition, general guidelines on entity-level controls (not specific to IT) and links to resources related to the popular Committee of Sponsoring Organizations (COSO) model of internal controls can be found on the website for the Institute of Internal Auditors (IIA) at www.theiia.org. Finally, your external auditors likely will have some published guidelines to share with you on this topic.

Master Checklist

The following table summarizes the steps listed herein for auditing entity-level controls.

Auditing Entity-Level Controls

	Checklist for Auditing Entity-Level Controls
❑	1. Review the overall IT organization structure to ensure that it provides for clear assignment of authority and responsibility over IT operations and that it provides for adequate segregation of duties.
❑	2. Review the IT strategic planning process to ensure that it aligns with business strategies. Evaluate the IT organization's processes for monitoring progress against the strategic plan.
❑	3. Determine whether technology and application strategies and roadmaps exist, and evaluate processes for long-range technical planning.
❑	4. Review performance indicators and measurements for IT. Ensure that processes and metrics are in place (and approved by key stakeholders) for measuring performance of day-to-day activities and for tracking performance against SLAs, budgets, and other operational requirements.
❑	5. Review the IT organization's process for approving and prioritizing new projects. Determine whether this process is adequate for ensuring that system acquisition and development projects cannot commence without approval. Ensure that management and key stakeholders review project status, schedule, and budget periodically throughout the life of significant projects.
❑	6. Evaluate standards for governing the execution of IT projects and for ensuring the quality of products developed or acquired by the IT organization. Determine how these standards are communicated and enforced.
❑	7. Ensure that IT security policies exist and provide adequate requirements for the security of the environment. Determine how those policies are communicated and how compliance is monitored and enforced.
❑	8. Review and evaluate risk-assessment processes in place for the IT organization.
❑	9. Review and evaluate processes for ensuring that IT employees at the company have the skills and knowledge necessary for performing their jobs.

Checklist for Auditing Entity-Level Controls *(continued)*

❏ 10. Review and evaluate policies and processes for assigning ownership of company data, classifying the data, protecting the data in accordance with their classification, and defining the data's life cycle.

❏ 11. Ensure that effective processes exist for complying with applicable laws and regulations that affect IT (such as HIPAA, Sarbanes-Oxley) and for maintaining awareness of changes in the regulatory environment.

❏ 12. Review and evaluate processes for ensuring that end users of the IT environment have the ability to report problems, are appropriately involved in IT decisions, and are satisfied with the services provided by IT.

❏ 13. Review and evaluate processes for managing third-party services, ensuring that their roles and responsibilities are clearly defined and monitoring their performance.

❏ 14. Review and evaluate processes for controlling nonemployee logical access.

❏ 15. Review and evaluate processes for ensuring that the company is in compliance with applicable software licenses.

❏ 16. Review and evaluate controls over remote access into the company's network (such as dial-up, VPN, dedicated external connections).

❏ 17. Ensure that hiring and termination procedures are clear and comprehensive.

❏ 18. Review and evaluate policies and procedures for controlling the procurement and movement of hardware.

❏ 19. Ensure that system configurations are controlled with change management to avoid unnecessary system outages.

❏ 20. Ensure that media transportation, storage, reuse, and disposal are addressed adequately by company-wide policies and procedures.

❏ 21. Verify that capacity monitoring and planning are addressed adequately by company policies and procedures.

❏ 22. Based on the structure of your company's IT organization and processes, identify and audit other entity-level IT processes.

PART II

Auditing Data Centers and Disaster Recovery

Information technology (IT) processing facilities, usually referred to as data centers, are at the core of most modern organizations' operations, supporting almost all critical business activities. In this chapter we will discuss the steps for auditing data center controls, including the following areas:

- Physical security and environmental controls
- Data center operations
- System and site resiliency
- Disaster preparedness

Background

Ever since the first general-purpose electronic computer (the Electronic Numerical Integrator and Computer, or ENIAC) was created in 1946, computer systems have had specific environmental, power, and physical security requirements. Beginning in the late 1950s, as mainframe computers became more widely available, data centers were created for the express purpose of meeting these requirements. Now, most organizations have their own data centers or co-locate their systems in a shared facility.

Today's data centers provide physical access control infrastructure, environmental controls, power and network connectivity, fire-suppression systems, and alarm systems. This data center infrastructure is designed to maintain a constant optimal computing environment. The auditor's role is to verify and validate that all the necessary systems and procedures are present and working properly to protect the confidentiality, integrity, and availability of the company's systems and data.

Data Center Auditing Essentials

A data center is a facility that is designed to house an organization's critical systems, which comprise computer hardware, operating systems, and applications. Applications are leveraged to support specific business processes such as order fulfillment, customer relationship management (CRM), and accounting. Figure 4-1 shows the relationships among data center facilities, system platforms, databases, applications, and business processes.

Figure 4-1
Data-processing
hierarchy

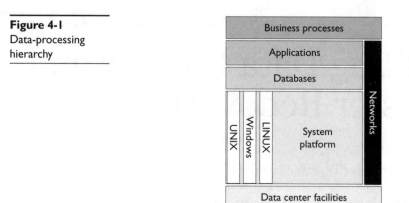

As you can see, data center facilities are at the foundation of the hierarchy, which is why it is so important that they have the necessary controls to mitigate risk. Major data center threats include the following:

- Natural threats such as weather events, flooding, earthquakes, and fire
- Manmade threats such as terrorist incidents, riots, theft, and sabotage
- Environmental hazards such as extreme temperatures and humidity
- Loss of utilities such as electrical power and telecommunications

You may notice that most of these threats are physical in nature. In this age of advanced technology, it is easy to forget the importance of physical controls and focus your energy on logical controls. However, even with excellent logical access controls in place, these physical threats can compromise your systems' security and availability.

For those who have not worked in a data center environment, data centers can be a little overwhelming. Particularly in large environments and co-located facilities, data center access might be experienced through intimidating man-traps (doors specifically designed to allow only one person through at a time), physical guards, biometric readers, and card-key-access authentication systems.

Once you pass into the computing environment, you should notice racks of computer systems sitting on a raised floor. Most of the time, miles of power and network cables are run beneath the raised floor, although many data centers run cables through open conduits that hang from the ceiling. You also will notice generators, large power conditioners, and UPS (uninterruptible power supply) devices or rooms filled with batteries to ensure that clean, uninterrupted power is available at all times. Most data centers have industrial-strength heating, ventilation, and air conditioning systems to maintain optimal temperature and humidity levels within the facility.

The brain of the data center facility is the data center control center. It usually consists of a series of consoles and computer monitors that are used to monitor temperature, humidity levels, power consumption, alarms, and critical system status. Many times, if the control center is actually physically located within the data center, the control center and tape operations may be the only areas consistently manned by data center personnel.

For the purpose of the data center audit, we will explore physical security and environmental controls; system and site resiliency controls; policies, plans, and procedures used in governing data center operations; and controls that enable disaster preparedness.

Physical Security and Environmental Controls

Data centers incorporate several types of facility-based controls, commonly referred to as physical security and environmental controls, including facility access control systems, alarm systems, and fire suppression systems. These systems are designed to prevent unauthorized intrusion, detect problems before they cause damage, and prevent the spread of fire.

Facility Access Control Systems

Facility access control systems authenticate workers prior to providing physical entry to facilities, with the goal of protecting the information systems that reside within the data center. Physical access control systems use the same concepts as logical access control systems for authentication based on something you know, something you have, or something you are. For example, the "something you know" may be a PIN code for a door. The "something you have" might include card-key systems or proximity badge systems, or you may have a physical key to unlock a door. In some cases, the access control system can be a standard key lock or simplex lock, although you'll see later that these are not preferred standalone mechanisms for controlling access. The "something you are" may include biometric devices that read fingerprints, hand geometry, and even retina characteristics to authenticate individuals who need to enter the facility.

Access control systems may use a man-trap to enforce the authentication mechanism. Man-traps consist of two doors that are separated by a corridor or a small closet-sized room. People entering the facility must first authenticate to open the door that allows them to enter the corridor. Once the first door closes behind them, they must authenticate again to open the door leading to the data center facility. The two doors cannot be open at the same time. Even if someone is able to circumvent security and gain access to the corridor via the first door, the person will be effectively trapped when the access control system blocks his or her access to the data center itself.

Alarm Systems

Because fire, water, extreme heat and humidity levels, power fluctuations, and physical intrusion threaten data center operations, data centers should implement several different types of alarm systems. Specifically, you will normally see the following types of alarms:

- Burglar alarms (with magnetic door, window, or cabinet sensors; motion sensors; and sometimes audio sensors)
- Fire alarms (usually heat and/or smoke-activated sensors broken into zones that cover different parts of the facility)
- Water alarms (usually with sensors beneath the raised floor, near bathrooms, or in water pipe ducts)

- Humidity alarms (normally with sensors disbursed throughout the facility)
- Power fluctuation alarms (with sensors near the logical point of entry)
- Chemical or gas alarms (sometimes in battery rooms and near air intakes)

These alarm systems usually feed into the data center operations center. During an alarm condition, the operator can drill down to specific sensors and reference a surveillance camera to isolate the cause of a problem.

Fire Suppression Systems

Because of the large amount of electrical equipment, fire is a major threat to data centers. Therefore, data centers normally are equipped with sophisticated fire-suppression systems and should have a sufficient number of fire extinguishers. Generally speaking, fire-suppression systems come in two varieties: water-based systems and gas-based systems.

System and Site Resiliency

Because the computer systems that reside in a data center are leveraged to automate business functions, they must be available any time the business operates. Therefore, data centers incorporate various types of controls to ensure that systems remain available to perform critical business operations. These controls are designed to protect power, the computing environment, and wide area networks (WANs).

Power

Clean power is absolutely critical to maintain computer operations. Power fluctuations such as spikes, surges, sags, brown-outs, and black-outs can damage computer components or cause outages. To mitigate this risk, data centers provide power redundancy in several layers, including the following:

- Redundant power feeds (connecting the data center to more than one power grid)
- Ground to earth (to carry power away from critical components during fault conditions)
- Power conditioning (to flatten out harmful spikes and sags in current)
- Battery backup systems or UPSs (to provide uninterrupted power in the event of power fluctuations, brown-outs, or black-outs)
- Generators (to provide electrical power during prolonged power outages)

Heating, Ventilation, and Air Conditioning (HVAC)

Extreme temperature and humidity conditions can cause damage to computer systems. Because computers require specific environmental conditions to operate reliably, HVAC systems are required controls. Data centers typically provide sophisticated redundant systems to maintain constant temperature and humidity and often provide double the required capacity.

Network Connectivity

Whether from internal networks or the Internet, users access information systems residing within data center facilities through network connections. Network connectivity is critical. More often than not, data center facilities have redundant Internet and WAN connections via multiple carriers. If one carrier experiences a network outage, service to the facilities can be provided by another carrier.

Data Center Operations

Although data centers are designed to be automated, they do require a staff to operate. As a result, data center operations should be governed by policies, plans, and procedures. The auditor should expect to find the following areas covered by policies, plans, and procedures:

- Physical access control
- System and facility monitoring
- Facility and equipment planning, tracking, and maintenance
- Response procedures for outages, emergencies, and alarm conditions

Disaster Preparedness

All data centers are susceptible to natural and manmade disasters. History shows that when disaster strikes a data center, the organizations such facilities serve come to a screeching halt. The auditor's job is to identify and measure physical and administrative controls at the facility that mitigate the risk of data-processing disruptions, including the following:

- System resiliency
- Data backup and restore
- Disaster recovery planning

 NOTE It is not within the scope of this chapter to cover business continuity. We instead focus on controls related to disaster recovery for the organization's IT environment, specifically related to systems housed within data centers.

Test Steps for Auditing Data Centers

The following topic areas should be addressed during the data center audit:

- Neighborhood and external risk factors
- Physical access controls
- Environmental controls
- Power and electricity

- Fire suppression
- Data center operations
- System resiliency
- Data backup and restore
- Disaster recovery planning

Test steps are detailed for each of these areas.

Neighborhood and External Risk Factors

When auditing a data center facility, you should first evaluate the environment in which the data center resides. The goal is to identify high-risk threats. For example, the data center you are auditing may be in the flight path of a regional airport, a Federal Emergency Management Agency (FEMA) flood zone, or a high-crime area. These types of environmental characteristics will reveal otherwise latent threats. In your audit, you will be looking for controls that reduce the likelihood of one of these threats being realized.

I. Review data center exterior lighting, building orientation, signage, fences, and neighborhood characteristics to identify facility related risks.

Data center facilities should provide a physically secure environment for personnel and information systems. A breach of physical security, whether through a bomb, a physical intrusion, or a weather-related event, would compromise information and personnel security.

How

Perform a physical inspection of the data center facility. Pay attention to how far the building is set back from the curb and whether or not barriers are in place to prevent cars from getting too close to the building. You're looking for controls that will reduce the risk of vehicle accidents or car bombs impacting the data center.

Determine on which floor of the building the data center resides. This information is important because below-ground and ground-level data centers are susceptible to flooding. Data centers on higher floors are more prone to lightning, wind, and tornado damage. The ideal is a single-story data center that is 5 feet or so above ground. If you're performing an audit of an existing data center, you obviously won't be able to get the auditees to move it just because you don't like the floor it's on; however, this information will help guide you in looking for compensating controls. For example, if the data center is below ground level, you will place extra focus on water-detection controls (discussed later in this chapter). This provides a great example of why it's valuable to be involved in your company's projects early. If you're invited to the table early during the development of a new data center, you might be able to influence the chosen location. Otherwise, all you can do is suggest controls to compensate for issues at the existing location.

Signage   Review exterior signage to determine whether it's obvious to a passerby that the facility contains a data center. Data centers should be anonymous, away from main thoroughfares, and inconspicuously marked, if marked at all. In fact, most data centers employ what the security industry calls *security through obscurity*. Maintaining relative anonymity will reduce the possibility of the facility becoming a target for espionage, theft, or sabotage. Review interior signage as well. In general, it's best not to guide visitors in the building to the data center, especially if the building has frequent visitors from outside the company.

Neighborhood   The next question is, "Who are the neighbors of the data center facility?" Is it located in a multitenant building, or is it a standalone structure? If neighbors are within a close proximity, in what sort of business are they engaged? A data center that is located next to a warehouse or manufacturing facility may have an increased risk of being affected by hazardous material spills or fires. The ideal is a standalone structure without any close neighbors. Again, it will be difficult to influence this if you're auditing an existing data center, but knowing this information will help you identify necessary compensating controls. For example, if you're in a multitenant facility, you will want to suggest that the data center have standalone, segregated utilities (such as power feeds) so that the other tenants won't have a potential negative impact on the data center's power supply, water supply, and so on.

Exterior Lighting   Evaluate exterior lighting. Proper lighting deters crime and loitering around the facility. Critical facilities should have exterior walls and parking lots illuminated uniformly at an intensity level that allows for viewing at a reasonable distance.

Fences   Evaluate the adequacy of fences around the facility for deterring intruders. A 3- to 4-foot fence will deter common trespassers. An 8-foot fence with barbed wire at the top will deter all but the most determined intruders.

2. Research the data center location for environmental hazards and to determine the distance to emergency services.

Environmental threats such as floods, severe weather, and transportation-related accidents can destroy or severely damage a data center. In the event of an emergency, rapid response from authorities is critical. Therefore, the proximity to fire stations, police stations, and hospitals is important.

How

Perform research to identify environmental hazards that may not be evident during the on-site visit. Look for information on the following areas:

- Flood elevations
- Weather and earth movement threats
- Proximity to transportation-related hazards

- Local crime rate
- Proximity to industrial areas
- Proximity to emergency services

If you're reviewing an existing facility, you probably won't be able to impact the existence of these characteristics, as it's usually not realistic to recommend that the data center be moved. However, you can use this information during the audit to determine compensating controls that should be put in place. Ideally, you'll be able to consult during the construction of a new data center and influence its location based on the existence of these factors. However, even if the data center has already been built, as an auditor, it is your responsibility to inform management about risks to the business. It is management's responsibility to decide where to spend limited resources in an effort to mitigate those risks. Even if it's not realistic to relocate the data center, it may be reasonable to suggest that additional monitoring and disaster recovery capabilities be put in place.

Flood Elevations   According to FEMA, floods are one of the most common hazards in the United States. Finding flood-zone information on the Internet is relatively easy.

NOTE   The following Internet resources are available to assist auditors in evaluating flood risks: http://hazards.fema.gov/ and http://msc.fema.gov/.

You should also identify any flooding hazards that are present as a result of the data center's location within the building. Determine what is located in the rooms immediately adjacent to and above the data center. Restrooms and other rooms involving frequent water usage introduce the threat of leaks and burst pipes flooding the data center.

Weather and Earth Movement Threats   Since different geographic zones are prone to different weather and earth movement hazards, you should understand which of these threats are prevalent in the geographic area in which the data center resides. For example, if the data center you are auditing is in Dallas, Texas, the threats would be tornados, flooding, and extreme heat, whereas in northern California the threat would come from earthquakes.

NOTE   Some excellent weather-related Internet resources include http://www.noaa.gov/, http://earthquake.usgs.gov/, and http://hazards.fema.gov/.

Proximity to Transportation-Related Hazards   Planes, trains, and automobiles represent another risk to data center operations. Specifically, research whether or not the data center you are auditing is in an airport flight path or if a rail line is near the facility. Though rare, planes do crash and trains do derail and can pose a risk. Maps and observation are good methods for identifying nearby transportation-related hazards.

Local Crime Rate   Obviously, if your data center is in a high-crime area, there is a higher risk of theft and other crimes. Therefore, another statistic to research is the local crime rate. If the area has a high crime rate, you may recommend mitigating controls such as reinforced fences, an increased presence of security personnel, closed-circuit television (CCTV), and perimeter alarm systems.

NOTE   Several excellent sources of online crime statistics are available at the following websites: www.ojp.usdoj.gov/bjs/dtdata.htm and www.cityrating.com/crimestatistics.asp.

Proximity to Industrial Areas   Many data center facilities are situated in industrial zones near factories and warehouses. These areas generally have a higher crime rate and a higher risk of hazardous material spills affecting data center operations. Therefore, if the data center is situated in an industrial area, you should evaluate the risks inherent to the area and determine any needed compensating controls. Similarly, within your own building, determine the usage of the rooms immediately adjacent to and above the data center. Manufacturing processes and other processes involving chemicals introduce the risk of chemical leaks and explosions.

Proximity to Emergency Services   When an emergency occurs within a data center, every minute that passes can be very costly. Therefore, it is important that you evaluate the distance to police stations, hospitals, and fire stations. This information can be obtained from the blue pages of the local phone book. Again, this is probably not an area you can influence after-the-fact, but it does provide good background information as you perform the rest of the audit, helping you gauge the level of capabilities you need on-site versus what you can rely on externally.

Physical Access Controls

Several information security incidents have occurred in which thieves gained unauthorized access to sensitive information by defeating physical access control mechanisms. Therefore, restricting physical access is just as critical as restricting logical access. In a data center environment, physical access control mechanisms consist of the following:

- Exterior doors and walls
- Access control procedures
- Physical authentication mechanisms
- Security guards
- Other mechanisms and procedures used to secure sensitive areas

3. Review data center doors and walls to determine whether they protect the facilities adequately.

A data center's first and most formidable line of defense should be the walls and doors used in its construction. Look closely at how well doors and walls protect against intrusion and other hazards such as projectiles or blasts.

How

Through interviews and observation, identify all potential entry points into the data center. Verify that walls and doors are adequately reinforced. Exterior walls should be reinforced with steel and concrete to protect the facility. If the data center resides within a building, the walls may be constructed of sheetrock but should be reinforced with steel to prevent intrusion. Exterior doors should also be reinforced and should be able to withstand intrusion attempts. Ideally, there should be no exterior-facing doors or walls, which provides an extra layer of protection against forced entry. You can attempt to influence this if consulting prior to data center construction.

Raised Floors and Drop Ceilings   Most data centers use either raised floors or drop ceilings to conceal ventilation ducts and power and network cables. Interior building walls sometimes are constructed with spaces below raised floor or spaces above drop ceilings left unwalled. This would allow someone attempting to gain unauthorized access to the secured area to remove either a floor tile or a section of the drop ceiling to crawl over or under the wall. This is a common oversight that can allow intruders to bypass your physical security controls. During the building tour, remove a section of raised floor and a ceiling tile at a data center wall to verify that walls extend from the structural floor to the structural ceiling. If they do not, you will need to encourage the addition of wall extensions or reinforced wire cages above and below the data center to prevent unauthorized entry.

Doors   Ensure that doors are force-resistant, preferably with magnetic locks. Review the location of each door's hinges. If they are on the outside of the room, ensure they are protected to prevent an intruder from removing the door by popping it off its hinges.

Man-traps are an effective means of controlling access to critical facilities. Verify through observation that man-traps exist where appropriate and that they are working properly. Man-traps are equipped with two locking doors with a corridor in between. To ensure security, one door should be required to be locked before the other is allowed to open. Obviously, the man-trap should be constructed of reinforced walls and doors as well.

Windows   Identify any windows looking into the data center and ensure that all are constructed with reinforced shatterproof glass. In general, windows looking in on the data center should be avoided, as they advertise the location of the data center to passers-by. If any windows provide a view into the data center from outside the building, determine whether they have been adequately covered with curtains or blinds or other obscuring mechanisms.

4. Evaluate physical authentication devices to determine whether they are appropriate and are working properly.

Physical authentication devices such as card-key readers, proximity badges, biometric devices, simplex (combination) locks, and traditional key locks serve to allow access to authorized personnel and keep out unauthorized personnel. The failure or misuse of these devices can allow unauthorized persons access to the data center or prevent authorized personnel from entering.

How

For each entry point into the data center, identify the physical authentication mechanism and ensure it has the following characteristics:

- Restricts access based on the individual's unique access needs or even restricts access to particular doors or to particular hours of the day
- Easily deactivated in the event an employee is terminated or changes jobs or in the event a key/card/badge is lost or stolen
- Difficult to duplicate or steal credentials

Obtain a sample of data center authentication device logs and verify that the device is logging the following information:

- User identification
- Date, time, and place of the access attempt
- Success or failure of the access attempt

Review processes for periodically reviewing and investigating these logs.

Card-Key and Proximity Devices   Card-key devices use magnetic stripes or radio frequency identification (RFID) chips to authenticate users who possess the card. Because a stolen card can be used for unauthorized authentication, a PIN-code device will preferably be coupled with the card-key reader. Verify that all card-key readers are working properly and are logging access attempts.

Biometric Devices   Biometric authentication devices have become more accurate and cost-effective over the past few years. As a result, more and more data centers are now employing the technology. Biometric devices are able to measure fingerprint, retina, and hand geometry. Because these biometric characteristics are unique to each individual, biometric authentication devices are difficult to defeat. Review the quality of the biometric system being used to determine whether an inordinate number of false negatives or any observed false positives have occurred.

Key Locks and Combination Locks   Traditional key locks and simplex (combination) locks are the weakest forms of physical authentication and should be avoided. These forms of physical authentication offer no way to identify who has access to the data center. Keys can be lost, stolen, borrowed, or copied. Combination codes can be shared or can be stolen via shoulder surfing (watching someone enter the code). These are also the most difficult credentials to revoke when an employee no longer needs access to the data center.

5. Ensure that physical access control procedures are comprehensive and being followed by data center and security staff.

Physical access control procedures govern employee and guest access to the data center facility. If physical access control procedures are incomplete or not enforced consistently, data center physical access will be compromised.

How

Review the following related to physical access control procedures:

- Ensure that access authorization requirements are documented and clearly defined for both employees and guests. Approval from one (or more) of a predefined set of knowledgeable individuals should be required before data center access is granted. Standards for what constitutes a need for ongoing data center access should be established. For example, an employee who needs only occasional (such as quarterly) access to the data center does not need ongoing access but can instead arrange to be escorted on the occasions when access is needed. The philosophy of "minimum necessary access" should be embraced when it comes to granting access to data center facilities.

- Verify that guest access procedures include restrictions on taking pictures and outline conduct requirements within the data center. Visitors should be required to sign a visitor log indicating their name, company, and reason for visiting and should be required to wear identification badges that are a different color from employee badges. Visitors should be escorted at all times and vendor service personnel (including cleaning personnel) should be supervised while on site.

- Review a sample of both guest access and employee ID authorization requests to ensure that access control procedures are followed.

- Review procedures for ensuring that data center access is removed (including the collection of physical devices such as badges, keys, and cards) when it is no longer required. This should be part of the termination checklist and will preferably be automated. It should also encompass changes of jobs within the company, so that employees don't retain data center access beyond the point when it is needed.

- Obtain a list of all individuals who have access to the data center, select a representative sample of employees with access to the data center, and determine whether access is appropriate.

- Determine whether management regularly reviews the physical access authorizations for validity. Management should periodically pull a list of people with data center access and review it for appropriateness. Review evidence that this is happening.

6. Ensure that burglar alarms and surveillance systems are protecting the data center from physical intrusion.

Burglar alarms and surveillance systems mitigate the risk of undetected physical intrusion by serving as a detective control as well as a deterrent for would-be intruders. The absence of these controls would increase the risk of theft and other criminal activities.

Most data centers employ either CCTV, audio surveillance systems, or a combination of the two. These systems typically feed into a guard station, where they are monitored by security personnel and recorded on either tape or a digital storage system. Data centers also often employ burglar alarms, generally through a series of sensors that are placed in strategic locations such as doors and hallways.

How

Review the placement of intrusion sensors, verifying that critical areas of the data center are covered adequately, and review maintenance logs to ensure that the system has been maintained and tested properly. Look for the following common types of sensors:

- Motion sensors that detect infrared motion
- Contact sensors that are placed on windows and doors to detect when they are opened or broken
- Audio sensors to detect breaking glass or changes in normal ambient noise
- Door prop alarms to detect when a data center door is left open for more than a specified length of time (typically 30 seconds)

Review camera quality and placement, ensuring that they are located at strategic points in the data center (such as each entry point). Verify that the surveillance systems are monitored and evaluate the frequency of the monitoring. Verify that the video surveillance is recorded for possible future playback and review tape rotation or mass-storage archival schedules.

These steps can be performed through a combination of document review and observation. The data center security manager should be able to provide this information.

7. Review security guard building round logs and other documentation to evaluate the effectiveness of the security personnel function.

Security guards can be one of the most effective physical access controls. They act as a deterrent and can also control facility access and respond to incidents with cognitive reasoning. If the security personnel function is ineffective, emergency response most likely would be slow and ineffective, doors could be left unlocked, and unauthorized personnel could have the opportunity to enter the data center facility.

How

Verify that documentation of building rounds, access logs, and incident logs/reports exist and that this information is recorded properly by obtaining samples from the security staff. Look for consistent entry and exit times, regular building tours, and comprehensive incident logs/reports. Visit the main security post to obtain this documentation.

PART II

8. Verify that sensitive areas within the data center are secured adequately. Ensure that all computer processing equipment essential to data center operations (such as hardware systems and power supply breakers) is located within the computer processing room or in a secure area.

Data centers typically have some areas that are more sensitive than others, such as equipment staging areas, generators, and computer systems that are processing sensitive information. If a large number of people have access to the data center, sensitive equipment may need to be segregated in high-security areas. If these areas are not adequately secured, information could be altered or disclosed to unauthorized personnel or destroyed due to a system failure caused by either sabotage or an accident.

If equipment essential to data center operations is not located within the data center (or an equally controlled area), someone without data center access may be able to adversely impact data center availability and/or access sensitive information.

How

Based on the number of people with access to the data center and the nature of the equipment contained therein, evaluate the need for access to be further segregated within the data center. For example, computer systems that process sensitive information may be locked within a cage or cabinet, with only a select number of personnel given access. During interviews and tours of the data center, verify that these areas are protected appropriately with proper access control mechanisms and, if appropriate, are monitored by CCTV cameras and/or alarm systems.

Review the location of all data center systems, including power supplies, HVAC equipment, batteries, production servers, and so on, and ensure all are located within the data center or an equally secured facility.

Environmental Controls

Computer systems require specific environmental conditions such as controlled temperature and humidity. Data centers are designed to provide this type of controlled environment. When auditing a data center, you should verify that there is enough HVAC capacity to service the data center even in the most extreme conditions.

9. Verify that HVAC systems maintain constant temperatures within the data center.

HVAC systems are used to provide constant temperature and humidity levels. Computer systems can be damaged by extremes in either. High humidity can cause corrosion of computer components, and low humidity can cause static electricity discharges that can short-circuit system boards. High temperatures can reduce the lifespan of computer equipment and result in system freezes and crashes.

How

Review the following areas:

- Temperature and humidity logs to verify that each falls within acceptable ranges over a period of time. In general, data center temperatures should range from 65 to 70°F (with temperatures above 85°F damaging computer equipment) and humidity levels should be between 45 and 55 percent. However, this will vary depending on the specifications of the equipment. Determine how the data center staff has established the parameters for the equipment.

- Temperature and humidity alarms to ensure data center personnel are notified of conditions when either factor falls outside of acceptable ranges. Sensors should be placed in all areas of the data center where electronic equipment is present. Ensure that sensors are placed in appropriate locations either by reviewing architecture diagrams or by touring the facility. Review maintenance and testing documentation to verify that the system is in good working order.

- HVAC design to verify that all areas of the data centers are covered appropriately. Determine whether the air flow within the data center has been modeled to ensure adequate and efficient coverage. Look for cold aisle and warm aisle configuration, which is a configuration of equipment racks where servers are faced such that hot and cold air are separated, thereby improving cooling efficiency.

- Configuration of the HVAC systems. The data center should use a self-contained independent air conditioning system that is isolated from other building systems and can be used with backup power. This will allow the HVAC controls to continue to function for the data center in the event of a power loss. Data center air conditioning ducts should be designed so as not to penetrate the perimeter walls. Otherwise, they could allow unauthorized access from outside the data center.

This information usually can be obtained from the facility manager.

10. Ensure that a water alarm system is configured to detect water in high-risk areas of the data center.

Water and electronic equipment do not mix. Data centers normally employ water sensors in strategic locations such as near water sources or under raised floors. Water sensors detect the presence of water and are designed to alert data center personnel prior to a major problem.

How

Identify potential water sources such as drains, air-conditioning units, exterior doors, and water pipes to verify that water sensors are placed in locations where they will mitigate the most risk. The facility manager should be able to point out both water sources and sensors during a tour of the facility. Review maintenance records to ensure that the alarm system is maintained periodically.

Floor plans indicating shut off valves for all water systems should be available. Data center managers should be aware of all water valves within the secured area. Determine whether this is the case.

Power and Electricity

Computer systems require uninterrupted, clean power to operate. Data centers typically employ several different types of controls to maintain clean power. These controls include the following:

- Redundant power feeds that provide power from two or more power stations
- Ground-to-earth to carry excess power away from systems during electrical faults
- Power conditioning systems to convert potentially dirty power to clean power
- Battery backup systems (UPSs) that provide immediate power, typically for short periods of time
- Generators to provide sustained power during extended power losses

11. Determine whether the data center has redundant power feeds.

Some data centers are built in locations where they can connect to more than one power station. When the power supplied by one feed is lost, the other often will remain live. As a result, redundant power feeds can be used to maintain utility power continuity.

How

This control is not always possible, but it is worth exploring with the data center facility manager during interviews.

12. Verify that ground-to-earth exists to protect computer systems.

Ungrounded electrical power can cause computer equipment damage, fire, injury, or death. These perils affect information systems, personnel, and the facility itself. Today, buildings that do not have grounded electrical outlets are probably in violation of building code. Unlike redundant power feeds, the ground-to-earth control should always be present. Ground-to-earth is a basic feature of all electrical installations that consists of a *green wire* that connects all electrical outlets to a rod that is sunk into the ground. When short circuits or electrical faults occur, excess voltage is passed through the ground wire safely into the ground rather than short-circuiting electrical equipment. This control should be present in any facility less than 30 years old or so, but it is definitely worth verifying. Older buildings that have not had electrical systems upgraded may not have an electrical ground, however. Electrical ground normally is required in building codes.

How

This information can be obtained by interviewing the data center facility manager or through observation.

13. Ensure that power is conditioned to prevent data loss.

Power spikes and sags damage computer systems and destroy information. Power conditioning systems mitigate this risk by buffering the spikes and sags. Clean power can be represented as a wave pattern with symmetric peaks and valleys. Normal utility power has a wave pattern with peaks and valleys that are far from symmetric, causing momentary spikes and sags. These spikes and sags shorten the life of electronic components and sometimes cause system faults. Power conditioning systems smooth out the wave pattern to make it symmetric.

How

Through interviews and observation, verify that power is being conditioned by either a power conditioning system (such as surge protectors) or a battery backup system.

14. Verify that battery backup systems are providing continuous power during momentary black-outs and brown-outs.

Power failures can cause data loss through abrupt system shutdowns. UPS battery systems mitigate this risk by typically providing 20 to 30 minutes of power as well as power conditioning during normal utility power conditions. Basically, they provide enough time for the generator (if available) to turn on and begin generating electricity, or for critical systems to be shut down gracefully to minimize data loss. They also perform a power conditioning function, because they logically sit in between utility power and computer center equipment. As a result, the batteries are actually powering the data center all the time. When utility power is live, the batteries are charged constantly. Conversely, when power is lost, they begin to drain.

How

Interview the data center facility manager and observe UPS battery backup systems to verify that the data center UPS system is protecting all critical computer systems and affords adequate run times (that is, make sure the batteries will run long enough for the generator to kick in and/or for critical systems to be shut down gracefully). In some cases, the UPS system may be able to initiate a graceful shutdown automatically when capacity reaches a certain threshold. Look for the existence and implementation of this feature.

Review a list of equipment tied into the UPS and ensure all critical systems are covered (such as critical production servers, network equipment, HVAC systems, fire detection and suppression systems, monitoring systems, badge readers, and so on).

15. Ensure that generators protect against prolonged power loss and are in good working condition.

Mission-critical data centers, by their nature, cannot withstand any power loss. Since it is impractical to install enough batteries to power the data center for more than an hour or two, generators allow the data center to generate its own power in the event of a prolonged loss of utility power.

Generators come in two common varieties: diesel-powered and natural gas– or propane-powered. Each has its benefits and drawbacks.

Diesel generators are most common but have a finite amount of fuel stored in their tanks. Diesel fuel is also a biohazard. Spillage could result in significant cleanup expenses. Also, if the generator is in close proximity to the data center, and a spill reaches the data center, it would be disastrous. These risks can be mitigated though fuel service contracts and spill barriers, however.

Natural gas generators run cleaner and theoretically have an infinite supply of fuel as long as the gas lines are intact. There is no danger of spills, but fire danger is increased. Natural gas generators are employed rarely, however, because of the expense.

Propane generators are also expensive but have a limited supply of fuel. Again, this can be mitigated with service contracts.

How

Through observation and interviews, verify that the data center has a generator. In addition, obtain the sustained and peak power loads from the facility manager and compare them with current power generation capacity. Generators should be able to produce at least double the sustained power load.

Determine the generators' ability to power operations for a sustained period of time by reviewing onsite fuel storage as well as service contracts for replenishing fuel. Review controls in place to mitigate the inherent risks for whichever type of fuel is being used (such as spill barriers if diesel fuel is used).

All types of generators require frequent maintenance and testing, so review both maintenance and test logs during a data center audit.

16. Evaluate the usage and protection of emergency power-off (EPO) switches.

EPO switches are designed to shut off power immediately to the computer and peripheral devices during emergencies, such as during a data center fire or emergency evacuation. If they are not adequately protected, it could result in inadvertent shutdown of the data center.

How

Through observation, review the EPO switch(es) for the data center. Ensure that they are clearly labeled and easily accessible, yet still secured from unauthorized or accidental usage. They should be inside the secured area and underneath some sort of shield to prevent accidental activation.

Fire Suppression

Since data centers face a significant risk from fire, they typically have sophisticated fire suppression systems, generally one of two types: gas-based systems and water-based systems. The data center relies on more than just fire suppression systems, however, as controls. Other fire suppression controls include the following:

- Building construction
- Fire extinguishers
- Proper handling and storage of hazardous materials

17. Ensure that data center building construction incorporates appropriate fire suppression features.

For more than 30 years, building codes have required that buildings be constructed in such a way as to resist fire. Fire suppression features include the following:

- Fire-rated walls and doors to prevent fire from moving from one area of a building to another
- Firestops where fire-rated walls or floor assemblies are sealed to prevent the spread of fire
- Standpipe fire hose systems to provide a ready supply of water for fire suppression

The absence of these features introduces the risk of a fire spreading more quickly and causing additional damage and possibly threatening lives.

How

Review the available fire suppression features built into the facility. The facility manager or local fire marshal should be able to provide information about wall/door fire rating and firestops. Standpipe water systems will be visible and observed easily during a building tour.

18. Ensure that data center personnel are trained in hazardous materials (hazmat) handling and storage and that hazmat procedures are appropriate. Also determine whether data center personnel are trained in how to respond to a fire emergency.

Hazardous and highly flammable materials are a common cause of fire. These materials include the following:

- Diesel and other fuels
- Solvents and thinners
- Propane or acetylene torches
- Chlorine or ammonia-based chemicals
- Glues and bonding compounds

These materials should be handled and stored in a proper manner to mitigate the risk of fire or spillage. Also, data center personnel should be trained in how to respond to a fire (such as knowledge of emergency numbers to call, when and how to activate fire suppression systems, and so on) to minimize the threat to equipment and human life.

How

Review hazmat incident reports and hazmat and fire response training materials and procedures, as well as interview data center staff.

Through observation, determine whether anything is being unnecessarily stored in or near the data center of a combustible nature (such as paper stock, toners, cleaners or other chemicals). If so, suggest that it be removed to reduce the need for hazmat procedures.

19. Verify that fire extinguishers are strategically placed throughout the data center and are maintained properly.

Fire extinguishers are often the first line of fire defense. In data centers, they should be placed in hallways and aisles every 50 feet or so. Three common types of extinguishers can be used: dry chemical–based, water-based, and inert gas–based. In most cases, data centers should use inert gas–based fire extinguishers, such as CO_2 extinguishers, because water and dry chemicals damage electrical equipment. A lack of usable fire extinguishers could result in a small fire getting out of control.

How

Review the locations of fire extinguishers, as well as a sample of the attached service tags, during a data center tour. Ensure the location of each fire extinguisher is marked appropriately and easily visible. Since many data centers contain racks that are at least 6 feet tall, a marker should identify the location of each fire extinguisher that is visible above the racks.

The data center facility manager also should be able to supply maintenance records. Fire extinguishers should be inspected at least annually.

20. Ensure that fire suppression systems are protecting the data center from fire.

All data centers should have a fire suppression system to help contain fires. Most systems are gas-based or water-based and often use multistage processes, in which the first sensor (usually a smoke sensor) activates the system and a second sensor (usually a heat sensor) causes a discharge of either water or gas.

Gas-Based Systems   Varieties of gas-based fire suppression systems include CO_2 FM-200 and CEA-410. Gas-based systems are expensive and often impractical, but their use does not damage electronic equipment.

Water-Based Systems   Water-based systems are less expensive and more common but can cause damage to computer equipment. To mitigate the risk of damaging all the computer equipment in a data center or in the extended area of a fire, fire suppression systems are designed to drop water from sprinkler heads only at the location of the fire. Four common types of fire suppression systems are used:

- **Wet pipe**   Pipes are always filled with water. This is the least desirable type of system for a data center, because a leaky pipe or broken sprinkler head would result in flooding.

- **Dry pipe**   Pipes are filled with air and are filled with water at the time of a discharge.

- **Preaction**   Pipes are filled at stage 1 activation and water is discharged during stage 2.

- **Deluge**   A dry pipe system that discharges a large amount of water to overwhelm a fire.

The absence of a fire suppression system would allow a fire to spread more quickly, resulting in more equipment loss and possibly loss of life.

How
Review system design, maintenance, and test records. This information can be obtained through a combination of interviews, document review, and observation. The data center facility manager should be able to provide the design, maintenance, and test documentation.

If water-based systems are used, determine whether the pipes above the data center are always filled with water (a wet pipe system). If so, determine what mitigating controls have been employed to minimize the chance of unintended water flow into the data center, such as from a broken sprinkler head or leaky pipe. For example, look for cages around the sprinkler heads, water flow sensors, and regular maintenance of the pipes.

If gas-based systems are used, determine the type of gas in use and ensure it is not harmful to humans if inhaled.

21. Verify that fire alarms are in place to protect the data center from the risk of fire.
Because of all the electrical equipment, fire can be a problem for data centers. Fire alarms alert data center personnel and local fire departments of a developing fire condition so that they can begin fire response procedures and evacuate the premise. A fire alarm failure would put data center operations and human lives at risk.

Data center fire alarm systems usually are multizone systems, which reduce the risk of false alarms due to a single malfunctioning sensor or zone. In such a system, sensors in two or more zones must detect the fire before an alarm sounds. Three types of sensors can be used:

- **Heat sensors**   Activate when temperature reaches a predetermined threshold or when temperatures rise quickly

- **Smoke sensors**   Activate when they detect smoke

- **Flame sensors**   Activate when they sense infrared energy or flickering of a flame

Smoke and heat sensors are most common.

Hand-pull fire alarms should also be strategically located (such as near all entrances) throughout the data center so that employees can raise an alarm when observing a fire condition.

How

Via physical observation and interviews, review fire alarm sensor type, placement, maintenance records, and testing procedures. Sensors should be located above and below the ceiling tiles and below the raised floor.

Observe whether hand-pull fire alarms are strategically located throughout the data center and review maintenance records and testing procedures.

Data Center Operations

Effective data center operations require strict adherence to formally adopted policies, procedures, and plans. The areas that should be covered include the following:

- Facility monitoring
- Roles and responsibilities of data center personnel
- Segregation of duties of data center personnel
- Responding to emergencies and disasters
- Facility and equipment maintenance
- Data center capacity planning
- Asset management

22. Review the alarm monitoring console(s), reports, and procedures to verify that alarms are monitored continually by data center personnel.

Alarm systems most often feed into a monitoring console that allows data center personnel to respond to an alarm condition before calling authorities, evacuating the building, or shutting down equipment. The absence of a monitoring console and appropriate response procedures would introduce the risk of an alarm condition going unnoticed.

How

Review alarm reports and observe the data center alarm-monitoring console to verify that intrusion, fire, water, humidity, and other alarm systems are monitored continually by data center personnel. Occasionally, the intrusion alarm is monitored by data center security staff. The main objective here is to verify that all applicable alarms are being monitored.

Review facility monitoring and response procedures to ensure that alarm conditions are addressed promptly. Facility monitoring procedures ensure that all critical alarm conditions are captured and acted on promptly. They should include a description of the alarm systems that will be monitored, as well as the steps that are to be taken in the event of all reasonably foreseeable alarms, including fire, intrusion, water, power outage, data circuit outage, system, and system component alarm conditions. Verify that alarm-condition response is clearly outlined for each type of alarm condition. Obtain the actual monitoring procedures as well as monitoring logs from data center facility management.

23. Verify that network, operating system, and application monitoring provides adequate information to identify potential problems for systems located in the data center.

System monitoring provides insight into potential problems resulting from capacity issues, misconfigurations, and system component failures. Inadequate system monitoring gives rise to the threat of security violations going undetected and system outages. Although this function typically is managed by IT service groups rather than data center personnel, monitoring is a critical component of sound operations for the systems in the data center. System monitoring encompasses the monitoring of network devices, intrusion detection systems, operating systems, system hardware, and applications. Whereas intrusion detection system monitoring is focused primarily on monitoring for security violations, network device, operating system, system hardware, and application monitoring is focused primarily on items that can affect the availability of a system, such as hard-disk usage, number of concurrent connections, and so forth. Therefore, when auditing monitoring system procedures, you need to understand the objective of the system.

How

Determine the criticality of specific system components within the data center and verify that monitoring systems provide near–real-time information to detect a problem with these system components. Determine how the computer systems are monitored and if an automated or manual problem log is maintained for hardware and software failures and downtime. Examples of items that may be monitored include system uptime, utilization, response time, and errors. In addition, review monitoring logs and reports to identify whether any components being monitored exceed predetermined thresholds and then verify that actions have been taken to remediate the condition. Monitoring logs and reports typically can be obtained from system support groups, network support groups, and security and application monitoring teams.

24. Ensure that roles and responsibilities of data center personnel are clearly defined.

Well-defined employee roles and responsibilities ensure that responsibility and accountability for data center functions are clear. Inadequate roles and responsibilities can result in unclear job boundaries and data center functions going unaddressed, which could increase the risk of system outages.

How
Review documentation and verify that all job functions are covered and that responsibilities associated with job functions are clearly defined. Data center facility management should be able to provide job descriptions, including roles and responsibilities.

25. Verify that duties and job functions of data center personnel are segregated appropriately.
Segregation of duties is a basic security precept of personnel management. The goal is to spread high-risk duties across two or more employees to reduce the risk of fraud or inadvertent errors. If high-risk functions are not segregated, the data center will have a higher degree of fraud risk.

How
Verify that high-risk job functions, such as access authorization, are segregated across two or more employees. These processes should be tracked with logs and forms that can be reviewed to verify that duties are segregated effectively.

26. Ensure that emergency response procedures address reasonably anticipated threats.
Data centers are faced with various threats, including the following:

- Fire
- Flood
- Physical or logical intrusion
- Power loss
- System failure
- Telecommunications outages

These and other identified threats should be addressed by emergency response plans. When a fire breaks out or a data center floor begins to flood, data center personnel need a clear plan to address the condition and minimize losses. Although used only during the unlikely event of an emergency, emergency response plans are absolutely critical for reducing the risk of an emergency escalating owing to improper response from data center personnel. For example, suppose a generator catches fire while being tested. Without clear procedures and proper training, you probably would witness employees running around in the heat of the moment, responding in a way that they think is most appropriate but most likely not working together to solve the problem. With clear emergency response procedures, such decisions would have already been considered, and employees would not be forced to make decisions in the heat of the moment, resulting in a more coordinated response.

How
Review response plans. Verify that plans are present for all foreseeable threats and ensure that response procedures are comprehensive and well thought out. Data center operations staff should be able to provide these plans. Observe whether emergency

telephone numbers are posted or easy to access and that they include outside police, fire departments, and other emergency response groups.

27. Verify that data center facility-based systems and equipment are maintained properly.

When not properly maintained, facility-based systems and equipment are prone to premature failure. These breakdowns can cause loss of information and system outages. As a result, maintenance is critical.

How

Review maintenance logs for critical systems and equipment. Critical systems and equipment should be maintained at least semiannually. The data center facility manager should be able to provide the maintenance logs.

Determine whether procedures are in place for daily or weekly cleaning of the data center, including regular cleaning under the raised data center floor and of computer equipment. Dirt and dust in the data center can negatively impact the functioning of computer equipment.

28. Ensure that data center personnel are trained properly to perform their job functions.

Data center personnel cannot be expected to be proficient if they are not afforded job training. When not trained properly, data center personnel are more likely to cause data loss or system outages due to mistakes.

How

Review training history and schedules. Ensure that training is relevant to job functions and that all data center personnel are afforded training. Determine whether there is ongoing communication of employee responsibilities with respect to confidentiality, integrity, availability, reliability, and security of all IT resources. Look for policies that prohibit eating, drinking, and smoking within the data center, or those that at least restrict such activity to special break areas. Also, look for signs posted stating such prohibitions.

Data center management should be able to provide access to training history and schedules. Review history for the past full year and schedules for the next six months.

29. Ensure that data center capacity is planned to avoid unnecessary outages.

Capacity planning ensures that procedures are in place to monitor and analyze factors that could impact the data center's current or future power, network, heating, ventilation, air-conditioning, and space requirements. Inadequate capacity planning could result in data loss, system outages, and/or delays in system deployments. Capacity management is a broad topic that was covered in detail in Chapter 3. A well-managed data center will be able to forecast how much rack space, network drops, network gear, electricity, and heating, ventilation, and air conditioning, just to name a few, are needed to support current and future operations.

How

Review monitoring thresholds and strategies that data center management uses to determine when facilities, equipment, or networks require upgrading. Data center management should be able to provide the capacity planning strategy and documented procedures, including thresholds for upgrading systems. Verify that these procedures are comprehensive and review evidence that they are being followed.

30. Verify that procedures are present to ensure secure storage and disposal of electronic media.

Electronic media often contain sensitive information that, if disclosed, would constitute a compromise of information security. As a result, media storage and disposal must be closely controlled. Improper storage of electronic media could also result in accidental corruption of the information stored on the media.

How

Ensure that the following media storage and disposal controls exist within the data center:

- Electronic media are stored in a dry, temperature-controlled, and secure environment.
- Electronic media containing sensitive information is encrypted and tracked as it moves from one location to another.
- Electronic media is degaussed, overwritten with a Department of Defense (DOD)–compliant electronic shredding utility, or physically destroyed prior to disposal.

You should be able to obtain media tracking, storage, and disposal records from data center management. Tour electronic media storage facilities within the data center to verify that appropriate access and environmental controls are in place. For more information regarding electronic media management, see Chapter 3.

31. Review and evaluate asset management for data center equipment.

Asset management is the controlling, tracking, and reporting of assets to facilitate accounting for the assets. Without effective asset management, the company will be subject to the increased expense of duplicate equipment if assets are available but not locatable. The company will also be subject to unnecessary lease expenses if leased equipment is not adequately tracked and returned on time. Similarly, without adequate asset management, end-of-life equipment conditions may not be noted, resulting in increased risk of hardware failure. Theft of equipment that is not tracked could go unnoticed.

How

Review and evaluate the data center's asset management policies and procedures, and ensure that they comply with company policy and encompass the following:

- **Asset procurement process**   Ensure that this process requires appropriate approvals prior to the purchase of hardware.
- **Asset tracking**   Ensure that the data center is using asset tags and has an asset management database.
- **Current inventory of all equipment**   Ensure that an inventory contains the asset number and location of all hardware, along with information about the equipment's warranty status, lease expiration, and overall lifecycle (that is, when it falls out of vendor support). Ensure that an effective mechanism is in place for keeping this inventory up to date. A sample of asset tags also should be inspected visibly and traced to the inventory.
- **Asset move and disposal procedures**   Ensure that unused equipment is stored in a secure manner.

System Resiliency

Most information systems that reside within data centers process information that requires high system availability. Data center controls ensure high availability relative to the facility, whereas redundant system components and sites are used to ensure system availability in relation to the computer hardware.

32. Ensure that hardware redundancy (redundancy of components within a system) is used to provide high availability where required.

Failure of system components will cause system outages and data loss. When high system availability is required, systems should contain redundant system components such as Redundant Array of Inexpensive Disks (RAID) and redundant power supplies.

How

Determine whether standards for data center hardware include requirements for redundant components. For a sample of systems within the data center, ensure that critical system components such as disk storage and power supplies are redundant wherever possible. Information about hardware redundancy can be found within system specification documents. Data custodians (administration personnel) should be able to provide this documentation.

33. Verify that duplicate systems are used where very high system availability is required.

If system downtime will result in significant costs or loss of revenue to the business and system downtime cannot be tolerated, duplicate (redundant) systems are used to provide for automatic failover in the event of a system crash. This should not be confused with the preceding step, which evaluates the redundancy of components within a single system. This step is referencing the potential need for duplicating the system in its entirety. For the most critical systems, these redundant systems might be placed at two or more separate locations, allowing information to be copied to alternative sites at set intervals such as daily or in real time.

When reviewing system redundancy, you need to determine the manner in which data is copied from the main system to duplicate systems. Because most systems with this level of criticality are database applications, we will focus on database redundancy. Three types of systems provide database transaction redundancy:

- **Electronic vaulting**   Provides periodic data copies through a batch process
- **Remote journaling**   Provides real-time parallel processing over a network connection
- **Database shadowing**   Provides real-time parallel processing over two or more network connections

How

For a sample of systems in the data center, ensure that the appropriate level of system redundancy is being used for the level of system availability that is required. Include redundancy of network connectivity for the data center in this analysis. System redundancy information usually can be obtained from system architecture documentation and interviews with data center and system administrators.

Data Backup and Restore

System backup is regularly performed on most systems. Often, however, restore is tested for the first time when it is required because of a system corruption or hard-disk failure. Sound backup and restore procedures are critical for reconstructing systems after a disruptive event.

34. Ensure that backup procedures and capacity are appropriate for respective systems.

Typically, backup procedures come in the form of backup schedules, tape rotations, and an off-site storage process. Depending on the *maximum tolerable downtime*, system backup schedules could be as frequent as real time or as infrequent as monthly. If systems are backed up and/or taken off-site less frequently than required on critical systems, an unacceptable amount of data will be lost in the event of a system failure or disaster.

Backup schedules typically are 1 week in duration, with full backups normally occurring on weekends and incremental or differential backups at intervals during the week. Tape rotations generally are 6 to 10 weeks in duration. Therefore, the organization will have the opportunity, for example, to retrieve a 6- or 8-week-old version of a file if needed. This can be critical if a file corruption isn't discovered until more than a week after the corruption occurred.

How

Determine whether systems are backed up periodically and the backups stored off-site in a secured location. Verify that processes are in place to determine the appropriate frequency of backup for each system in the data center and to ensure the backup media have adequate space to store the appropriate system contents. Verify that backups are being performed and taken off-site in alignment with organizational backup practices and the requirements of each system. System backup procedures and logs can be obtained from data center staff. Consider retrieving and reviewing a sample of backup system logs.

35. Verify that systems can be restored from backup media.

There is no reason to back up information unless restore is possible; unfortunately, however, organizations rarely test backup media to ensure that system restore works properly. Backup media failure rates are high, especially with magnetic tapes. If it is not possible to restore from backup media, data will be lost.

How

Ask a system administrator to order backup media from off-site storage facilities and observe the restoration of data from the media to a test server. Review the restore logs to verify that all files were restored.

36. Ensure that backup media can be retrieved promptly from off-site storage facilities.

Often, backup media cannot be retrieved from off-site storage facilities. This is due to backup media being marked improperly or placed in the wrong location. This situation can cause either undue delay in restoring systems or a complete loss of data.

How

Verify that backup media can be retrieved within the time frames set forth in the service level agreement with the off-site storage vendor. This can be accomplished by reviewing the logs from recent retrieval requests or requesting retrieval during the audit and measuring the results. Also, ensure that a perpetual inventory is maintained of all tapes stored off-site.

Disaster Recovery Planning

The goal of disaster recovery planning is to reconstitute systems efficiently following a disaster, such as a hurricane or flood.

37. Ensure that a disaster recovery plan (DRP) exists and is comprehensive and that key employees are aware of their roles in the event of a disaster.

If a disaster strikes your only data center and you don't have a DRP, the overwhelming odds are that your organization will suffer a large enough loss to cause bankruptcy. Disaster recovery, therefore, is a serious matter.

PART II

How

Auditing DRPs can be difficult because of the complexity of successfully recovering data center operations. Perform the following steps:

- Ensure that a DRP exits.

- Verify that the DRP covers all systems and operational areas. It should include a formal schedule outlining the order in which systems should be restored and detailed step-by-step instructions for restoring critical systems. These instructions should provide sufficient detail that they could be followed by most any system administrator.

- Review the last data center threat assessment to verify that the DRP is still relevant and addresses the current risk to the data center.

- Ensure that disaster recovery roles and responsibilities are clearly defined.

- Verify that salvage, recovery, and reconstitution procedures are addressed.

- If an emergency operations center is used, verify that it has appropriate supplies, computers, and telecommunications connectivity.

- Ensure that emergency communications are addressed in the plan. This should include a contact list of all personnel to be notified in the event of a disaster, along with phone numbers. Personnel to be notified of a disaster could include key decision-making personnel, personnel who will be involved in the recovery, equipment vendors, and contacts at alternate processing facilities.

- Verify that the DRP identifies a critical recovery time period during which business processing must be resumed before suffering significant or unrecoverable loss. Validate that the plan provides for recovery within that time period.

- Determine whether the plan includes criteria for determining whether a situation is a disaster and procedures for declaring a disaster and invoking the plan.

- Verify that a current copy of the DRP is maintained at a secured, off-site location.

- Review the results of the last disaster recovery exercise.

This information can be obtained from reviewing the actual DRP or from interviewing the data center facility manager or disaster recovery planner.

38. Ensure that DRPs are updated and tested regularly.

If plans are not tested, there is no assurance that they will work when needed. Plans should be tested and updated at least annually, sometimes more frequently for organizations that are upgrading or procuring new systems, conducting mergers or acquisitions, or adding new lines of business. Failure to update or test DRPs will result in slower recovery times in the event of a disaster.

PART II

How

Review the update or version history that usually is included in the front of the plan. Plans should be updated at least annually. Likewise, review disaster recovery test documentation to verify that tests are performed at least annually. This information usually accompanies the plan in either electronic or paper form.

39. Verify that parts inventories and vendor agreements are accurate and current.

When disasters occur, organizations are faced with the task of recovering from scratch systems that often are completely destroyed. This requires hardware, software, and backup media. To speed up the process, data centers should keep certain equipment (such as servers and parts) at off-site facilities and enter into vendor agreements to receive expedited equipment in the event of a disaster. Often this spare equipment will be kept at a "hotsite," where systems are available and ready to use at an alternate data center to expedite recovery.

How

Review spare equipment inventories and vendor agreements to ensure that both are current for existing systems. Vendor agreements should accompany the DRP. Spare equipment inventories can be obtained from asset management or system personnel.

40. Ensure that emergency operations plans address various disaster scenarios adequately.

Several types of disasters can occur at a data center. The common ones include fire, flood, and other weather-related events. Different types of events will require different salvage and recovery efforts. Emergency operations plans should reflect any reasonably anticipated scenario. Inaccurate emergency operations plans increase recovery times.

How

Verify that any reasonably anticipated scenario is covered by emergency operations plans and that those plans accurately reflect specific needs relating to each scenario. This analysis can be performed by interviewing disaster recovery planners or simply by reviewing emergency operations plans.

Knowledge Base

Several additional resources offer information about data centers and related controls. A number of good websites provide information about potential hazards (such as flood hazards) for specific geographic areas and general information on emergency and disaster activities:

- hazards.fema.gov
- msc.fema.gov

- www.fema.gov
- www.noaa.gov
- earthquake.usgs.gov

The Green Grid is a consortium of IT companies and professionals seeking to improve energy efficiency in data centers. Some useful background and guidelines for data center power efficiency can be found at its website at www.thegreengrid.org.

Disaster recovery is a deep discipline. While we touched on best practices and provided high-level audit procedures, several resources can be used by auditors for additional information, including the following:

Resource	Website
The Disaster Recovery Journal	www.drj.com
Disaster Recovery Institute International	www.drii.org
Disaster Recovery World	www.disasterrecoveryworld.com
ISACA	www.isaca.org

Master Checklists

The following table summarizes the steps listed herein for auditing data centers and disaster recovery.

Auditing Data Centers

Checklist for Auditing Data Centers
❏ 1. Review data center exterior lighting, building orientation, signage, fences, and neighborhood characteristics to identify facility-related risks.
❏ 2. Research the data center location for environmental hazards and to determine the distance to emergency services.
❏ 3. Review data center doors and walls to determine whether they protect data center facilities adequately.
❏ 4. Evaluate physical authentication devices to determine whether they are appropriate and are working properly.
❏ 5. Ensure that physical access control procedures are comprehensive and being followed by data center and security staff.
❏ 6. Ensure that intrusion alarms and surveillance systems are protecting the data center from physical intrusion.
❏ 7. Review security guard building round logs and other documentation to evaluate the effectiveness of the security personnel function.
❏ 8. Verify that sensitive areas within the data center are secured adequately. Ensure that all computer processing equipment essential to data center operations (such as hardware systems, power supply breakers, and so on) is located within the computer processing room or in a secure area.

Checklist for Auditing Data Centers (*continued*)

❏   9. Verify that heating, ventilation, and air-conditioning (HVAC) systems maintain constant temperatures within the data center.

❏   10. Ensure that a water alarm system is configured to detect water in high-risk areas of the data center.

❏   11. Determine whether the data center has redundant power feeds.

❏   12. Verify that ground-to-earth exists to protect computer systems.

❏   13. Ensure that power is conditioned to prevent data loss.

❏   14. Verify that battery backup systems are providing continuous power during momentary black-outs and brown-outs.

❏   15. Ensure that generators protect against prolonged power loss and are in good working condition.

❏   16. Evaluate the usage and protection of emergency power-off (EPO) switches.

❏   17. Ensure that data center building construction incorporates appropriate fire suppression features.

❏   18. Ensure that data center personnel are trained in hazardous materials (hazmat) handling and storage and that hazmat procedures are appropriate. Also determine whether data center personnel are trained in how to respond to a fire emergency.

❏   19. Verify that fire extinguishers are strategically placed throughout the data center and are maintained properly.

❏   20. Ensure that fire suppression systems are protecting the data center from fire.

❏   21. Verify that fire alarms are in place to protect the data center from the risk of fire.

❏   22. Review the alarm monitoring console(s), reports, and procedures to verify that alarms are monitored continually by data center personnel.

❏   23. Verify that network, operating system, and application monitoring provides adequate information to identify potential problems for systems located in the data center.

❏   24. Ensure that roles and responsibilities of data center personnel are clearly defined.

❏   25. Verify that duties and job functions of data center personnel are segregated appropriately.

❏   26. Ensure that emergency response procedures address reasonably anticipated threats.

❏   27. Verify that data center facility-based systems and equipment are maintained properly.

❏   28. Ensure that data center personnel are trained properly to perform their job functions.

❏   29. Ensure that data center capacity is planned to avoid unnecessary outages.

❏   30. Verify that procedures are present to ensure secure storage and disposal of electronic media.

❏   31. Review and evaluate asset management for data center equipment.

❏   32. Ensure that hardware redundancy (redundancy of components within a system) is used to provide high availability where required.

❏   33. Verify that duplicate systems are used where very high system availability is required.

❏   34. Ensure that backup procedures and capacity are appropriate for respective systems.

Checklist for Auditing Data Centers *(continued)*

❑   35. Verify that systems can be restored from backup media.

❑   36. Ensure that backup media can be retrieved promptly from off-site storage facilities.

❑   37. Ensure that a disaster recovery plan (DRP) exists and is comprehensive and that key employees are aware of their roles in the event of a disaster.

❑   38. Ensure that disaster recovery plans are updated and tested regularly.

❑   39. Verify that parts inventories and vendor agreements are accurate and current.

❑   40. Ensure that emergency operations plans address various disaster scenarios adequately.

Auditing Routers, Switches, and Firewalls

The network is the fundamental backdrop of your IT operations infrastructure, allowing data to transverse between users, data storage, and data processing. Routers, switches, and firewalls work together to enable data transfer while protecting networks, data, and end users. This chapter discusses how to review these critical pieces of your infrastructure while helping you to do the following:

- Unravel the complexity of network equipment.
- Understand critical network controls.
- Review specific controls for routers, switches, and firewalls.

Background

Routers, switches, and firewalls join and protect our networks, but how did we end up with this interconnected network of devices?

It started in 1962, when Paul Baran of the RAND Corporation was commissioned by the U.S. Air Force to study how to maintain control over aircraft and nuclear weapons after a nuclear attack. This project was primarily meant to be a military network that would allow the armed forces to maintain communication with other commands throughout the United States in the event of a catastrophe. The new network carried the objective of allowing the armed forces to maintain control of nuclear weapons needed to launch a counterattack.

In 1968, ARPA (Advanced Research Projects Agency) awarded the ARPANET (Advanced Research Projects Agency Network) contract to BBN (Bolt, Beranek, and Newman). The physical network was constructed in 1969, linking four nodes: the University of California at Los Angeles, Stanford Research Institute (SRI), the University of California at Santa Barbara, and the University of Utah. The network was wired together using only 50-kbps circuits. From there, the Internet was developed and flew into modern society; today it serves as the backbone of every major company on the planet. In 1973, development began on the protocol later termed the *Transmission Control Protocol/Internet Protocol* (TCP/IP), but it was 1977 before it was demonstrated. This new protocol was created to allow diverse computer networks to interconnect and communicate with each other. Ten years later, in 1983, TCP/IP became the core Internet Protocol on ARPANET.

ARPANET was divided into two networks, MILNET and ARPANET. MILNET was intended to serve the needs of the military, and ARPANET was intended to support the advanced research component that later was to include commerce. We've come a long way since the 1960s. Just 30 years later, in the early 1990s, you could order pizza and manage your bank account online. By the early 2000's, these activities were commonplace.

In the next section we will uncover how these components work using simple explanations and analogies.

Network Auditing Essentials

Networks enable hosts to communicate using specialized hardware optimized for delivering data from one host to another. Fundamentally, the hardware is a computer running an operating system designed to move data. Network devices such as routers, switches, and firewalls have the basic components you would find in your typical server, except they are highly customized. These devices contain specialized processors with embedded instructions designed to process data movement in a fast and efficient manner. They also have memory, an operating system, and a means for configuring the device.

Networking giants in recent years have answered the call for simplicity and created sexy graphical user interfaces (GUIs) to compliment the fearsome command line access used to interact with, and configure, network devices. However, regardless of the method, you are still configuring the operating system for a device that essentially is a computer designed to move data.

Let's start our review of network auditing essentials with a discussion covering protocols and the *International Standards Organization*'s (ISO) *Open System Interconnection* (OSI) model to gain a better understanding of routers, switches, and firewalls. This review will help you work with your network team to audit your networking environment. We will stick to simple analogies and examples while avoiding complex issues. It can take years to master advanced networking concepts. The purpose of this section is to help an auditor who's completely new to networking quickly understand the differences between how routers, switches, and firewalls work.

Protocols

Hosts communicate with each other by first using a common language, or protocol. The hardware and software that handles the communication has to know how to communicate among the different devices on the network. Protocols define rules by which devices agree for communication. A simple analogy might be a friend who speaks in a different language. For example, if my friend speaks only French, I will either agree to speak in French or use an interpreter (called a gateway in network parlance) to communicate with my friend.

You may have noticed that many different protocols are used. Why? Each protocol has features designed into it to make the protocol more efficient at communicating specific types of data or allowing for specific functions.

OSI Model

The seven-layer OSI model describes how data moves from one system to another system. This model helps describe how to build applications, protocols, and equipment that move data from your application to the physical wire, across hundreds or thousands of miles, to an application on the other side.

Two common layered models are the ISO OSI model and the TCP/IP model. The TCP/IP model has five layers that loosely relate to the layers in the ISO OSI model. For the purposes of this chapter, we will discuss and stick with the ISO OSI seven-layer model (Table 5-1). Keep in mind that this is just a model and that real implementations of protocols do not always align perfectly with the seven steps that follow.

Layer	Common Name	Description
Layer 7	Application	Represents the end user application such as HTTP, File Transfer Protocol (FTP), Simple Mail Transport Protocol (SMTP), or Telnet.
Layer 6	Presentation	Handles formatting, encryption, compression, and presentation of data to the application. Examples include Secure Sockets Layer (SSL) and Transport Layer Security (TLS).
Layer 5	Session	Deals with the setup and management of sessions between computer applications. Examples include named pipes, NetBIOS, and session establishment for TCP.
Layer 4	Transport	Deals with transport issues, such as getting to the destination in one piece, and error control. TCP and User Datagram Protocol (UDP) are perhaps the best-known examples in this layer.
Layer 3	Network	Routes packets between networks. Examples include IP, Internet Control Message Protocol (ICMP), IP Security (IPSec), and Address Resolution Protocol (ARP). Routers operate at this layer typically using IP addresses.
Layer 2	Data Link	Links data on hosts from one location to another, typically on the local area network (LAN) but sometimes on the wide area network (WAN) too. Examples include Ethernet, Token Ring, Fiber Distributed Data Interface (FDDI), Frame Relay, and Asynchronous Transfer Mode (ATM). Switches and bridges operate at this layer, typically using Media Access Control (MAC) addresses.
Layer 1	Physical	Defines the physical link, cabling, and binary transmission. Modulation and flow control occur at this layer.

Table 5-1   Simplified OSI Model Description

Routers and Switches

Two key hardware components of networks are switches and routers. Let's take a step back and discuss routers and switches, starting with an analogy.

An Oversimplified Switching and Routing Analogy

Consider your local school full of classrooms. Students can broadcast their name out to everyone in their own class, and everyone in the classroom can hear the speaker. The classroom is their own *broadcast domain*, and it doesn't take long for the people in the classroom to know each other's personal names. However, several communication challenges arise when the size of the classroom, or *broadcast domain*, becomes too large. Let's assume our teacher is superhuman and all classroom communications are handled by the teacher, representing the function of a switch on our network. Our classroom is controlled, but how do we route traffic *between* classrooms?

The next scenario is about *routing traffic between* classrooms. Each of the classrooms has its own number assigned to the classroom. Let's assume a hall monitor handles traffic between classrooms, taking a message from one teacher and delivering it to another teacher to hand off to the student. The hall monitor represents the function of a router on our network.

Routers

Routers connect and route data between networks using Layer 3 network addresses, usually IP addresses. Routers operate at OSI Layer 3. Once data is routed to the destination network, the data goes to a switch where the destination host resides. The switch uses the destination host's MAC address, at OSI Layer 2, to send data the rest of the way to the host.

Switches

A switch is an extension of the concept of a hub. A hub takes a frame that it receives on any given port and repeats it out to every port on the hub. A switch has a learning feature, whereby it learns the MAC address for each host plugged into the switch ports. Once it knows this information, the switch will repeat a frame only out to the port that contains the correct destination MAC address. Everything at the switch level typically is handled with the MAC address, represented by OSI Layer 2. Each of the layers is encapsulated by the next layer, as shown in Figure 5-1.

Computer networks are composed of interconnected LANs, which are simply groups of computers, printers, and other equipment connected to the same network. Devices may be assigned physically or logically to the same LAN based on location (such as a building or small geographic office) or function (such as device management or financial applications). Hosts on the network have various applications and protocols that rely on broadcasts, which are a way of addressing all hosts that are in the same *broadcast domain*. If all hosts were on the same LAN on a network of thousands, you could saturate your network with broadcast traffic.

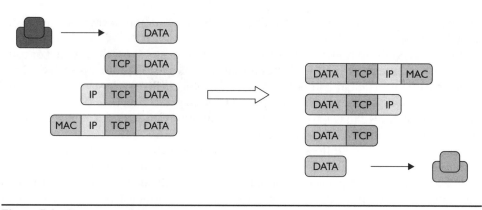

Figure 5-1 Data encapsulation

Routers, by definition, separate broadcast traffic domains (broadcast domains), and many switches also have this powerful capability of controlling broadcast domains. These switches essentially separate ports (and therefore hosts connected to those ports) into little groups. These groups form virtual networks, or *virtual LANs* (VLANs), which limit broadcast traffic to the VLAN. Side effects include additional security features, whereby you can use Access Control Lists (ACLs) and firewalls to control traffic into and out of the VLAN. VLANs aren't necessary to control traffic, but if you have set up a VLAN, you can control traffic into and out of that VLAN.

VLANs can be used on most types of switches to further segment networks connected to the switch. Routing between these VLANs can be performed by routers separate from the switch or, in some cases, integrated into the switch. Switches that can switch packets between VLANs without the use of an external router are known as *Layer 3 switches.*

VLANs are extremely powerful. Think of VLANs as the ability to separate a physical switch into multiple logical switches. Additionally, VLANs can be shared within the same network among multiple physical switches and routers, allowing two geographically separated devices to exist logically on the same virtual network.

VLANs allow network administrators to create segregated networks based on levels of trust or types of traffic. For example, you can create a separate VLAN for managing sensitive hosts and prevent general access to the management console of network equipment or sensitive appliances. Breaking up the network into smaller LANs also generally helps to reduce the number of broadcasts that individual hosts are required to process, and VLANs also allow network administrators to move a host with a logical change in the switch rather than a cable move.

Routers

We now need a way to route traffic between networks. Routers forward packets between different networks. Eventually, the packaged data, or *packet*, reaches the remote LAN and then finally arrives at the host on the other side. Each router between you and the remote host simply looks at the IP address header information, located at Layer 3, to see where to send it next.

Features specific to routers enable them to communicate across the Internet or company network. Routers dynamically build routing tables using protocols such as Open Shortest Path First (OSPF) and Border Gateway Protocol (BGP). These enable the routers to send packets in the direction they need to go to get to the other side as quickly as possible. Routers also may have ACLs and quality-of-service (QOS) features. The association between routers and switches is shown in Table 5-2.

Despite some of the differences between them, switches and routers typically are managed in similar manners using similar syntax and have many of the same concerns from an audit perspective. Keep in mind the purpose of the device as you step through the audit, and this will help you to determine what additional steps, if any, you might want to perform.

Firewalls

Hundreds of firewalls on the market span several dozen vendors and several dozen applications. However, all are essentially designed to help segment networks and users into appropriate security zones. It's confusing even to try simplifying the types of firewalls that exist, and for the purposes of this book we will stick to the National Institute of Standards and Technology (NIST) Publication 800-41-Rev1.

A correctly deployed firewall in key areas protects information assets from unnecessary risk. Network firewalls are essential in their role of protecting the network. Firewalls can be used for perimeter protection or for creating concentric rings of various levels of trust within a network. Firewalls also can help to establish a protected area of your network that is accessible to the public or only certain partners. Firewalls have developed into specialized functions that include protecting virtualized machines from each other on virtual networks or protecting web hosts from network attacks specifically targeting web traffic.

Packet Filtering Firewalls

Packet filtering firewalls are essentially routers operating at Layer 3 using set ACLs. Decisions are made to allow and disallow traffic based on the source and destination IP address, protocol, and port number.

Layer	Name	Equipment Used	Depends on	Example
Layer 3	Network	Routers	IP Address—WAN	198.133.219.25
Layer 2	Data Link	Switches	MAC Address—LAN	00-14-22-F5-04-16

Table 5-2 Routers and Switches

Stateful Inspection Firewalls

Stateful inspection, also stateful packet inspection (SPI) or dynamic packet-filtering firewalls, operate at Layers 3 and 4. Your router at home allows you to establish and maintain a session externally with another address. The "state" refers to identifying and tracking sessions that occur in Layers 4 and 5. The rules are changed dynamically when you establish an outbound connection to enable packets from the destination IP address to be returned to you. All other traffic is stopped from reaching your computer, protecting you from the dangers inherent in the Internet.

Application Firewalls

Application-level firewalls combine the functionality of the typical firewall operating in the lower OSI layers with the power and deep inspection of application awareness. Now, based on information at the application level, such as known malicious traffic, decisions can be made to allow or disallow traffic. An example might be an appliance or host that screens web traffic before it hits your web server. Based on the behavior and content of the web traffic, decisions might be made dynamically to refuse access to the web server.

Application-Proxy Gateway

Application-proxy gateways manage conversations between hosts, acting as an intermediary at the application level of the OSI model. Because proxies reestablish conversations to the destination, they effectively can hide the source of a conversation. Proxies might enforce authentication, logging, or content rules. One of the advantages of application-proxy gateways is the potential ability to stop an encrypted session, decode the data, read the data in clear-text, encode the data, and then reinitiate an encrypted session to the destination. This is extremely resource-intensive and performance requirements become a concern for these applications.

Additional Firewall Technologies

Additional types of firewalls discussed in greater detail in NIST Publication 800-41-Rev1 demonstrate the specialization that has occurred in the firewall market. These firewall technologies include Dedicated Proxy Servers, Virtual Private Networking, Network Access Control, Unified Threat Management, Web Application Firewalls, and Firewalls for Virtual Infrastructures.

 NOTE   NIST Publication 800-41-Rev1, "Guidelines on Firewalls and Firewall Policy," can be found at http://csrc.nist.gov/publications/PubsSPs.html.

Auditing Switches, Routers, and Firewalls

The audit steps are divided into *general steps* and *specific steps*. The general audit steps are applicable to network equipment in general, followed by specific sections for routers, switches, and firewalls. Work through the first section of general controls regardless of your audit and then move to the specific section(s) you need to complete the audit.

 NOTE The general networking audit steps need to be performed regardless of what networking device you audit. These steps apply to routers, switches, and firewalls, regardless of what layer they operate on and regardless of where they are located in your network.

General Network Equipment Audit Steps

Begin the audit by asking the network engineers for a copy of the configuration file and the version of the device you intend to audit. For routers and switches, frequently, nearly all the information you want is located in the configuration file, and it prevents you from having to log onto the device repeatedly.

 NOTE Many of the examples that follow are from the Cisco IOS. Your networking equipment may be different, but the concepts generally are the same. Your network engineers should know when differences occur and can show you adequate supporting documentation so that you feel confident that your network is secure and operating as it should.

1. Review controls around developing and maintaining configurations.

This step is a catch-all that addresses configuration management, the overarching concept of maintaining the secure configuration of the firewall. Failure to maintain a secure configuration subjects the firewall to lapses in technology or processes that affect the security of your network. Review any changes on the firewall immediately to ensure that the change did not unintentionally degrade performance or otherwise hurt the security of the assets the firewall is protecting.

How

Discuss change-management practices with network administrators. Ensure that changes are planned, scheduled, documented (including the purpose of the change), and approved prior to implementation. Ensure that the company's configuration change-management policies and processes are followed. See Chapter 3 for more information.

Note that this step lightly covers routine patch cycles, which is specifically covered again in Step 2. Discuss the following as applicable with the administrator to ensure that proper configuration management controls are in place:

- Security mailing lists are monitored.

- The latest patches are applied in a routine patch cycle under the guidance of written and agreed-on policies and procedures.

- A configuration guideline exists for the equipment in the environment and is strictly followed. Exceptions are carefully documented and maintained.

- Regular vulnerability scanning from both internal and external perspectives is conducted to discover new risks quickly and to test planned changes to the environment.

- Regular internal reviews of the configuration are conducted to compare the existing infrastructure with the configuration guide.

- Regular status reports are issued to upper management documenting the overall security posture of the network.

Having a strong configuration standard is critical to a secure network. Network equipment, including routers, switches, and firewalls, has many configuration options that affect security and are rarely secure out of the box. Taking the time to understand these options and how to configure them to your environment is fundamental to maintaining a sound and secure network.

2. Ensure that appropriate controls are in place for any vulnerabilities associated with the current software version. These controls might include software updates, configuration changes, or other compensating controls.

This step goes beyond configuration changes and targets specifically software updates and any associated vulnerabilities. This step is where you as an auditor will research critical vulnerabilities associated with the software and ensure that appropriate controls are in place, such as a software update, a configuration change, or other compensating control.

Note that it isn't necessary to install each and every update, but you generally should keep your network equipment current. As vulnerabilities become known to the security community, they are documented in various online databases such as the National Vulnerability Database (NVD) located at http://nvd.nist.gov. These lists should be checked, and if the version of code being used is found to have some known vulnerabilities, the device should be patched or have other mitigating controls employed to protect the network device and your network.

How

Discuss the software version information with the network administrator and the status of any pending patches or upgrades. Check the software and version against the NVD. Note and discuss any potential issues with the network administrator.

3. Verify that all unnecessary services are disabled.

Running unnecessary services can leave you susceptible to performance- and security-related risks. This is true of any host or device and adds to the attack surface available to potential attackers.

How

Discuss unnecessary services with the network administrator, and review the configuration of the device. If the device depends on another platform (for example, some firewalls), ensure that the underlying platform also has all unnecessary services disabled.

Discuss any exceptions with the administrator, and determine what additional risk exposure might exist and whether exceptions are necessary. For any other services enabled, discuss with the administrator to verify that there is a legitimate business need for the service. Services should be enabled only when needed. Refer to the vendor's website for the best source of required services and those that might be considered security risks. Note the presence or absence of these services.

4. Ensure that good SNMP management practices are followed.

Simple Network Management Protocol (SNMP) represents an often-overlooked way to obtain full administrative access to a network device. This step may not be applicable to your equipment if the equipment doesn't support SNMP management or it is disabled.

How

Discuss SNMP management practices with your network administrator. SNMP Versions 1 and 2 send the community string in clear text, and the packets are unauthenticated. SNMP Version 3 adds message integrity, authentication, and encryption to the packets. However, all versions have suffered from security issues. Refer to Cisco's website and carefully review the suggested compensating controls listed under "Workarounds" at http://www.cisco.com/warp/public/707/cisco-sa-20080610-snmpv3.shtml.

SNMP community strings should follow standard password policies for strength and change frequency. Management with SNMP should be restricted with an access list, and no management should be allowed from an untrusted network.

5. Review and evaluate procedures for creating user accounts and ensuring that accounts are created only when there's a legitimate business need. Also review and evaluate processes for ensuring that accounts are removed or disabled in a timely fashion in the event of termination or job change.

This step has a wide scope, covering controls around account usage and management. Inappropriately managed or used accounts could provide easy access to the network device, bypassing other additional security controls to prevent malicious attacks. This step should cover policies and procedures that are essential to ensure that only authorized administrators can log into a network device and that once logged in, they have the proper privilege level. Login procedures should adhere to strong authentication, authorization, and accounting (AAA).

How

Discuss with the administrator and verify with the administrator's help that appropriate policies and procedures exist to add and remove account access to the device. Accounts should be controlled such that only those authorized to have access can log onto the device. Unused accounts, if applicable, should be removed from the configuration of the network device or completely disabled in accordance with your organization's account management policies.

Also review the process for removing accounts when access is no longer needed. The process could include a periodic review and validation of active accounts by system administrators and/or other knowledgeable managers. Obtain a sample of accounts, and verify that they are owned by active employees and that those employees' job positions have not changed since the account's creation.

In general, accounts should never be shared among administrators. This can present risk in that you lose accountability for actions taken on the system. Strong account policies always should be enforced by the network device. Additionally, discuss login procedures with the administrator to ensure that all users are managed appropriately using roles and that actions are logged appropriately. In general, individual IDs should be created for every person requiring access to the network device, or the network device should use a central authentication server for these accounts, sometimes called an *AAA server*. RADIUS (Remote Authentication Dial-In User Service) and TACACS+ (Terminal Access Controller Access-Control System Plus) are examples of AAA servers.

Some network infrastructures may use TACACS+ for AAA on routers and switches. This system allows anyone with a Remote Access Services (RAS)–enabled NT account to log onto the router in nonprivileged mode. An additional "enable" password is then required for privileged access. An example configuration file entry if TACACS+ servers are used might be this:

```
tacacs-server host <IP Address>
```

Individual IDs might look something like this in the configuration file:

```
username <name> password 7 <encrypted password>
```

These IDs should be created with a privilege level of 1 (which is the default), forcing the enable password to be required for additional access.

6. Ensure that appropriate password controls are used.

Weak and unencrypted passwords allow attackers to guess or read passwords easily in plaintext. Strong password controls are essential to protecting network equipment. Older versions of network software allowed storing passwords in clear-text by default. You probably won't see this, but you should verify that passwords are securely stored with the administrator.

How

Discuss password controls with the network administrator, and consult existing policies and procedures. Ensure that complex passwords are used, stored with MD5 hashes or similar encryption where possible, and changed with appropriate periodicity (such as every 90 days). Passwords used for privileged modes of operation should never be the same as any other password used on the device.

Finally, ensure that appropriate controls exist so that the same password isn't shared on a large number of devices throughout your network. Passwords shared on the WAN should not be used on the LAN.

7. Verify that secure management protocols are used where possible.

Telnet sends all its information in clear-text, allowing passwords and other information to be viewed with a sniffer. SNMP Versions 1 and 2 are similar. Secure alternatives are SSH, IPSec, and SNMPv3. While it is imperative that secure protocols be used from an untrusted network, it is also important on the inside as well.

How

Discuss management procedures with the network administrator, and review the configuration of the network device. Ensure that policies and procedures exist to manage routers, switches, and firewalls as securely as possible. Secure Shell (SSH) Protocol, another secure management protocol, or an out-of-band management system should be used for remote administration.

8. Ensure that current backups exist for configuration files.

Keep copies of the all network device configurations in a readily accessible, secure location—this is critical! These files contain any comments that can help to give perspective to the configuration settings and filters. You can change filters with much more ease and accuracy when you can refer back to the old configuration files. These backups also can be invaluable for diagnosing and recovering from unexpected network failures.

How

Discuss policies and procedures with the network administrator, and ask to see where the current configurations are kept. Verify with the administrator that the backup repository contains the latest configurations shown on the routers and switches. The configuration files should be stored in a secure location to which only the network team and appropriate administrators have access.

9. Verify that logging is enabled and sent to a centralized system.

Logs should be collected for AAA and system events. Logs should also be sent to a secure host to prevent tampering with the information. Failure to keep logs may prevent administrators from properly diagnosing a network issue or malicious behavior.

How

Discuss logging with the network administrator, and review the configuration file. Ensure that appropriate log levels are used. Log levels range from 0 to 7 on Cisco equipment. Log level 0 would log only emergencies during which the system was unusable, and log level 7 is debug-level logging.

Logging is identified by the following:

```
logging host <ip address>
```

AAA logging is identified in Cisco configuration files by the following:

```
aaa accounting
```

SNMP traps are identified by the following:

```
snmp-server host [log host] [version] [community string] [trap-type]
snmp-server enable traps [trap-type]
```

10. Evaluate use of Network Time Protocol (NTP).

Use the NTP provides time synchronization for the timestamp on all logged events. These timestamps are invaluable in reporting and troubleshooting.

How

Discuss the use of NTP with the administrator, and review the configuration file. For ease of management, standardize all clocks to a single time zone. The following indicates that NTP is enabled. Notice that the key option is used with authentication.

```
ntp server <ip address> key <key>
```

11. Verify that a banner is configured to make all connecting users aware of the company's policy for use and monitoring.

A warning banner that clearly marks the router or switch as private property and disallowing unauthorized access is essential should a compromise ever result in legal action.

How

Verify with the administrator and a review of the device configuration that all connecting users are made aware of the company's policy for use and monitoring. Confirm that the motd or login banner does not disclose any information about the company or network device. This information should be reserved for the exec banner after a successful login.

For Cisco equipment, you would review the configuration file for either the banner motd or the banner login. These do basically the same thing with minor differences. The motd banner is displayed before the login banner, but both appear to the end user before the login prompt. The motd banner can be disabled on a per-line basis, whereas the login banner cannot.

12. Ensure that access controls are applied to the console port.

Logical access can be gained via the console port with poor physical access controls to the router or switch. Often the console port will have no password for convenience. Ensure that a password is used to provide an additional layer of defense beyond the physical controls. A password is imperative if the location is not physically secure.

How

Discuss access controls with the administrator. Verify that physical access to the console port is protected and logically that the console port is password-protected. There are actually several different ways to do this; here is an example of a Cisco router or switch configuration:

```
line con 0
password xxxxxxxxxxx (to use a password only)
login local (to use a locally defined username and password)
login authentication <name of authentication server list>
password 7 xxxxxxxxxxxxxxx
```

If AAA authentication is used, make sure that the line starts with aaa authentication login default. Failure to include default could mean that login on the console port is allowed without any password. Typically, TACACS+ will be tried first with local as a backup.

13. Ensure that all network equipment is stored in a secure location.

Anyone with physical access to a network device might be able to gain full logical access using well-documented password recovery procedures. Someone also could unplug cables or otherwise disrupt service. Additionally, access should be limited to prevent non-malicious accidents (such as tripping over a cable) from disrupting service.

How

Visually observe the location of the network equipment, and discuss physical access to the equipment with the network administrator.

14. Ensure that a standard naming convention is used for all devices.

Standard naming conventions make troubleshooting and finding issues easier. Standard naming conventions also help to make managing the environment easier as the organization grows.

How

Discuss the naming conventions used with the network administrator.

15. Verify that standard, documented processes exist for building network devices.

Documented processes provide repeatability of secure designs and higher quality workmanship, helping to prevent common mistakes that might lead to a service disruption or network compromise.

How

Discuss documented policies and procedures for building network equipment with the network administrator. If possible, verify using a recent build that the process was followed.

Additional Switch Controls: Layer 2

The following are additional test steps for switches, or Layer 2 devices.

1. Verify that administrators avoid using VLAN 1.

By default, all ports on a Cisco switch are members of VLAN 1. Avoiding the use of VLAN 1 prevents network intruders from plugging into unused ports and communicating with the rest of the network.

How

Discuss this practice with the administrator, and review the configuration file for the existence of VLAN 1.

2. Evaluate the use of trunk autonegotiation.

A trunk on a switch joins two separate VLANs into an aggregate port, allowing traffic access to either VLAN. There are two trunking protocols: 802.1q, which is an open standard, and ISL, which was developed by Cisco. Some switch types and software versions are set to autotrunking mode, allowing a port to attempt automatically to convert the link into a trunk. Dynamic Trunking Protocol (DTP) might help to determine which trunking protocol the switch should use and how the protocol should operate. If this is the case, generally speaking, all the VLANs on the switch become members of the new trunked port. Disabling trunk autonegotiation mitigates the risks associated with a VLAN-hopping attack, whereby someone in one VLAN is able to access resources in another VLAN.

How

Discuss with the network administrator, and review the configuration file. Five best practices may help you to decide if the trunk autonegotiation is set appropriately on the ports in your switch. The examples and practices come from the "NSA Switch Configuration Guide."

1. Do not use the DTP if possible. Assign trunk interfaces to a native VLAN other than VLAN 1.

```
Switch(config)# interface fastethernet 0/1
Switch(config-if)# switchport mode trunk
Switch(config-if)# switchport trunk native vlan 998
```

2. Put nontrunking interfaces in permanent nontrunking mode without negotiation.

```
Switch(config)# interface fastethernet 0/1
Switch(config-if)# switchport mode access
Switch(config-if)# switchport nonegotiate
```

3. Put trunking interfaces in permanent trunking mode without negotiation.

```
Switch(config)# interface fastethernet 0/1
Switch(config-if)# switchport mode trunk
Switch(config-if)# switchport nonegotiate
```

4. Specifically list all VLANs that are part of the trunk.

```
Switch(config)# interface fastethernet 0/1
Switch(config-if)# switchport trunk allowed vlan 6, 10, 20, 101
```

5. Use a unique native VLAN for each trunk on a switch.

```
Switch(config)# interface fastethernet 0/1
Switch(config-if)# switchport trunk native vlan 998
Switch(config)# interface fastethernet 0/2
Switch(config-if)# switchport trunk native vlan 997
```

3. Verify that Spanning-Tree Protocol attack mitigation is enabled (BPDU Guard, Root Guard).

Risks associated with this type of attack include giving an attacker the ability to use the Spanning-Tree Protocol to change the topology of a network. The Spanning-Tree Protocol is designed to prevent network loops from developing. The switch will learn the network topology and move a port through four stages—block, listen, learn, and forward—as it ensures that an endless loop isn't developing in the network traffic patterns.

How

Discuss with the network administrator, and review the configuration file. For access ports, look for the following configuration:

```
spanning-tree portfast
spanning-tree bpdufilter enable
spanning-tree bpduguard enable
```

For downlink ports to other switches, look for the following configuration:

```
spanning-tree guard root
```

4. Evaluate the use of VLANs on the network.

VLANs should be used to break up broadcast domains and, where necessary, to help divide resources with different security levels.

How

Discuss the application of VLANs with the network administrator. Devices at different security levels ideally should be isolated on separate switches or Layer 2 devices. For example, if you have equipment that, for some reason, cannot be protected with the company's standard antivirus software and security patches, you could place that equipment on a separate VLAN.

5. Disable all unused ports and put them in an unused VLAN.

This setup prevents network intruders from plugging into unused ports and communicating with the rest of the network.

How

Discuss this practice with the network administrator.

6. Evaluate use of the VLAN Trunking Protocol (VTP) in the environment.

VTP is a Layer 2 messaging protocol that distributes VLAN configuration information over trunks. VTP allows the addition, deletion, and renaming of VLANs on a network-wide basis. A network attacker could add or remove VLANs from the VTP domain as well as create Spanning-Tree Protocol loops. Both situations can lead to disastrous results that are very difficult to troubleshoot. This would not have to be a malicious event. A switch with a higher configuration version number in its VTP database has authority over other switches with a lower number. If a lab switch such as this one were placed on the production network, you might accidently reconfigure your entire network.

How

Discuss use of the VTP with the network administrator to ensure that passwords are used if the VTP is necessary. VTP should be turned off if it's not used. The VTP mode of a switch can be server, client, or transparent. Use transparent mode unless client or server is required.

If VTP is necessary, domains should be set up for different areas of the network and passwords should be enabled. Look for these lines in the configuration file:

```
vtp domain domain_name
vtp password Some_strong_password
```

7. Verify that thresholds exist that limit broadcast/multicast traffic on ports.

Configuring storm controls helps to mitigate the risk of a network outage in the event of a broadcast storm.

How

Discuss with the administrator and review the configuration file for the presence of `storm-control [broadcast | multicast | unicast] level`.

Additional Router Controls: Layer 3

The following are additional test steps for routers, or Layer 3 devices.

1. Verify that inactive interfaces on the router are disabled.

Inactive interfaces that should be disabled include LAN and WAN interfaces such as Ethernet, Serial, and ATM. Open interfaces are possible sources of attack if someone plugs into the interface.

How

Discuss policies and procedures with the network administrator to ensure that this is a common practice. Ask the administrator for examples. The command `shutdown` is used to disable interfaces.

2. Ensure that the router is configured to save all core dumps.

Having a core dump (an image of the router's memory at the time of the crash) can be extremely useful to Cisco tech support in diagnosing a crash and possibly detecting that an attack was the root cause.

How

Discuss how the router handles core dumps with the network administrator. The core dumps should be located in a protected area that is accessible only to the network administrator, because disclosure of important information could occur. You might review the configuration file for something similar to the following. Note that Trivial FTP (TFTP) and Remote Copy Protocol (RCP) also may be options here, but FTP is recommended.

```
exception protocol ftp
exception dump <ip address of server>
ftp username <username>
ftp password <password>
```

NOTE Note that core dumps will cause the router to take longer to reboot after a crash because of the time it takes to dump the core file to the server.

---

3. Verify that all routing updates are authenticated.

Authentication ensures that the receiving router incorporates into its tables only the route information that the trusted sending router actually intended to send. It prevents a legitimate router from accepting and then employing unauthorized, malicious, or corrupted routing tables that would compromise the security or availability of the network. Such a compromise might lead to rerouting traffic, a denial of service, or simply access to certain packets of data to an unauthorized person.

How

The authentication of routing advertisements is available with Routing Information Protocol (RIPv2), OSPF, intermediate system to intermediate system (IS-IS), Enhanced Interior Gateway Routing Protocol (EIGRP), and BGP. Most allow the use of plaintext authentication or an MD5 hash. The MD5 method should be used to prevent passwords from being sniffed.

RIPv2 authentication is configured on a per-interface basis. Look in the configuration file for something like this:

```
router rip
version 2
key chain name_of_keychain
key 1
key-string string
interface ethernet 0
ip rip authentication key-chain name_of_keychain
ip rip authentication mode md5
```

OSPF authentication is configured on a per-area basis with keys additionally specified per interface. Look in the configuration file for something like this:

```
router ospf 1
area 0 authentication message-digest
interface ethernet 0
ip ospf message-digest-key 1 md5 authentication_key
```

BGP authentication is configured on a per-neighbor basis. Look in the configuration file for something like this (MD5 is the only option, so it does not need to be specified):

```
router bgp 1
neighbor ip_address or peer_group_name password password
```

4. Verify that IP source routing and IP directed broadcasts are disabled.

IP source routing allows the sender of an IP packet to control the route of the packet to the destination, and IP directed broadcasts allow the network to be used as an unwitting tool in a smurf or fraggle attack.

How

Discuss the router configuration with the network administrator. An example configuration for disabling IP source routing might look something like this for Cisco routers:

```
no ip source-route
```

You should see the following on each interface in the configuration file for Cisco routers to disable IP directed broadcasts:

```
no ip directed-broadcast
```

Additional Firewall Controls

The following are additional test steps for firewalls. Note that some of these controls might be handled by a router in conjunction with a firewall, but a router by itself is a poor firewall for the perimeter of a corporate network.

1. Verify that all packets are denied by default.

All packets on a firewall should be denied except for packets coming from and headed to addresses and ports that are all explicitly defined. This is a much stronger defensive position than trying to keep track of what rules you have set up to block each specific address or service. For example, external SNMP queries from outside your network targeted to a router inside your network would be denied by default if the only traffic you allowed into your DMZ was to a web server.

How

Verify with the firewall administrator that all packets are denied by default. Ask the administrator to show you in the configuration how this is set up.

2. Ensure that inappropriate internal and external IP addresses are filtered.

Traffic coming from the internal address space should not have external addresses as the source address. Likewise, traffic coming from outside the network should not have your internal network as the source address.

How

Verify with the help of the firewall administrator that all packets entering from the exterior with source IP addresses set up for internal networks are denied. Likewise, all packets coming from the interior with source IP addresses not set up for the interior should be denied. Additionally, firewalls should hide internal Domain Naming Service (DNS) information from external networks.

3. Evaluate firewall rule sets to provide appropriate protection.

Failure to manage your firewall rules may expose you to unnecessary risk from open or inappropriate access. It wasn't long ago that a few hundred firewall rules was considered inexcusable and difficult to manage. Today, many organizations have several hundred, or even thousands, of firewall rules on a single appliance. Firewall rules quickly accumulate and are difficult to remove because administrators are afraid to break applications, forget why specific rules exist, or simply can't navigate the complexity of hundreds of rules. Don't underestimate the importance of this step.

How

Interview the administrator and discuss what tools and processes exist to manage the configuration management process and the change management process. Verify that appropriate controls are in place to identify the purpose of the existing firewall rules. Change controls have already been covered by this point in the audit. However, this is a great opportunity to review the importance of change controls with the administrator.

At some point in the growing complexity of large data sets, such as hundreds of firewall rules across dozens of firewalls, specialized technologies and automated processes must be considered to support firewall management. Several excellent products are on the market, shown in Table 5-3, that can help administrators avoid mistakes and manage firewall rules in large environments. Some auditors may want to run vulnerability scans on the firewall and try various methods of using Nmap to reach assets that should be blocked. These approaches are a fine supplement; however, remember that although the current state of the firewall may secure your assets, the broken firewall management processes in place could leave your organization bleeding without you ever knowing it. Both are important. You need to be assured that your technical controls are effective now and that they will continue to be effective because of the additional controls in place to manage system changes.

Tools and Technology

These tools can be quite helpful and guide you toward parts of your configuration file that might need further review. A strong case could be made that new configuration files should be tested with good peer reviews and tools such as those listed here. Many

Table 5-3 Firewall Management Solutions	Product	Company	Website
	FireMon	Secure Passage	www.securepassage.com
	SecureTrack	Tufin	www.tufin.com
	Firewall Analyzer	Algosec	www.algosec.com
	Firewall Assurance	Skybox Security	www.skyboxsecurity.com
	Playbook	Matasano Security	www.matasano.com/playbook

general vulnerability scanners also test commonly exploited vulnerabilities for networking platforms.

Tool	Website
Wireshark	www.wireshark.org
Nmap	http://insecure.org
TeraTerm Pro	http://hp.vector.co.jp/authors/VA002416/teraterm.html
"Top 100 Network Security Tools"	http://sectools.org

NOTE Automated tools can be quite harmful to production environments. Exercise care, and design the test in a manner that will not affect production systems.

Knowledge Base

Resource	Website
Cisco documentation	www.cisco.com/univercd/home/home.htm
Cisco conventions	http://www.cisco.com/en/US/tech/tk801/tk36/technologies_tech_note09186a0080121ac5.shtml
The Internet Engineering Task Force (IETF)	www.ietf.org
National Vulnerability Database	http://nvd.nist.gov
Assigned port numbers, essential for reading access lists	www.iana.org/assignments/port-numbers
Valid but unassigned IP blocks	www.iana.org/assignments/ipv4-address-space
Original ISO OSI Standard (s020269_ISO_IEC_7498-1_1994(E).zip) and many others	http://standards.iso.org/ittf/PubliclyAvailableStandards
NIST publications	http://csrc.nist.gov/publications/PubsSPs.html

Master Checklists

The following tables summarize the steps listed herein for auditing routers, switches, and firewalls.

General Network Equipment Audit Steps

These controls should be evaluated in addition to performing the specific steps in the following checklists as they apply. For example, if you were to audit a switch, router, or firewall, you would perform the steps in the following checklist and then additionally perform the steps under the appropriate checklist for switches, routers, or firewalls.

Checklist for Auditing Network Equipment

❏ 1. Review controls around developing and maintaining configurations.

❏ 2. Ensure that appropriate controls are in place for any vulnerabilities associated with the current software version. These controls might include software updates, configuration changes, or other compensating controls.

❏ 3. Verify that all unnecessary services are disabled.

❏ 4. Ensure that good SNMP management practices are followed.

❏ 5. Review and evaluate procedures for creating user accounts and ensuring that accounts are created only when there is a legitimate business need. Also review and evaluate processes for ensuring that accounts are removed or disabled in a timely fashion in the event of termination or job change.

❏ 6. Ensure that appropriate password controls are used.

❏ 7. Verify that secure management protocols are used where possible.

❏ 8. Ensure that current backups exist for configuration files if applicable.

❏ 9. Verify that logging is enabled and sent to a centralized system.

❏ 10. Evaluate use of the Network Time Protocol (NTP).

❏ 11. Verify that a banner is configured to make all connecting users aware of the company's policy for use and monitoring.

❏ 12. Ensure that access controls are applied to the console port.

❏ 13. Ensure that all network equipment is stored in a secure location.

❏ 14. Ensure that a standard naming convention is used for all devices.

❏ 15. Verify that standard, documented processes exist for building network devices.

Auditing Layer 2 Devices: Additional Controls for Switches

These controls should be evaluated in addition to performing the general steps for auditing network equipment.

Checklist for Auditing Layer 2 Devices: Additional Controls for Switches

❏ 1. Verify that administrators avoid using VLAN 1.

❏ 2. Evaluate the use of trunk autonegotiation.

❏ 3. Verify that Spanning-Tree Protocol attack mitigation is enabled (BPDU Guard, Root Guard).

❏ 4. Evaluate the use of VLANs on the network.

❏ 5. Disable all unused ports, and put them in an unused VLAN.

❏ 6. Evaluate use of the VTP in the environment.

❏ 7. Verify that thresholds exist that limit broadcast/multicast traffic on ports.

Auditing Layer 3 Devices: Additional Controls for Routers

These controls should be evaluated in addition to performing the general steps for auditing network equipment.

Checklist for Auditing Layer 3 Devices: Additional Controls for Routers
❑   1. Verify that inactive interfaces on the router are disabled.
❑   2. Ensure that the router is configured to save all core dumps.
❑   3. Verify that all routing updates are authenticated.
❑   4. Verify that IP source routing and IP directed broadcasts are disabled.

Auditing Firewalls: Additional Controls

These controls should be evaluated in addition to performing the general steps for auditing network equipment.

Checklist for Auditing Firewalls: Additional Controls
❑   1. Verify that all packets are denied by default.
❑   2. Ensure that inappropriate internal and external IP addresses are filtered.
❑   3. Evaluate firewall rule sets to provide appropriate protection.

Auditing Windows Operating Systems

The Windows operating system has grown from humble beginnings and evolved into one of the world's most pervasive operating system for servers and clients. This chapter covers the basic components of a Windows server audit and includes a quick audit for Windows clients.

We will discuss the following:

- A brief history of Windows development
- Windows essentials: learning about the target host
- How to audit Windows servers
- How to audit Windows clients
- Tools and resources for enhancing your Windows audits

Background

Microsoft and IBM worked jointly to develop OS/2 in the early 1990s, but the relationship turned sour. Microsoft and IBM split up and went separate directions, with Microsoft later releasing Windows NT in July 1993. Microsoft's server line as we know it today finds its roots in these humble beginnings. Windows NT was the professional version of the Windows operating system targeting company and government organizations.

The server market evolved from Windows NT to Windows Server 2000, Windows Server 2003, and then Windows Server 2008. What this means for the auditor is that many versions of the operating system are used in most large environments. It's highly recommended to find the time to familiarize yourself with the operating systems in your particular environment. Not all utilities work on all systems. In some situations, hosts might exist on your network that are no longer supported by Microsoft. Additional controls should be in place to protect these systems, such as technologies that prevent network attacks or malware propagation.

Microsoft Windows products cover nearly two dozen categories. The Enterprise focus breaks down into Client Infrastructure, Server Infrastructure, and Comprehensive Management. Comprehensive Management is an important strategic focus by Microsoft to integrate management into Microsoft System Center, including Configuration

Manager, Operations Manager, Data Protection Manager, Virtual Machine Manager, and Service Manager. The strategic focus includes simplified management platforms targeting midsize and small businesses, called Microsoft System Center Essentials and Microsoft Intune.

Windows Auditing Essentials

The material in this chapter requires a basic understanding of the components that compose the Windows environment. In addition, your role as an auditor and advisor will significantly improve if you understand how to approach a comprehensive audit of a Windows platform.

Figure 6-1 illustrates how the operating system serves as a vehicle for supporting applications. Many components surrounding the operating system should be considered in a complete review. For example, consider the danger of poorly maintained or configured applications. The more applications you add to the platform, the more potential trouble areas you have as an auditor as you increase your attack surface area. Several chapters in this book are devoted to applications that you might want to consider for your audit. In addition, the hardware, storage, and network affect the performance and protection of the operating system. Finally, the surrounding controls and management of the environment affect the support, risk, compliance, and business alignment of the server.

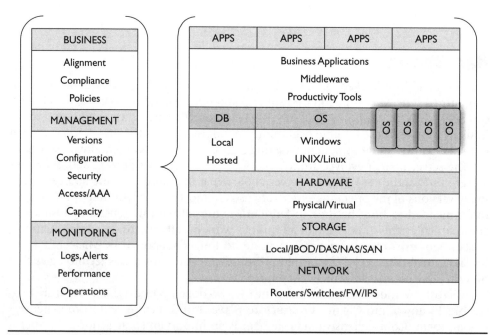

Figure 6-1 Model for auditing hosts

Consider scheduling time on your calendar to use and learn any of the tools discussed in this chapter. You might be surprised at how easy most of them are to use and how much more efficient you become because you know the shortcuts to getting just the information you want. Sometimes it's too easy as auditors to continue using what you've always used because it works, instead of looking at new methods for improving your efficiency. After you've done a little homework, you can ask your company administrators to show you the ropes. Most administrators of any caliber actually enjoy doing this. You can be assured that if you show up to an administrator's office asking about an obscure tool, you'll get his or her attention, and one of you will walk away a little wiser for the visit.

Command-Line Tips

Those of you who are comfortable with the command line on a UNIX machine may appreciate installing UNIX functionality using Cygwin from www.cygwin.com, which allows you to access several utilities such as `ls`, `sed`, `grep`, `more`, and `cat`. It's also possible to create scripts based on these binaries, located in the bin directory, to manipulate the text output from standard Windows utilities. Finally, as long as you understand the risks involved, you power users may even want to add the <drive>:\cygwin\ bin directory to the environment path.

NOTE If you like the command line and enjoy scripting, take advantage of the resources located in Microsoft's scripting center website at www.microsoft.com/technet/scriptcenter/default.mspx.

Essential Command-Line Tools

Several tools should be in every administrator's back pocket. Keep in mind that with today's complex firewalls and malware protection, not all these tools may work properly. Test every tool in a lab environment prior to running it on a production network.

NOTE The various tools discussed in this chapter can be powerful. Follow best practices. Learn how these tools work on another computer off the network in a test environment prior to using them on your own computer or production network and systems.

Resource Kit Tools

The Windows 2003 and earlier resource kit tools are beyond this chapter's scope and are not discussed here. Windows 2008 did not ship with a general administration resource kit. Many of the tools you would have found useful have been supplemented with much more robust or powerful tools that are now part of the command line, one of the Remote Server Administration Tools, or are handled by a more powerful Sysinternals tool.

The old Windows 2003 Resource Kit contains more than 120 different tools for administering and troubleshooting systems, managing Active Directory, configuring security features, and much more. You can still download the Resource Kit tools from Microsoft's website, but you should carefully test any tool that you intend to use to make sure it will not disrupt your environment.

 NOTE Microsoft offers outstanding command-line help at http://technet .microsoft.com/en-us/library/cc754340(WS.10).aspx. Type **help cmd** from the command prompt for general information about using the command line in Windows.

Sysinternals Tools

The Sysinternals tools, bought by Microsoft in 2006, help administrators and auditors perform complex tasks and detailed analysis. You can download Sysinternals tools from the website at www.sysinternals.com. Dozens of tools are available for remote administration, network analysis, process and registry monitoring, and other tasks. Several companies include a subset of these tools as part of the standard build for servers and clients.

Other Tools

Many, many other tools are available as well, some of which are listed here and discussed in the various audit steps. You can script nearly everything in the following audit, and in some cases, you may find that you have commercial configuration management tools that can perform a detailed analysis of the system to the standard set in the following discussions. You will still find it helpful to sample critical servers and individually test them for appropriate controls.

One interesting tool, the Windows Forensic Toolchest (WFT), written by Monty McDougal, serves as a wrapper for command-line tools. It can handle any of the tools listed here or others you may want to add. WFT is referenced as part of the SANS forensic track. You can learn more about it from www.foolmoon.net/security (and you might get a discount if you tell him you learned about it from this book).

Common Commands

Table 6-1 presents a list of command-line tools used throughout this chapter.

Server Administration Tools

Remote Server Administration Tools (RSAT) enable a Windows 7 client to manage roles and features running on Windows Server 2003 and 2008 systems. RSAT is comparable in functionality to the Windows Server 2003 Administrative Tools Pack and Remote Server Administration Tools for Windows Vista. Most of the tools in the Adminpak were used for Active Directory (AD) domain-specific administration. If the subject of the audit is part of the AD infrastructure, these tools may be of use. RSAT allows administrators to perform remote server management functions and includes several great tools that are otherwise difficult to duplicate in functionality.

Tool	Description	Where to Get It
psinfo	List system information, including installed service packs, patches, applications, and drive information	www.sysinternals.com
Systeminfo	List system information	Native command
Pslist	List running processes	www.sysinternals.com
psservice	List all installed services	www.sysinternals.com
cmdkey	Create, list, or delete stored credentials	Native command
Netsh	Display or modify network configuration	Native command
netstat	Provide network information	Native command
psservice	List service information	www.sysinternals.com
Sc	Tool for talking with service controller	Native command
DumpSec	GUI and command-line "Swiss army knife" of the security settings	http://somarsoft.com
tcpview	GUI view of processes mapped to ports	www.sysinternals.com
procexp	Powerful GUI process explorer	www.sysinternals.com
Fport	Command line view of processes mapped to ports	www.foundstone.com/ knowledge/ proddesc/fport.html
schtasks	List scheduled tasks at the command line	Native command
bootcfg	List boot partition information	Native command
pendmoves	List file move operations scheduled for the next reboot	www.sysinternals.com
autoruns	List everything scheduled to start when your computer starts up—the GUI version	www.sysinternals.com
autorunsc	List everything scheduled to start when your computer starts up—the command-line version.	www.sysinternals.com
rsop.msc	Open the resulting set of security policies on your host when run from the Start | Run box or command line	Native command
secpol.msc	Open just the local computer policy	Native command
Pwdump	Dump Windows password hashes into a format usable by nearly all free and commercial password crackers	http://openwall.com/passwords

Table 6-1   Common Commands Used in this Chapter

 NOTE   You can easily add the Microsoft Windows RSAT to your desktop or laptop computer. Just visit Google, type **Microsoft Remote Server Administration Tools** in the search field, and follow the link to Microsoft's downloads page. After downloading the installer package onto your computer, you need to run the file as an administrator to install the tools onto your system.

Performing the Audit

The key to a successful audit of Windows servers or clients is to review the host thoroughly by itself and in conjunction with the many other possible connections that pass data to and from the host.

The following audit steps focus only on the host and do not cover extensive reviews of overlying applications or trust relationships with outside systems. Also not covered are data input and data output methods or their validity. You would deal with these on a per-host basis using techniques and tools covered elsewhere in this book. The steps shown here are typical of many server audits and represent a good tradeoff between the number of risks covered and the amount of time it takes to review the host.

 NOTE The test steps in this chapter focus on testing the logical security of Windows boxes, as well as processes for maintaining and monitoring that security. However, other internal controls are also critical to the overall operations of a computing environment, such as physical security, disaster-recovery planning, backup processes, change management, and capacity planning. These topics are covered in Chapter 4 and should be included in your audit if they have not already been covered effectively in a separate data center or entity-level controls audit.

Test Steps for Auditing Windows

In an ideal world, you would audit against a reference set of controls and information covering every possible configuration setting. However, we don't live in an ideal world, and most of us don't have that much time per host. The test steps in this chapter are a recommended list of items to evaluate. From experience, we know that debate abounds regarding auditing Windows. Can a Windows server be secured? What makes your steps better than someone else's steps? The steps covered here have worked for several companies.

Many auditing programs fail to balance effective audits and effective time management. Related to time management, notice that we spend a lot of time discussing various ways to script the results. Configuration management tools can also be leveraged by the audit team to review scores of servers very quickly, and some audit packages promise the same. The only concerns here regard ensuring that all of the controls that impact the business are covered, and occasionally validating the results of the tools with your own independent reviews.

Setup and General Controls

The following represents a check of the overall system setup and other general controls to ensure overall system compliance with your organization's policy. These are mostly general, high-level controls, such as making certain that the system runs company-provisioned firewall and antivirus programs.

1. Obtain the system information and service pack version and compare with policy requirements.

Policies were written and approved to make your environment more secure, easily manageable, and auditable. Double-check the basic configuration information to ensure that the host is in compliance with policy. Older operating systems increase the difficulty in managing the server and increase the scope of administrator responsibilities as he or she attempts to maintain control over disparate operating system (OS) versions. Maintaining standard builds and patch levels greatly simplifies the process of managing the servers.

How

You could find this information using built-in command-line tools, hunting through the graphical user interface (GUI), and searching the registry. However, two efficient ways to pull up this information include the Sysinternals tool `psinfo` and the native tool `systeminfo`. Go to sysinternals.com and download the pstool package. Use one of these tools to retrieve this information, and then compare the results with your organization's policies and requirements.

 NOTE Download `pstools` from www.sysinternals.com/Utilities/PsTools .html. The tool psinfo is part of this set of tools. You may want to use several tools from Sysinternals for auditing your servers.

2. Determine whether the server is running the company-provisioned firewall.

Failure to use a firewall subjects the client to network attacks from malware, attackers, and curious people.

How

Most of the time, a check of the processes on the system shows that the company-provisioned firewall is installed and running on the system. An easy way to script this check is to run the Sysinternals tool `pslist`. Do this by running `pslist <process name>` on the system, and search for the appropriate running process by specifying the process you want to find.

For many organizations, the firewall is centrally managed and the same across all hosts in a group. You may want to verify the configuration of the firewall on the host.

If you are using the Windows Firewall, learn the `netsh` command set, which allows scripted output and changes to the firewall. Try running `netsh firewall show config` to see the overall configuration of the firewall on the host and whether the firewall is configured for particular adapters. Use `netsh firewall show` to see other available options for the `netsh firewall` tool.

3. Determine whether the server is running a company-provisioned antivirus program.

Running software other than company-provisioned software may cause instabilities in the enterprise software environment on the laptop or desktop. Failure to have antivirus protection may allow harmful code or hacking tools to run on the computer that violate company policy.

How

A visual check of the system tray shows that an antivirus program is installed and running on the system. As mentioned earlier, an easy way to script this check is to run `pslist` from Sysinternals on the system and search for the running process:

```
pslist rtvscan
PsList 1.26 - Process Information Lister
Copyright (C) 1999-2004 Mark Russinovich
SysInternals - www.SysInternals.com
Process information for CA-CDAVIS:
Name  Pid Pri Thd Hnd Priv  CPU Time  Elapsed Time
Rtvscan  244 8 53 569 26212  0:07:16.640  85:27:32.223
```

Depending on the nature of your audit, you also might want to check the configuration of the antivirus program on the host. For many organizations, the antivirus program is managed centrally and is the same across all hosts. One thing to be careful about with antivirus programs is the ability to exclude certain files or folders from monitoring. This is an easy way to get around the antivirus program.

4. Ensure that all approved patches are installed per your server management policy.

If all the OS and software patches are not installed, widely known security vulnerabilities could exist on the server.

How

Use `systeminfo` or `psinfo -s` to pull this information up for you, and then compare the results against the policies and requirements of your organization. You can use the output to compare with existing SMS/SCCM, patchlink, and other patch-management data. You could also compare the output with data from a vulnerability scanner to identify possible disparities.

5. Determine whether the server is running a company-provisioned patch-management solution.

Again, running software other than company-provisioned software may cause instabilities in the enterprise software environment on the laptop or desktop. Failure to have a company-provisioned patch-management solution may prevent the server from receiving the latest patches, allowing harmful code or hacking tools to run on the computer.

How

A visual check of the processes in the Task Manager usually shows that the company-provisioned patch-management system for servers is installed and running on the system. For example, this may be evidenced by the existence of the process in the Task Manager or the output of `pslist`. Some organizations like to enable automatic updates, which is also easily checked by looking for "Automatic Updates" in the Control Panel. You can also verify whether the system shows up on the Microsoft System Center Configuration Manager (SCCM) console and validate the last patch cycle applied to a given machine.

6. Review and verify startup information.

Rogue partitions, processes, or programs in violation of your policies can sometimes be found during system startup. In addition, malware will sometimes make use of the next reboot to install kits deeper into the OS.

How

Several utilities can help you dissect what the next reboot will do to the system. Two excellent tools include `pendmoves`, and `autoruns`. You can use `pendmoves` by itself without any switches to understand what file moves are planned for the next system restart.

`Autoruns` is the GUI version of `autoruns`. When you use `autoruns` from the command line, it might be easier to output it to a comma-separated values (CSV) file with the `-c` switch and view the results inside Excel. It might be difficult to appreciate the power of `autoruns` until you use the GUI `autoruns` version to see the information it's capable of uncovering for you.

Review Services, Installed Applications, and Scheduled Tasks

Running services, installed applications, and automated tasks that are beyond the scope of the server's stated purpose increase the complexity of maintaining the server and provide additional attack vectors. Unknown services, applications, and tasks may be indications that a server was compromised. These should be reviewed routinely.

7. Determine what services are enabled on the system, and validate their necessity with the system administrator. For necessary services, review and evaluate procedures for assessing vulnerabilities associated with those services and keeping them patched.

Enabling network services creates a new potential vector of attack, therefore increasing the risk of unauthorized entry into the system. Therefore, network services should be enabled only when there is a legitimate business need for them.

New security vulnerabilities are discovered and communicated frequently to the Windows community (including potential attackers). If the system administrator is not aware of these alerts and does not install security patches, well-known security vulnerabilities could exist on the system, providing a vector for compromising the system.

 NOTE This is one of the most critical steps you will perform. Unnecessary and unsecured network services are the number one vector of attack on Windows servers.

How

The tools shown in Table 6-2 reveal key pieces of information to help you identify services and how they are used. Netstat reveals the active sockets on your computer listening for external communications. Psservice, sc, and DumpSec list the running services. Next, you can map the running services to the open ports using tcpvcon. Finally, procexp is also capable of showing you much of this information but cannot be scripted. It is mentioned here because of its powerful capabilities and because it is free.

These may seem like a lot of utilities, but it's worth your time to look through them to decide what information you need for your audit. In general, if the system is being used in the AD domain, ensure that the Group Policy Object (GPO) policy rules are periodically reviewed. These rules are applied to any system that joins the domain/specific branch.

You can use the native netstat command by typing netstat -an at the command line. Look for lines containing LISTEN or LISTENING. The host is available for incoming connections on these TCP and UDP ports. You can find a list of services using such tools as psservice, which is very much like the netstat service on *NIX systems.

Other utilities that map processes to port numbers include the built-in sc (try sc query type= service) command and tcpvcon from Sysinternals. We recommend tcpvcon from Sysinternals. The "Tools and Technology" section a bit later offers information about where to find these tools and more. You can run tasklist /svc

Tool	Description	Where to Get It
Netstat	Provide network information	Native Windows command
Psservice	List service information	www.sysinternals.com
Sc	Native tool for talking with service controller	Native Windows command
DumpSec	GUI and command-line "Swiss army knife" of the security settings	www.somarsoft.com
Tcpvcon	CLI view of processes mapped to ports	www.sysinternals.com
Tcpview	GUI view of processes mapped to ports	www.sysinternals.com
Procexp	Powerful GUI process explorer	www.sysinternals.com

Table 6-2 Tools for Viewing Service Information

if you quickly want to map existing process IDs to running services. If you want to know absolutely everything about a process, download and run the Sysinternals Process Explorer.

Once you have obtained a list of enabled services, discuss the results with the system administrator to understand the need for each service. Many services are enabled by default and therefore were not enabled consciously by the system administrator. For any services that are not needed, encourage the administrators to disable them. The Microsoft snap-in for the management console can be launched by typing **services.msc** from the Run option on the Start menu.

8. Ensure that only approved applications are installed on the system per your server management policy.

Administrators must manage the set of applications installed on their hosts for the following reasons:

- Not all applications play well together.
- Applications may have a dependency that's not installed.
- More applications mean more areas of potential compromise.

Unmanaged or unknown applications also may have configuration or coding issues that make the server vulnerable to compromise. For example, a poorly managed application could be missing patches, could allow access to a privileged process, or could inadvertently create a covert channel for an unprivileged user.

How

Use the results from the output of `psinfo -s`, which includes information about the installed applications. You might also consider looking through Process Explorer. Compare your findings with organizational policy and discuss them with the administrator.

9. Ensure that only approved scheduled tasks are running.

Scheduled tasks can stay hidden for weeks until an administrator takes the time to view the running scheduled tasks on the host. Scheduled tasks created by malicious or unknowing sources could damage host or network resources.

How

Note that reading scheduled tasks from the command line doesn't show you what the task is really going to do. The task can be called anything an attacker wants to call it while setting it up. That being said, you can view tasks from the command line using `schtasks`:

```
The current directory is C:\>
schtasks
TaskName    Next Run Time   Status
============================= ======================= ===========
Malicious Task  12:27:00 PM, 6/13/2011
```

Administrators should note that running the old AT on the command line on this server doesn't list Malicious Task. Get in the habit of using schtasks to view tasks. If you really want to understand in-depth exactly what each task does, you need to open the properties of each task independently. From there, you also can see the target file and review several other settings. Choose Start | Search and type **schedule**. Then select Task Scheduler. Alternatively, you could type taskschd.msc at the command line to open the Task Scheduler.

Account Management and Password Controls

Account management and password controls are fundamental components of server management. Tracking users over time is a difficult task, and a common method for gaining access to systems that a user should never have had access to in the first place.

10. Review and evaluate procedures for creating user accounts and ensuring that accounts are created only for a legitimate business need. Review and evaluate processes for ensuring that accounts are removed or disabled in a timely fashion in the event of termination or job change.

If effective controls for providing and removing access to the server are not in place, it could result in unnecessary access to system resources. This, in turn, places the integrity and availability of the server at risk.

How

Interview the system administrator, and review account-creation procedures. This process should include some form of verification that the user has a legitimate need for access. Take a sample of accounts from the password file, and review evidence that they were approved properly prior to being created. Alternatively, take a sample of accounts from the password file, and validate their legitimacy by investigating and understanding the job function of the account owners.

You should also review the process for removing accounts when access is no longer needed. This process could include an automated feed from the company's human resources (HR) system providing information on terminations and job changes. Or the process could include a periodic review and validation of active accounts by the system administrator and/or other knowledgeable managers. Obtain a sample of accounts from the password file, and verify that they are owned by active employees, and that those employees' job positions have not changed since the account's creation.

Additional controls may be appropriate in your environment to monitor the use of sensitive administrator accounts. Review these controls if they are determined to be a critical part of your audit.

I I. Ensure that all users are created at the domain level and clearly annotated in the active directory. Each user should trace to a specific employee or team.

Most user accounts should be administered centrally by a domain controller, with the possible exception of accounts created on isolated systems that are not a member of a domain (such as some DMZs). This increases network security because account provisioning and deprovisioning can be controlled.

How

You can view the accounts by opening `compmgmt.msc` from the command line or with a tool such as `DumpSec` using the following syntax:

```
DumpSec.exe /rpt=users /saveas=fixed /outfile=users.txt
```

 NOTE Download `DumpSec` from www.somarsoft.com. The same executable that launches the GUI is used from the command line. You can include `DumpSec` in a script by including the binary with your script when you run the script. Learn about the different command-line options by going to the help file under Help | Contents and selecting Command-Line options.

Discuss your findings with the administrator, and pay close attention to accounts that should exist outside the domain. The only accounts that should exist outside the domain are the built-in guest and administrator accounts unless required by an application.

12. Review and evaluate the use of groups, and determine the restrictiveness of their use.

Groups can greatly simplify the provisioning and deprovisioning process for adding or removing user access to systems as users join and leave a team. However, old members sometimes hang around inside a group when they leave a team.

How

Review the contents of the groups on the system for appropriate membership while you're looking through the accounts using the method in the preceding step. Remember that in an Active Directory environment, groups can be nested, and you need to check the membership of the nested groups. In general, this is a good time to investigate the use of shared accounts. Such accounts present risk in that you lose accountability for actions taken on the system. However, in some situations, this is unavoidable, such as with certain software on a manufacturing floor. Organizations dealing with personally identifiable information (PII), Payment Card Industry (PCI), or Health Insurance Portability and Accountability Act (HIPPA) should closely examine their use of shared accounts.

PART II

Additionally, ensure that the IT security team, investigations team, and appropriate support personnel have administrative access to the server. This may not pertain to all organizations, and there may be some exceptions. These users should be placed into a group and not added as individual users to the server.

NOTE Although mentioned earlier, it bears repeating that it's common to have exception requests that document exceptions to policy. This is fine as long as the requests are documented with the specific accepted risks and the appropriate management sign-off on the request. Many large organizations require the highest levels of management to sign-off on such requests to discourage exceptions to policy.

13. Review and evaluate the strength of system passwords.

If passwords on the system are easy to guess, it is more likely that an attacker will be able to break into that account, obtaining unauthorized access to the system and its resources. A key mitigating control for many organizations is the use of two-factor authentication.

How

All accounts should have passwords. The methods used to test these controls depend on the password-provisioning process and controls enabled on the servers and Active Directory. At a minimum, you should review system settings that provide password controls such as those mentioned in the next step.

You can retrieve and test Windows password hashes in several ways. You should, however, be careful and play it safe. Password dump, or `pwdump`, is one commonly used tool to dump password hashes from systems (see download information in the accompanying note). Different versions work using different methods. The tool works well, but even the latest version may have problems on your server, crashing your system. This has happened to highly customized servers. Test everything in a nonproduction environment first.

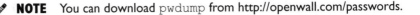

NOTE You can download `pwdump` from http://openwall.com/passwords.

Perhaps the easiest way to get your software asset management (SAM) and SYSTEM files is to copy them from the C:\WINDOWS\repair directory. Select the files with the CTRL key pressed, and then CTRL-drag them to another folder or USB drive.

Cracker	Cost	Comments
John	Free	www.openwall.com. A fast brute-force cracker that supports dictionaries and is accessed from the command line.
Rcrack	Free	Code is originally from Zhu Shuanglei at www.antsight.com/zsl/rainbowcrack. Built into a lot of tools such as Cain and Abel (www.oxid.it). You must find, generate, or buy tables.
Ophcrack	Free	Sometimes buggy, but free and quick. Comes with rainbow tables; download at http://ophcrack.sourceforge.net.

Table 6-3   Common Password Crackers

As for cracking the passwords, once you have the hashes, you can attempt to crack the passwords with one of the password crackers listed in Table 6-3. Several of these will take the SAM and SYSTEM files as direct inputs, dump the hashes, and perform the crack.

14. Evaluate the use of password controls on the server, such as password aging, length, complexity, history, and lockout policies.

Password controls are essential to enforcing password complexity, length, age, and other factors that keep unauthorized users out of a system.

How

You'll find the account policies as they affect your system by typing `rsop.msc` at the command line. When the window opens, choose Computer Configuration | Windows Settings | Security Settings | Account Policies. In general, verify that the policies listed in Table 6-4 are set in accordance with your local policies. Some common settings are listed.

Policy	Setting
Minimum password age	1 day
Maximum password age	90–180 days
Minimum password length	8 characters
Password complexity	Enabled
Password history	10–20 passwords remembered
Store passwords using reversible encryption	Disabled, if possible, but understand and test this before making this decision
Account lockout duration	10–30 minutes
Account lockout threshold	10–20 attempts
Reset account lockout after	10–30 minutes

Table 6-4   Account Policies

Review User Rights and Security Options

Microsoft ships with a robust ability to configure user rights and security options. These are only effective, however, if they are configured properly.

15. Review and evaluate the use of user rights and security options assigned to the elements in the security policy settings.

The default installation of Windows Server 2003 has 39 user rights settings and 70 security options. Windows Server 2008 grew to 44 user right settings and 78 security options. These settings and options allow broad, sweeping, and powerful changes to how the host behaves under many different situations.

 CAUTION Be careful here. It is possible to lock yourself out, disable critical internal processes, and limit necessary functionality. It's strongly recommended that you thoroughly test any changes you make here in a test environment with any applications that may even possibly depend on the settings running on the system.

How

You'll find the security policies as they affect your system by typing `rsop.msc` or `secpol.msc` at the command line. After the GUI opens, choose Computer Configuration | Windows Settings | Security Settings | Local Policies. Remember that you can export these settings by right-clicking the folder icon and selecting Export List. Another helpful command-line option is to type `.gpresult` to get a summary of group policy settings.

Evaluate the settings you found with the policies for your organization. Several guides suggest recommended settings, including Microsoft's website, the built-in security templates, the Center for Information Security guides (www.cisecurity.org), and of course, SANS (www.sans.org). The bottom line here is that you need to decide what your organization is looking to accomplish and audit against these settings. If your organization isn't using these settings at all, you should take the initiative to spearhead a project to look into them. Here are some common settings for both.

Common security options include the following:

- Renaming guest and administrator accounts
- Disabling the guest account
- Choosing not to display the last logged on user
- Prompting the user to change the password before expiration
- Refusing enumeration of SAM accounts and shares by anonymous
- Refusing to store network credentials (be careful with this!)
- Changing local-area network (LAN) manager responses (be careful with this!)

Common user rights assignments include the following:

- Changing who can access the computer across the network
- Defining who can log on locally
- Denying access to the computer from the network

- Denying logon through terminal services
- Defining who can take ownership of file or other objects

Network Security and Controls

Network access to servers must be controlled.

16. Review and evaluate the use and need for remote access, including RAS connections, FTP, Telnet, SSH, VPN, and other methods.

Not all remote access technologies are created equal, and until encrypted networks become the standard, clear-text protocols should be eliminated where possible. Although newer equipment and savvy network administrators can help mitigate the risk of eavesdropping on network traffic, the real risk of catching that traffic still exists, especially on the same broadcast domain.

Certain protocols such as File Transfer Protocol (FTP) and Telnet transmit all information in clear-text, including user ID and password. This could allow someone to obtain this information by eavesdropping on the network. Nonessential remote access connections should be limited or eliminated and clear-text administrative communications eliminated. Exceptions should be limited to business-driven cases on which senior management is willing to sign-off and formally accept the risk of clear-text and remote access.

Modems in particular, or Remote Access Services (RAS) access, bypass corporate perimeter security (such as firewalls) and allow direct access to the machine from outside the network. They present significant risk to the security of the machine on which they reside and can also allow the modem user to access the rest of the network. Allowing dial-in modems to be placed on a production machine is dangerous. Using a virtual private network (VPN) is a much better idea—preferably a VPN with two-factor authentication.

How

View the output of the services and port-mapping tools, and discuss these with the administrator. Ask the administrator about the remote access policies and the different methods of access. Question the need for any clear-text communications that aren't driven by business needs. In some cases, clear-text communications exist and are difficult to remove because of a legacy application, or the traffic just isn't that important. However, where possible, an encrypted protocol should be used instead. For Microsoft hosts, encrypted protocols include the Remote Desktop Protocol (RDP), Citrix (ICA protocol), Secure Shell (SSH), and Secure Sockets Layer (SSL), among many others.

On a Windows server, you can find information about remote access by choosing Start | Administrative Tools | Routing and Remote Access.

 NOTE The use of secure protocols is particularly important in a DMZ and other high-risk environments. The auditor may determine that they are of less importance on the internal network. However, it is still advisable to use secure protocols even on internal networks to minimize attacks from within.

17. Ensure that a legal warning banner is displayed when connecting to the system.

A legal logon notice is a warning displayed whenever someone attempts to connect to the system. This warning should be displayed prior to actual login and should say something similar to this: "You're not allowed to use this system unless you've been authorized to do so." Verbiage of this sort may be needed to prosecute attackers in court.

How

Log into your account using each available service that provides access, such as remote desktop, Telnet, and SSH. Determine whether a warning banner is displayed. Interview the system administrator to determine whether the verbiage for this warning banner has been developed in conjunction with the company's legal department.

18. Look for and evaluate the use of shares on the host.

Inappropriate or open shares may needlessly compromise personal or company data. You need to identify all shares, shared directories, and permissions. For example, it's not uncommon to find open shares on a network with personal, group ranking, or payroll information. This type of data never should be kept on an open share.

How

Use the Microsoft Management Console (MMC) snap-in under Start | Administrative Tools or by typing `compmgmt.msc` at the command line. When the MMC opens, go to Computer Management | System Tools | Shared Folders to view open shares, sessions, and files.

Alternatively, you can script this with `DumpSec`. The first command lists the shares, and the second lists the shared directories. You still should verify the share permissions manually, especially for manually created shares.

```
DumpSec.exe /rpt=shares /saveas=fixed /outfile=TempFile01
DumpSec.exe /rpt=allsharedirs /saveas=fixed /outfile=TempFile02
```

You also can view a list of shares by running the command `net share`. You can view remotely opened files by running `psfile` from Sysinternals or use the command `net file`. If you have a large set of shares on a server and want to spot-check it for inappropriate content, consider indexing the shared volume using a tool such as `dtSearch`. After the indexing is completed, you can run instant searches across the entire volume. This tool is familiar to forensic examiners and built into several products. You can find out more about it at www.dtsearch.com.

For each share you find, determine whether the permissions are appropriate. Disallow public shares where the NT-authenticated users group has full control permissions.

19. Ensure that the server has auditing enabled per your organization's policies.

Auditing provides evidence in the aftermath of an event and helps with troubleshooting issues on the host. Ideally, an event-correlation engine would filter and produce meaningful data for the system administrator. Until that day comes, it is important that you have auditing enabled to provide a record for what happens on the host.

How

You should view your audit settings manually with the MMC Group Policy snap-in. If you want, you can export the settings by right-clicking the Audit Policy folder icon and selecting Export List. Recommended settings are shown in Table 6-5.

Enable object access auditing only if you know how to use this feature. You should monitor only as much as is necessary to meet your needs. You can quickly fill your logs and tax your system with meaningless overhead if this is misused. Desired Configuration Manager (DCM) from Microsoft can also be helpful for those running SCCM.

You would use the following syntax for DumpSec at the command line:

```
DumpSec.exe /rpt=policy /saveas=fixed /outfile=policies.txt
```

20. Review and evaluate system administrator procedures for monitoring the state of security on the system.

If the system administrator doesn't monitor his or her systems for changes or regularly attempt discovering issues in these systems, security vulnerabilities could exist, and security incidents could occur without his or her knowledge. By *monitoring*, we mean actively watching for issues (detection) and actively searching them out (finding vulnerabilities).

Audit Policy	Audit Settings	
Audit account logon events	Success	Failure
Audit account management	Success	Failure
Audit directory service access	Not defined	
Audit logon events	Success	Failure
Audit object access	Not defined or failure	
Audit policy change	Success	Failure
Audit privilege use		Failure
Audit process tracking	Not defined	
Audit system events	Success	Failure

Table 6-5 Common Audit System Settings

Monitoring also provides a snapshot of the current security level of the system (from a network services standpoint). The world of network vulnerabilities is an ever-changing one, and it is unrealistic to create a static audit program that will provide an up-to-date portrait of vulnerabilities that should be checked. Therefore, a scanning tool that is updated frequently is the most realistic mechanism for understanding the current security state of the machine. In addition, if the system administrator has a security patching process in place, this scan will provide at least some validation as to the effectiveness of that process.

How

Interview the system administrator and review any relevant documentation to get an understanding of security monitoring practices. You can perform numerous levels and methods of security monitoring; although they don't all need to be performed, some level of monitoring is important. The monitoring level required should be consistent with the criticality of the system and the inherent risk of the environment (for example, a web server in the DMZ should have more robust security monitoring than a print server on the internal network). The system administrator is responsible for monitoring his or her hosts for issues such as those you have been auditing for throughout the audit steps in this chapter.

If security monitoring is performed, assess the frequency of the monitoring and the quality with which it is performed. Look for evidence that the security monitoring tools are actually used. Review recent results, and determine whether they were investigated and resolved. Leverage the results of the rest of the audit in performing this assessment. For example, if you found significant issues in an area they were supposedly monitoring, it might lead to questions as to the effectiveness of that monitoring.

Network Vulnerability Scanning and Intrusion Prevention

Network vulnerability scanning and monitoring can be a very effective control, particularly when you use correlation tools such as RSA enVision to monitor identified vulnerabilities correlated with attempted attacks.

Network accessible vulnerabilities are dangerous because they can be exploited by anyone on the network. Several great scanners are on the market, such as Qualys and Tenable Network Security's Nessus scanner. Auditing a host with a scan for vulnerabilities lets you see the host from the network's perspective, validates your findings, and can show you things that you didn't find. This is true for both Windows and UNIX systems. Many of these companies offer free trial versions of the scanner prior to purchase. The Nessus scanner is practically free depending on your needs, but you need a host on which to install the scanner. The Qualys scanner is particularly easy to use for Windows users. Both have received positive reviews from industry peers.

Even though many of these tools are designed to have nondisruptive settings and don't require access to the system, you should always inform the appropriate IT personnel (such as the system administrator, the network team, and IT security) that you plan to run the tool, receive their approval, and schedule with them execution of the tool. There is always a chance that the scanning tool will interact in an unexpected fashion with a port and cause a disruption, so it is important that others are aware of your activities. These tools almost always should be run in a "safe" (nondisruptive) mode in a production environment so that the tools do not attempt to exploit any vulnerabilities discovered. On rare occasions, you will want to run an actual exploit to get more accurate results, but this should be done only with buy-in from and coordination with the system owner and administrator.

21. If you are auditing a larger environment (as opposed to one or two isolated systems), determine whether there is a standard build for new systems and whether that baseline has adequate security settings.

Consider auditing a system freshly created from the baseline. One of the best ways to propagate security throughout an environment is to ensure that new systems are built correctly before moving into testing or production.

How

Through interviews with the system administrator, determine the methodology used for building and deploying new systems. If a standard build is used, consider auditing a newly created system using the steps in this chapter. Here is where something like Microsoft's Configuration Manager best comes into play; you can report on the deviations from the baseline and work on auditing just the deltas. Additionally, this is also the time to ask your virtualization administrators for information about the baselines they use to create virtual servers.

 NOTE Consider discussing an approval process for new standard builds in which an auditor would look over the changes and perform a full audit of new images. This is a great way for the audit team to create a working relationship with the Windows server team.

22. Perform the steps from Chapter 4 as they pertain to the system you are auditing.

In addition to auditing the logical security of the system, you need to ensure that appropriate physical controls and operations are in place to provide for system protection and availability.

How

Reference the steps from Chapter 4, and perform those that are relevant to the system being audited. For example, the following topics are likely to be pertinent:

- Asset inventory
- Physical security
- Environmental controls
- Capacity planning
- Change management

- Backup processes
- Disaster recovery planning

How to Perform a Simplified Audit of a Windows Client

The following steps provide a very quick method for verifying the image used for provisioning new computers for the end user. This audit isn't designed to cover or catch everything, but it does give the auditor a quick view of the client's health. These checks lean heavily on the Microsoft Baseline Security Analyzer and your external scanner of choice. If you would like a more comprehensive view of the system, you can perform many of the steps in the preceding section pertaining to servers.

Perform the following steps using a freshly built computer and through interviews with a local technician responsible for provisioning new computers.

1. Determine whether the client is running the company-provisioned firewall.

Running software other than company-provisioned software may cause instabilities in the enterprise software environment on the laptop or desktop. Failure to have a firewall subjects the client to network attacks from malware, attackers, and curious people.

How

Usually, a visual check of the processes in the Task Manager shows that the company-provisioned firewall is installed and running on the system. An easy way to script this check is to run `pslist` from Sysinternals on the system and search for the service. See the same step executed for servers in the preceding section for more information.

If you are using the Windows Firewall, learn the `netsh` command set, which allows scripted output and changes to the firewall. Try running `netsh firewall show config` to see the overall configuration of the firewall on the host and whether the firewall is configured for particular adapters. Use `netsh firewall show` to see other available options for the `netsh firewall` tool.

2. Determine whether the client is running a company-provisioned antivirus program.

Running antivirus software other than company-provisioned software may cause instabilities in the enterprise software environment on the laptop or desktop. Failure to have antivirus software may allow harmful code or hacking tools to run on the computer that violate company policy.

How

A visual check of the system tray shows that antivirus software is installed and running on the system. As mentioned earlier, an easy way to script this check is to run `pslist` from Sysinternals on the system and search for the specific running process. Be wary of customized configurations such as excluding directories and files from normal protections offered by the antivirus software.

3. Determine whether the client is running a company-provisioned patch-management solution.

Again, running software other than company-provisioned software may cause instabilities in the enterprise software environment on the laptop or desktop. Failure to have a company-provisioned patch-management solution may prevent the client from receiving the latest patches, allowing harmful code or hacking tools to run on the computer.

How

A visual check of the processes in the Task Manager usually shows that the company-provisioned patch-management system for client computers is installed and running on the system. For example, this may be evidenced by the existence of the process in the task manager or `pslist`. Some organizations like to enable automatic updates, which is also easily checked by looking for Automatic Updates in the Control Panel.

4. Determine whether the client is equipped with the minimum recommended service pack, hotfixes, and software.

Failure to install the latest hotfixes and service packs as recommended by Microsoft or other software vendors you use in your environment may allow harmful code to run on the computer or prevent legitimate software from working properly.

How

Perhaps the easiest way to check this is with the utility `psinfo`. This utility has several powerful switches that allow for checking for installed software or hotfixes and then outputting the information into a comma-separated file that opens nicely in Excel. Keep in mind that the `pstools`, `psinfo` included, are designed to be run remotely to manage hosts across the network. The options allow for checking against all computers in the local domain, in a file, or on a single host. The following is a partial output of `psinfo`:

```
The current directory is C:\PERL>
psinfo
PsInfo v1.73 - Local and remote system information viewer
Copyright (C) 2001-2005 Mark Russinovich
SysInternals - www.SysInternals.com
System information for \\CA-CDAVIS:
Uptime:      0 days 10 hours 42 minutes 25 seconds
Kernel version:   Microsoft Windows XP, Multiprocessor Free
Product type:     Professional
Product version:       5.1
Service pack:     2
Kernel build number:    2600
Registered organization:
Registered owner:      Christopher Davis
Install date:     4/19/2006, 1:57:31 PM
IE version:       6.0000
```

5. Ensure that the client has all the following according to the Microsoft Baseline Security Analyzer (MBSA).

The MBSA does a great job of auditing a single host quickly for some of the more grievous errors we commit as administrators. For example, we know that incomplete patch installations may cause instabilities in the enterprise software environment on the laptop or desktop. MBSA will check for this and many other common mistakes, such as the following:

- **Active accounts with blank or weak passwords**   Blank and weak passwords create easy targets for attackers.

- **Using file systems older than NTFS**   Older file systems are easier to compromise because they don't support granular file permissions.

- **Autologin enabled**   Autologin allows attackers to boot directly and easily into the computer.

- **Guest accounts enabled**   Guest accounts usually have weak passwords and are easily compromised.

- **Anonymous access**   Anonymous access allows attackers to access and profile the computer without an audit trail.

- **Logon auditing**   When enabled, logon auditing provides an audit trail of who has attempted to log onto the computer.

- **IIS enabled**   IIS is complicated to configure securely correctly, and some users won't take the time to do this, even if they know they should.

How

Download MBSA from http://technet.microsoft.com/en-us/security/cc184924.aspx and run the tool. Consult the results of the MBSA scan for possible errors. You should get back results stating the following:

- No incomplete software update installations were found.

- No users have blank or simple passwords.

- All hard drives are using the NTFS file system.

- Autologin is not configured on the computer.

- Guest account is disabled on the computer.

- Computer is properly restricting anonymous access.

- Logon success and logon failure auditing are both enabled.

- IIS is not running on the computer.

6. Scan the system using a commercial-grade network scanner.

Remotely scanning the computer allows you to have a more complete picture of the computer's possible avenues of compromise than you get by simply checking everything locally to the host.

How

Several great scanners are on the market. You need to scan your hosts. Auditing a host with a scan for vulnerabilities

- enables you to see the host from the network's perspective.
- validates your findings.
- may show you issues that you didn't find during the normal audit.

This is true both for Windows and UNIX systems. Many companies offer free trial versions of the scanner prior to purchase. The Nessus scanner is practically free depending on your needs, but you need a host on which to install the scanner.

7. Evaluate physical security controls during a walk-through.

Physical security controls are required usually according to some company policy, and just as important, they help to protect computers from easy physical compromise. There are three common areas for improving physical security inside the building:

- Cable locks should be used on laptops.
- Users should be logged out of their workstations.
- Passwords should not be written down anywhere.

How

Conduct a random walk-through of the work site once during working hours and once after working hours. During the walk-through, observe the use of cable locks, users logged out of their workstations, and whether or not passwords are written down in plain site.

Cable locks may not be an issue if other controls are in place, but most companies can relate to the occasional laptop "walking off" the job site. Cable locks are cheap and a great deterrent to "honest thieves."

Users should show the company some love and log out of their workstations by pressing WINDOWS KEY-L. This key combination quickly locks the computer and prevents others from walking behind the user and using the user's privileges.

Users quite often write down passwords and place them in readily available or obvious locations. There are too many stories of people who never intended to be dishonest, but then they couldn't resist the "open password" and got into trouble. Consider the use of second-factor authentication tokens or free utilities such as `keepass` (http://keepass.sourceforge.net) that store passwords inside an encrypted vault.

Tools and Technology

Several of the tools mentioned in this chapter are free and easily accessible. You are encouraged to download them and play with them on your personal machine, but be careful. Some of them are powerful and should be tested in the bulletproof superman testing network prior to use in a production environment. Table 6-6 lists some of the tools you might consider as you look into auditing Windows.

Resource	Website
Microsoft Script Center	www.microsoft.com/technet/scriptcenter/default.mspx
Microsoft Command-line Reference	http://technet.microsoft.com/en-us/library/cc754340(WS.10).aspx
Microsoft Sysinternals Tools	http://www.sysinternals.com (Redirects to Microsoft Technet)

Table 6-6 Tools and Technology: Auditing Windows

Knowledge Base

The following table shows additional resources where you can obtain information about Windows environments and related controls. Microsoft has a tremendous amount of information on its website for general consumption. Additionally, the community of helpful enthusiasts and social forums continues to grow.

Resource	Website
Microsoft Server and Tools	www.microsoft.com/servers/home.mspx
Microsoft TechNet	www.technet.com
Microsoft System Center	www.microsoft.com/systemcenter
Windows Intune	www.microsoft.com/online/windows-intune.aspx
Microsoft Tech-Ed Online	www.msteched.com
Windows Products	www.microsoft.com/windows/products
TCP/IP Fundamentals for Windows	http://technet.microsoft.com/en-us/library/cc307741.aspx
Secure Windows Server	http://technet.microsoft.com/en-us/library/dd548350(WS.10).aspx
Windows Firewall with Advanced Security	http://technet.microsoft.com/en-us/library/dd772715(WS.10).aspx
Microsoft Security Assessment Tool	http://technet.microsoft.com/en-us/security/cc185712.aspx
Microsoft Baseline Security Analyzer	http://technet.microsoft.com/en-us/security/cc184924.aspx
The Center for Information Security	www.cisecurity.org
Computer Security Resource Center	http://csrc.nist.gov
KeePass Password Tool	http://keepass.sourceforge.net

Master Checklists

The following tables summarize the steps listed earlier for auditing Windows servers and clients.

Auditing Windows Servers

Checklist for Auditing Windows Servers

❑   1. Obtain the system information and service pack version, and compare with policy requirements.

❑   2. Determine whether the server is running the company-provisioned firewall.

❑   3. Determine whether the server is running a company-provisioned antivirus program.

❑   4. Ensure that all approved patches are installed per your server management policy.

❑   5. Determine whether the server is running a company-provisioned patch-management solution. Using the patch-management solution, validate the patched history of the client, if possible.

❑   6. Review and verify startup information.

❑   7. Determine what services are enabled on the system and validate their necessity with the system administrator. For necessary services, review and evaluate procedures for assessing vulnerabilities associated with those services and keeping them patched.

❑   8. Ensure that only approved applications are installed on the system per your server management policy.

❑   9. Ensure that only approved scheduled tasks are running.

❑   10. Review and evaluate procedures for creating user accounts and ensuring that accounts are created only when there's a legitimate business need. Also review and evaluate processes for ensuring that accounts are removed or disabled in a timely fashion in the event of termination or job change.

❑   11. Ensure that all users are created at the domain level and clearly annotated in the active directory. Each user should trace to a specific employee or team.

❑   12. Review and evaluate the use of groups, and determine the restrictiveness of their use.

❑   13. Review and evaluate the strength of system passwords.

❑   14. Evaluate the use of password controls on the server, such as password aging, length, complexity, history, and lockout policies.

❑   15. Review and evaluate the use of user rights and security options assigned to the elements in the security policy settings.

❑   16. Review and evaluate the use and need for remote access, including RAS connections, FTP, Telnet, SSH, VPN, and other methods.

❑   17. Ensure that a legal warning banner is displayed when users connect to the system.

❑   18. Look for and evaluate the use of shares on the host.

❑   19. Ensure that the server has auditing enabled per your organization's policies.

❑   20. Review and evaluate system administrator procedures for monitoring the state of security on the system.

❑   21. If you are auditing a larger environment (as opposed to one or two isolated systems), determine whether a standard build is available for new systems and whether that baseline has adequate security settings. Consider auditing a system freshly created from the baseline.

❑   22. Perform the steps from Chapter 4 as they pertain to the system you are auditing.

PART II

Auditing Windows Clients

Checklist for Auditing Windows Clients

❑   1. Determine whether the client is running the company-provisioned firewall.

❑   2. Determine whether the client is running a company-provisioned antivirus program.

❑   3. Determine whether the client is running a company-provisioned patch-management solution.

❑   4. Determine whether the client is equipped with the minimum recommended service pack, hotfixes, and software.

❑   5. Ensure that the client has all the following according to the Microsoft Baseline Security Analyzer (MBSA).

❑   6. Scan the system using a commercial-grade network scanner.

❑   7. Evaluate physical security controls during a walk-through.

Auditing Unix and Linux Operating Systems

This chapter discusses the steps required for auditing Unix- and Linux-based operating systems (also referred to as *nix systems*) and includes the following:

- The history of Unix and Linux
- Basic commands for getting around in the *nix environment
- How to audit Unix and Linux systems, focusing on the following main areas:
  - Account management and password controls
  - File security and controls
  - Network security and controls
  - Audit logs
  - Security monitoring and general controls
- Tools and resources for enhancing your *nix audits

Background

Unix dates back to 1969, when it was developed by employees at AT&T for the purpose of providing an environment in which multiple users could run programs. Strong security was not one of the goals of its development.

In the late 1970s, students at University of California, Berkeley, made extensive modifications to the AT&T Unix system, resulting in the *Berkeley Software Distribution (BSD)* Unix variant, which became very popular in academic circles. Around the same time, AT&T began a push to develop its Unix operating system into a legitimate commercial product called *AT&T System V* (or just *System V*).

During the 1980s, as commercial interest in the Unix operating system grew, companies faced the dilemma of deciding which of the two versions of Unix to adopt. Sun Microsystems' SunOS and Digital Equipment Corporation's Ultrix were based on the BSD. Other companies that tried to develop a Unix-based OS, including Hewlett-Packard (HP), IBM, and Silicon Graphics, used System V as their standard. Microsoft developed a third version of Unix, called *Xenix,* and licensed it to Santa Cruz Operations (SCO). Xenix was based on a prior version of the AT&T Unix operating system.

All these versions of Unix obviously resulted in confusion in the industry and frustration for vendors who were attempting to develop software for use on Unix-based platforms. This resulted in the merging of some versions, beginning with Xenix and AT&T's System V in 1988. Next was a merger of AT&T and Sun's versions, called System V Release 4 (SVR4), which was to be compatible with programs written for either System V or BSD. Sun later named its proprietary version of this operating system Solaris. Not to be left out, a number of the other companies, such as IBM and HP, formed an organization called the Open Software Foundation (OSF), whose mission was to put control of Unix in the hands of a not-for-profit group. The OSF operating system (OSF/1) was never widely adopted, and the individual companies continued to develop and use their own proprietary Unix variants, such as IBM's AIX, HP's HP-UX, SCO Unix, and IRIX.

Linux, a "Unix-like" operating system, came on the scene with a Usenet posting in 1991 by its author, Linus Torvalds. Strictly speaking, Linux is a *kernel* and not an operating system, because what Torvalds developed was the piece that allows other programs to run. Most of these other programs that allow the system to be truly usable came from the GNU project. Hence, many people refer to Linux as *GNU/Linux* when speaking of it as an entire OS, but since this subject is a bit of a religious war, we won't discuss it further here.

From these humble, hobbyist beginnings in 1991, Linux grew to a 1.0 release in 1994. But even before the 1.0 release, a number of Linux "distributions" were developed, combining the Linux kernel with applications and system utilities. Some examples of today's popular distributions are Red Hat, Ubuntu, Debian, SUSE, and Gentoo. Although many aspects of all Linux distributions are identical or very similar, they included some differences as well, such as package management and the init system. Support models differ as well, and when you pay for a Linux distribution, you're typically paying for the support because the software itself is free. This free software, combined with the ability to run on generic x86/64-bit based hardware, has made Linux a compelling choice for both enterprise and personal computing needs.

 NOTE As you can see from this history, there are many variations of the Unix and Linux OSs. Although the information and concepts in this chapter are generic and applicable to all versions, it would take more space than is feasible to note the nuances for each *nix version. This chapter therefore focuses on Solaris (Unix) and Red Hat (Linux), where version-specific commands and examples are required.

Unix and Linux Auditing Essentials

If you are new to the Unix world, you'll find it helpful to obtain access to a Unix/Linux system while reading through this section. Try the commands for yourself to become familiar with them.

Windows users can easily turn their machine into a Linux system without altering the Windows file system. Just download and burn one of the many bootable Linux CDs, such as the popular Knoppix (www.knoppix.org), and boot into a full-featured Linux distribution. If you have a spare PC to work with, visit http://distrowatch.com and select Major Distributions. You'll find a wealth of information about the various free distributions available there.

> **NOTE** When you're learning these commands, remember that you can access help at any time by typing `man <commandname>` for comprehensive help or `<commandname> --help` for abbreviated help.

Key Concepts

Before we start digging into the details, let's establish some key concepts upon which we can build:

- Everything in Unix is a file. For example, if you type in a command and press ENTER, you are actually executing a file within the system that has the same name as the command you entered. And if you attach a device, such as a printer or storage, to your Unix system, it will be represented on the system as a file.

- There is only one file system within any given Unix system, and the root of that file system is the directory called /. Every directory and every file branches off this root directory. Since everything in Unix is a file, if you do a recursive listing off of the / directory, you will see every component of the system.

- The system administrator (or superuser) account in Unix is called "root." This account has full control over the system.

- If you can alter a file that someone is executing, you can easily capture his or her account.

File System Layout and Navigation

The file system can be thought of as a tree, and the base of every tree is its root. So the root directory, designated /, is the trunk from which other directories branch. Every Unix system has a root directory, but you will find some variance in what you see from there. Table 7-1 lists some common directories that you usually will find.

Several essential commands typed at the command prompt can be helpful for navigating Linux and Unix file systems. The most essential commands are shown in Table 7-2 along with some common and helpful switches.

Directory	Description
/bin	Location of most of the system binaries (programs)
/sbin	Contains binaries that are reserved for use by privileged accounts
/etc	Contains system configuration files
/boot	Contains location of the kernel in many systems
/home	Typical location for user home directories
/var	Contains information that programs need to track as they run (such as the process ID on the system); usually contains log files as well
/lib	System and application libraries that aren't executed directly but are used by applications as they run
/opt	Includes many installed add-on packages
/usr	Another place for user-added packages; often duplicates many of the top-level directories within itself, so you'll have /usr/etc, /usr/bin, and so on; documentation is often placed into /usr/share
/root	Often contains the home directory for the root account
/tmp	Temporary directory that any user typically can access; often cleared when the system is booted
/mnt	Remote file systems may be mounted here
/dev	Represents the concept that everything is a file, so you will find device files here representing the hardware in your system
/proc	This pseudo-file system doesn't exist on a physical disk, but contains memory-resident information about both the processes running on a system and the system itself

Table 7-1 Common Unix and Linux Directories

NOTE When navigating a *nix system, the presence or absence of the leading / in the path is very important; if present, it serves to anchor the path at the root directory. Thus, if you are currently in /usr, cd /bin and cd bin will take you to two different places (/bin and /usr/bin, respectively). These are known as *absolute* or *relative path names*. The absolute path always starts with / and traces the entire path from the root directory. The relative path, with no leading /, starts with the present directory.

Command	Meaning	Description	Tips for Use
cd	Change directory	Changes directory location as you would from the Windows command prompt	cd ~ changes directory to user's home directory . signifies current directory .. signifies parent directory
ls	List directory contents	Lists the contents of a directory along with information such as ownership, permissions, file size, and so on, when used with the -l option	ls -l uses long listing format for the files within the directory ls -ld provides the long listing format for the directory itself ls -al provides the long listing format for all directory contents, including hidden files ls -alR provides a recursive directory listing, using the long listing format and displaying hidden files ls -altr provides the long listing format, displaying the directory's contents in reverse chronological order
pwd	Print working directory	Displays the current working directory on the screen	Auditors can use this command when copying screen output for an audit to show on workpapers where they are working on the system
more cat less	Lists file contents	Lists the contents of a file	cat displays all the file's contents at once more displays the file's contents one page at a time less displays the file's contents one page at a time and allows backward navigation
ypcat	List NIS file contents	Lists the contents of a centralized NIS file	Displays the contents of the NIS password and group files if you're using NIS for centralized account management
su	Switch user	Allows a user to switch to another user ID	Works only if you have "root" access or if you know the password of the account to which you want to switch

Table 7-2 Common Linux and Unix Navigation Commands

PART II

File System Permissions

File and directory permissions can be separated into user, group, and world permissions. In other words, each file and directory has permissions set for the owner of the file, for the group associated with the file, and for everyone else (often called "world" or "other"). Each of these entities can be granted read, write, and/or execute access. Both files and directories have their own permission sets. You can see how this can get tricky, but remember that the most restrictive set of permissions wins every time. For example, if a file has world-read permissions but is restricted under its parent directory to disallow world-read permissions, then the world (meaning everyone) will not be able to read the file.

You will notice that these permissions are shown in two ways. Some places use three sets of `rwx` for read, write, and execute. The three sets are for the owner, group, and world. An example might be `rwxr-xr--`. This means that the file's owner has read, write, and execute permissions on the file; the file's group has read and execute permissions; and everyone else has read permissions. Another example might be `rw-r-----`. This means that the file's owner has read and write permissions on the file, the file's group has read permissions, and everyone else has no permissions.

Other places use a three-digit number such as `754`, which is identical to the `rwxr-xr--` and is shown in Figure 7-1. For those who never studied binary numbers, just remember that read is worth 4 points, write is worth 2, and execute is worth 1. Add them up for each set (that is, owner, group, and world), and you have your permissions. Thus `754` is a way to say, "I don't mind if other people read this file and if those in my group run this file, but only I should be able to modify it." As additional examples, permissions of `rw-r-----` would be represented as `640` and `rwxrwxrwx` would be represented as `777`.

Finally, note that file permissions are not completely independent of the permissions of the directory that contains the file. This interaction is illustrated in Figure 7-2. For example, if you have `rwx` access to a file, but that file is sitting in a directory to

Permissions on a file or directory:

	Owner			Group			World		
Available permissions	Read	Write	Execute	Read	Write	Execute	Read	Write	Execute
Assigned permissions	r	w	x	r		x	r		
Binary (1 = Yes, 0 = No)	1	1	1	1		1	1		
Decimal value	4	2	1	4		1	4		
Cumulative result	7			5			4		
Resulting permissions:				754 (or)			rwxr-xr--		

Figure 7-1 Unix permissions

Figure 7-2
Interaction between file and directory permissions

		Directory Permissions			
		-	r	x	wx
File Permissions	-	No access	No access	No access	Delete file
	r	No access	No access	Read data	Delete file or read data
	w	No access	No access	Add to or clear data	Delete file or add to or clear data
	rw	No access	No access	Update data	Delete file or update data
	x	Can't execute	Can't execute	Execute	Delete file or execute

which you have no access, then you will not be able to read, write to, delete, or otherwise access the file. Conversely, if you have no access to a file, but that file is sitting in a directory to which you have write and execute access, you will be able to delete that file, as the combination of write and execute access is what allows a user to delete files from and add files to a directory. In this scenario, you would be able to delete the file and then create a new file with the same name within that directory, opening up the possibility of file spoofing. It is therefore critical when you're evaluating the security of a file to evaluate related directory permissions.

NOTE Execute permissions on all parent directories back to / are required of a user to perform operations on a file within that path. For example, permissions are 777 on a file in /home/andrew, but permissions in the andrew directory are 700. Non-root users other than Andrew will not be able to read or delete that file.

Users and Authentication

Access to a Unix system is typically controlled by means of a username and password. This authentication information may be kept on the local file system, or it may be kept in a central location on the network, where many systems can access the same information. In the simplest case, where all the information is local, we typically would consider three files, /etc/passwd, /etc/shadow, and /etc/group.

PART II

Field	Use
account	Represents the user to the system. This name is used when the user logs in.
password	Encrypted password. It may be kept in /etc/shadow instead; if so, this field simply will contain an *, x, !, or other character.
UID	Numeric user ID.
GID	Numeric group ID for the user's primary group.
GECOS	Optional field used to store arbitrary additional information about the account. A typical use would be the real name and/or employee ID of the user.
directory	Location of the user's home directory.
shell	User's default shell, the command-line environment that interprets commands and passes them to the kernel.

Table 7-3 Components of a Unix Password File

Unix Password File

The /etc/passwd file (Table 7-3) contains account information for all users. Each account on the local system will have a single line in the /etc/passwd file. The system refers to this file when a user attempts to authenticate.

Lines in /etc/password have this format:

```
account:password:UID:GID:GECOS:directory:shell
```

Unix Shadow File

By design, the /etc/passwd file (Table 7-4) allows world read access. Therefore, if the encrypted password is kept in that file, any user on the system would be able to download all users' encrypted passwords and attempt to crack them using freely available password cracking software. To mitigate this risk, most systems store the encrypted password inside a shadow password file, which is readable only by root. The shadow password file is complementary to the /etc/passwd file, with a corresponding line for each user.

Lines in /etc/shadow have this format:

```
account:password:lastchange:min:max:warn:inactive:expired:reserved
```

Field	Use
account	Name representing the user to the system.
password	Encrypted password; $*LK*$ indicates that the account is locked.
lastchange	Number of days since the password was changed.
min	Minimum number of days allowed between password changes.
max	Maximum number of days allowed between password changes.
warn	Number of days before max, at which point the user will be warned to change his or her password.
inactive	Number of days of inactivity after which the user's account will be disabled.
expired	Number of days since January 1, 1970, that the account has been disabled.
reserved	An extra field that is not used.

Table 7-4   Components of a Unix Shadow File

Unix Group File

The /etc/group file (Table 7-5)contains information on groups on the system.

Lines in /etc/group use this format:

```
name:password:GID:users
```

LDAP, NIS, or NIS+

In more complicated cases, credentials can be checked against an authentication database located on the network; typically, this is Lightweight Directory Access Protocol (LDAP), Active Directory, Network Information System (NIS), or NIS+. You may be

Field	Use
name	Name of the group.
password	Group password, if one is used.
GID	Numeric group ID.
users	List of users who are members of the group, although members of the group who are assigned to it through their GID in /etc/password (see Table 7-3) won't necessarily be on this list.

Table 7-5   Components of a Unix Group File

able to determine whether one of these is used in preliminary discussions with the system administrator, or you may want to look at the systems yourself.

Determine whether NIS, NIS+, or LDAP is used by looking at the line beginning with `passwd` in `/etc/nsswitch.conf`. The presence of `nis`, `nisplus`, or `ldap` on that line indicates use of those protocols. These typically will be present in addition to `files`, which refers to the local password file. You also may see `compat`, which enables the use of + and – in the local password file for NIS/NIS+. If `compat` mode is used, then a + at the beginning of a line in /etc/passwd would indicate that NIS/NIS+ is being used. Review of the `passwd_compat` entry in /etc/nisswitch.conf should allow you to distinguish between the two. Note that local access can show you only what you need to know about local Unix authentication. You may need more information to determine the effectiveness of a network authentication scheme such as NIS or LDAP. For these, you may want to do a separate review of the particular authentication infrastructure.

Network Services

To understand areas of potential risk in your environment, you must know the avenues by which a system can be accessed, and you need to be able to determine what network services are enabled on the system. On most systems, you can use the `netstat` command to see this information. The most generic usage would be `netstat -an`, which will list a lot of information. Services running on Transmission Control Protocol (TCP) ports that are listening for external connections usually will say `LISTEN` in the output. User Datagram Protocol (UDP) ports may say `IDLE` on some systems such as Solaris. On Linux, look for UDP ports that have a listed `Remote Address` of `0.0.0.0`.

Once you have identified the open ports, you should determine what applications (often called *daemons*) are running on them. You often can determine this by mapping the port to the list of well-known ports maintained by Internet Assigned Numbers Authority (IANA) at www.iana.org/assignments/port-numbers. However, you should be aware that, for example, even though TCP port 25 is supposed to be for SMTP, there's no reason you can't run a web server on that port instead. If you have any questions about port number assignment, ask the system administrator. You also may want to use some of the tools listed in the "Tools and Technology" section later in this chapter that can automate the process of identifying open ports and the applications running on them.

Test Steps for Auditing Unix and Linux

The following audit steps are divided into five sections:

- Account management and password controls
- File security and controls
- Network security and controls
- Audit logs
- Security monitoring and general controls

> **NOTE**   The test steps in this chapter focus on testing the logical security of
> Unix and Linux boxes as well as processes for maintaining and monitoring that
> security. However, other internal controls are critical to the overall operations
> of a Unix/Linux environment, such as physical security, disaster recovery
> planning, backup processes, change management, capacity planning, and system
> monitoring. These topics are covered in Chapter 4 and should be included
> in your audit of the Unix/Linux environment if they have not already been
> covered effectively in a separate data center or entity-level IT controls audit.

Account Management and Password Controls

Most of the steps in this section require some form of testing over the system's password file. Prior to commencing work on these steps, the auditor should determine whether the system is using only its local password file (/etc/passwd) or some additional form of centralized account management such as NIS or LDAP. If the latter form is used, the auditor must execute the following steps on both the centralized password file and the local password file. The same concept applies for the steps that reference the group file.

In the "How" sections of the following steps, we will not attempt to specify the commands for every possible centralized account management system, because there are a number of vendor-specific tools. We will include the details for pulling information from NIS, which is the most common of these systems, as an example. If your company uses a different tool, such as NIS+ or LDAP, you will need to work with your system administrator and review the documentation for these systems to determine the equivalent commands. However, the concepts described here for the local and NIS password and group files will apply.

1. Review and evaluate procedures for creating Unix or Linux user accounts and ensuring that accounts are created only when there's a legitimate business need. Also, review and evaluate processes for ensuring that accounts are removed or disabled in a timely fashion in the event of termination or job change.

If effective controls are not in place for providing and removing access to the server, it could result in users having unnecessary access to system resources. This, in turn, places the integrity and the availability of the server at risk.

How

Interview the system administrators, and review account creation procedures. This process should include some form of verification that every user has a legitimate need for access. Take a sample of accounts from the password file, and review evidence that they were approved properly prior to being created. Alternatively, take a sample of accounts from the password file and validate their legitimacy by investigating and understanding the job function of the account owners.

Also review the process for removing accounts when access is no longer needed. This process could include an automated feed from the company's human resources (HR) system providing information on terminations and job changes. Or the process could include a periodic review and validation of active accounts by the system administrators and/or other knowledgeable managers. Obtain a sample of accounts from the password file, and verify that they are owned by active employees and that those employees' job positions have not changed since the account's creation.

2. Ensure that all user IDs in the password file(s) are unique.

If two users have the same user ID (UID), they can fully access each other's files and directories and can "kill" each other's processes. This is true even if they have different usernames. The operating system uses the UID to identify the user. It merely maps the username to the corresponding UID in the password file.

How

For local accounts, use the command `more /etc/passwd`, and review the entries to ensure that there are no duplicate UIDs. If NIS is used, the command `ypcat passwd` also should be used so that NIS UIDs can be examined.

The following command will list any duplicate UIDs found in the local password file:

```
cat /etc/passwd | awk -F: '{print $3}' | uniq -d
```

3. Ensure that passwords are shadowed and use strong hashes where possible.

For the system to function appropriately, the password file needs to be world readable. This means that if the encrypted passwords are contained within the file, every user on the system will have access to them. This, in turn, gives users the opportunity to copy the encrypted passwords and attempt to crack them via password-cracking tools that are freely available on the Internet. Given enough time, a brute-force cracking tool can guess even the most effective password. Also consider the form of the passwords. The crypt routine traditionally used for Unix passwords is a relatively weak form of encryption by today's standards, and the maximum effective password length is eight characters. A better choice is to use MD5 hashes, which are difficult to crack and allow more than eight characters for the password.

How

To determine whether a shadow password file is being used, type the `more /etc/passwd` command to view the file. Look within the password field for all accounts. If each account has an "∗" or "x" or some other common character in it, the system uses a shadow password file. The shadow password file will be located at /etc/shadow for most systems. Systems using NIS create some special problems that make the use of shadowed passwords more difficult, and older systems cannot shadow these passwords at all. If NIS is used in your environment, consult with the system administrator to discuss the possibilities of shadowing these passwords. If it is not possible to do so, consider other password-related policies.

MD5 is now the default hash on many Linux systems. The crypt form can be recognized because it is always 13 characters long; an MD5 hash in /etc/passwd or /etc/shadow will be prepended with the characters 1 and is longer.

4. Evaluate the file permissions for the password and shadow password files.

If a user can alter the contents of these files, he or she will be able to add and delete users, change user passwords, or become a superuser by changing his or her UID to 0. If a user can read the contents of the shadow password file, he or she can copy the encrypted passwords and attempt to crack them.

How

View the file permissions for these files by using the ls -l command on them. The /etc/passwd file should be writable only by "root," and the /etc/shadow file also should be readable only by "root."

5. Review and evaluate the strength of system passwords.

If passwords on the system are easy to guess, it is more likely that an attacker will be able to break into that account, thus obtaining unauthorized access to the system and its resources.

How

Review system settings that provide password composition controls. For Solaris systems, the password policy is usually set in /etc/default/passwd. Use a more command on this file, and view the PASSLENGTH parameter to determine minimum password length. Compare the value of this parameter with your company's IT security policy. Most Linux systems have /etc/login.defs, which provides basic controls such as minimum password length and maximum password age for locally created accounts.

Unfortunately, the standard Unix passwd program does not provide strong capabilities for preventing weak passwords. It will prevent a user from choosing his or her username as a password but not much else. Through discussions with the system administrator, you can determine whether other tools have been implemented either to replace or enhance the native passwd functionality for password composition requirements. One stronger possibility is npasswd, a replacement for passwd. Npasswd is currently hosted at www.utexas.edu/cc/unix/software/npasswd/. Additional controls also can be provided through PAM (Pluggable Authentication Modules) by the use of pam_cracklib, pam_passwdqc, or a similar module (pam_cracklib is included in many Linux distributions). Look for lines beginning with password in /etc/pam.conf or the configuration files in /etc/pam.d/ to get an idea of what's in use on the system you're auditing. Perform a more command on these files to view their contents.

Consider obtaining a copy of the password file and the shadow password file and executing a password-cracking tool against the encrypted passwords to identify weak passwords. See the "Tools and Technology" section later in this chapter for information on password-cracking tools. Use good judgment in interpreting the results, because a brute-force cracking tool will eventually crack any password if given enough time. If the password files have been shadowed, you really need to worry only about truly weak passwords that are obvious and easy to guess. These sorts of passwords likely will be guessed within the first 30 to 60 minutes by someone running a password-cracking program. On the other hand, if the password files have not been shadowed, you likely will want to run the program for much longer, because anyone with access to the system will have the ability to do the same thing.

6. Evaluate the use of password controls such as aging.

It is important to change passwords periodically for two primary reasons. First, without aging, an attacker with a copy of the encrypted or hashed passwords will have an unlimited amount of time to perform an offline brute-force cracking attack. Second, someone who already has unauthorized access (through cracking or just password sharing) will be able to retain that access indefinitely.

How

Review system settings that provide password aging controls. For Solaris systems, the password policy is usually set in /etc/default/passwd. Perform a `more` command on this file and view the `MAXWEEKS` parameter to determine the maximum age for passwords and the `MINWEEKS` parameter to determine the minimum age for passwords. Minimum age is important to prevent a user from changing his or her password and then immediately changing it back to its previous value. View the settings of these parameters and compare them with your company's IT security policy.

Most Linux systems have /etc/login.defs, which provides basic controls such as minimum password length and maximum password age for locally created accounts. Additional controls can be provided through PAM by the use of `pam_cracklib`, `pam_passwdqc`, or a similar module (`pam_cracklib` is included in many Linux distributions). Look for lines beginning with `password` in /etc/pam.conf or the configuration files in /etc/pam.d/ to get an idea of what's in use on the system you're auditing. Perform a `more` command on these files to view their contents.

The "root" account generally will not be subject to automatic aging to prevent the possibility of the account being locked. However, a manual process should be in place for periodically changing the password in accordance with company policy. Review the process for changing this password, and look for evidence that this process is being followed. Also audit the process that is used by the system administrators to document and communicate the root passwords, as these will likely be shared between the members of the team.

7. Review the process used by the system administrator(s) for setting initial passwords for new users and communicating those passwords.

When new user accounts are created, the system administrator must assign an initial password to that user. If that password is easy to guess, it could allow the account to be hacked, resulting in unauthorized access to the server and its resources. If the initial password is not communicated via a secure channel, it could allow others to view the password and obtain unauthorized access to the account.

How

Interview the system administrator, and review documentation to understand the mechanism used for creating initial passwords. Ensure that this mechanism results in passwords that are difficult to guess and that comply with your company's IT security policy.

Also, review the channels used for communicating the new passwords to users. Ensure that unencrypted transmissions are not used. Finally, it is often a good idea for the user to be required to change his or her password immediately on first login. Interview the system administrator to determine whether or not this is done. Accounts can be expired, thus forcing the user to change his or her password on the next login by the use of `passwd -f` on Solaris and `passwd -e` on Linux. These commands will expire a user's account immediately, forcing the user to change it on the next login. These are not items that can really be checked for, other than asking the system administrator how he or she does things.

8. Ensure that each account is associated with and can be traced easily to a specific employee.

If the owner of an account is not readily apparent, it will impede forensic investigations regarding inappropriate actions performed by that account. If multiple people use an account, no accountability can be established for actions performed by that account.

How

Review the contents of the password file(s). The owner of each account should be obvious, with the user's name or other unique identifier (such as employee number) either used as the username or placed in the GECOS field. Question any accounts that seem to be shared, such as guest or application accounts. If accounts such as these are required, they should be configured with restricted shells and/or such that a user cannot directly log into them (thus requiring the user to log in as himself or herself first and then using `su` or `sudo` to access the shared account, creating an audit trail).

9. Ensure that invalid shells have been placed on all disabled accounts.

This is only a significant risk if trusted access is allowed (see the "Network Security and Controls" section later in the chapter). If trusted access is allowed, a user with a certain username on one system (the trusted system) can log into an account with that same username on another system (the trusting system) without entering a password. This can be done as long as the user account on the trusting system has a valid shell defined to it, even though the account may have been disabled. Therefore, if a system administrator disables an account but leaves it with a valid shell, a user on a remote, trusted system with the same username still could access that account.

How

View the contents of the password files (via the `more` command). If an account has been disabled, it will show an "`*`," "`*LK*`," or something similar in the password field (remember to look in the shadow password file if it is being used). For those accounts, review the contents of the shell field. If it contains anything other than `/dev/null`, `/bin/false`, or something similar, the account probably still can access a valid shell or program.

10. Review and evaluate access to superuser (root-level) accounts and other administration accounts.

An account with root-level access has the ability to do anything with the system, including deleting all files and shutting the system down. Access to this ability should be minimized. Other accounts may exist on the system for the purpose of administering specific applications and also should be tightly controlled to prevent system disruption.

How

Review the contents of the password files, and identify all accounts with a UID of 0. Any account with a UID of 0 is treated by the system as if it were the "root" account. Question the need for any account besides "root" to have a UID of 0. Determine via interviews who knows the passwords to the "root" and other UID 0 accounts, and evaluate the appropriateness of this list.

Review the password file for the existence of other administration accounts (such as "oracle"). You likely will have identified potential candidates when performing Step 8. Determine via interviews who knows the passwords to these accounts and evaluate for appropriateness.

Many environments use `sudo` or a similar tool to allow users to perform certain functions with elevated privileges. This is a useful way to allow a user to perform specific system administration duties without granting the user full root access. Even for users who require full root access, `sudo` can be configured to allow a user to run all commands with root access, allowing the user to perform system administration from his or her own account instead of logging into the "root" account. This is useful for audit trail purposes.

If `sudo` is used, review the /etc/sudoers file to evaluate the ability of users to run commands as "root" (and other sensitive accounts) with the `sudo` command. The `sudo` tool can be used to grant specific users the ability to run specific commands as if they were "root" (or any other account for that matter). This is generally preferable to giving users full root access.

The basic format of an entry in the sudoers file would look something like this:

Andrew `ALL=(root) /usr/bin/cat`

Micah `ALL=(ALL) ALL`

In this example, user Andrew would be allowed to run the command `/usr/bin/cat` as the user root on all systems, and user Micah would be allowed to run any command as any user on any system. Many other options will not be covered here. Consult the man page for sudoers for more information.

If `sudo` or an equivalent tool is used, review processes for managing the sudoers file (or equivalent). This file can quickly become complex, with lots of lines, each granting access to specific elevated privileges to specific users, and outdated. It therefore requires management similar to what you expect to see with firewall rule sets and the like. Look for processes to review, validate, and clean up the entries periodically in this file. If your Unix environment is large (it consists of a large number of servers), it may be preferable to implement some form of centralized sudoers file that is referenced by all systems rather than attempting to maintain the file on each individual system.

Finally, it is important that you review the use of trusted access for root and other administrative accounts. See Steps 28 and 29 for information on testing for trusted access.

11. Review and evaluate the usage of groups and determine the restrictiveness of their usage.

This information will provide a foundation for evaluating file permissions in later steps. If all users are placed in one or two large groups, then group file permissions are not very useful. For example, if all users are part of one large group, a file that allows group "write" permissions effectively allows world "write" permissions. However, if users are placed in selective, well-thought-out groups, group file permissions are effective controls.

How

Review the contents of the /etc/group, /etc/passwd, and related centralized files (such as NIS) using the more (such as more /etc/passwd) and, for NIS, ypcat (such as ypcat passwd and ypcat group) commands.

Look at the password as well as the group files to get an idea of group assignments, because user primary group assignments from the password file do not need to be relisted in the group file. In other words, if a user is assigned to the "users" group in the /etc/passwd file, there is no need to list him or her as a member of that group in the /etc/group file. Therefore, to obtain a full listing of all members of the "users" group, you must determine who was assigned to that group in the /etc/group file and also determine who was assigned to that group in the /etc/passwd file (along with any NIS, LDAP, and so on, equivalents being used in your environment). It is important to note that a group does not need to be listed in the group file in order to exist. It is therefore necessary to identify all group IDs (GIDs) in the password file and determine the membership of those groups. If you rely on the group file to identify all groups on the system, you may not receive a complete picture.

12. Evaluate usage of passwords at the group level.

Group-level passwords allow people to become members of groups with which they are not associated. If a group has a password associated with it in the group file, a user can use the newgrp <group name> command and will be prompted to enter that group's password. Once the password is entered correctly, the user will be given the rights and privileges of a member of that group for the duration of the session. There is generally little need for this functionality, because users are usually granted membership to whichever groups they need to access. Creating a group-level password creates another vector of attack on the system by creating the opportunity for users to hack the group-level passwords and escalate their privileges.

How

Review the contents of the group file(s) by using `more /etc/group` for the local file and `ypcat group` for NIS. If the groups have anything other than a common character (such as an "*" or even nothing) in the password field (the second field for each entry), passwords are being used. If group-level passwords are being used, speak to the system administrators to understand the purpose and value of using such passwords, and review the process for restricting knowledge of these passwords.

To look for passwords in /etc/group, you could use this command in your audit script:

```
awk -F: '{if($2!="" && $2!="x" && $2!="*")print "A password is set for group
"$1" in /etc/group\n"}' /etc/group
```

13. Review and evaluate the security of directories in the default path used by the system administrator when adding new users. Evaluate the usage of the "current directory" in the path.

A user's path contains a set of directories that are to be searched each time the user issues a command without typing the full pathname. For example, suppose the `ls` command on your system is located at /bin/ls. To execute this program and view the permissions in the /home directory, you could type `/bin/ls /home`. By typing in the exact location of the file, you are using the full pathname. However, we rarely do this. Instead, the norm is to type `ls /home`. In this case, the user's path is the mechanism for finding the file that is to be executed.

For example, let's say that your path looks like this:

```
/usr/bin:/usr/local/bin:/bin
```

This means that when you type in a command, the operating system will first look for a file by that name in /usr/bin. If the file doesn't exist there, it will next look in /usr/local/bin. If it still doesn't find a file by that name there, it will look in /bin. If it is still unsuccessful, the command will fail. Thus, in our example, we have attempted to execute the `ls` command, which is located in /bin. The system will first look for a file called `ls` in the /usr/bin directory. Since there is no file in that directory, it will look in the /usr/local/bin directory. Since the file is not there either, it will look in /bin. A file called `ls` is in /bin on our system, so the operating system will attempt to execute that file. If the permissions on that file grant you execute permissions, you will be allowed to run the program.

Attackers who can write to a directory in a user's path can perform filename spoofing. For example, if the directory that contains the `ls` command is not secured, an attacker could replace the `ls` command with his or her own version. Alternatively, if the "current directory" (meaning whatever directory the user happens to be in at the time the command is executed) or another unprotected directory is placed early in the user's path, the attacker could place his or her own version of the `ls` command in one of these and never have to touch the real `ls` command.

Because of all this, directories in the path should be user- or system-owned and should not be writable by the group or world.

A "." or an empty entry (a space) represents the "current directory," which means whatever directory the user happens to be in at the time he or she executes a command. Since this is an unknown, it is generally safer to leave this out of the path. Otherwise, an attacker could trick a user or administrator into switching to a specific directory and then executing a common command, a malicious version of which could be located in that directory.

Each user has the ability to set his or her path in his or her initialization files. However, most users will never touch their paths, and it is important for the system administrator to provide a default path that is secure.

How

The easiest way to view your own path is by typing `echo $PATH` at the command line. The default setting for users' paths may be found in /etc/default/login, /etc/profile, or one of the files in /etc/skel. Ask the system administrator where the default setting is kept if you are unsure. If the user has modified his or her path, this typically will be done in one of the dot-files in the home directory. Look at the contents of such files as .login, .profile, .cshrc, .bash_login, and so on. A quick way to look is to use the command `grep "PATH=" .*` in the user's home directory. A user's home directory can be determined by viewing his or her entry in the password file.

Once you know the name of the file that contains the path, view the contents of the file using the `more` command. The `ls -ld` command can then be performed on each directory in the path to view directory permissions. The directories should be writable only by the user and system accounts. Group and world write access should not be allowed (unless the group contains only system-level accounts).

14. Review and evaluate the security of directories in root's path. Evaluate the usage of the "current directory" in the path.

If a user can write to a directory in root's path, it is possible that the user could perform filename spoofing and obtain access to the root account. See Step 13 for further explanation of this concept.

How

Have the system administrator display root's path for you (using the `echo $PATH` command when logged in as root), and then review the permissions of each directory using the `ls -ld` command. All directories in root's path should be system-owned and should not be group or world writable (unless the group contains only system-level accounts such as `bin` and `sys`). The "current directory" generally should not be part of root's path.

The following will print the permissions of root's path (assuming that the script is executed as root) and warn if there is a "." in the path or if one of the directories is world writable:

```
#!/bin/sh
for i in `echo $PATH | sed 's/:/ /g'`
do
if [ "$i" = . ]
```

```
then
echo -e "WARNING: PATH contains .\n"
else
ls -ld $i
ls -ld $i | awk '{if(substr($1,9,1)=="w")print "\nWARNING - " $i " in
root'\'s' path is world writable"}'
fi
done
```

15. Review and evaluate the security of user home directories and configuration files. They generally should be writable only by the owner.

User config files are basically any file located in the user's home directory that starts with a dot (.), commonly called *dot-files*. These files define the user's environment, and if a third party can modify them, privileged access to the account can be obtained. For example, when a user first logs in, commands within his or her .login, .profile, .bashrc, or other file (depending on the shell) are executed. If an attacker is able to modify one of these files, he or she can insert arbitrary commands, and the user will execute those commands at the next login. For example, commands could be executed that copy the user's shell to another file and make it Set UID (SUID) (a concept that will be explained in step 18). The attacker then would be able to execute this new file and "become" that user. Access to these files also allows the attacker to change the user's path or create malicious aliases for common commands by modifying these files. Other config files, such as .cshrc and .kshrc, are executed at login, when a new shell is run, or when someone uses the su command to switch to the user's account. The ability to insert arbitrary commands into these files results in a similar risk as with the .login and .profile files.

Another config file that should be locked down is the .rhosts file. This file provides trusted access (access without the use of a password) to the user's account from specific accounts on specific other systems. A person who can modify this file can gain trusted access to the user's account.

Even though specific risks were not mentioned for other dot-files, it is generally a good idea to keep them locked down. There is generally no legitimate reason that others should be modifying a user's config files.

Access to a user's home directory also should be locked down. If an attacker has write privileges to the directory, he or she will have the ability to delete any of the user's config files and replace them with his or her own versions.

How

The location of user home directories can be obtained from the account entries in the password file. The ls -ld command should be performed on each directory to view directory permissions. The ls -al command should be performed on each directory to view the permission on the files (including the config files) within the directory.

File Security and Controls

16. Evaluate the file permissions for a judgmental sample of critical files and their related directories.

If critical files are not protected properly, the data within these files can be changed or deleted by inappropriate users. This can result in system disruption or unauthorized disclosure and alteration of proprietary information.

How

Using the `ls -l` command, examine the permissions on critical system files and their related directories. Generally, the most critical files within the Unix and Linux operating systems are contained in the following directories:

- /bin, /usr/bin, /sbin, /usr/sbin, and/or /usr/local/bin (programs that interpret commands and control such things as changing passwords)

- /etc (files that contain information such as passwords, group memberships, and trusted hosts and files that control the execution of various daemons)

- /usr or /var (contain various accounting logs)

For these directories and the files contained therein, question the need for write access to be granted to anyone other than system administration personnel.

In addition, other critical data files (such as files containing key application data and company proprietary information) will likely be on the system you are auditing and should be secured. Interview the system administrator to help identify these.

For ease of use and to get a full picture of the file system, you can ask the system administrator to run the `ls -alR` command (recursive file listing) against the entire file system and place the results in a file for you. You can then view the contents of this file in performing this and other steps. The system administrator must do this because only the superuser can access the contents of all directories.

You might want to look for several variations that are short of a full `ls -alR`. If, for example, you want to find all world-writable files (excluding symbolic links, or symlinks), use `find / -perm -777 ! -type l -print`. Check the man pages to get more ideas on how you can use that command in your audit.

17. Look for open directories (directories with permission set to `drwxrwxrwx`) on the system and determine whether they should have the sticky bit set.

If a directory is open, anyone can delete files within the directory and replace them with their own files of the same name. This is sometimes appropriate for /tmp directories and other repositories for noncritical, transitory data; however, it is not advisable for most directories. By placing the sticky bit on the directory (setting permissions to `drwxrwxrwt`), only the owner of a file can delete it.

How

Examine directory permissions within the recursive file listing obtained from the preceding step, and search for open directories. (In the listing of `ls -alR`, note that the directory permissions will be listed next to the ".".) To find just directories with world-write permissions, you can use the command `find / -type d -perm -777`. For any such directories discovered, discuss the function of those directories with the system administrator, and determine the appropriateness of the open permissions.

18. Evaluate the security of all SUID files on the system, especially those that are SUID to "root."

SUID files allow users to execute them under the privileges of another UID. In other words, while that file is being executed, the operating system "pretends" that the user executing it has the privileges of the UID that owns the file. For example, every user needs the ability to update the password file to change passwords periodically. However, it would not be wise to set the file permissions of the password file to allow world-write access, because doing so would give every user the ability to add, change, and delete accounts. The `passwd` command was therefore created to give users the ability to update their passwords without having the ability to alter the rest of the password file. The `passwd` file is owned by "root" and has the SUID bit set (`-rwsr-xr-x`), meaning that when users execute it, they do so using the privileges of "root."

If an SUID file is writable by someone other than the owner, it may be possible for the owning account to be compromised. Other users could change the program being run to execute arbitrary commands under the file owner's UID. For example, a command could be inserted such that the owner's shell is copied to a file and made to be SUID. Then, when the attacker executed this copied shell, it would run as if it were the owner of the SUID file, allowing the attacker to execute any command using the privilege level of the captured account.

How

For Solaris and Linux, a full list of SUID files can be viewed by using the following command:

```
find / -perm -u+s
```

Note that the results of this command will not be complete unless it is run by someone with superuser access.

Review the file permissions for those programs, particularly for those that are SUID to root. They should be writable only by the owner.

Also question the need for any programs that are SUID to a user account. There should be little reason for one user to run a program as if he or she were another user. Most SUID programs are SUID to root or some other system or application account. If you see a program that is SUID to a user account, it is possible that this program is being used to capture that user's account.

19. Review and evaluate security over the kernel.

The kernel is the core of the operating system. If it can be altered or deleted, an attacker could destroy the entire system.

How

Use the `ls -l` command on the location of the kernel for the system you are auditing. It should be owned and writable only by the superuser. The kernel could be stored in a number of possible locations. Some common kernel names are /unix (AIX), /stand/ vmunix (HP), /vmunix (Tru64), /kernel/genunix (Solaris), and /boot/vmlinuz (Linux). Ask the system administrator for the location of the kernel on the system you are auditing.

20. Ensure that all files have a legal owner in the /etc/passwd file.

Each time a file is created, it is assigned an owner. If that owning account is subsequently deleted, the UID of that account still will be listed as the owner of the file unless ownership is transferred to a valid account. If another account is created later with that same UID, the owner of that account will, by definition, be given ownership of those files.

For example, suppose that Grant (UID 226) creates the file /grant/file. UID 226 (Grant) is listed as the owner of this file. Grant is then fired, and his account is deleted. However, ownership of his file is not transferred. The operating system still considers UID 226 to be the owner of that file, even though that UID no longer maps to a user in the password file. A few months later, Kate is hired and is assigned UID 226. The system now considers Kate to be the owner of the file /grant/file, and she has full privileges over it. If /grant/file contains highly sensitive information, this could be a problem. To avoid this problem, before deleting an account, the system administrators should disposition all files owned by that account, either by deleting them or by transferring ownership.

How

Have the system administrator perform the `quot` command (which has to be run by the superuser). This command will show all file owners on the system. Review this list, and ensure that a username, and not a UID, is shown for every entry. If a UID appears, it means that there is no entry in the password file for that UID, which means that the password file could not convert the UID into a username. If a user is added later to the password file with that UID, that user would have ownership of these files.

 NOTE The `quot` command is not available on all versions of Unix and Linux. If this is the case, the output of a `ls -alR` command will need to be reviewed manually to see if any files list an invalid username as the owner.

21. Ensure that the `chown` command cannot be used by users to compromise user accounts.

The `chown` command allows users to transfer ownership of their files to someone else. If a user can transfer an SUID file to another user, he or she then will be able to execute that file and "become" the user. For example, if a user copies his or her shell, makes it SUID and world-executable, and then transfers ownership to "root," then, by executing that file, the user becomes "root."

How

Many versions of Unix allow only the superuser to execute `chown`. Many others do not allow SUID bits to be transferred to another user. To determine whether these controls are in place on the machine you are auditing, perform the following in order:

1. Review the password file and determine where your shell is located (it probably will be something like /bin/csh or /usr/bin/sh).

2. Run the command `cp <shell file name> ~/myshell` to create a copy of your shell file in your home directory.

3. Run the command `chmod 4777 ~/myshell` to make your new shell file SUID and world executable.

4. Choose another user from the password file to transfer ownership to, preferably a fellow auditor.

5. Run the command `chown <new owner name> ~/myshell`, which will attempt to transfer ownership of the file to another user.

6. Run the command `ls -l ~/myshell` to see whether you transferred ownership successfully and, if so, whether the SUID bit also transferred.

7. If the SUID bit transferred to another owner, execute the file by typing `/myshell`. This will execute the shell.

8. Run the command `whoami`. This should show that you are now the other user and have taken over his or her account.

9. If this happens, the system administrator will need to contact his or her vendor for a fix.

22. Obtain and evaluate the default umask value for the server.

The umask determines what permissions new files and directories will have by default. If the default umask is not set properly, users could inadvertently be giving group and/or world access to their files and directories. The default should be for files to be created securely. Privileges then can be loosened based on need and conscious decisions by the users (as opposed to their being unaware that their new files and directories are not secure).

How

The default may be set in /etc/profile or in one of the files in /etc/skel. However, the easiest test is often just to view the umask value for your own account because this usually will be a representation of the default value for all new users. This can be done using the umask command.

The umask basically subtracts privileges when files and directories are created using the modular format of file permissions and assuming that the default is for all files and directories to be created fully open (777 permissions). In other words, with a umask of 000, all new files and directories will be created with default permissions of 777 (777 minus 000), meaning full access for the owner, group, and world.

For example, if the umask is set to 027, it will result in the following default permissions for newly created files and directories:

Normal default	777
Minus the umask	027
Default permissions on this server	750

This provides full access to the owner, read and execute access to the group, and no access to the world.

At a minimum, the default system generally should be set to a value of 027 (group write and all world access removed) or 037 (group write/execute and all world access removed).

23. Examine the system's crontabs, especially root's, for unusual or suspicious entries.

A *cron* executes a program at a preset time. It is basically the Unix or Linux system's native way of letting you schedule jobs. The *crontab* (short for cron table) contains all the crons scheduled on the system. Crons can be used to create time bombs or to compromise the owning account. For example, if an attacker managed to compromise a user's account, he or she could set up a cron that would copy the user's shell nightly and make it SUID and then delete this copy of the shell 15 minutes later. The attacker then could regain access to the account daily during that time period, but security-monitoring tools would not detect it unless the tools happened to run in that 15-minute window. An example of a time bomb would be a case where a system administrator is fired or quits and schedules a cron that crashes the system to run 6 months later.

How

The crontabs should be located within directory /usr/spool/cron/crontabs or /var/spool/cron/crontabs. By performing the ls -l command on this directory, you will be able to list the contents. Each account with a crontab will have its own file in this directory. The contents of these files can be viewed with the more command. This will allow you to see the commands that are being executed and the schedule for that execution. Based on file permissions, you may need the administrator to display the contents of the crontabs. Also, depending on the level of your Unix knowledge, you may need the administrator's help in interpreting the contents of the files.

24. Review the security of the files referenced within crontab entries, particularly root's. Ensure that the entries refer to files that are owned by and writable only by the owner of the crontab and that those files are located in directories that are owned by and writable only by the owner of the crontab.

All crons are run as if the owner of the crontab is running them, regardless of the owner of the file being executed. If someone besides the owner of the crontab can write to a file being executed by the crontab, it is possible for an unauthorized user to gain access to those accounts by altering the program being executed to cause the crontab owner to execute arbitrary commands (such as copying the cron owner's shell and making it SUID). For example, if root's crontab has an entry that executes the file /home/barry/flash, and that file is owned by "Barry," then "Barry" has the ability to add any command he wants to the flash file, causing "root" to execute that command the next time the cron is executed.

If a crontab is executing a file that is in a directory that is not secure, this would allow other users to delete the program being run and replace it with their own, again potentially resulting in the owner of the crontab executing arbitrary commands.

How

The contents of each user's crontab should be reviewed (see the preceding step for more information). The `ls -l` command should be performed on each file being executed in a crontab, and the `ls -ld` command should be executed for each of the directories containing those files.

25. Examine the system's scheduled atjobs for unusual or suspicious entries.

Atjobs are one-time jobs that are scheduled to run some time in the future. They operate much like cron jobs (except that they are executed only once) and can be used to create time bombs.

How

The atjobs should be located within directory /usr/spool/cron/atjobs or /var/spool/cron/atjobs. By performing the `ls -l` command on this directory, you can list the contents. The contents of these files can be viewed with the `more` command. This will allow you to see the commands that are being executed and the schedule for that execution. Based on file permissions, you may need the administrator to display the contents of the atjobs. Also, depending on the level of your Unix knowledge, you may need the administrator's help in interpreting the contents of the files.

Network Security and Controls

26. Determine what network services are enabled on the system, and validate their necessity with the system administrator. For necessary services, review and evaluate procedures for assessing vulnerabilities associated with those services and keeping them patched.

Whenever remote access is allowed (that is, whenever a network service is enabled), it creates a new potential vector of attack, therefore increasing the risk of unauthorized entry into the system. Therefore, network services should be enabled only when there is a legitimate business need for them.

New security holes are discovered and communicated frequently to the Unix/Linux community (including potential attackers). If the system administrator is not aware of these alerts, and if he or she does not install security patches, well-known security holes could exist on the system, providing a vector for compromising the system.

NOTE This is one of the most critical steps you will perform. Unnecessary and unsecured network services are the number one vector of attack on *nix servers. They will allow someone who has no business being on the system either to gain access to the system or to disrupt the system.

How

Use the `netstat -an` command, and look for lines containing LISTEN or LISTENING. These are the Transmission Control Protocol (TCP) and User Datagram Protocol (UDP) ports on which the host is available for incoming connections. If LSOF is present on the system (more common on Linux), then `lsof -i` can be used.

Once you have obtained a list of enabled services, talk through the list with the system administrator to understand the need for each service. Many services are enabled by default and therefore were not enabled consciously by the system administrator. For any services that are not needed, encourage the administrator to disable them.

Understand the process used to keep abreast of new vulnerabilities for enabled services and to receive and apply patches for removing those vulnerabilities. Common sources for vulnerability announcements include vendor notifications and Computer Emergency Response Team (CERT) notices. CERT covers the high-profile vulnerabilities, but you really should be getting notifications from your OS and add-on software vendors to ensure adequate coverage. Information on this process can be gathered via interviews and review of documentation.

If you need to validate a specific patch or package version, you can view installed packages and patches via the following commands:

- **Solaris** `showrev -p` will list the patches that have been applied; these can be cross-referenced with the patches listed in the security advisory from Sun.
- **Linux** `rpm -q -a` (Red Hat or other distributions using RPM) or `dpkg --list` (Debian and related distributions) will show the versions of installed packages.

Note that software can be installed outside the package-management system provided by the vendor, in which case these commands won't show you the requisite information. If you need to find the version of an executable, try running the command with the `-v` switch. In most cases, this will show you version information that you can compare with information in vulnerability notices.

A network scan of existing vulnerabilities also can be used to help validate the effectiveness of the patching process. See the next step for further details.

Consider the configuration of the services, not just whether they are allowed. The proper configuration of certain services such as Network File System (NFS), anonymous File Transfer Protocol (FTP), and those that allow trusted access and root login are discussed later in this chapter. Space restrictions prevent us from detailing the proper configuration of every potential service (plus new vulnerabilities are discovered all the time). This is why the use of a network scanning tool is a critical component of an effective audit. Such a tool will keep up with and test for the latest vulnerabilities for you.

27. Execute a network vulnerability-scanning tool to check for current vulnerabilities in the environment.

This will provide a snapshot of the current security level of the system (from a network services standpoint). The world of network vulnerabilities is an ever-changing one, and it is unrealistic to create a static audit program that will provide an up-to-date portrait of vulnerabilities that should be checked. Therefore, a scanning tool that is updated frequently is the most realistic mechanism for understanding the current security state of the machine. In addition, if the system administrator has a security-patching process in place, this scan will provide validation as to the effectiveness of that process (or as to whether it is really being executed).

How

See the "Tools and Technology" section later in this chapter for information on potential network vulnerability-scanning tools. Even though many of these tools are designed to be nondisruptive and do not require access to the system, you should always inform the appropriate IT personnel (such as the system administrator, the network team, and IT security) that you plan to run the tool, and then get their approval and schedule with them a time to execute the tool. Scanning tools can interact in an unexpected fashion with a port and cause a disruption, so it is important that others be aware of your activities. These tools should usually be run in a "safe" (nondisruptive) mode such that they do not attempt to exploit any vulnerabilities discovered. On rare occasions, you will want to run an actual exploit to get more accurate results, but this should be done only with buy-in from and coordination with the system owner and administrator.

28. Review and evaluate the usage of trusted access via the /etc/hosts.equiv file and user .rhosts files. Ensure that trusted access is not used or, if deemed to be absolutely necessary, is restricted to the extent possible.

Trusted access allows users to access the system remotely without the use of a password. Specifically, the /etc/hosts.equiv file creates trust relationships with specific machines, whereas the .rhosts file creates trust relationships with specific users on specific machines.

For example, if system "Trusting" has an /etc/hosts.equiv file that lists machine "Trusted" as a trusted host, then any user with an account using the same username on both systems will be able to access "Trusting" (the trusting machine) from "Trusted" (the trusted machine) without the use of a password. Thus, if the username "Hal" exists on both machines, the owner of the "Hal" account on "Trusted" will be able to access the "Hal" account on "Trusting" without using a password. Keep in mind that the key is the account name. If John Jones has an account on both machines, but one has the account name "jjones" and the other has the account name "jjonzz," then the trust relationship won't work. The operating system won't acknowledge them as the same account.

The .rhosts files work similarly except that they are specific to a user. Each user can have a .rhosts file in his or her home directory that provides trusted access to his or her account. If username "Barry" on system "Trusting" has a .rhosts file in his home directory and that .rhosts file lists system "Trusted," then the "Barry" account on "Trusted" will be able to access the "Barry" account on "Trusting" without using a password. Alternatively, system and username pairs can be listed in the .rhosts file. The .rhosts file for "Barry" on "Trusting" could list username "Wally" on system "Trusted." This would mean that the "Wally" account on "Trusted" would be able to access the "Barry" account on "Trusting" without using a password.

If the system you are auditing has trust relationships with other machines, the security of the trusting system depends on the security of the trusted system. If the accounts that are trusted are compromised, then, by definition, the accounts on the system you are auditing will be compromised as well. This is the case because access to the trusted machine provides access to the trusting machine. It is best to avoid this sort of dependency if at all possible.

 NOTE If NIS is used, it is also possible to grant trusted access to specific netgroups (groups of usernames).

Trusted access can also be used to bypass controls over shared accounts. As discussed in other steps, shared accounts can be locked down such that su or sudo are required for access. However, if a user has access to a shared account via one of these mechanisms and then creates a .rhosts file for that account granting trusted access to his or her personal account, the user will be able to bypass the need to use su or sudo to access the account.

The first option should be to eliminate trusted access. If it becomes obvious to the auditor that this is not feasible in the environment, the steps in the "How" section that follows can be used to mitigate the risk.

NOTE Trusted access works via the usage of the Berkeley r commands (for example, rlogin, rsh, and rexec). These commands are designed to look for trusted relationships automatically via .rhosts and /etc/hosts.equiv files when executed. If a trusted relationship doesn't exist, these commands will require the entry of a password. If trusted relationships do exist, these commands will not require the entry of a password.

How
Examine the contents of the /etc/hosts.equiv file and any .rhosts files on the system. The contents of the /etc/hosts.equiv file can be viewed by using the more/etc/hosts.equiv command. To find .rhosts files, you will need to view the contents of each user's home directory via the ls -l command (the location of user home directories can be found in the password file) to see whether a .rhosts file exists. The contents of any .rhosts files found can be viewed by using the more command. If file permissions restrict you from viewing the contents of these files, you will need to have the system administrator perform these commands for you.

Discuss the contents of these files with the system administrator to understand the business need for each entry. Encourage the administrator to delete any unnecessary entries or preferably to eliminate the use of trusted access altogether. For essential trusted relationships, discuss the possibility of using trusted Secure Shell (SSH) keys, which is generally a preferred alternative to hosts.equiv and .rhosts (see the next step for more details).

Ensure that none of the files contain the + sign. This symbol defines all the systems on the network as trusted and enables them all to log on without using a password (if there is an equivalent username on the trusting server). If the + sign exists in the /etc/hosts.equiv file, then any user (except "root") on any system on the network who has the same username as any of the accounts on the trusting system will be able to access the account without using a password. If the + sign exists in a .rhosts file, any user on any system on the network who has the same username as the owner of the .rhosts file will be able to access the account without using a password. This includes the "root" account, so a .rhosts file with a + in root's home directory is usually a particularly bad idea.

For any legitimate and necessary trust relationships, determine whether the administrator is comfortable in knowing that each system to which trusted access is given is as secure as the system being audited. As mentioned earlier, the system's security depends on the security of any system being trusted. System administrators generally should not give trusted access to systems they do not control. If they do, they should take steps to obtain assurance as to the security and integrity of the systems being trusted either by performing their own security scans or by conducting interviews with the system administrator of the trusted system.

If trusted hosts are needed in the /etc/hosts.equiv file, ensure that trusted users are not specified in this file. In some versions of Unix, a trusted user specified in this file will be allowed to log into the system as any username (except "root") without entering a password.

If trusted access is allowed, usernames in the password files must be consistent across each system involved in the trusted relationship. Determine whether this is the case. If system2 trusts system1, then username "Bob" on system1 can log in as username "Bob" on system2 without entering a password. If "Bob" on system1 is Bob Feller, while "Bob" on system2 is Bobby Thompson, then Bobby Thompson's account now has been compromised.

Ensure that the /etc/hosts.equiv and .rhosts files are secured properly (using the `ls -l` command). The /etc/hosts.equiv file should be owned by a system account (such as "root") and writable only by that account. If others can write to this file, they could list unauthorized machines in the trusted hosts list. The .rhosts files should be owned by the account in whose home directory they sit and should be writable only by that account. If a user can write to another user's .rhosts file, that user could make himself or herself, or someone else, trusted to log into that user's account from another machine.

Ensure that entries use the fully qualified domain name for systems being trusted (such as "rangers.mlb.com" instead of just "rangers"). An entry that does not use the fully qualified domain name could be spoofed by a machine with the same host name but a different domain.

Review processes used by the system administrators to detect and review any new trusted access established on the system. They should detect and review any new .rhosts files or entries and any new /etc/hosts.equiv entries.

29. Review and evaluate the usage of trusted access via SSH keys.

Trusted access via SSH keys is conceptually the same as trusted access via .rhosts files discussed in the preceding step, and is generally preferred if trusted access is required. It lets users access the system remotely via SSH without the use of a password, creating trust relationships with specific users on specific machines.

To establish a trust relationship via SSH keys, a user creates (or more likely uses an SSH key generation command to create) a subdirectory in his or her home directory on the trusted machine called .ssh and places two files within that directory: *id_rsa* is the private key and *id_rsa.pub* is the public key (if DSA is being used instead of RSA, replace *rsa* with *dsa* in those filenames). The user then places the text from the public key file into a file called authorized_keys2 in the .ssh subdirectory of the home directory on the machine that the user wants to access (which becomes the trusting machine). Once this is done, the user will be able to access the trusting machine (the machine on which he or she created an authorized_keys2 file in his or her home directory) from the trusted machine (the machine containing the user's public and private key files) via SSH without the use of a password.

NOTE These default filenames (authorized_keys2, id_rsa, id_rsa.pub) can vary depending on the version of SSH being used and can even be changed by the user in some versions of SSH. Although this step is written using these standard filenames, talk with your administrator to understand the specifics for the environment you're auditing.

If the system you are auditing has trust relationships with other machines, the security of the trusting system depends on the security of the trusted system. If the accounts that are trusted are compromised, then, by definition, the accounts on the system you are auditing will be compromised as well. This is the case because access to the trusted machine provides access to the trusting machine. It is best to avoid this sort of dependency if at all possible.

Trusted access can also be used to bypass controls over shared accounts. As discussed in other steps, shared accounts can be locked down such that su or sudo are required for access. However, if a user has access to a shared account via one of these mechanisms and then places his or her personal public key in the shared account's authorized_keys2 file, the user will then be able to bypass the need to use su or sudo to access the account.

The first option should be to eliminate trusted access. If it becomes obvious to the auditor that this is not feasible in the environment, the steps in the "How" section below can be used to mitigate the risk.

How

Examine the contents of any authorized_keys2 files on the system. To find these files, you will need to view the contents of each user's home directory's .ssh subdirectory via the ls -l command (the location of user home directories can be found in the password file) in order to see whether an authorized_keys2 file exists. The contents of any authorized_keys2 files found can be viewed by using the more command. File permissions should restrict you from viewing the contents of these files, so you will likely need to have the system administrator perform these commands for you.

Discuss the contents of these files with the system administrator to understand the business need for each entry. Encourage the administrator to delete any unnecessary entries or preferably to eliminate the use of trusted access altogether.

For any legitimate and necessary trust relationships, determine whether the administrator is comfortable in knowing that each system to which trusted access is given is as secure as the system being audited. As mentioned earlier, the system's security depends on the security of any system being trusted. System administrators generally should not give trusted access to systems they do not control. If they do, they should take steps to obtain assurance as to the security and integrity of the systems being trusted either by performing their own security scans or by conducting interviews with the system administrator of the trusted system.

Ensure that the authorized_keys2 files and related .ssh subdirectories are secured properly (using the ls -l command). They should be owned by the account in whose home directory they reside and should be writable only by that account. If a user can write to another user's authorized_keys2 file, the user could set up additional trust relationships for the other user's account. For many versions of Unix, trusted access via SSH keys will not work unless permissions on these files and directories are set to 600.

Ensure that all id_rsa files on the system and related .ssh subdirectories are secured properly (using the `ls -1` command). The files should be owned by the account in whose home directory they reside and should be readable and writable only by that account. If a user can read another user's private key file, that user could use that information to spoof the other user and access trust relationships that user has established with other servers.

Passphrases can also be used to restrict further what activities can be performed using this form of trusted access. Talk with your administrator to determine whether passphrases are being used and to what extent. If they are being used, it will be important that you review the strength of and controls over those passphrases.

Review processes used by the system administrators to detect and review any new trusted access established on the system. They should detect and review any new authorized_keys2 files or entries.

Additional controls can be established over this function, depending on the version of SSH being used, such as disallowing key-based authentication or requiring any keys that are to be used for user authentication to be stored in a centralized location (instead of in various accounts' home directories). Talk with the administrator and perform research to determine what features are available and have been enabled in your environment.

30. If anonymous FTP is enabled and genuinely needed, ensure that it is locked down properly.

Anonymous FTP allows any user on the network to get files from or send files to restricted directories. It does not require the use of a password, so it should be controlled properly.

How

To determine whether anonymous FTP is enabled, examine the contents of the password file(s). If you see an "ftp" account in the password file and the FTP service is enabled, then anonymous FTP is available on the system. Once an anonymous FTP user has logged in, he or she is restricted only to those files and directories within the "ftp" account's home directory, which is specified in ftp's password entry (we'll assume that the home directory is at /ftp for this step). The "ftp" account should be disabled in the password file and should not have a valid shell.

Ensure that the FTP directory (/ftp) is owned and writable only by "root" and not by "ftp." When using anonymous FTP, the user becomes user "ftp." If "ftp" owns its own files and directories, anyone using anonymous FTP could alter the file permissions of anything owned by "ftp." This can be determined by performing the `ls -1` command on the "ftp" home directory. "Ftp" should own only the /ftp/pub directory.

Examine the permissions of the /ftp directory and the subdirectories (by using the `ls -l` command).

- The /ftp/pub directory should have the sticky bit set so that people cannot delete files in the directory.
- The /ftp directory and its other subdirectories should be set with permissions at least as restrictive as `dr-xr-xr-x` so that users can't delete and replace files within the directories.

Ensure that the /ftp/etc/passwd file contains no user entries (just "ftp") or passwords (by performing the `more` command on the file). Otherwise, anyone on the network can see usernames on the server and use those for attacking the system. It should not allow group or world write permissions (`ls -l /ftp/etc/passwd`).

Other files outside of the /ftp/pub directory should not allow group or world write access (verify by using the `ls -l` command).

Attackers could transfer large files to the /ftp directories and fill up the file system (to commit a denial-of-service attack and/or prevent audit logs from being written). The system administrator should consider placing a file quota on the "ftp" user or placing the /ftp home directory on a separate file system.

31. If NFS is enabled and genuinely needed, ensure that it is secured properly.

NFS allows different computers to share files over the network. Basically, it allows directories that are physically located on one system (the NFS server) to be mounted by another machine (the NFS client) as if they were part of the client's file structure. If the directories are not exported in a secure manner, the integrity and availability of that data can be exposed to unnecessary risks.

How

NFS use can be verified by examining the /etc/exports file or the /etc/dfs/dfstab file (using the `more` command). If this file shows that file systems are being exported, then NFS is enabled.

Because NFS authorizes users based on UID, UIDs on all NFS clients must be consistent. If, for example, Cathy's account is UID 111 on the system being audited, but Bruce's account is UID 111 on an NFS client, then Bruce will have Cathy's access level for any files that are exported (because the operating system will consider them to be the same user). After determining which systems can mount critical directories from the system you're auditing, you will need to work with the system administrator to determine how UIDs are kept consistent on those systems. This may involve obtaining a copy of each system's password file and comparing UIDs that appear in both the NFS server and an NFS client. Note that the same risk exists and should be investigated for GIDs.

Review the /etc/exports file or the /etc/dfs/dfstab file (using the `more` command):

- Ask the system administrator to explain the need for each file system to be exported.

- Ensure that the `access=` option is used on each file system being exported. Otherwise, any machine on the network will be able to access the exported file system. This option should be used to specify the hosts or netgroups that are allowed to access the file system.

- Ensure that read-only access is given where possible using the `ro` option (note that read/write is the default access given if read-only is not specified).

- Ensure that root access is not being given to NFS clients (that is, the `root=` option is not being used) unless absolutely necessary and unless the NFS clients have the same system administrator as the server. The `root=` option allows remote superuser access for specified hosts.

- Ensure that root accounts logging in from NFS clients are not allowed root access. You should not see `anon=0`, which would allow all NFS clients superuser access.

Review the contents of the /etc/fstab or the /etc/vfstab (or /etc/checklist for HP systems) file (using the `more` command) to see if the system you are auditing is importing any files via NFS. If it is, ensure that the files are being imported "nosuid." If SUID files are allowed, the NFS client could import a file that is owned by "root" and has permissions set to `rwsr-xr-x`. Then, when a user on the NFS client runs this program, it will be run as that client's superuser. The root user on the NFS server could have inserted malicious commands into the program, such as a command that creates a .rhosts file in the client "root" user's home directory. This .rhosts file then could be used by the NFS server to obtain unauthorized superuser access to the NFS client. Note that if the system administrator is the same on both the NFS client and the NFS server, this is not a big risk.

On all these NFS steps, the auditor should use good judgment. The criticality of the files being exported should influence the scrutiny with which the auditor reviews them.

32. Review for the use of secure protocols.

Certain protocols (such as Telnet, FTP, remote shell [rsh], rlogin, and remote copy [rcp]) transmit all information in clear-text, including UID and password. This could allow someone to obtain this information by eavesdropping on the network.

How

Review the list of services that are enabled and determine whether `telnet`, `ftp`, and/ or the "`r`" commands are enabled. If so, via interviews with the system administrator, determine the possibility of disabling them and replacing them with secure (encrypted) alternatives. Telnet, rsh, and rlogin can be replaced by SSH; FTP can be replaced by Secure File Transfer Protocol (SFTP) or Secure Copy Protocol (SCP); and rcp can be replaced by SCP.

NOTE The use of secure protocols is particularly important in a DMZ and other high-risk environments. The auditor may determine that it is of less importance on the internal network. However, it is still advisable to use secure protocols even on internal networks to minimize attacks from within.

33. Review and evaluate the use of .netrc files.

The .netrc files are used to automate logons. If a confidential password is placed in one of these files, the password may be exposed to other users on the system.

How

The following command can be used to find and print the contents of all .netrc files on the system. You likely will need to have the system administrator run this command to search the entire system.

```
find / -name '.netrc' -print -exec more {} \;
```

For any .netrc files found, review the file contents. If read access is restricted, you will need the system administrator to do this for you. Look for indications of passwords being placed in these files. If you find them, review file permissions via the `ls -l` command, and ensure that no one besides the owner can "read" the file. Even if file permissions are locked down, anyone with superuser authority will be able to read the file, so it's better to avoid using these files at all. However, if they exist and are absolutely necessary, the auditor should ensure that they have been secured to the extent possible.

34. Ensure that a legal warning banner is displayed when a user connects to the system.

A *legal logon notice* is a warning displayed whenever someone attempts to connect to a system. This warning should be displayed prior to actual login and basically should say, "You're not allowed to use this system unless you've been authorized to do so." Verbiage of this sort may be needed to prosecute attackers in court. Unfortunately, court rulings have dictated that you must specifically tell someone not to hack your system or you can't prosecute them for doing so.

How

Log into your account using each available mechanism that provides shell access, such as Telnet and SSH. Determine whether a warning banner is displayed. The text for this banner frequently is located in files such as /etc/issue and /etc/sshd_config (or /etc/openssh/sshd_config). Via interviews with the system administrator, determine whether the verbiage for this warning banner has been developed in conjunction with the company's legal department.

35. Review and evaluate the use of modems on the server.

Modems bypass corporate perimeter security (such as firewalls) and allow direct access to the machine from outside the network. They present significant risk to the security of the machine on which they reside and also may allow the modem user to "break out" of the machine being audited and access the rest of the network. Allowing dial-in modems to be placed on a production machine is usually a bad idea. It is almost always preferable to have access to a machine channeled through standard corporate external access mechanisms such as a virtual private network (VPN) or Remote Access Services (RAS).

How

Unfortunately, there is no reliable method of determining whether a modem is connected to a machine outside of physical inspection. If physical inspection is not practical, the next best option is to interview the system administrator to understand whether modems are used. If they are used, alternative mechanisms for allowing external access to the machine should be investigated. If a dial-in modem is deemed truly necessary, consider implementing compensating controls such as dial-back to trusted numbers (that is, when a call is received, the machine hangs up and dials back to a trusted number) and authentication.

Audit Logs

36. Review controls for preventing direct "root" logins.

Because several people usually know the "root" password, if they are allowed to log in directly as the "root" account, no accountability exists for actions performed by that account. If inappropriate actions are performed by the "root" account, there will be no way to trace those actions back to a specific user. It is preferable to force people to log in as themselves first and then use su or sudo to access the "root" account.

How

Review the wtmp log (by performing the more command on /usr/adm/wtmp, /var/adm/wtmp, or /etc/wtmp depending on the type of system) to verify that there are no direct "root" logins. The last command can be used to view the contents of this file on most systems. Exceptions would be direct logins from the console, which may be needed for emergencies.

Review settings for preventing direct "root" logins via telnet and rlogin.

- The file /etc/default/login can be used to disable direct "root" logins on Solaris machines. If this file is available, the CONSOLE= parameter should be set to the pathname of a nonexistent device. If the administrator wants to place the pathname of the actual console device (the terminal directly linked to the Unix machine) into this parameter, the console should be in a secure location. The contents of this file can be viewed by executing the more /etc/default/login command.

- On Linux and HP systems, the /etc/securetty file can be used to prevent direct logins as "root." The contents of the file should contain all terminals that are allowed direct "root" login. The file should exist but be empty. Sometimes the system administrator will want to allow direct "root" login from the console terminal. This is acceptable, as long as the console is in a secure location. The contents of this file can be viewed by executing more /etc/securetty.

Review settings for preventing direct "root" logins via SSH. The /etc/sshd_config or /etc/openssh/sshd_config file is used for this purpose. Review the contents of this file using the more command. Look for the PermitRootLogin parameter. If this parameter is set to a value of no, "root" logins are not permitted. If the parameter is not there or is set to a value of yes, "root" logins are permitted.

Review settings for preventing direct "root" logins via FTP. This can be done by placing a "root" entry in the /etc/ftpusers file. Review the contents of this file using the more command.

37. Review the su and sudo command logs to ensure that when these commands are used, they are logged with the date, time, and user who typed the command.

The su command is a tool used frequently by attackers to try to break into a user's account. The sudo command allows authorized users to perform specific commands as if they were "root." The use of both commands should be logged to ensure accountability and to aid in investigations.

How

Attempt to perform a more command on the su log. However, the log may be protected, so you may not be able to do this. If this is the case, have the system administrator provide you with a copy of the log and perform the command on it. For some systems, the su log will be at /usr/adm/sulog, /var/adm/sulog, or /var/log/auth.log. For other systems, the /etc/default/su file will determine where the su log will be kept.

- Ensure that this file exists and is capturing information on su usage (such as who performed the command, to what account they switched, the date and time of the command, and indications as to whether or not the command succeeded).

- Question any instance of one user su-ing to another user's account. There should be little to no reason for one user to attempt to su to another user's account on the system. Most su commands should be issued from an administrator's account to "root" or from a user account to an application ID.

View the sudo log to ensure that it is capturing information on sudo usage (such as who performed the command, what command was performed, and the date and time of the command). By default, the sudo logs are written to the syslog, but this can be changed in /etc/sudoers, so check for the location on your system (using the more command).

38. Evaluate the syslog to ensure that adequate information is being captured.

If system audit logs are not kept, there will be no record of system problems or user activity and no way to track and investigate inappropriate activities.

How

View the contents of the /etc/syslog.conf file using the `more` command. The /etc/syslog. conf file determines where each message type is routed (to a filename, to a console, and/or to a user). At a minimum, `crit` and `err` messages related to `auth` (authorization systems—programs that ask for usernames and passwords), `daemon` (system daemons), and `cron` (cron daemon) probably should be captured, along with `emerg` and `alert` messages.

Each syslog message contains, in addition to the program name generating the message and the message text, the facility and priority of the message.

Following are some of the common potential syslog facilities (that is, the type of system function):

- `kern`   Kernel
- `user`   Normal user processes
- `mail`   Mail system
- `lpr`   Line printer system
- `auth`   Authorization systems (programs that ask for usernames and passwords)
- `daemon`   System daemons
- `cron`   cron daemon

Following are the potential priority levels that indicate the severity of the message:

- `emerg`   Emergency condition (such as an imminent system crash)
- `alert`   Immediate action needed
- `crit`   Critical error
- `err`   Normal error
- `warning`   Warning
- `notice`   Not an error but special handling needed
- `info`   Informational message
- `debug`   Used when debugging programs

Notice that these are listed in descending order—most critical to least critical. When specifying a logging level, the level encompasses that level and higher, so logging at the debug (lowest) level, for example, also would log all other levels. An asterisk for the facility or level indicates that all facilities or levels are logged.

On HP systems, the /etc/btmp file contains invalid login attempts. Determine whether this file exists. If not, it should be created. On Solaris, the file /var/adm/login-log will log any time a user tries to log into the system but types a bad password five times in a row (by default—the number can be configured in the /etc/default/login file). If this file does not exist, it should be created.

PART II

39. Evaluate the security and retention of the wtmp log, sulog, syslog, and any other relevant audit logs.

If the audit logs are not secure, then unauthorized users could change their contents, thus damaging the logs' usefulness during investigations. If logs are not retained for an adequate period of time, the administrator may be unable to investigate inappropriate activities and other system issues if needed.

How

The locations of the log files are discussed in previous steps in this section. Perform a `ls -l` command on those files. They usually should be writable only by "root" or some other system account.

Interview the system administrator to determine retention, which could be either online or offline. It is generally preferable to retain these security logs for at least 3 to 6 months to allow for adequate history during investigations.

40. Evaluate security over the utmp file.

The utmp log keeps track of who is currently logged into the system and includes information regarding what terminals from which users are logged in. By changing the terminal name in this file to that of a sensitive file, an attacker can get system programs that write to user terminals to overwrite the target file. This would cause this sensitive file to be corrupted.

How

Perform an `ls -l` command on the utmp file, which is usually located at /etc/utmp on Unix systems and at /var/run/utmp on Linux systems. The file should be owned by "root" or another system account and should allow only owner write.

Security Monitoring and General Controls

41. Review and evaluate system administrator procedures for monitoring the state of security on the system.

If the system administrator does not have processes for performing security monitoring, security holes could exist, and security incidents could occur without his or her knowledge.

How

Interview the system administrator, and review any relevant documentation to get an understanding of security monitoring practices. Numerous levels and methods of security monitoring can be performed. Although all monitoring levels and methods do not need to be performed, you should see some level of monitoring, which should be consistent with the criticality of the system and the inherent risk of the environment. (For example, a web server in the DMZ should have more robust security monitoring than a print server on the internal network.) Basically, you want to know how the system administrator is monitoring for problems such as what you've been auditing for throughout the other audit steps in this chapter.

Following are four primary levels of monitoring. Potential tools for performing these types of monitoring are discussed in the "Tools and Technology" section later in this chapter.

- **Network vulnerability scanning**   This is probably the most important type of security monitoring in most environments. It monitors for potential vulnerabilities that could allow someone who has no business being on the system either to gain access to the system or disrupt the system. Since these vulnerabilities can be exploited by anyone on the network, you need to be aware of them and close them down.

- **Host-based vulnerability scanning**   This is scanning for vulnerabilities that would allow someone who's already on the system to escalate his or her privileges (such as exploit the "root" account), obtain inappropriate access to sensitive data (owing to poorly set file permissions, for example), or disrupt the system. This type of scanning generally is more important on systems with many nonadministrative end users.

- **Intrusion detection**   This monitoring detects unauthorized entry (or attempts at unauthorized entry) into the system. Baseline monitoring tools (such as Tripwire) can be used to detect changes to critical files, and log-monitoring tools can be used to detect suspicious activities via the system logs.

- **Intrusion prevention**   This type of monitoring detects an attempted attack and stops the attack before it compromises the system. Examples include host Intrusion Prevention System (IPS) tools and network-based IPS tools such as Tipping Point.

If security monitoring is being performed, assess the frequency of the monitoring and the quality with which it is performed. Look for evidence that the security monitoring tools actually are used and acted on. Review recent results, and determine whether they were investigated and acted on. Leverage the results of the rest of the audit in performing this assessment. For example, if you found significant issues in an area that is supposedly being monitored, it might lead to questions as to the effectiveness of that monitoring.

42. If you are auditing a larger Unix/Linux environment (as opposed to one or two isolated systems), determine whether a standard build exists for new systems and whether that baseline has adequate security settings. Consider auditing a system freshly created from the baseline.

One of the best ways to propagate security throughout an environment is to ensure that new systems are built right. In this way, as new systems are deployed, you have confidence that they initially have the appropriate level of security.

How

Through interviews with the system administrator, determine the methodology used for building and deploying new systems. If a standard build is used, audit a newly created system using the steps in this chapter.

43. Perform steps from Chapter 4 as they pertain to the system you are auditing.

In addition to auditing the logical security of the system, you should ensure that appropriate physical controls and operations are in place to provide for system protection and availability.

How

Reference the steps from Chapter 4, and perform those that are relevant to the system being audited. For example, the following topics are likely to be pertinent:

- Physical security
- Environmental controls
- Capacity planning
- Change management
- System monitoring
- Backup processes
- Disaster recovery planning

Tools and Technology

The open-source community has provided numerous valuable tools that an auditor can take advantage of to increase both the accuracy and efficiency of his or her work. Some of the most commonly used tools for auditing *nix systems are listed below with a few tips on their use.

Nessus

The Nessus network vulnerability scanner written by Renaud Deraison first appeared in 1998 and was arguably the most advanced and most popular open-source network vulnerability-assessment tool. Beginning with version 3.0, Nessus is now closed-source and is owned by Tenable Security. The current version is still free to use, but registration/payment will get you faster access to the latest plug-ins and vulnerability checks. The source to the 2.x stream is still open, and others have already picked up on its development. In a nutshell, Nessus operates by looking for open ports on the target host, trying to identify the services running on those ports, and then testing those services for specific vulnerabilities. The server operates on Unix/Linux only, but clients to control the server are also available for Windows.

For more information, see www.nessus.org and www.openvas.org.

NMAP

NMAP can be a handy way to check for open ports on a server without running an all-out vulnerability scanner such as Nessus, perhaps to test the rules of a host-based firewall. NMAP affords the user many options, and the man page is a must-read to understand them all.

For more information, see www.insecure.org/nmap.

Chkrootkit

Chkrootkit is designed to identify both known rootkits running on a system and "suspicious" files or processes. It can be run in the course of an audit to check for possible compromises and also can be suggested to the system administrator as a tool that could be run on a regular basis for security monitoring. Its effectiveness is enhanced if run from a read-only file system with trusted, statically linked binaries.

For more information, see www.chkrootkit.org. Also see www.netadmintools.com/art279.html. (The author used the instructions on this site, with a few minor tweaks in the build process probably owing to differing versions, to create static binaries for a trusted chkrootkit package.)

Crack and John the Ripper

If checking the strength of user-chosen passwords is part of your audit scope, you'll want to take a look at these two tools. Alec Muffett's Crack dates back to the early 1990s and is widely known and distributed. John the Ripper, however, generally is faster and more full-featured. Either probably will get the job done in most cases. Consider adding wordlists to the dictionaries of these tools, including non-English wordlists, to enhance their efficacy.

For more information, see ftp.cerias.purdue.edu/pub/tools/unix/pwdutils/crack and www.openwall.com/john.

Tiger and TARA

Tiger and TARA are host-based vulnerability scanning tools that can automate performance of a number of the test steps in this chapter, allowing you to avoid tedious manual execution and analysis of each step. Tiger is a security tool originally developed at Texas A&M University. TARA is a variant of Tiger.

For more information, see savannah.nongnu.org/projects/tiger and www-arc.com/tara.

Shell/Awk/etc

Although not a tool in the same sense as the others, the *nix shell can prove valuable, especially with the help of additional tools such as awk or sed, which can chop up and process text output from commands. Much of the required information to perform the steps in this audit program could be obtained by the use of a shell script. This script can be provided to the system administrator, who would run it as "root," providing the output to the auditor. Using logical operations to test the values returned can even automate the evaluation process, returning a simple pass/fail grade for some of the steps. A simple example is found in step 2, where the passwd file is checked for duplicate UIDs.

Knowledge Base

If you're interested in learning more about the subject of auditing *nix operating systems, many resources are available in print and on the Internet.

One of the "go to" books on Unix security is *Practical UNIX & Internet Security*, by Simson Garfinkel, Gene Spafford, and Alan Schwartz, published by O'Reilly Media. This book provides an excellent overview of the topic, along with detailed guidance on how to secure the Unix environment.

Another excellent print resource is *Essential System Administration*, by Æleen Frisch, published by O'Reilly Media. This book is written for *nix administrators but also can serve as an excellent guide for auditors who are looking for details on how to implement many of the concepts discussed in this chapter.

Many websites are devoted to Unix; the problem is wading through them to determine which ones can be most useful. Following are some to consider:

Website	Description
isaca.org	Standards and security guidance
www.sans.org/rr/	Certifications and other documents from SANS
www.sans.org/top20	SANS top 20 vulnerabilities
www.nsa.gov/ia/guidance/security_ configuration_guides/index.shtml	Security configuration guides from the National Security Agency
csrc.nist.gov/publications/PubsSPs.html	Security guidelines from the National Institute of Standards and Technologies
www.insecure.org/tools.html	Top 75 security tools as generated from a survey of NMAP users
seclists.org/	List of lists; good security-oriented mailing lists
www.securityfocus.com/	Mailing lists, news, vulnerabilities
cve.mitre.org/	Along with the vulnerability database section of security focus, offers a good place to begin research on potential vulnerabilities

Remember that Google is your friend, and a wealth of information is available on the Internet about how Unix and Linux systems work. For example, try searching for **command list unix**.

Master Checklists

This chapter covers several methods for auditing Unix hosts and their variants. Because there are so many variants, it is impossible to list every occurrence you'll run across. Here is a list of the items we reviewed in this chapter.

Auditing Account Management and Password Controls

Checklist for Auditing Account Management and Password Controls
❑   1. Review and evaluate procedures for creating Unix or Linux user accounts and ensure that accounts are created only when there's a legitimate business need. Also review and evaluate processes for ensuring that accounts are removed or disabled in a timely fashion in the event of termination or job change.
❑   2. Ensure that all UIDs in the password file(s) are unique.
❑   3. Ensure that passwords are shadowed and use strong hashes where possible.
❑   4. Evaluate the file permissions for the password and shadow password files.
❑   5. Review and evaluate the strength of system passwords.
❑   6. Evaluate the use of password controls such as aging.
❑   7. Review the process used by the system administrator(s) for setting initial passwords for new users and communicating those passwords.
❑   8. Ensure that each account is associated with and can be traced easily to a specific employee.
❑   9. Ensure that invalid shells have been placed on all disabled accounts.
❑   10. Review and evaluate access to superuser ("root"-level) accounts and other administration accounts.
❑   11. Review and evaluate the use of groups, and determine the restrictiveness of their use.
❑   12. Evaluate the use of passwords at the group level.
❑   13. Review and evaluate the security of directories in the default path used by the system administrator when adding new users. Evaluate the use of the "current directory" in the path.
❑   14. Review and evaluate the security of directories in root's path. Evaluate the use of the "current directory" in the path.
❑   15. Review and evaluate the security of user home directories and config files. They generally should be writable only by the owner.

Auditing File Security and Controls

Checklist for Auditing File Security and Controls

❑   16. Evaluate the file permissions for a judgmental sample of critical files and their related directories.

❑   17. Look for open directories (directories with permission set to `drwxrwxrwx`) on the system, and determine whether they should have the sticky bit set.

❑   18. Evaluate the security of all SUID files on the system, especially those that are SUID to "root."

❑   19. Review and evaluate security over the kernel.

❑   20. Ensure that all files have a legal owner in the /etc/passwd file.

❑   21. Ensure that the `chown` command cannot be used by users to compromise user accounts.

❑   22. Obtain and evaluate the default umask value for the server.

❑   23. Examine the system's crontabs, especially the "root" crontab, for unusual or suspicious entries.

❑   24. Review the security of the files referenced within crontab entries, particularly the root crontab. Ensure that the entries refer to files that are owned by and writable only by the owner of the crontab and that those files are located in directories that are owned by and writable only by the owner of the crontab.

❑   25. Examine the system's scheduled atjobs for unusual or suspicious entries.

Auditing Network Security and Controls

Checklist for Auditing Network Security and Controls

❑   26. Determine what network services are enabled on the system, and validate their necessity with the system administrator. For necessary services, review and evaluate procedures for assessing vulnerabilities associated with those services and keeping them patched.

❑   27. Execute a network vulnerability scanning tool to check for current vulnerabilities in the environment.

❑   28. Review and evaluate the use of trusted access via the /etc/hosts.equiv file and user .rhosts files. Ensure that trusted access is not used or, if deemed to be absolutely necessary, is restricted to the extent possible.

❑   29. Review and evaluate the usage of trusted access via SSH keys.

❑   30. If anonymous FTP is enabled and genuinely needed, ensure that it is locked down properly.

❑   31. If NFS is enabled and genuinely needed, ensure that it is secured properly.

❑   32. Review for the use of secure protocols.

❑   33. Review and evaluate the use of .netrc files.

❑   34. Ensure that a legal warning banner is displayed when a user connects to the system.

❑   35. Review and evaluate the use of modems on the server.

Auditing Audit Logs

Checklist for Auditing Audit Logs

❑   36. Review controls for preventing direct "root" logins.

❑   37. Review the `su` and `sudo` command logs to ensure that when these commands are used, they are logged with the date, time, and user who typed the command.

❑   38. Evaluate the syslog to ensure that adequate information is being captured.

❑   39. Evaluate the security and retention of the wtmp log, sulog, syslog, and any other relevant audit logs.

❑   40. Evaluate security over the utmp file.

Auditing Security Monitoring and General Controls

Checklist for Auditing Security Monitoring and General Controls

❑   41. Review and evaluate system administrator procedures for monitoring the state of security on the system.

❑   42. If you are auditing a larger Unix/Linux environment (as opposed to one or two isolated systems), determine whether a standard build exists for new systems and whether that baseline has adequate security settings. Consider auditing a system freshly created from the baseline.

❑   43. Perform steps from Chapter 4 as they pertain to the system you are auditing.

PART II

Auditing Web Servers and Web Applications

The explosive growth in the Internet has also driven an explosive growth in development tools, programming languages, web browsers, databases, and different client-server models. The unfortunate result is that complex models often require additional controls to secure the model. This chapter covers the absolute bare minimum set of controls that should be reviewed. This chapter covers the following:

- How to audit a web server
- How to audit a web application

Background

Few technology inventions have changed our lives as much—or as quickly—as web applications. The web interface has grown from static pages to an incredibly interactive blend of capabilities driven by an army of creative programmers. In the late 1980s, the concept of the World Wide Web began its humble beginnings with Tim Berners-Lee and Robert Caillieau. By 1991, the first web server was installed in the United States to communicate with the NeXT computer in Switzerland.

The early rapid development of the Internet is broadly attributed to the need to share information that would accelerate development across scientific research departments. Later, development and growth were driven by business opportunities. Entrepreneurs soon found new business models in the Internet and were able to take advantage of people's need to send and receive information and multimedia instantly.

Web Auditing Essentials

The 2010 Verizon Data Breach Incident Report identified the web as the most common attack vector for successful company breaches, accounting for a full 54 percent of all attacks. These web attacks further accounted for 92 percent of all records compromised across all attack categories. Web servers are common targets. They are difficult to properly secure, and they often contain company secrets, personal information, or cardholder data.

Remember that auditing, as much as we would like to believe otherwise, isn't an exact science, and auditing web servers is one area in which this is apparent. The audit procedures in this chapter attempt to use a subset of the tools and technologies available to identify common risks in the system or processes around the system. There are dozens of tools and resources available to assist you in performing a more robust audit of your specific application. Avoid becoming ineffective as you try to cover too much with too few resources and knowledge.

As a final word of caution, the following steps should be considered a starting point for your audit. Web application penetration testing tools should be utilized along with proper training. Additional layered controls, such as a Web Application Firewall (WAF), are strongly recommended.

One Audit with Multiple Components

A complete web audit is really an audit of three primary components, including the server operating system, web server, and web application. These three components are shown in Table 8-1. Additional components such as a supporting database or relevant network infrastructure may also be appropriate to consider as part of your audit.

The first component we discuss is the underlying platform or operating system on which the web server and application are installed and operate. Next is the web server itself, such as Internet Information Services (IIS) or Apache, that is used to host the web application. Finally, we cover an audit of the web application. The web application for our purposes includes associated development frameworks such as ASP.NET, Java, Python, or PHP and applicable content management systems (CMS) such as Drupal, Joomla, or WordPress.

A major difficulty with reviewing web applications has to do with the number of possible interacting components which may exist within the framework of the website. Volumes could be written about every web server and web application framework in existence and the individual settings for each one. We will cover the concepts, show some examples, and leave it to you to understand how to apply the concepts to your unique situation.

A wealth of languages and structures are available for web application development, complicating the audit process. However, several tools and methods are also available to help us determine what needs attention. The steps that follow cover these tools and methods. Keep in mind that if the following steps don't fit with your intentions, you should review Chapter 13, which covers auditing applications. Chapter 13 is intentionally geared toward conceptually breaking down complex or infrequent audits.

Web Audit Component	Key Concerns
Web platform	Security of the operating system, physical and network protection to the host
Web server	Default settings, sample code, general misconfigurations, logging
Web application	Development framework security settings, default application settings, input validation, incorrectly serving up data, access to company confidential data, general misconfigurations

Table 8-1 Web Auditing Components

Part 1: Test Steps for Auditing the Host Operating System

The host operating system audit should be conducted in conjunction with the audit of the web server and web application(s). Please see Chapters 6 and 7 on Windows or Unix as appropriate for the audit of the platform.

 NOTE The platform component of the audit is as important as the audit of the web server and the web applications. Please refer to the Chapters 6 and 7 on auditing UNIX and Windows servers.

Part 2: Test Steps for Auditing Web Servers

Each step may or may not apply to your web server, but you need to take the time to determine this. We examine the applications that are running on the web server in a separate audit that follows this one.

1. Verify that the web server is running on a dedicated system and not in conjunction with other critical applications.

A compromised web host may allow the attacker to compromise other applications on your web server. You should use a dedicated machine for your web server. For example, you would never want to install your web server on a domain controller.

How

Identify and discuss each application with the administrator. Carefully consider the legitimate business need to allow other applications to remain on the same host as the web server. If these applications must coexist, consider bringing each of the additional applications into the scope of the audit.

2. Verify that the web server is fully patched and updated with the latest approved code.

Failure to run adequately patched systems subjects the web server to unnecessary risk of compromise from vulnerabilities that may have been patched with updated code releases.

How

Every organization has its own patch-management systems and policies. Verify that the web server is running the latest approved code with the help of the administrator according to the policies and procedures in the environment. Also review the policies and procedures for appropriate and timely demands for keeping and verifying that systems are up to date with the latest code releases. Also identify and document with the help of the administrator any special patches/engineering binaries that have not been released for general availability by the vendor.

3. Verify that unnecessary services, modules, objects, and APIs are removed or disabled. Running services and modules should be operating under the least privileged accounts.

Unnecessary services, modules, objects, and APIs present additional attack surface area, resulting in more opportunities for malicious attackers and malware.

How

Discuss and verify, with the help of the administrator, that unnecessary services are disabled and that the running services are operating under the least privileged account possible. Verify that File Transfer Protocol (FTP), Simple Mail Transport Protocol (SMTP), Telnet, extra server extensions, and Network News Transfer Protocol (NNTP) services are disabled if they are not required. You can use `netstat` or a more robust process to port-mapping utility. Many web servers have robust management interfaces whereby you can review additional installed modules and plugins.

Review logs and configuration files to validate that only necessary modules are enabled. Question the need for anything else that might be running.

4. Verify that only appropriate protocols and ports are allowed to access the web server.

Minimizing the number of protocols and ports allowed to access the web server reduces the number of attack vectors available to compromise the server.

How

Discuss with the administrator and verify with the administrator's help that only necessary protocols are allowed to access the server. For example, the TCP/IP stack on the server should be hardened to allow only appropriate protocols. NetBIOS and Server Message Block (SMB) should be disabled on IIS servers. Note any additional controls that may be in place, such as firewall rules or network Access Control Lists (ACLs) to limit the protocols and ports allowed to access the web server. In general, only TCP on ports 80 (HTTP) and 443 (SSL) should be allowed to access the web server. In addition, in certain cases it may be necessary to review the negotiated ciphers allowed by Secure Sockets Layer (SSL) transactions. Review these decisions with the administrator.

5. Verify that accounts allowing access to the web server are managed appropriately and hardened with strong passwords.

Inappropriately managed or used accounts could provide easy access to the web server, bypassing other additional security controls that prevent malicious attacks. This is a large step with a wide scope, covering controls around account use and management.

How

Discuss and verify with administrator that unused accounts are removed from the server or completely disabled. The administrator's account on Windows servers should be renamed, and all accounts should be restricted from remote login except for those used for administration.

The root account on UNIX-flavored hosts (Linux, Solaris, and so on) should be strictly controlled and never used for direct remote administration. Never run Unix web servers such as Apache under the root account. They should be run under a distinct user and group such as www-apache:www-apache. Please see Chapter 7 for more information about the root account.

In general, accounts never should be shared among administrators, and administrators should never share their accounts with users. Strong account and password policies always should be enforced by the server and by the web server application.

Additional considerations for IIS web servers include ensuring that the IUSR_ MACHINE account is disabled if it is not used by the application. You also should create a custom least-privileged anonymous account if your applications require anonymous access. Configure a separate anonymous user account for each application if you host multiple web applications.

6. Ensure that appropriate controls exist for files, directories, and virtual directories.

Inappropriate controls for files and directories used by the web server and the system in general allow attackers access to more information and tools than should be available. For example, remote administration utilities increase the likelihood of a web server compromise.

How

Verify that files and directories have appropriate permissions, especially those containing the following:

- Website content
- Website scripts
- System files (such as %windir%\system32 or web server directories)
- Tools, utilities, and software development kits

Sample applications and virtual directories should be removed. Discuss and verify with the administrator that logs and website content are stored on a nonsystem volume where possible.

Also verify that anonymous and everyone groups (world permissions) are restricted except where absolutely necessary. Additionally, no files or directories should be shared out on the system unless necessary.

7. Ensure that the web server has appropriate logging enabled and secured.

Logging auditable events helps administrators to troubleshoot issues. Logging also allows incident response teams to gather forensic data.

How

Verify with the administrator that key audit trails are kept, such as failed logon attempts. Ideally, these logs should be relocated and secured on a different volume than web server. Log files also should be archived regularly. They should be analyzed regularly, preferably by an automated tool in large IT environments.

8. Ensure that script extensions are mapped appropriately.

Scripts might allow an attacker to execute the code of his or her choice, potentially compromising the web server.

How

Verify with the web administrator that script extensions not used by the web server are mapped to a 404 web page handler or simply denied altogether. Examples of extensions that you may or may not use include .idq, .htw, .ida, .shtml, .shtm, .stm, .idc, .htr, and .printer.

9. Verify the validity and use of any server certificates in use.

Server-side certificates enable clients to trust your web server's identity or that your web server is who you say your server is supposed to be. Old or revoked certificates suggest that your website may or may not be valid to end users.

How

Verify with the help of the administrator that any certificates are used for their intended purpose and have not been revoked. Certificate data ranges, public key, and metadata all should be valid. If any of these have changed, consider the need for a new certificate that reflects your current needs.

Part 3: Test Steps for Auditing Web Applications

This section represents an approach to the application audit as represented by the Open Web Application Security Project (OWASP) Top 10.

According to its website, OWASP is "dedicated to enabling organizations to develop, purchase, and maintain applications that can be trusted." OWASP maintains a tremendous amount of information that can help you to develop an audit program for your web applications. The OWASP Top Ten are regarded as a set of *minimum* standards to be reviewed during an audit. Do not blindly follow the steps in this section.

Your web application design may call for additional testing including a partial or full code review, third-party penetration testing, commercial scanners, or open source tools. Each of these can offer some additional assurance that your application is correctly designed and configured. Consider the business value of the web application and invest in the appropriate resources to ensure that your application is secure. Additional guidance on how to effectively find vulnerabilities in web applications are provided in the OWASP Testing Guide and the OWASP Code Review Guide found at www.owasp.org.

Application design drives the importance of the following steps. We assume that interactions occur between the web server and the user. These interactions may come from logging into the application or serving user-requested data.

> **NOTE** Keep in mind that the audience of this book varies greatly in technical abilities, and an attempt has been made to simplify the content in this section as much as possible for the majority of the readers. You will find further guidance by visiting www.owasp.org to determine what scope and toolset are most appropriate for your environment.

1. Ensure that the web application is protected against injection attacks.

Injection attacks allow a web client to pass data through the web server and out to another system. For example, in a SQL injection attack, SQL code is passed through the web interface, and the database is asked to perform functions out of bounds of your authorization. Several websites have coughed up credit card and Social Security card information to hackers who have taken advantage of injection attacks.

Failure to realize the power of injection attacks and to review your systems for the likelihood of being exploited may result in the loss of critical and sensitive information.

How

Discuss injection attacks with the administrator and web application development team as appropriate to ensure that they understand how such attacks work, and then ask how they are guarding against injection attacks. No tool can review and discover every possible injection attack on your web application, but you still can defend your system against such attacks. The following defense methods could also be listed under the next audit step, reviewing cross-site scripting:

- Validate all input using positive validation methods whereby you reject any input that does not match the expected input, such as values, length, and character sets.

- Perform a code review if possible for all calls to external resources to determine whether the method could be compromised.

- Commercial tools are available that may help find injection vulnerabilities, such as acunetix (www.acunetix.com). These tools are powerful and may find well-known attacks, but they will not be as helpful as performing a solid code review. Another tool that may be helpful is Burp Suite from www.portswigger. net. Burp Suite is a powerful tool and should be part of your toolset.

- Consider hiring third-party help if the application is particularly sensitive, you lack the resources, or you need to verify items such as regulatory compliance.

> **NOTE** These steps apply to the application development life cycle as much as they apply to an existing application. Payment Card Industry (PCI) requires compliance with OWASP for your existing web applications, but that starts on the drawing board before the first line of code is written.

2. Review the website for cross-site-scripting vulnerabilities.

Cross-site scripting (XSS) allows the web application to transport an attack from one user to another end user's browser. A successful attack can disclose the second end user's session token, attack the local machine, or spoof content to fool the user. Damaging attacks include disclosing end user files, installing Trojan horse programs, redirecting the user to some other page or site, and modifying the presentation of content.

How

XSS attacks are difficult to find, and although tools can help, they are notoriously inept at locating all the possible combinations of XSS on a web application. By far the best method for determining whether your website is vulnerable is by doing a thorough code review with the administrator.

If you were to review the code, you would search for every possible path by which HTTP input could make its way into the output going to a user's browser. The key method used to protect a web application from XSS attacks is to validate every header, cookie, query string, form field, and hidden field. Again, make sure to employ a positive validation method.

CIRT.net contains two tools, Nikto and a Nessus plug-in, that you might be able to use to help you partially automate the task of looking for XSS vulnerabilities on your web server. Keep in mind that these tools are not as thorough as conducting a complete code review, but they can at least provide more information to those who don't have the skill set, resources, time, and dollars to conduct a complete review. Nikto is available from www.cirt.net/code/nikto.shtml. Burp Suite and many other commercial tools that may help also are available.

NOTE Always keep in mind that these tools may find well-known attacks, but they will not be nearly as good as performing a solid code review.

If you don't have the internal resources available to perform a code review, particularly on a homegrown application, and you believe that the data on the website warrants a deep review, then you may consider hiring third-party help.

3. Review the application for broken authentication and session management vulnerabilities.

Account credentials and session tokens must be protected. Attackers who can compromise passwords, keys, session cookies, or other tokens can defeat authentication restrictions and assume other users' identities and level of authorized access.

How

Discuss with the administrator the authentication mechanism used to authenticate users to the web application. The web application should have built-in facilities to handle the life cycle of user accounts and the life cycle of user sessions. Verify that helpdesk functionality, such as lost passwords, is handled securely. Walk through the implementation with the administrator, and then ask the administrator to demonstrate the functionality to you.

The following list of guiding principles may be helpful when it comes to checking the authentication mechanism used on a website. These continue to maintain relevance despite the many advances in web design and products that promise secure user and session management:

- When a user enters an invalid credential into a login page, don't return which item was incorrect. Show a generic message instead such as, "Your login information was invalid!"

- Never submit login information via a GET request. Always use POST.

- Use SSL to protect login page delivery and credential transmission.

- Remove dead code and client-side viewable comments from all pages.

- Do not depend on client-side validation. Validate input parameters for type and length on the server, using regular expressions or string functions.

- Database queries should use parameterized queries or properly constructed stored procedures.

- Database connections should be created using a lower privileged account. Your application should not log into the database using sa or dbadmim.

- One way to store passwords is to hash passwords in a database or flat file using SHA-256 or greater with a random SALT value for each password.

- Prompt the user to close his or her browser to ensure that header authentication information has been flushed.

- Ensure that cookies have an expiration date, and do not store passwords in clear-text.

TIP OWASP's Guide to Authentication is maintained online at www.owasp.org/index.php/Guide_to_Authentication.

4. Verify that proper object reference and authorization controls are enforced.

Web applications may use the actual name or database key as a reference to an object in the web application or database containing sensitive information or access. The best practice is to use indirect references to objects. After a user is authenticated to the web server, the web server determines what kind of access the user should have and to what parts of the website the user should have access. Failure to enforce access controls (authorization) to each direct object reference may allow an attacker to step out of authorized boundaries, accessing other users' data or administering unauthorized areas. Specifically, attackers should not be allowed to change parameters used during an authorized user session to access another user's data. Client proxy and other tools allow attackers to view and change data during sessions.

How

Automated tools may help some, but a code review is by far the most effective method for identifying these issues. The reality for most audit teams is that few have the hours or skill required to comb through the code to identify the use of direct and indirect object references, or authorized access in general. Tools that may be helpful include Paros Proxy from www.parosproxy.org and Burp Suite. Both have ample documentation available describing how to use them.

A quick check for homegrown applications is to discuss policy requirements with the administrator. Failure to have a policy or other written documentation for a homegrown application is the first red flag strongly suggesting that access controls are not correctly enforced. Access controls are complicated and difficult to get right without carefully documenting your desired results.

5. Verify that controls are in place to prevent Cross Site Request Forgery (CSRF or XSRF).

Cross Site Request Forgery attacks exploit the trust a website has for the authenticated user. Attackers exploit this trust by sending embedded images, scripts, iframe elements, or other methods to call a command that executes on the web server while you are logged in with your credentials. Making matters worse for the user, this type of attack originates from the IP address of the user, and any logged data will appear as if the logged-in user entered it.

Web servers should validate the source of web requests to minimize the risk from attackers attempting to create authenticated malicious web requests that originate from sources outside the control of the web application. Here is an example of how this type of attack might look as an image request:

```
<img src="http://mybank.com/transfer?acct=mine&amt=100&to=attacker">
```

How

Discuss with the web application developer or web administrator the methodology used for uniquely creating tokens for each link and form for state-changing functions. Information generated by the client browser, such as the IP address or session cookie, is not a valid token because these can be included in forged requests. Without an unpredictable token, the web application is most likely subject to this type of attack.

Several tools can act as a proxy and allow you to see the content posted from your client to the remote web server. One such tool is Paros Proxy. If you can repeatedly replay the same URL over time to achieve the same result, then your application may be vulnerable.

Another method used by professional web testers is to review the handling of requests during a code review. The preferred method for handling the unique token is outside of the URL, such as in a hidden field. OWASP provides tools for developers to create applications that securely create and manage unique tokens.

6. Review controls surrounding maintaining a secure configuration.

This is a catch-all that addresses configuration management, the overarching concept of maintaining the secure configuration of the web server. Failure to maintain a secure configuration subjects the web server to lapses in technology or processes that affect the security of the web platform and web application.

How

Perform the web platform and server audit, and discuss any issues noted with the administrator. Determine whether any of the issues noted are due to inadequate configuration management. Discuss the following with the administrator to ensure that proper configuration management controls are in place:

- Security mailing lists for the web server, platform, and application are monitored.

- The latest security patches are applied in a routine patch cycle under the guidance of written and agreed-to policies and procedures.

- A security configuration guideline exists for the web servers, development frameworks, and applications in the environment covering default account management, installed components, and security settings and is strictly followed. Exceptions are carefully documented and maintained.

- Regular vulnerability scanning from both internal and external perspectives is conducted to discover new risks quickly and to test planned changes to the environment.

- Regular internal reviews of the server's security configuration are conducted to compare the existing infrastructure with the configuration guide.

- Regular status reports are issued to upper management documenting the overall security posture of the web servers.

A strong server configuration standard is critical to a secure web application. Take the time to understand the available security settings and how to configure them for your environment.

 TIP Secure web applications start with secure development processes. Check out OWASP's Open Software Assurance Maturity Model (SAMM) project online at www.owasp.org/index.php/SAMM.

7. Verify that secure cryptographic storage mechanisms are used correctly.

Web applications often want to obfuscate or encrypt data to protect sensitive data and credentials. The challenge is that there are two parts to encryption schemes: the black box that does the magic and the implementation of the black box into your web application. These components are difficult to code properly, frequently resulting in weak protection.

How

Begin the discussion with the web administrator by reviewing the sensitivity of the data you want to protect. Additionally consider whether any industry or regulatory drivers require data encryption. Discuss in detail with the developer or review documentation with the administrator to validate that appropriate mainstream acceptable encryption mechanisms are implemented into your web application. Proprietary schemes are generally considered to be inappropriate for compliance to standards and regulations. Most professional auditing organizations will flag proprietary algorithms and implementations.

Ensure that the level of encryption is equivalent to the level of data you want to protect. If you need to protect extremely sensitive data such as credit card data, you are required to use actual encryption instead of a simple algorithm that obfuscates the data.

 NOTE *Obfuscation* simply refers to creative ways of hiding data without using a key. Encryption is considered to be far more secure than obfuscation. Encryption uses tested algorithms and unique keys to transform data into a new form in which there is a little or no chance of re-creating the original data without a key. Sound complicated? Free and peer-reviewed packages exist for commonly used programming languages and web services to enable secure encryption. The result is that your data is much more difficult to steal with properly implemented encryption than it is with obfuscation.

8. Verify that proper controls are in place to restrict URL filtering.

These controls enforce role-based access to protected and sensitive areas of your web applications. Missing or incorrectly configured restrictions to sensitive URLs may allow an attacker to change the URL to access private or privileged pages. Appropriate filtering ensures that only authenticated users have access to each restricted page that they are authorized by their role to view. An attacker, who may be an authorized system user, should not be able to change the URL to view information outside of his or her role.

How

Each web page type, or web form, should be tested with authenticated and anonymous users to verify that only authenticated users have access—and only to what they are authorized to view. Verify and map out access to privileged pages, and then verify that authentication is required to access each page. Verify that once an authenticated user accesses a page type that the authenticated user is appropriately restricted to just the pages to which the user should have access.

 NOTE Mitre.org maintains a Common Weakness Enumeration (CWE) entry on this topic, CWE-285: Improper Access Control (Authorization), located at http://cwe.mitre.org/data/definitions/285.html.

9. Evaluate transport layer protection mechanisms (network traffic encryption) to protect sensitive information.

Private conversations are private only if nobody else can listen to them. Until encrypted networks become the standard, clear-text protocols should be eliminated where possible. Although newer equipment and savvy network administrators can help mitigate the risk of eavesdropping on network traffic, the real risk of catching that traffic still exists, especially on the same VLAN or broadcast domain.

Certain protocols such as HTTP, FTP, and Telnet transmit all information in clear-text, including any requested user IDs and passwords. This could allow someone to obtain this information by eavesdropping on the network. Clear-text communications in general should be minimized where possible and only secure protocols should be allowed for private pages.

How

Connect to various private pages and verify that the connections made to the web application are secured using protocols such as SSL/TLS. Port-mapping tools can be used to monitor specific connections to the web application from the client. You can view the output of these tools and discuss your results with the administrator. OpenSSL can also be used to validate available ciphers and versions.

Ask the administrator about the web services access policies and the different methods of access for private areas of the web application, with the focus on ensuring that each access method and ongoing communications with the web application are performed using secure protocols. Secure access methods during authentication ensures that the user information (such as user ID) and authentication tokens (such as password) are encrypted. Secure communications prevents data from being viewed by eavesdroppers. Ask the administrator about session cookies to verify that the secure flag is set to prevent the browser from sending them in the clear.

Question the need for any clear-text communications. There may be extreme cases where clear-text communications exist and are difficult to remove because of a legacy application or the traffic just isn't that important. However, where possible, an encrypted protocol should be used instead. Exceptions should be extremely rare and limited to business-driven cases where senior management is willing to sign-off on and formally accept the risk of clear-text communications. Encrypted communications are absolutely required under some conditions with no exceptions. Packages exist for nearly every scenario to encrypt communications.

 NOTE The use of secure protocols are particularly important for externally facing web applications and others hosted in high-risk environments. The auditor may determine that the web application is of less importance on isolated secured internal networks. However, it is still advisable that secure protocols be used, even on internal networks, to minimize attacks from within the organization. In many cases, regulations and standards (such as HIPAA and PCI) forbid the use of clear-text communications.

OWASP suggests avoiding pages combining SSL and clear-text traffic. Many sites still serve mixed pages, and the pop-up messages tend to be confusing for the users. Worse, it begins to desensitize users to pop-up messages while browsing secure sites. Furthermore, the server certificates should be legitimate, current, and properly configured for the appropriate web servers and domains that the web application uses.

10. Review the web application redirects and forwards to verify that only valid URLS are accessible.

Using an unchecked redirect, attackers may be able to redirect users to the attacker's website using a URL that looks as if it comes from your domain. This is a preferred method for phishing scams to make requests appear valid by using the attacked organization's address in the first portion of the crafted URL. This is sometimes used in conjunction with a URL shortening service for the target website to obfuscate the malicious intent of the URL.

```
http://www.mydomain.com/redirect.asp?url=badsite.com
```

In some cases, an unchecked forward can send a user to a privileged page that would otherwise be inaccessible if additional authorization controls are implemented incorrectly.

```
http://www.mydomain.com/somepage.asp?fwd=adminsite.jsp
```

How

Review with the administrator the use of any redirects and forwards within the web application to determine whether there are ways to avoid their use or implement safe controls around their use. Automated scanners may be used to automatically scan and verify a website for the proper handling of redirects and forwards.

Note that redirects and forwards are called transfers in Microsoft's .NET framework. OWASP recommends ensuring the supplied value is valid and authorized for the user when redirects and forwards cannot be avoided. Blind redirects and forwards are dangerous, and controls should limit the destination of both. There are many ways to implement redirects and forwards securely, but they should never be implemented blindly.

NOTE Mitre.org maintains a Common Weakness Enumeration (CWE) related to this topic, CWE-601: URL Redirection to Untrusted Site ('Open Redirect'), located at http:// cwe.mitre.org/data/definitions/601.html.

Additional Steps for Auditing Web Applications

The following steps were part of the original OWASP checklist and discussed in the first edition of this book. The consensus feedback during the update of this material was to include it for the reader's benefit. They remain relevant and appropriate to consider for your web application.

11. Verify that all input is validated prior to use by the web server.

Information must be validated before being used by a web application. Failure to validate web requests subjects the web server to increased risk from attackers attempting to manipulate input data to produce malicious results.

How

Discuss with the web application developer or web administrator the methodology used for input validation for the application you are testing.

There are several tools that effectively act as a proxy and allow you to see much of the content posted from your client to the remote web server. One such tool is Paros Proxy, located at www.parosproxy.org.

Another method used by professional web testers is to understand the movement of data during a code review. This isn't something that should be taken lightly because it may be beyond the scope of what you are trying to accomplish. There is a tradeoff that you as an auditor are going to have to make regarding the amount of effort you put into this versus the cost of the data you are protecting.

In general, two ways to look at validation methods are negative methods and positive methods. Negative methods focus on knowing what bad input to filter out based on the known bad. The problem with negative filtering is that we don't know now what tomorrow's vulnerabilities and input methods will bring. Positive filtering is much more effective and involves focusing on validating the data based on what they should be. This is similar in approach to a firewall that denies everything except what should be accepted.

Common items for positive filtering include criteria you might find in a database or other places that accept data. These include criteria such as

- Data type (e.g. string, integer, and real)
- Allowed character set
- Minimum and maximum length
- Whether null is allowed
- Whether the parameter is required or not
- Whether duplicates are allowed
- Numeric range
- Specific legal values (e.g., enumeration)
- Specific patterns (e.g., regular expressions)

12. Evaluate the use of proper error handling.

Improperly controlled error conditions allow attackers to gain detailed system information, deny service, cause security mechanisms to fail, or crash the server.

How

Improper error handling generally is a function of having detailed plans in place during development of the application to centralize and control all input methods. Ask the administrator how error handling was designed into the web application and how errors are handled internally as the application interfaces with other compartmentalized functions. For example, how would the web application handle an error generated by the database? Does it make a difference whether the database is hosted internally by the application as opposed to hosting the database externally on another server? How does the application handle input validation errors? What about username and password errors?

Error handling is often better controlled if it is centralized as opposed to compartmentalizing it across several interworking objects or components. Error handling should be deliberate and show structure during a code review. If the error handling looks haphazard and like an afterthought, then you may want to look much more closely at the application's ability to handle errors properly.

Tools and Technology

There are several reasons why an automated product can fail to thoroughly audit every possible component of your web server, but that doesn't mean these products should be ignored. Code reviews actually may go very fast for experienced coders, but this depends on many variables. For example, how experienced is the coder? How well does the reviewer understand the web application? How well does the reviewer understand the constructs of the programming language used for the application? How complex is the application? What external interfaces exist, and how well does the reviewer understand these external interfaces?

If you live and play in this world, code reviews may be easy for you. If you live and play in many worlds, you may want to consider augmenting your searches with automated tools, especially if you don't have the budget to get the help you know that you need. Part of the difference between a good engineer and a great engineer is resourcefulness. Just because you don't have the money doesn't mean you can't take advantage of the tools and community around you.

 NOTE Automated tools can be quite harmful to production environments. Exercise care, and design the test in a manner that will not affect production systems.

Automated tools can be quite helpful and guide you toward parts of your web platform or web application that needs further review. A strong case can be made that new applications should be tested with good code reviews and tools such as those listed here. This list only scratches the surface of what's out there. Many general vulnerability scanners also test commonly exploited vulnerabilities.

Tool	Website
BackTrack	www.backtrack-linux.org
Burp Suite	http://portswigger.net/burp/
Samurai Web Testing Framework	http://samurai.inguardians.com
Web Sleuth	www.sandsprite.com/Sleuth
Paros Proxy	www.parosproxy.org
WebInspect	www.spidynamics.com/products/webinspect (redirects to HP)
Nikto	www.cirt.net/nikto2
XSS plug-in for Nessus	www.nessus.org/plugins/index.php?view=single&id=39466
Apache JMeter	http://jakarta.apache.org/jmeter
Google Skipfish	http://code.google.com/p/skipfish

Knowledge Base

Below you will find additional resources where you can obtain information about web application environments and related controls. Many vendors maintain a tremendous amount of information on their website for general consumption. Additionally, the community of helpful enthusiasts and social forums continues to grow.

Website	Website
Apache website	www.apache.org
Microsoft IIS website	www.microsoft.com/windowsserver2003/iis
IIS answers	www.iisanswers.com
UrlScan tool for IIS	http://technet.microsoft.com/en-us/security/cc242650.aspx
Open Web Application Security Project (OWASP)	www.owasp.org
OWASP Application Security Verification Standard	www.owasp.org/index.php/OWASP_Application_Security_Verification_Standard_(ASVS)
Web Application Security Consortium	www.webappsec.org
Common Weakness Enumeration (CWE)	cwe.mitre.org
CGI Security	www.cgisecurity.net
Security Guidance for IIS	http://technet.microsoft.com/en-us/library/dd450371(WS.10).aspx
IIS Lockdown Tool	http://technet.microsoft.com/en-us/library/dd450372(WS.10).aspx
Google Code University— Web Security	http://code.google.com/edu/security

Master Checklists

The following tables summarize the steps for auditing web servers and web applications.

Auditing Web Servers

Checklist for Auditing Web Servers
❑   1. Verify that the web server is running on a dedicated system and not in conjunction with other critical applications.
❑   2. Verify that the web server is fully patched and updated with the latest approved code.
❑   3. Verify that unnecessary services, modules, objects, and APIs are removed or disabled. Running services and modules should be operating under the least privileged accounts.
❑   4. Verify that only appropriate protocols and ports are allowed to access the web server.
❑   5. Verify that accounts allowing access to the web server are managed appropriately and hardened with strong passwords.
❑   6. Ensure that appropriate controls exist for files, directories, and virtual directories.
❑   7. Ensure that the web server has appropriate logging enabled and secured.
❑   8. Ensure that script extensions are mapped appropriately.
❑   9. Verify the validity and use of any server certificates in use.

Auditing Web Applications

Checklist for Auditing Web Applications
❑   1. Ensure that the web application is protected against injection attacks.
❑   2. Review the website for cross-site-scripting vulnerabilities.
❑   3. Review the application for broken authentication and session management vulnerabilities.
❑   4. Verify that proper object reference and authorization controls are enforced.
❑   5. Verify that controls are in place to prevent Cross Site Request Forgery (CSRF or XSRF).
❑   6. Review controls surrounding maintaining a secure configuration.
❑   7. Verify that secure cryptographic storage mechanisms are used correctly.
❑   8. Verify that proper controls are in place to restrict URL filtering.
❑   9. Evaluate transport layer protection mechanisms (network traffic encryption) to protect sensitive information.
❑   10. Review the web application redirects and forwards to verify that only valid URLS are accessible.
❑   11. Verify that all input is validated prior to use by the web server.
❑   12. Evaluate the use of proper error handling.

Auditing Databases

In this chapter we discuss auditing the lockboxes of company information. We will discuss how to conduct audits on the following components that affect the operational security of your data stores:

- Database permissions
- Operating system security
- Password strength and management features
- Activity monitoring
- Database encryption
- Database vulnerabilities, integrity, and the patching process

Background

The term *database* typically refers to a relational database management system (RDBMS). Database management systems (DBMS) maintain data records and their relationships, or indexes, in tables. Relationships can be created and maintained across and among the data and tables.

The more generic term *database* can be applied to any collection of data in any structured form. For instance, a flat file that contains customer records can serve as a database for an application. However, in this chapter, we focus on auditing a full-blown RDBMS.

Typically, an audit includes a fairly in-depth review of various areas, including the perimeter, the operating system, policies, and so on. If time allows, an audit might cover one or two of the most critical databases. Databases are complex beasts requiring patience and technical know-how to audit and secure properly. However, neglecting a database audit is a serious error. Databases are the virtual lockboxes of the information age. Where do organizations store their most valuable assets? Not in perimeter devices, not in an e-mail system, and not in a flat file. They are stored in a database. When you hear about a security breach and sensitive data being stolen, ask yourself where that data "lived" when it was attacked? In a database!

Databases live both a blessed and a cursed existence. Databases are blessed because they are rarely exposed to the types of attacks that your web servers, firewalls, and other systems confront. Databases should be and almost always are buried deep and far behind the firewall. Most organizations are smart enough to know not to place their most valuable data out in the unsecured public network. Of course, some attacks, such as SQL injection, can easily make their way through a firewall and hit the database.

Databases are cursed for the same reasons. Because databases are so far behind the firewall, securing and auditing your databases are often considered afterthoughts, something to be done if you have extra time and maybe just on one or two critical databases. This has led to a situation in which database security typically is left in a shabby condition. The typical database administrator believes that the database is far enough behind the firewall that even rudimentary security measures aren't necessary.

The secured perimeter might serve as enough protection for the database in a perfect world. Unfortunately, we don't live in a perfect world, and the firewall is no longer a valid "last line of defense." Focus is now shifting to protecting data right where it sits—in the database. As an auditor, you are likely to find that the database is the weak link in the security chain. And, luckily, a few relatively simple recommendations can create vast improvements in database security.

Database Auditing Essentials

To audit a database effectively, you need a basic understanding of how a database works. You need to understand a broad set of components to audit a database properly. Here's a little history lesson.

In the early 1990s, applications were written using the client-server model, which comprised a desktop program connecting over a network directly to a database backend. This was referred to as a *two-tier application*. In the late 1990s, *three-tiered applications* became the norm. This new model consisted of a web browser connecting to a middle-tier web application. The middle tier then connected to the database backend. Three-tiered applications were a great step forward. It meant that custom software didn't need to be installed on every client workstation, and software updates could be applied to a central server. Clients could run any operating system that supported a basic browser. Moreover, in the three-tiered model, securing the database was much simpler.

Of course, the infrastructure required by the database to support two-tier applications still exists in database backends for three-tiered applications. The danger now exists that an attacker will circumvent the web application to attack the backend database.

Common Database Vendors

Typically, an audit engagement will focus on one or two database vendors, such as Oracle or DB2. However, any medium-sized or large organization typically will use a sampling of many different database platforms. Following is a summary of the most common databases and vendors, along with a short overview of each.

Oracle

Oracle Corporation is the largest database vendor and supplies an entire series of databases. In addition, Oracle Corporation has grown beyond standard database software to provide a variety of products including but not limited to web servers, development tools, identity-management software, a collaboration suite, and multiple enterprise resource planning (ERP) solutions.

In the database market, the Oracle Database has one of the largest install bases and an impressive feature set. The database comes in multiple flavors, including Standard Edition, Enterprise Edition, OracleLite, Express Edition, and others. Most Oracle databases you audit will be either Standard Edition or Enterprise Edition. The features are fairly similar; however, the advanced features in Enterprise Edition are changing constantly, so you will need to access the Oracle website to check the exact feature sets included in the version you are auditing.

Oracle also has branched out into other databases, having purchased several other database vendors, including the following:

- Sleepycat Software, which maintains Berkeley DB, an open-source, embedded database
- MySQL (from their Sun Microsystems acquisition)
- The TimesTen In-Memory Database
- InnoDB, a transaction engine for the MySQL database

IBM

IBM is another of the largest database vendors, although IBM's database software is a small piece of the company's business. IBM's main database is the DB2 product line that comprises two main products:

- DB2 Universal Database, providing database software for AIX, Linux, HP-UX, Sun, and Windows
- DB2 Universal Database for z/OS, providing software for the mainframe

A lot of confusion surrounds the nomenclature of these two products. Typically, people refer to Universal DB (UDB) as the Linux, Unix, and Windows version and DB2 as the mainframe version. This is a misnomer, because UDB is actually a term used for all of IBM's latest DB2 software. Understand what people mean when they use these terms, but try to use the correct terms to avoid confusion.

IBM also maintains the Informix Dynamic Server. Informix was, for a brief period of time, the second most popular database prior to its acquisition by IBM. Owing to some misgovernance issues, Informix fell out of favor and hit hard times. These days Informix is rarely used for new database installations, but there is a large installed base within many enterprises, and you should expect Informix to exist for quite some time into the future because of legacy application and operational dependence.

IBM also maintains one of the first commercially available database management systems, Information Management System (IMS). IMS dates back to 1969 and is not actually a relational database but rather a hierarchical database. IMS typically runs on the mainframe and does not usually work in a client-server model.

MySQL

MySQL is an open-source database used extensively in small or medium-sized web applications. MySQL was developed under the GNU Public License by MySQL AB, a privately held Swedish company. MySQL has a large and growing grassroots following and is the *M* in the *LAMP* (Linux, Apache, MySQL, and PHP) open-source web platform. MySQL AB was purchased by Sun in February 2008, and Sun was later purchased by Oracle in 2010, making MySQL an Oracle product.

MySQL traditionally has been a bare-bones database, providing a small fraction of the functionality available from other database vendors. From the security perspective, this is good, because MySQL does exactly what it was meant to do very well—and little else. Administration costs are relatively low, and MySQL provides adequate performance for all but the most demanding web applications.

MySQL AB is investing heavily in the MySQL database. MySQL 5.0 has added significant functionality, including stored procedures, views, and triggers. It is one of the simplest databases to secure from hacking because of the small attack surface it exposes. In addition, MySQL source code is available for anyone to see, which has led to a relatively secure and vulnerability-free code base. Vulnerabilities have been discovered in the MySQL source code, but security holes are discovered early in the life cycle of each release and are patched quickly.

MySQL AB also offers a second open-source database called MaxDB, which is designed specifically as a high-reliability backend for SAP systems.

Sybase

Sybase was acquired by SAP in 2010 to help SAP compete with Oracle. Sybase produces several databases, including the following:

- The flagship Sybase Adaptive Server Enterprise, database, designed for enterprise databases
- Sybase Adaptive Server Anywhere, designed as a lighter-weight database

Sybase originally partnered with Microsoft to develop the early versions of its database system, which was referred to at the time as *Sybase SQL Server* on Unix and *Microsoft SQL Server* on Windows. As of version 4.9, Microsoft and Sybase split the code line and went their separate ways.

Sybase has expanded beyond databases as well. The company offers various developer tools and a web application server and currently is focused on the delivery of data to mobile devices. Although the company has lost significant market share to the competition in the database market, it continues to maintain a presence in many places, and its databases will continue to exist for a long time.

Microsoft

Microsoft SQL Server is one of the most popular databases owing to its low price tag and its simplistic administration model, as well as the sheer momentum of Microsoft. Microsoft SQL Server comes in several flavors:

- Microsoft SQL Server 7.0 is an older version of the product with a few legacy installations still in existence.

- Microsoft SQL Server 2000 (a.k.a. SQL Server 8.0) was Microsoft's main database version for five years. As such, it is heavily entrenched in a large number of enterprises.

- Microsoft SQL Server 2005 provided a rich new set of security features among other functionality over its predecessor.

- Microsoft SQL Server 2008 is the latest in Microsoft's line and continues to have a wide adoption through its strong integration with other Microsoft products.

- The *Microsoft Database Engine* (MSDE) is a free version of SQL Server providing a backend for independent software vendors (ISVs) to embed databases in their applications. Because MSDE is free, it is embedded in a large number of applications and is very common. With the delivery of SQL Server 2005, MSDE has been renamed to *SQL Server 2005 Express Edition*.

Microsoft SQL Server is often referred to as *SQL, SQL Server, MSSQL,* and even *MS SQL Server*. Although it's best to stick to the proper nomenclature to avoid confusion, it's important that you also understand the common, although incorrect, lingo.

Because Microsoft SQL Server is so easy to install and administer, it is often used by people with relatively little knowledge about securing it properly. This can lead to problems, not because Microsoft SQL Server is insecure, but because many people using it haven't taken even the most basic steps to protect it.

Database Components

Each database vendor has a slightly different implementation of the various database components. However, the theories and principles apply to all the different platforms fairly universally. We will cover enough of these basics to give you a bird's eye view. From there, you should have enough background to follow a technical guide on a specific database platform. Following are the major pieces of the database that you will need to understand as an auditor.

Program Files

A database is implemented as a software system, and as such, it comprises a core set of operating system files. These files include the executable files that will run the database management system. It also may contain other nonexecutable program files such as help files, source and include files, sample files, and installation files.

These files should be protected, because the database relies on their integrity. They should be guarded from any form of modification—particularly any executable files. Access controls should be as restrictive as possible on the directory that holds these files. Ideally, only database administrators should have access to this directory.

Configuration Values

Databases rely heavily on configuration settings to determine how the system operates. Protecting these settings is important, because if the configuration can be manipulated, security can be subverted.

Configuration values reside in a variety of places, including the following:

- In operating system text files
- In the data files
- On Windows, stored in the registry
- In environment variables

Configuration values are used for a wide range of settings, such as these:

- Setting the type of authentication or trust model
- Setting which groups are database administrators
- Determining password management features
- Determining the encryption mechanism used by the database

Verifying the integrity of configuration values is a critical component of any audit.

Data Files

Databases need to store the data they hold in physical operating system files that typically comprise a series of files. The format of the files is typically proprietary, and the data files contain information such as the following:

- Data being stored
- Pointers from one field to the next field or from one row to the next row
- Index data, including pointers from the index to the physical data

 NOTE Indexes contain a subset of the data to which they point. This means that if an attacker can access the index, he or she may not need access to the physical data itself. Ensure that access to any index is protected to the same degree as the data itself.

Usually, the database dictionary is stored in these data files, so any access to these files can be used to circumvent controls built into the database.

Client/Network Libraries

An important component of any database system is the client. Typically, the client is located on a remote system from the database. The client also can connect from the local system, which is frequently the case with batch processes.

In order for a client to connect to the database, a client library or driver is required on the client's machine. This usually consists of a set of executables such as DLLs and shared objects, as well as an API that the client can use to connect to the database. The client libraries are hard to protect because they usually exist on remote systems where access controls are much more difficult to maintain. However, it is very important to maintain the integrity of the client drivers in locations from where administrators or even regular users will be connecting.

One weak point in the security model is the integrity of the client libraries. If the client drivers can be manipulated, credentials can be stolen fairly easily. Client drivers can be trojaned, or even something as simple as a keyboard logger on the client system can lead to a compromise of the database.

Communication over the network also requires network drivers on the database. These drivers are another point of focus for the auditor, because they are the avenue that the attacker will use to access the database.

Backup/Restore System

Backups are a very important piece of every database platform. Failure in some component of the database is not a question of *if* but *when*. Whether the problem is a hardware or a software failure, having a backup is critical to restoring the system. Backups contain a copy of the database. The backup can be to a separate file, to a tape, or to another storage facility.

Data is commonly stolen from, lost, or leaked through the backup facility. Backups often are secured by encrypting the data as they are written to a file or by encrypting the entire file after it is written. Storing the encryption key then becomes important to securing the backup properly. Just as important is ensuring that you have properly backed up the encryption keys along with the data so that the backup can be restored properly. If you can't restore the files, the backup becomes worthless. Backups that cannot be restored result in a loss of utility.

SQL Statements

Structured Query Language (SQL) is used to access data in a relational database. Technically, SQL should be pronounced as three separate letters "S-Q-L," but the pronunciation "sequel" has become so commonplace it is also accepted as correct. SQL is a set-based language, meaning that it works on a set of data at a time. It is not a procedural language, meaning that it does not have any procedural components such as while loops, if statements, for loops, and so on. Most database platforms do have extensions to SQL to provide procedural components. For instance, Oracle has PL/SQL, and Sybase and Microsoft SQL Server have Transact-SQL.

SQL statements are used to pull data from the database. SQL is built around four core statements:

- **SELECT**   View a subset of data from a table
- **INSERT**   Add new data to a table
- **UPDATE**   Modify existing data in a table
- **DELETE**   Remove a subset of data from a table

The statement you will need to understand best is `SELECT`. The basic syntax of the `SELECT` statement is

```
SELECT <COLUMN LIST> FROM <TABLE NAME> WHERE <CONDITION>
```

In this statement, `<COLUMN LIST>` is a comma-separated list of column names that will be displayed. As a shortcut, you can use an asterisk to display all columns in the output. `<TABLE NAME>` is replaced with the name of the table to be displayed. `<CONDITION>` and the word `WHERE` are optional. If you do not indicate a `WHERE` clause, all rows in the table are returned. Using the `WHERE` clause, you can `SELECT` only the rows you want to include.

An example of selecting the first and last names of all employees who earn more than $20,000 is shown here:

```
SELECT FIRST_NAME, LAST_NAME FROM EMPLOYEES WHERE SALARY > 20000
```

`SELECT` statements can get much more complex than this. Your audit typically does not need to go much deeper than this, however.

Database Objects

A database comprises a variety of objects, each with a unique task or purpose. Understanding each object is not necessary, but you should have a grasp of the common object types.

Following are the most common types of database objects. Each database platform also has many proprietary object types, such as table spaces, schemas, rules, sequences, and synonyms. You should review the specific documentation for your database platform for more details.

- **Table** Stores rows of data in one or more columns.
- **View** A `SELECT` statement on top of a table or another view that creates a virtual table. Views can change the number or order of columns, can call functions, and can manipulate data in a variety of ways.
- **Stored procedure/function** Procedural code that can be called to execute complex functionality within the database. Functions return values. Procedures do not return values. Stored procedures are very efficient for data access.
- **Trigger** Procedural code that is called when a table is modified. Can be used to perform any actions, including modifications to other tables, when data are changed.
- **Index** Mechanism to provide fast lookup of data. Indexes are complex objects, and their proper tuning is critical to database performance.

Data Dictionary

The database stores metadata about itself, called the *data dictionary* or sometimes the *system tables*. The metadata tells the database about its own configuration, setup, and objects. Note that the metadata does not say anything about the content of the information in the database, only about the format of the database. The format of the data dictionary is static. The data dictionary does contain metadata about its own structure, but its format is not something that can be modified easily.

The metadata in the data dictionary is designed to be manipulated. Rarely is the data dictionary manipulated directly. Instead, special stored procedures with complex validation logic are used to manipulate the system tables. Direct access to the system tables is dangerous, because even a small misstep could corrupt the data dictionary, leading to serious database problems.

The data dictionary defines the rest of the database, specifying objects such as users, groups, and permissions. The data dictionary defines the structure of the database, including specifying where physical files are stored on disk, the names of tables, column types and lengths, and the code for stored procedure, trigger, and views.

Test Steps for Auditing Databases

Before you conduct the audit, you will need a few basic tools. You should have a checklist of the items you need to verify. You can create your own checklist, you can find checklists on the Internet, or you can even use the basic checklist we provide here.

Start off by meeting with and discussing the audit with the database administrator (DBA). Clearly, the DBA is not going to be excited about the idea of being audited. Therefore, do your best to approach the DBA in as friendly a way as possible. Make sure that the DBA understands that you are there to help, not hinder, his or her work.

Databases are very often 24/7 systems, meaning they are not allowed any downtime. You'll encounter pushback on anything you want to do that could, with even the remotest possibility, affect database availability. The first time you as the auditor bring down the database, your job becomes infinitely more difficult.

Be ready to optimize the time you will be accessing the system. Ensure that any account you are given on the system runs with only the permissions you need. Immediately after you are completed with any work, have the DBA lock the account. Don't delete the account—simply lock it until you are officially done with the audit. Then, if you do need to gather more information, the DBA can simply unlock the account rather than re-create it.

Perform as much work offline as possible. Ideally, you want to download the system tables, password hashes, files permissions, and all other information onto a local source. Then you can disconnect from the database and perform your audit steps offline with no risk of affecting the database. For instance, you want to ensure that you never do password strength testing on the database; the password hashes can be downloaded, and password strength testing can be done offline.

By you showing the DBA this level of caution with the database, he or she will, hopefully, give you the professional courtesy of letting you do your job. Being at odds with the DBA can result in an audit that provides little value to the organization.

Now that you are equipped with some background on databases, we need a plan for performing an audit. Many of the steps covered here are almost identical to steps you would perform on an operating system or network audit, but they need to be placed in the context of the database. Some steps are unique to the database.

Setup and General Controls

1. Obtain the database version and compare with your corporate policy requirements. Verify that the database is running a database software version the vendor continues to support.

Policies were written and approved to make an environment more secure, easily manageable, and auditable. Double-check basic configuration information to ensure that the database is in compliance with the organization's policy. Older databases increase the difficulty in managing the environment and increase the scope of administrator responsibilities as he or she attempts to maintain control over disparate database versions. Maintaining standard builds and patch levels greatly simplifies the process of managing the databases. In addition, many legacy databases run versions of database software that are no longer supported by the database vendor. This becomes a problem when a security vulnerability is released, and the database cannot be patched because no patches for the older versions are available from the vendor.

How

Through conversations with the DBA and review of your company's IT standards and policies, determine what database versions and platforms are recommended and supported by your company. Verify with the database vendor which versions and platforms are supported and whether patches for new security issues will be provided. Inventory the versions of the database that are run, and check for any databases that fall under the unsupported versions. Ideally, you want to keep the databases upgraded to supported versions.

2. Verify that policies and procedures are in place to identify when a patch is available and to apply the patch. Ensure that all approved patches are installed per your database management policy.

Most database vendors have regularly scheduled patch releases. You must be prepared for the scheduled releases so that you can plan appropriately for testing and installation of the patches. If all the database patches are not installed, widely known security vulnerabilities could exist on the database.

How

Interview the DBA to determine who reviews advisories from vendors, what steps are taken to prepare for the patches, and how long the patches are tested before being applied to the production databases. Ask to review notes from the previous patching cycle.

Obtain as much information as possible about the latest patches, and determine the scope of the vulnerabilities addressed by the patches. Compare the available patches with the patches applied to the database. Talk with the DBA about steps taken to mitigate potential risk if the patches are not applied in a timely manner. Many DBAs attempt to mitigate the need to patch by removing components of the system they determine to have vulnerabilities. Although this is a great practice because it does reduce the security risk, it should not be accepted as a long-term replacement for patching.

Databases pose an interesting dilemma with regard to patching for most organizations. Many databases run on a 24/7 schedule, so they have no allowance for downtime. This means that no time is available to bring down the database to apply the patches.

The other major complication for database patching is that testing new patches is typically a 3- to 6-month process. Databases typically are so critical that patches cannot be installed without thorough testing. Given a quarterly patch cycle, the DBAs full-time job easily could become testing and applying new patches, and this likely will become a full-time job for DBAs moving forward, just as today teams of people are dedicated to patching our Windows and Unix systems.

One solution to the downtime problem has been the use of *clustering*. In a clustered environment, a single node in the cluster can be taken offline, patched, and brought back online. This can work, but it introduces complexity to the process. Regardless of the solution, patches related to control weaknesses must be understood and the control weaknesses must be appropriately dealt with to protect the database.

3. Determine whether a standard build is available for new database systems and whether that baseline has adequate security settings.

One of the best ways to propagate security throughout an environment is to ensure that new systems are built correctly before moving into testing or production.

How

Through interviews with the system administrator, determine the methodology used for building and deploying new systems. If a standard build is used, consider auditing a newly created system using the steps in this chapter.

NOTE Consider discussing an approval process for new standard builds in which an auditor would look over the changes and perform a full audit of new images. This is a great way for the audit team to create a working relationship with the database management team.

Operating System Security

Other sections of this book are dedicated to operating system security, so we'll discuss it only briefly here. Start with the premise that a database not secured can be used to break into the operating system. Conversely, an unsecured operating system can be used to break into the database. Locking down one but not the other fails to provide proper security to either. Still, the database should get the most focus on because the database is the most "valuable" target in your network.

NOTE Refer to Chapters 6 and 7 for detailed steps on auditing the security of the operating system on which the database resides.

4. Ensure that access to the operating system is properly restricted.

The best situation is to have the operating system dedicated to the database only. No users other than DBAs should have access to connect to the operating system from a Secure Shell (SSH), File Transfer Protocol (FTP), or any other method outside the application. For most applications, users should not be able to update the database directly (that is, outside of the application). All updates to Oracle data should usually be performed via the application. Direct update of the data outside of the application could corrupt the database, and users usually have to reason to update data outside of the application. This can be accomplished by having a generic database ID for the application, which would perform updates to the database on behalf of the user (based on the user's authority within the application).

How

Verify with the administrator that all access to the operating system is restricted to DBAs only. Verify that any shell access occurs over a secure protocol, preferably SSH. Check for any accounts on the operating system that should be removed.

5. Ensure that permissions on the directory in which the database is installed, and the database files themselves, are properly restricted.

Inappropriate access and updates to the database's underlying database files can result in massive disruption of the database. For example, any direct alteration via the operating system of the data files containing the actual database data will corrupt the database. Also, in Oracle, redo log files allow for recovery of uncommitted data in the event of a database crash and control files are used by the database to do such things as locate the last redo log and locate the data files. Any direct updates of these files through the operating system could damage database functionality or prevent the database from being brought up. Each DBMS has its own specific startup, logging, and configuration files, and it is critical that these files be protected to ensure the ongoing availability and integrity of the database.

How

Verify that permissions on the directory to which the database is installed are as restrictive as possible and owned by the appropriate DBA account. Unfortunately, some database functionality was written without security in mind, and we can break database functionality by making file permissions too restrictive.

In Windows, similar measures should be taken. File permissions on the directory in which the database is installed should be limited to the permissions of the account the database runs under. Ensure that the "Everyone" or "Anonymous" user does not have any permissions on database files. In addition, make sure that all drives being used to store database files use NTFS.

In an ideal situation, even the DBA would not need permissions on the underlying operating system files. However, given the need for the DBA to work with database files and backups, patch the database, and accomplish other chores, the DBA will need some access to the operating system files. Privileged users who do not need access to the operating system should not been granted permissions to it.

Retrieve a list of file permissions on all database files and the directories in which they reside, either by connecting to the operating system and pulling this information yourself or by obtaining the information from the administrator. Review the listing to find any excessive privileges. On Unix, check that permissions are set to be no more permissive than 770. If you revoke all permissions for "Everyone," many programs may break, so be careful. Setting tight security is a good goal, but you may have to set exceptions to this policy, and be sure to document the reasons for exceptions. For Windows, make sure that permissions are not given to "Everyone." The best practice is to grant permissions to the DBAs who require access only.

6. Ensure that permissions on the registry keys used by the database are properly restricted.

For database platforms running on Windows, you must properly secure the registry keys being used by the database. The registry keys are used to store configuration values that are important to the secure functioning of the database. Make sure that only the account under which the database runs has permission to edit, create, delete, or even view these registry keys.

How

Review the security permissions through the Registry Editor, through a command-line utility such as GetDACL, or by obtaining the information from the administrator. After retrieving a complete list of the permissions, review it to ensure that no excessive permissions exist.

Account and Permissions Management

Review Database Accounts

Account management is difficult at any level just because you have to provision and remove users in a timely manner. Add the complexity of a database, and account creation, management, authentication, authorization, and auditing can be difficult at best. The challenge of managing accounts coupled with the inherent risk of the sensitive data typically stored in a database makes this section of the audit particularly important.

7. Review and evaluate procedures for creating user accounts and ensuring that accounts are created only with a legitimate business need. Also review and evaluate processes for ensuring that user accounts are removed or disabled in a timely fashion in the event of termination or job change.

Effective controls should exist for providing and removing access to the database, limiting unnecessary access to database resources.

How

Interview the database administrator, and review account-creation procedures. This process should include some form of verification that the user has a legitimate need for access. Ensure that access to DBA-level accounts and privileges are minimized.

Review a sample of accounts and evidence that accounts are approved properly prior to being created. Alternatively, take a sample of accounts and validate their legitimacy by investigating and understanding the job function of the account owners. Ensure that each user on the system has his or her own user account. No guest or group accounts should exist. If a large number of database accounts exists, question the need. Application end users should generally be accessing the database through the application and not by direct database access.

Also review the process for removing accounts when access is no longer needed. This process could include a mechanism by which user accounts are removed on terminations and job changes. The process could include a periodic review and validation of active accounts by the system administrator and/or other knowledgeable managers. Obtain a sample of accounts, and verify that they are owned by active employees and that those employees' job positions have not changed since the account's creation.

Password Strength and Management Features

Many database platforms maintain their own authentication settings. Ensure that passwords and the authentication mechanism do not become the weak link in the chain.

Other database platforms integrate with the operating system or some other security subsystem to provide authentication. For instance, DB2 Universal DataBase (UDB) does not maintain its own usernames and passwords, instead using the operating system or Resource Access Control Facility (RACF) for authentication. Microsoft SQL Server in Windows mode uses Windows authentication. This does not mean that users are not maintained in the database. Usernames continue to be maintained in the database because there needs to be a mapping of the users to groups as well as permissions and other database settings. However, the authentication happens at the operating system level instead of in the database.

Using integrated operating security for any of the database platforms has many pros and cons. Pros include the following:

- Operating system authentication typically is more robust than database authentication.
- Operating system authentication typically includes more password management features.
- Password management features are more likely to be implemented already at the operating system level.

Cons include the following:

- Authentication is out of the DBA's hands.
- A user with an operating system account can access the operating system of the database if it is not configured properly.

8. Check for default usernames and passwords.

The first basic item to audit for is default usernames and passwords. This continues to be an issue for databases. At least five database worms have been based on propagating through databases using default usernames and passwords. Table 9-1 classifies these default usernames and passwords into a few categories. Literally thousands of these default passwords can be found on various security websites.

How

Verify that all default usernames and passwords have been removed or locked, or that the passwords have been changed. Free and commercial utilities and tools are available to verify this.

9. Check for easily guessed passwords.

Users often choose passwords that can be easily guessed by automated programs or clever hackers. The most common passwords used to be *password* and *secret*. People are more clever these days and select more secure passwords, but it is still important to ensure that passwords cannot be found in a dictionary or easily guessed.

How

Run a password strength test on password hashes to determine whether any passwords are easily guessed. If you detect passwords that are found in a dictionary or can be guessed, talk with the DBA about user awareness practices and about implementing password strength-checking practices. Refer to step 10 for system configuration settings that can help strengthen passwords.

Category	Description
Default database password	Created in a standard database install. Can depend on the installed components of the database. Most of the latest versions of databases have eliminated default database passwords, but default passwords continue to be a serious concern in older versions of database software.
Sample or example passwords	Many samples, examples, and demonstrations of new or existing features are shown in SQL scripts that include creation of a test or sample account.
Default application password	When you install third-party products on top of a database, the products often install and run using a default username and password to access the database. These are known to hackers and serve as a common access route.
User-defined default password	When a new account is created, the password is often set to an initial value and then reset on first use. Problems arise when an account is created but never accessed. Ensure that passwords set on new accounts are random, strong passwords.

Table 9-1 Default Passwords

10. Check that password management capabilities are enabled.

Many of the database platforms provide support for rich password management features. Oracle leads this area by including capabilities for the following features:

- Password strength validation functions
- Password expiration
- Password reuse limits
- Password expiration grace time
- Password lockout
- Password lockout reset

If you do not configure these settings, they will not provide any additional security. By default, these features are not enabled.

How

Select the configuration values from the database. Ensure that each password management feature is enabled and configured for an appropriate value for the environment and in accordance with your company's policies. You will need to review the documentation for the database platform to determine the exact password management features available and the commands required to view them.

Review Database Privileges

Database privileges are slightly different from operating system permissions. Privileges are managed using GRANT and REVOKE statements. For instance, the following SQL statement gives USER1 the permission to SELECT from the SALARY table:

```
GRANT SELECT ON SALARY TO USER1
```

The REVOKE statement is used to remove permissions that have been granted:

```
REVOKE SELECT ON SALARY FROM USER1
```

The GRANT statement can be used selectively to give permissions, such as SELECT, UPDATE, DELETE, or EXECUTE. This allows you to grant access to read the data in the table but limit the ability to modify the table. GRANT and REVOKE also can be used more selectively on a column-by-column basis.

11. Verify that database permissions are granted or revoked appropriately for the required level of authorization.

If database permissions are not restricted properly, inappropriate access to critical data may occur. Database permissions also should be used to restrict people from using subsystems in the database that may be used to circumvent security. Security best practices dictate that permissions should be granted on a need-only basis. If permission is not specifically needed by an account, it should not be granted.

How

Talk with the database administrator to determine which user accounts are required to have access to what data. Some administrators may need access, some accounts may be used by a web application to access the data, and some accounts may be used by batch jobs. Accounts that do not require permissions or access should be locked, disabled, or even removed.

12. Review database permissions granted to individuals instead of groups or roles.

Database best practices dictate that you should attempt to grant permissions to roles or groups, and those permissions, in turn, should be granted to individuals within those roles or groups. Use of roles or groups to allocate permissions reduces the chance of making administrative mistakes and allows for easier maintenance of security controls. When new permissions need to be granted, they can be granted to a single group rather than to multiple accounts. In addition, when a user changes jobs, it is straightforward to revoke the role or group and grant new individuals access within the role or group.

How

Select the list of permissions from the database dictionary. Review for any permissions granted to an account or user. Check that privileges are granted to roles or groups. Individual users can then be granted permissions by assigning them to roles or groups as needed.

You also will need to download the list of roles/groups and users/accounts to determine which are allowed to be granted. The lists of users and groups are stored in the data dictionary.

13. Ensure that database permissions are not implicitly granted incorrectly.

Database permissions can flow from many sources. For instance, ownership of an object grants implicit full control over that object in a database. Privileges such as SELECT ANY TABLE allow access to all data and can lead to unauthorized access to data. If you do not have a complete understanding of how database permissions are implicitly granted, permissions may be granted in a way that was not intended.

How

Review the specifics of the permission model for the database platform and verify that permissions are inherited appropriately. Also review system privileges that allow access to data, such as SELECT ANY TABLE or granting a privileged role to a user. Document permissions that are implicitly as well as explicitly granted to ensure that permissions are not allowed when they are not appropriate.

14. Review dynamic SQL executed in stored procedures.

Access to an object also can be gained by running stored procedures or functions. On Microsoft SQL Server, when executing code objects, access to any other objects owned by the stored procedure owner is allowed. On Oracle, running a stored procedure allows you to access objects as the stored procedure owner. This can be dangerous if stored procedures are not constructed properly and can be manipulated.

How

With the DBA's assistance, review stored procedures, specifically looking for issues such as SQL injection or any form of dynamic SQL. Restrict use of dynamic SQL in procedures that run with elevated privileges. In addition, ensure that any and all access to stored procedures that run under elevated privileges are being logged.

In a large data warehouse environment, the auditor should work with the DBA and application owner to identify a sampling of critical paths and then look for dynamic SQL in stored procedures.

15. Ensure that row-level access to table data is properly implemented.

Relational databases are designed to grant permissions on a table or column. Unfortunately, they are not well designed to restrict access to a subset of rows in a table. When you grant a user SELECT privileges on a table, the user will be able to read every row in the table.

Several technologies can be used to help manage this problem. For instance, Oracle offers virtual private databases (VPDs) that you can use to limit access to specific rows. You also can use views programmatically to restrict rows returned based on the user's context. A common and practical approach is to use stored procedures to access tables. Using this strategy, the DBA does not need to grant permissions on the table, preventing the user from attempting to circumvent the stored procedure.

How

This will likely be a joint effort between the DBA and application owner, particularly in larger environments. Discuss with the appropriate administrators the method of row-level access controls in the database. Ensure that a user cannot access data in a table without proper authorization if the user circumvents the application or stored procedure providing access. Access the database through a user's account to verify that the "effective" ability of the user is as intended.

16. Revoke PUBLIC permissions where not needed.

Many of the built-in stored procedures and functions in a database are granted to the PUBLIC group by default. Each database has a slightly different implementation of a PUBLIC group—generically, it represents everyone in the database. This means that permissions granted to PUBLIC apply to everyone.

This has led to many security issues in databases. Many of the built-in procedures may not appear dangerous and have no practical use for ordinary users. Security best practices dictate that you should restrict all access unless explicitly needed. If a procedure contains functionality that is not needed, it should not be granted to any users. This is especially important for permissions granted to PUBLIC.

Remember that if you revoke permissions that are needed, you may end up breaking necessary functionality. Blindly revoking all PUBLIC permissions is a recipe for disaster.

How

Start by gathering a list of all permissions, highlighting those granted to PUBLIC. Discuss with the DBA which procedures and features of the database are being used or may be used in the future. Then determine how much risk would be introduced by revoking permissions from objects that are clearly not needed. If everyone agrees to have the permissions revoked, it makes sense to revoke them. Always make a backup and provide an undo script that can be used to roll back any changes if you later determine that you need those permissions or something unexpectedly breaks.

Data Encryption

Data encryption is applied to three distinct areas, or states. *Data in motion* describes data in transit across the network and is often encrypted using protocols such as Secure Sockets Layer (SSL). *Data at rest* describes data resident on storage, such as inside a database, and can be encrypted with a number of algorithms such as the Advanced Encryption Standard (AES). *Data in use* describes data processing in applications.

17. Verify that network encryption is implemented.

Network encryption serves two main purposes: to protect authentication credentials as they move across the network and to protect the actual data in the database as it moves over the network. The network is not a secure environment—IP addresses can be spoofed, and network traffic can be redirected and sniffed. It is critical that network traffic be encrypted not just over the external network but also on your intranet.

How

Verify that the network and client drivers have been configured to support encrypting network traffic using protocols such as SSL. Verify settings at both the client and the database. In some cases, you may need to sample the traffic to demonstrate the encryption.

18. Verify that encryption of data at rest is implemented where appropriate.

Encryption of data at rest involves encrypting data as it is stored in the database. Arguably, encryption of data at rest is more important than other forms of encryption, because the lifetime of data on disk or in the database is much longer than the lifetime of data on the network. If you look at where data is most likely to be stolen, you'll see that it is stolen directly from the database while at rest and not while traversing the network.

How

Verify that data that should be encrypted is encrypted properly. Also review the location where the encryption keys are stored, because the strength of encryption relies on the strength of protection of the encryption keys. If the encryption keys are stored with the encrypted data, an attacker can subvert the security simply by extracting the encryption keys.

Check the disaster recovery plan to ensure that encryption key management is included as a component. A mistake you do not want your DBA to make is to implement encryption features but fail to include key management in the backup procedures. Failing to back up encryption keys properly results in the inability to recover a database backup.

Monitoring and Management

Regulations require that access to sensitive data be properly monitored. Regulations such as PCI, HIPAA, and Sarbanes-Oxley have had a significant and positive impact on companies that store sensitive data.

19. Verify the appropriate use of database auditing and activity monitoring.

Ultimately, regardless of whether an outside organization has mandated database monitoring, if the stored data is of significant business value, the database should probably have appropriate monitoring in place to identify malicious attacks and inappropriate use of data.

A number of methods can be used to monitor activity:

- Enabling native auditing in the database

- Monitoring network traffic of audit database activity

- Reviewing transaction logs to build an audit trail from the database

Each method has particular strengths and weaknesses. For instance, native auditing is relatively inexpensive, because it is typically included with the database. Other solutions are more expensive but meet requirements or provide capabilities, such as context intelligence whereby an attack can be identified, which native auditing fails to provide.

How

Auditing can take many forms:

- **Access and authentication auditing** Determine who accessed which systems, when, and how.

- **User and administrator auditing** Determine what activities were performed in the database by both users and administrators.

- **Suspicious activity auditing** Identify and flag any suspicious, unusual, or abnormal access to sensitive data or critical systems.

- **Vulnerability and threat auditing** Detect vulnerabilities in the database, and then monitor for users attempting to exploit them.

- **Change auditing** Establish a baseline policy for database, configuration, schema, users, privileges, and structure, and then find and track deviations from that baseline.

Review the implemented methods of monitoring with the DBA and discuss the sensitivity of the data. Activity monitoring should align with the business value of the information stored in the database and with the policies and requirements of the organization.

Review a list of sensitive data in the database, and verify that auditing is properly enabled for sensitive data. Consider reviewing a list of sensitive transactions for a specific period of time to demonstrate the ability of the monitoring system to audit such events.

20. Evaluate how capacity is managed for the database environment to support existing and anticipated business requirements.

Technical and business requirements for databases can change quickly and frequently, driven by changes in infrastructure, business relationships, customer needs, and regulatory requirements. Inadequate database infrastructure places the business at risk of losing important data and may impede critical business functions.

How

Verify that capacity requirements have been documented and agreed to with customers. Review processes for monitoring capacity usage, noting when it exceeds defined thresholds. Requirements may be evaluated or captured in part by the same team responsible for the storage environment. Evaluate processes for responding and taking action when capacity usage exceeds established thresholds. Discuss the methods used to determine present database requirements and anticipated growth. Review growth plans with the administrator to verify that the hardware can meet the performance requirements, capacity requirements, and feature requirements to support infrastructure and business growth.

21. Evaluate how performance is managed and monitored for the database environment to support existing and anticipated business requirements.

Database performance is driven by several factors, including the physical storage media, communication protocols, network, data size, CPU, memory, storage architecture, encryption strategies, and a host of other factors. Inadequate database infrastructure places the business at risk of losing important data and may impede critical business functions that need either more storage or better performance.

How

Regular periodic performance reviews of the processor, memory, and IO/network bandwidth loads on the database architecture should be performed to identify growing stresses on the architecture. Verify that performance requirements have been documented and agreed to with customers. Review processes for monitoring performance and noting when performance falls below defined thresholds. Evaluate processes in place for responding and taking action when performance falls below established thresholds. Discuss the methods used to determine present performance requirements and anticipated changes.

NOTE Reviewing capacity management and performance planning are critical steps in this audit. Ensure that the administrator has a capacity management plan in place and verify that performance needs are appropriate for the organization.

Tools and Technology

Although you can perform most of your audit using manual methods, you'll often find it helpful to use a set of tools to perform repetitive or technical chores. Tools allow you to spend more time working on results instead of wrestling with the technical details. Auditing and monitoring tools can provide the raw materials that you need to analyze and interpret. This is the added value that a human auditor brings when using one of these tools.

Auditing Tools

Tools are useful for looking for vulnerabilities and patches. Two perspectives on scanning a database for vulnerabilities and patches are common: to look for and document as many vulnerabilities as possible, and to deemphasize vulnerabilities and instead focus on what patches you have installed. At the end of the day, you need to know what patches you haven't applied and you need to identify critical vulnerabilities and misconfigurations.

It's also important that you understand that network and operating system auditing tools fail miserably at helping with database audits. Why is this? Databases are complex beasts. They have their own access-control systems, their own user accounts and passwords, their own auditing subsystems, and even their own network protocols. Generic scanners simply do not have the expertise to provide more than a cursory look at the database.

A number of tools, such as the following, are specialized to help the auditor run audits on a database:

Database Auditing Tool	Website
AppDetective by Application Security, Inc.	www.appsecinc.com
NGSAuditor and NGSSquirrel by NGS Software, Ltd.	www.ngssoftware.com/home.aspx

Monitoring Tools

Many tools are designed to assist you with database activity monitoring. As an auditor, you have influence over the use of these tools to record and detect unauthorized or malicious access to sensitive data. You will need to determine what regulations apply to the database and then translate them into specific items that can be implemented as native auditing or more in-depth activity monitoring.

Database monitoring solutions include approaches that monitor the database passively by watching the network or by using a client installed on the host. Some monitoring solutions use a hybrid approach combining these two methods. IBM's hybrid solution, for example, maintains an impressive set of features and reports but requires an agent to work in conjunction with the Audit Vault server in a best practices setup. Although IBM states that the does not significantly harm database performance, many DBAs are wary of auditing databases using a client and would rather use an appliance that watches traffic over the network. Recognizing this, IBM acquired Gardium in late 2009. The product uses a network appliance that watches database traffic transparently, monitoring transactions, security events, and privileged access, without placing a client on the database host.

Several tools provide technology for monitoring activity in the database:

Monitoring Tool	Website
DbProtect from Application Security, Inc.	www.appsecinc.com/products/dbprotect
Guardium	www.guardium.com
AuditDB from Lumigent	www.lumigent.com/solutions/database-auditdb.html
SecureSphere from Imperva	www.imperva.com/products/products.html

Auditors also need to understand the tools available to meet database encryption requirements. There are several vendors that provide solutions in this area. The most innovative and impressive solution is probably from Vormetric because of their deployment and management model. Vormetric deploys without any application coding or knowledge, and can simultaneously manage database and file encryption permissions integrated with your LDAP, such as the following:

Data Encryption Tool	Website
Vormetric	www.vormetric.com
DbEncrypt from Application Security, Inc.	www.appsecinc.com/products/index.shtml
Defiance Security Suite from Protegrity	www.protegrity.com/DefianceSecuritySuite
Encryptionizer from NetLib	www.netlib.com
DataSecure from SafeNet	www.safenet-inc.com/Products/Data_Protection/Data_Encryption_and_Control/DataSecure.aspx

Knowledge Base

Database security information is not nearly as vast as that for network or operating system security. You can find enough detail to get the job done effectively, however.

Following is a list of books that can help you understand database security in databases. If you do need to run an audit, you can review one of the books that applies to your specific database platform.

- *Oracle Security Handbook,* by Marlene L. Theriault and Aaron C. Newman
- *Oracle Security Step-by-Step,* by Pete Finnigan
- *The Database Hacker's Handbook,* by David Litchfield, Chris Anley, Bill Grindlay, and John Heasman

- *Implementing Database Security and Auditing*, by Ron Ben Natan
- *SQL Server Security*, by Chip Andrews, David Litchfield, Chris Anley, and Bill Grindlay
- *SQL Server Security Distilled*, by Morris Lewis
- *SQL Server Security: What DBAs Need to Know*, by K. Brian Kelley
- *Oracle Privacy Security Auditing*, by Arup Nanda and Donald Burleson
- *Effective Oracle Database 10g Security by Design*, by David Knox
- *Special Ops: Host and Network Security for Microsoft, UNIX, and Oracle*, by Erik Birkholz
- *MySQL Security Handbook*, by John Stephens and Chad Russell
- *Cryptography in the Database: The Last Line of Defense*, by Kevin Keenan
- *Database Security*, by Maria Grazia Fugini, Silvana Castano, and Giancarlo Martella
- *Database Security and Auditing: Protecting Data Integrity and Accessibility*, by Sam Afyouni

Many online technical guides are also available. These guides are often free, up-to-date, and can be accessed from anywhere. Of course, they are also typically incomplete and not nearly as comprehensive as the books just listed.

Resource	Website
Oracle Database Security Checklist, by Oracle Corporation	www.oracle.com/technology/deploy/security/database-security/pdf/twp_security_checklist_database.pdf
SANS Oracle Security Checklist	www.sans.org/score/oraclechecklist.php
Ten Steps to Securing SQL Server 2000	www.microsoft.com/sql/techinfo/administration/2000/security/securingsqlserver.asp
SQLSecurity.com Checklist	www.sqlsecurity.com
NIST Security Checklists	web.nvd.nist.gov/view/ncp/repository
DISA Checklists	iase.disa.mil/stigs/checklist/
ISACA Auditing Guidelines	www.isaca.org
Links to papers and presentations covering Oracle security	www.petefinnigan.com/orasec.htm
Oracle security website	www.oracle.com/technology/deploy/security/index.html

Most database vulnerabilities discovered and fixed can be credited to a relatively small subset of security researchers. Although some groups, including many of the database vendors, view this work as "malicious," security researchers have done the database security market a huge service, and to top it all off, they have done it free of charge. The database vendors themselves have gone as far as to threaten lawsuits and revoke partnership agreements, and they have been particularly vocal about telling customers about how security researchers are "evil." The silver lining is that these security researchers are watchdogs in the community, and many simple security vulnerabilities have been eliminated or at least reduced because of their work. Of course, the vendors have been dragged into securing and fixing their databases kicking and screaming the whole way.

The most prominent database security research teams include the following:

Research Team	Website
Argeniss Information Security	www.argeniss.com
Red-Database-Security	www.red-database-security.com
Application Security, Inc., Team SHATTER	www.appsecinc.com/aboutus/teamshatter/index.html
NGS Research	www.ngssoftware.com
Pentest Limited	www.pentest.co.uk
Pete Finnigan	www.petefinnigan.com
Integrigy	www.integrigy.com
Chip Andrews	www.sqlsecurity.com

These websites serve as the most definitive source of vulnerability information on databases. If you have a question about a particular vulnerability, search these locations, and you're likely to find an answer.

As always, never forget the most up-to-date source of database security—Google. Simply search on any term of interest such as "Oracle Exploits" or "Auditing MySQL." Google provides a great list of resources to explore to help you do your job.

Master Checklist

The following table summarizes the steps listed herein for auditing databases.

Auditing Databases

Checklist for Auditing Databases
☐   1. Obtain the database version and compare it against policy requirements. Verify that the database is running a version the vendor continues to support.
☐   2. Verify that policies and procedures are in place to identify when a patch is available and to apply the patch. Ensure that all approved patches are installed per your database management policy.
☐   3. Determine whether a standard build is available for new database systems and whether that baseline has adequate security settings.
☐   4. Ensure that access to the operating system is properly restricted.
☐   5. Ensure that permissions on the directory in which the database is installed, and the database files themselves, are properly restricted.
☐   6. Ensure that permissions on the registry keys used by the database are properly restricted.

Checklist for Auditing Databases

❑ 7. Review and evaluate procedures for creating user accounts and ensuring that accounts are created only when there's a legitimate business need. Also review and evaluate processes for ensuring that accounts are removed or disabled in a timely fashion in the event of termination or job change.

❑ 8. Check for default usernames and passwords.

❑ 9. Check for easily guessed passwords.

❑ 10. Check that password management capabilities are enabled.

❑ 11. Verify that database permissions are granted or revoked appropriately for the required level of authorization.

❑ 12. Review database permissions granted to individuals instead of groups or roles.

❑ 13. Ensure that database permissions are not implicitly granted incorrectly.

❑ 14. Review dynamic SQL executed in stored procedures.

❑ 15. Ensure that row-level access to table data is implemented properly.

❑ 16. Revoke PUBLIC permissions where not needed.

❑ 17. Verify that network encryption is implemented.

❑ 18. Verify that encryption of data at rest is implemented where appropriate.

❑ 19. Verify the appropriate use of database auditing and activity monitoring.

❑ 20. Evaluate how capacity is managed for the database environment to support existing and anticipated business requirements.

❑ 21. Evaluate how performance is managed and monitored for the database environment to support existing and anticipated business requirements.

Auditing Storage

This chapter covers auditing storage and begins with an overview of common storage technologies. The storage audit combines the concerns of the platform and the data. The platform has similar control requirements as those found in a server. The data has unique control requirements because of the necessity to keep appropriate controls in place for different classes of data. This chapter covers the following:

- A brief technical overview of storage
- How to audit the storage environment
- Tools and resources for enhancing your storage audits

Background

Storage extends the boundaries of the computing environment to allow data to be shared among users and applications. Storage platforms have grown so efficient that servers can use the storage environment, as opposed to the storage native to the server and other forms of direct attached storage, for their primary storage requirements. Figure 10-1 illustrates the consolidation of data management across the data center to fewer points, simplifying management overhead with the use of shared storage.

The storage environment continues to evolve, as traditionally disparate technologies and storage platforms are combined into a single unit that manages both file data and application data within the same unit. Protocol smart switches capable of moving data at blistering speeds have broken bottlenecks to consolidating environments, which in turn enables downsizing of the data center. Add to this mix cool technologies such as data deduplication, storage virtualization, and solid state drives, and it's easy to see why good storage administrators are in high demand.

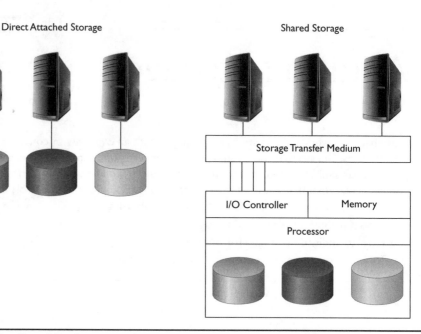

Figure 10-1   Consolidated storage architecture

Storage Auditing Essentials

To understand the material in this chapter you need to understand the basic components that make up the storage environment. Your role as an auditor and advisor will significantly improve if you understand the major technology trends that challenge traditional storage models.

Key Storage Components

Storage infrastructure includes components associated with the host, network, and storage that work in conjunction to provide storage facilities to users and applications.

Redundant Array of Independent Disks (RAID)

RAID storage techniques allow multiple drives to be combined to provide more storage options than would be provided by a single disk, including more capacity, redundancy, and performance. The storage controller manages multiple drives in one of several configurations classified as RAID *levels*.

RAID-0: Striping   Striping is a technique that offers the best performance of any RAID configuration. In a striped array, data is interleaved across all the drives in the array. If a file is saved to a RAID-0 array, the array distributes the file across the logical drive comprised of multiple physical disks. In Figure 10-2, the file would span across all six disks. From a performance perspective, RAID-0 is the most efficient because it can

Figure 10-2 RAID-0: Striping across six disks

write to all six disks at once. The drawback to RAID-0 is its lack of reliability. Any single disk failure results in the loss of all of that data stored in the array.

RAID-1: Mirroring RAID-1 is a disk array in which two disks are maintained as identical copies. The disks are mirrored to each other to protect against a drive failure. With mirroring, whatever you write to one drive gets written simultaneously to another. Thus, you always have an exact duplicate of your data on the other drive, as shown in Figure 10-3. RAID-1 is the most reliable of the RAID disk arrays because all data is mirrored after it is written; however, you can use only half of the storage space on the disks. Although this may seem inefficient, RAID-1 is the preferred choice for data that requires the highest possible reliability.

RAID-5: Reliability with Parity RAID-5 is a striped disk array, similar to RAID-0 in that data is distributed across the array; however, RAID-5 also includes additional data about the contents of the drives called *parity*. With parity, a mechanism maintains the integrity of the data stored in the array, so that if one disk in the array fails, the data can be reconstructed from the remaining disks. Parity is used to reconstruct data on a drive that has failed. RAID-5 is shown in Figure 10-4.

RAID-5 is a reliable storage solution. The RAID controller adds a parity byte to all binary information written to the array. These parity bytes add up either to an even or odd number. The controller can determine whether the information has been compromised in any way. If it has, it can replace the data automatically.

RAID-10: High Performance Striping with Mirrored Segments RAID-10 is implemented as a RAID-0 (striped array) whose segments are RAID-1 (mirrored) arrays. The result delivers high performance by striping RAID-1 segments and provides

Figure 10-3
RAID-1: Mirroring

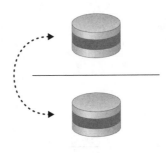

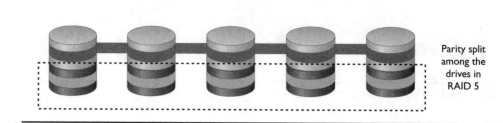

Figure 10-4 RAID-5: Reliability with parity

same fault tolerance as RAID-1. The number of drives makes RAID-10 very expensive, and the array comes with a high overhead. RAID-10 might be used to support a database server requiring high performance with fault tolerance. RAID-10 is shown in Figure 10-5.

Table 10-1 offers a summary of common RAID levels.

DAS, NAS, SAN, and CAS

Direct Attached Storage (DAS) is storage directly attached to the server by connectivity media such as parallel Small Computer System Interface (SCSI) cables. The media can either be internal drives or a dedicated RAID or JBOD (just a bunch of disks). This type of storage is the most limited and doesn't allow for the efficiencies that the other types of storage offer, because the storage is accessible only to the attached server.

A *Network Attached Storage (NAS)* device runs an operating system specifically designed to handle files and make them accessible to the network. NAS is also known as file storage and is often accessed by users and applications as mapped drives. Common protocols used in a NAS include Network File System (NFS) for UNIX operating systems and Common Internet File System (CIFS) for Microsoft operating systems. Common NAS vendors include EMC and NetApp.

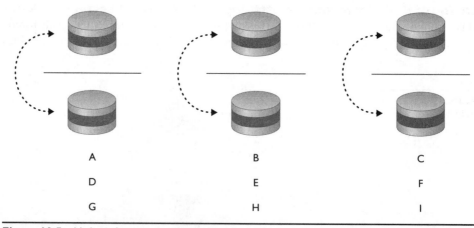

Figure 10-5 High performance striping with mirrored segments

Level	Techniques	Description	Pros/Cons
RAID-0	Disk striping	Data is distributed in stripes that are sent to each disk in the array.	Best performance; No fault tolerance.
RAID-1	Disk mirroring	Data on one drive is mirrored on another.	100% redundancy of data Slower performance and 50% loss of storage space
RAID-5	Block level striping with distributed parity	Data and parity are striped in blocks across all disks.	High Read data transaction rates Complex controller design
RAID-10	Disk striping and mirroring	Striped array's segments are RAID 1 arrays.	Offers redundancy along with high performance Common for high I/O databases

Table 10-1   Common RAID Levels

A *Storage Area Network (SAN)* is a scalable and flexible storage subsystem generally available to more than one host at the same time. The SAN operates using unique block-level communication protocols that require special hardware to work properly. The SAN comprises specialized devices such as host bus adapters (HBAs) in the host servers, switches that help route storage traffic, and disk storage subsystems that understand how to manage the special protocols required for SAN storage. Common protocols used in a SAN include SCSI and Fibre Channel (FC).

Table 10-2 compares SAN and NAS. Common SAN vendors include EMC, Hitachi, and IBM.

The trend among storage vendors is to collapse as much complexity as possible into fewer components that have the capability to handle the functionality traditionally split among different product lines. For example, EMC has gone to great lengths to embed NAS and SAN technologies into the same storage array, allowing the same chassis to perform functions that traditionally were split among NAS and SAN. The marketed long-term result is a solution that has a lower total cost of ownership, smaller footprint, and lower operating costs. Be aware of these and other trends that are discussed under "Key Storage Concepts."

Content Addressed Storage (CAS) is object-oriented storage designed specifically for archival storage of unique items that are not intended to be changed after they are stored. CAS is common for medical images and archival data for retention purposes. EMC coined the name CAS with its Centera archive product, which can be set up to allow data to be written to the storage and never to be deleted, preventing malicious or unintentional deletion of archived data.

Key Storage Concepts

The following are important storage concepts that are gaining momentum. Storage is changing—permanently—to become smarter, faster, smaller, and more efficient.

Comparison	Storage Area Network	Network Attached Storage
Storage type	Block based	File based
Protocols	SCSI, iSCSI, HyperSCSI, Fibre Channel, ATA over Ethernet (AoE)	NFS (Sun), CIFS (MS)
File sharing	Large amounts of data	Easier file sharing
Power to use	Less processing power	More processing power
Traditional cost	$$$$	$$
Performance	High performance, more predictable	Less predictable, cost efficient
Access	Usually abstracted by a file system or database management system for use by applications and end users	Directly useable by end users as a "file share" or applications that don't need the throughput of SAN

Table 10-2 Comparison of SAN and NAS

Recovery Point Objective and Recovery Time Objective

Recovery Point Objective (RPO) determines how much data you will lose should an incident occur. Recovery Time Objective (RTO) determines how long it will take to recover data should an incident occur. Figure 10-6 shows how these two work together to determine how an incident might impact an organization.

Tiered Storage

The *cost* of storage media is proportional to the *performance* of the media. Flash storage is the fastest media, and it's perfect for extreme performance environments. However, the cost (and some quirky side effects related to capacity decay over time) make flash a poor choice for archiving data for long periods of time. You can buy different types of storage media for the same massive storage environment and classify your storage according to performance requirements. The storage array can then put data on the appropriate media for the performance that's required. Several different data-tiering models can be used.

Data Deduplication

Data deduplication technologies find duplicates at some level, whether identical files or identical components, blocks, streams, or sequential bits, and substitute duplicate copies with a pointer to a single copy of the data. For example, consider an e-mail sent to ten people with an attachment. Either the attachment can be saved ten times, or the attachment can be saved once with nine pointers to the original copy.

Figure 10-6 Recovery Point Objective and Recovery Time Objective

Several methods, technologies, and vendors can be used for deduplicating and reducing the size of the data stored. They vary greatly in overhead, complexity, deployment, and effectiveness. Some, such as EMC's Avamar, identify redundant data at the source, minimizing backup data before it is sent over the LAN/WAN. Other solutions are placed next to the storage target to identify and manage redundant data at the target. Regardless of the solution, data deduplication is an important strategy component for effective capacity utilization. The results are reduced capacity requirements, smaller footprints, and reduced operational costs.

Green Storage

The objective of green storage is ostensibly to conserve resources and the environment, but it also lets you get more out of your storage infrastructure for less money. Using smart technologies and architectures, companies are shrinking the amount of space, equipment, energy, and administrative overhead required to manage storage.

Business needs and compliance requirements drive the need for redundancy. Many companies store ten times more data than they actually use. RAID-10, backups, development, snapshots, overprovisioning, compliance archives, and disaster recovery sites continue to increase the amount of storage used. The good news is that technologies and architecture decisions can drastically reduce this number, cutting in half the amount of storage required.

The use of storage virtualization, compression, thin provisioning, nonmirrored RAID, deduplication, and resizable volumes can help reduce the storage footprint in a data center. This in turn reduces the energy requirements. Going green can also save a company operational and administrative costs of maintaining and managing storage. These discussions should be part of your capacity planning interview with the administrator.

Storage Virtualization

Traditional storage requires heavy administrator overhead and detailed knowledge of physical paths, device information, and data locations. Storage virtualization is an abstraction of detail that separates layers between the host's needs and the storage. Location and implementation are transparent to the host. The result is improved delivery and quality (up time) of the storage infrastructure while increasing utilization and reducing capital cost and management overhead. Storage virtualization is a broad and somewhat complex topic, because of the many vendors and implementations available, but you should be aware of the architecture. Storage virtualization is growing in popularity and is here to stay.

Test Steps for Auditing Storage

The following storage audit is designed to review critical controls that protect the confidentiality, integrity, or availability of storage for the supported systems and users that rely on the storage. Dozens of storage vendors—from Dell, to EMC, to Hitachi, to SUN—cover every vertical of the market. Each of the steps that follow apply to some extent; however, use your judgment to determine the depth to which you decide to take any one step. For example, an auditor reviewing high-performance storage supporting a business critical web application might spend more time asking questions and reviewing vendor-specific analysis output that verifies the storage has the capacity and performance necessary to handle peak loads.

Setup and General Controls

1. Document the overall storage management architecture, including the hardware and supporting network infrastructure.

The team responsible for managing storage should maintain documentation illustrating the storage architecture and how the storage interfaces with the rest of the environment. This information should include data covering supported systems and the connecting network infrastructure. This information will be used by the auditor to help interpret the results of subsequent audit steps.

How

Discuss and review existing documentation with the administrator.

2. Obtain the software version and compare it against policy requirements.

Review the software version to ensure that the host is in compliance with policy. Older software may have reliability, performance, or security issues and increases the difficulty in managing the storage platforms. Additionally, disparate software versions may increase the scope of administrator responsibilities as he or she attempts to maintain control over the different versions running on the storage platforms.

How

Work with the administrator to obtain this information from the system and review vendor documentation. Ensure that the software is a version the vendor continues to support and does not contain widely known and patchable vulnerabilities that would bypass existing controls. Additionally, verify that the current running version does not contain performance or reliability issues that would affect your environment. Review any mitigating factors with the administrator, such as issues that have not been fixed but are not applicable to the environment.

3. Verify that policies and procedures are in place to identify when a patch is available and to evaluate and apply applicable patches. Ensure that all approved patches are installed per your policy.

Most storage vendors have regularly scheduled patch releases. You need to be prepared for the scheduled releases so that you can plan appropriately for testing and installation of the patches. If all the patches are not installed, widely known security vulnerabilities or critical performance issues could exist.

How

Interview the administrator to determine who reviews advisories from vendors, what steps are taken to prepare for the patches, and how long the patches are tested before being applied to the production storage systems. Ask to review notes from the previous patching cycle.

Obtain as much information as possible about the latest patches through conversations with the administrator and a review of vendor documentation, and determine the scope of the vulnerabilities addressed by the patches. Compare the available patches with the patches applied to the storage platform. Talk with the administrator about steps taken to mitigate potential risk if the patches are not applied in a timely manner.

4. Determine what services and features are enabled on the system and validate their necessity with the system administrator.

Unnecessary services and features increases risk exposure to misconfigurations, vulnerabilities, and performance issues and complicate troubleshooting efforts.

How

Today's storage systems range from the very simple to the extremely complex. Work closely with the storage administrator to discuss enabled services and their applicability to the environment. Review and evaluate procedures for assessing vulnerabilities associated with necessary services and keeping them patched.

Account Management

5. Review and evaluate procedures for creating administrative accounts and ensuring that accounts are created only when there's a legitimate business need. Also review and evaluate processes for ensuring that accounts are removed or disabled in a timely fashion in the event of termination or job change.

Effective controls should govern account creation and deletion. Inappropriate or lacking controls could result in unnecessary access to system resources, placing the integrity and availability of sensitive data at risk.

How

Interview the system administrator, and review account-creation procedures. This process should include some form of verification that the user has a legitimate need for access. Take a sample of accounts and review evidence that they were approved properly prior to being created. Alternatively, take a sample of accounts and validate their legitimacy by investigating and understanding the job function of the account owners.

Review the process for removing accounts when access is no longer needed. This process could include a semiautomatic process driven by the company's Human Resources (HR) Department providing information on terminations and job changes. Or the process could include a periodic review and validation of active accounts by the system administrator and/or other knowledgeable managers. Obtain a sample of accounts and verify that they are owned by active employees and that each employee has a legitimate business requirement for administrative access.

6. Evaluate the process and policies used for granting and revoking access to storage.

Written policies should govern the process used to create new storage allocations, including approval processes and procedures for setting up the new work area and the users who should have access to the new storage allocation. Policies or procedures should also exist for "cleaning up" or removing rights that are no longer needed when a project is completed. Failure to manage storage allocation could unnecessarily expend storage capacity, and failure to govern rights management may allow users who should no longer have access to storage to maintain inappropriate levels of access.

How

Discuss policies and procedures for granting and revoking access to workspaces with the storage administrator.

Storage Management

7. Evaluate how capacity is managed for the storage environment to support existing and anticipated business requirements.

Technical and business requirements for storage can change quickly and frequently, driven by changes in infrastructure, business relationships, customer needs, and regulatory requirements. Inadequate storage infrastructure places the business at risk of losing important data and may impede critical business functions that need more storage.

How

Verify that capacity requirements have been documented and that customers have agreed to them. Review processes for monitoring capacity usage and noting when it exceeds defined thresholds. Evaluate processes in place for responding and taking action when capacity usage exceeds established thresholds. Discuss the methods used to determine present storage requirements and anticipated growth. Review growth plans with the administrator to verify that the hardware can meet the performance, capacity, and feature requirements to support infrastructure and business growth.

Business drivers may affect the storage infrastructure design and architecture:

- Retention requirements may change because of new compliance drivers.
- Business continuity and disaster recovery plans may require faster response times and less data loss.
- Virtualization projects may require more storage.
- New high-performance databases may demand tiered storage technologies as you add faster spindles or Solid State Drives (SSDs) to support high-performance business requirements.
- Growing backup needs over strained networks might require a data deduplication solution to minimize the impact to the network.

8. Evaluate how performance is managed and monitored for the storage environment to support existing and anticipated business requirements.

Storage performance is driven by several factors, including the physical storage media, communication protocols, network, data size, CPU, memory, RAID architecture, data tiering strategies, and a host of other factors. Inadequate storage infrastructure places the business at risk of losing important data and may impede critical business functions that need either more storage or better performance.

How

Regular periodic performance reviews of the processor, memory, and bandwidth loads on the storage architecture should be performed to identify growing stresses on the architecture. Verify that performance requirements have been documented and that customers have agreed to them. Review processes for monitoring performance and noting when performance falls below defined thresholds. Evaluate processes in place for responding and taking action when performance falls below established thresholds. Discuss the methods used to determine present performance requirements and anticipated changes.

 NOTE Reviewing capacity management and performance planning is one of the most critical steps in this audit. Ensure that the administrator has a capacity management plan in place and verify that performance needs are appropriate for the organization.

9. Evaluate the policies, processes, and controls for data backup frequency, handling, and remote storage.

Processes and controls should meet policy requirements, support Business Continuity/ Disaster Recovery (BC/DR), and protect sensitive information. Data backups present monumental challenges for organizations, particularly when it comes to the central data repositories in the organization, namely the databases and storage platforms. Vendors offer several solutions to manage the frequency, handling, and remote storage of data and system backups. The implemented solution mix should be appropriate to meet the stated goals of the BC/DR plans.

How

Review policy requirements for meeting Recovery Point Objectives (RPOs), which affect how much data might be lost from a disaster, and Recovery Time Objectives (RTOs), which affect how long it will take to restore data after a disaster occurs. The RPOs and RTOs should be aligned with the BC/DR programs.

Additional Security Controls

10. Verify that encryption of data-at-rest is implemented where appropriate.

Encryption of data-at-rest involves encrypting data as it is stored. This step isn't appropriate for all environments and may be covered by other controls or applications. Encryption of data-at-rest is more important than other forms of encryption because the lifetime of data on disk is much longer than the lifetime of data on the network. If you look at where data is most likely to be stolen, it is directly from the storage while at rest and not while traversing the network.

How

Verify data that should be encrypted is encrypted properly. Additionally, review the location where the encryption keys are stored, because the strength of encryption relies on the strength of protection of the encryption keys. If the encryption keys are stored with the encrypted data, an attacker can subvert the security simply by extracting the encryption keys.

Check the disaster recovery plan to ensure that encryption key management is included as a component. A mistake you do not want your administrator to make is to implement encryption features but fail to include key management in the backup procedures. Failing to back up encryption keys properly may result in the inability to recover a backup.

11. Verify that network encryption of data-in-motion is implemented where appropriate.

Policy requirements may require encrypted traffic for applications that contain sensitive information or for backing up storage to another location. Network encryption is implemented for two main reasons: to protect authentication credentials as they move across the network, and to protect the actual data as it moves over the network. The network is not a secure environment—IP addresses can be spoofed, and network traffic can be redirected and sniffed.

How

Review policy requirements with the administrator and determine if any of the storage data is required to be encrypted in transit. If the storage contains sensitive data, verify that network traffic used to back up or replicate the storage is encrypted.

12. Evaluate the low-level and technical controls in place to segregate or firewall highly sensitive data from the rest of the storage environment.

Controls should exist that restrict access to sensitive information such as cardholder data (CHD), personally identifiable information (PII), source code, and other types of proprietary data, including administrative rights to the host. If encryption is used, describe it here and evaluate the handling of keys, including the granting and revocation of rights, keys, and certificates.

How

Review controls in place with the storage administrator to separate sensitive data. Review auditing and log management procedures for administrative access to the storage environment that could bypass intended controls. Consider compensating controls such as data encryption in the environment specific to an application. Identify technical and administrative controls that force separation between sets of data. Strong controls will prevent comingling of disparate data types and create actionable, nonrepudiated logs when these controls are bypassed.

13. Review and evaluate system administrator procedures for security monitoring.

The storage administrator should regularly monitor the environment for changes and also review the environment for security vulnerabilities. A poor monitoring program could allow security incidents to occur without the administrator's knowledge. By *monitoring*, we mean actively watching for issues (detection) and actively searching them out (finding and mitigating vulnerabilities).

How

Interview the system administrator and review relevant documentation to gain an understanding of security monitoring practices. Several methods of security monitoring may be performed. The level of monitoring should be consistent with the criticality of the system and the inherent risk of the environment. (For example, a storage environment supporting critical financial data should have robust security monitoring.) The system administrator is responsible for monitoring the environment to identify activity and trends that might prevent critical issues.

If security monitoring is performed, assess the frequency of the monitoring and the quality with which it is performed. Look for evidence that the security monitoring tools are actually used appropriately. It may be possible to review recent events and determine whether the events were investigated. Leverage the results of the rest of the audit in performing this assessment. For example, if you found significant issues in an area the administrator was supposedly monitoring, you might question the effectiveness of that monitoring.

14. Perform the steps from Chapter 4, "Auditing Data Centers and Disaster Recovery," as they pertain to the system you are auditing.

In addition to auditing the logical security of the system, you should ensure that appropriate physical controls and operations are in place to provide for system protection and availability.

How

Reference the steps from Chapter 4, and perform those that are relevant to the system being audited. For example, the following topics are likely to be pertinent:

- Asset inventory
- Physical security
- Environmental controls
- Capacity planning
- Change management
- System monitoring
- Backup processes
- Disaster recovery planning

Knowledge Base

Following are additional resources where you can obtain information about storage and related controls. The vendors offer a tremendous amount of information on their websites for general consumption.

Resource	Website
Storage Networking Primer	www.snia.org/education/storage_networking_primer
RAID Primer	www.acnc.com/04_00.html
RAID Recovery Guide	www.raidrecoveryguide.com
EMC	www.emc.com

Resource	Website
EMC Powerlink	www.emc.com/support-training/support/emc-powerlink.htm
NetApp	www.netapp.com
NetApp NOW	now.netapp.com
HP	www.hp.com
HP Support	welcome.hp.com/country/us/en/support_task.html
Storage Glossary	enterprisestorageforum.webopedia.com

Master Checklists

The following checklist summarizes the steps for auditing storage.

Checklist for Auditing Storage

❑ 1. Document the overall storage management architecture, including the hardware and supporting network infrastructure.

❑ 2. Obtain the software version and compare it against policy requirements.

❑ 3. Verify that policies and procedures are in place to identify when a patch is available and to evaluate and apply applicable patches. Ensure that all approved patches are installed per your policy.

❑ 4. Determine what services and features are enabled on the system and validate their necessity with the system administrator.

❑ 5. Review and evaluate procedures for creating administrative accounts and ensuring that accounts are created only when there's a legitimate business need. Also review and evaluate processes for ensuring that accounts are removed or disabled in a timely fashion in the event of termination or job change.

❑ 6. Evaluate the process and policies used for granting and revoking access to storage.

❑ 7. Evaluate how capacity is managed for the storage environment to support existing and anticipated business requirements.

❑ 8. Evaluate how performance is managed and monitored for the storage environment to support existing and anticipated business requirements.

❑ 9. Evaluate the policies, processes, and controls for data backup frequency, handling, and remote storage.

❑ 10. Verify that encryption of data-at-rest is implemented where appropriate.

❑ 11. Verify that network encryption of data-in-motion is implemented where appropriate.

❑ 12. Evaluate the low-level and technical controls in place to segregate or firewall highly sensitive data from the rest of the storage environment.

❑ 13. Review and evaluate system administrator procedures for security monitoring.

❑ 14. Perform the steps from Chapter 4, "Auditing Data Centers and Disaster Recovery," as they pertain to the system you are auditing.

PART II

Auditing Virtualized Environments

Innovations in operating system virtualization and server hardware permanently changed the footprint, architecture, and operations of data centers. This chapter discusses auditing virtualized environments, and begins with an overview of common virtualization technologies and key controls. The virtualization audit combines the concerns of the hypervisor and the guest operating systems. Although the focus of this chapter is the hypervisor and server virtualization, you can apply many of the same steps and concepts to desktop virtualization. We make the assumption that these system components are under your control. You should reference Chapter 14, "Auditing Cloud Computing and Outsourced Operations" for guidance on how to ensure outsourced virtualized environments are properly managed and secured.

This chapter covers the following:

- A brief technical overview of virtualization
- How to audit the virtualization environment
- Tools and resources for enhancing your virtualization audits

Background

Virtualization allows the separation of the operating system from the hardware, using a layer called a *hypervisor* to sit between the hardware and the operating system. The hypervisor abstracts the physical hardware and presents the hardware you specify to the operating system. The resulting abstraction of the operating system from the specific physical server provides tremendous creative freedom for backing up, copying, restoring, and moving running operating systems, complete with their installed applications. Figure 11-1 illustrates the separation of virtual machines from the physical hardware. Notice that complete abstraction from the hardware allows for some interesting hardware clustering scenarios and also enables the groundwork for sharing hardware resources with an outside cloud computing environment.

Figure 11-1
Virtualization model

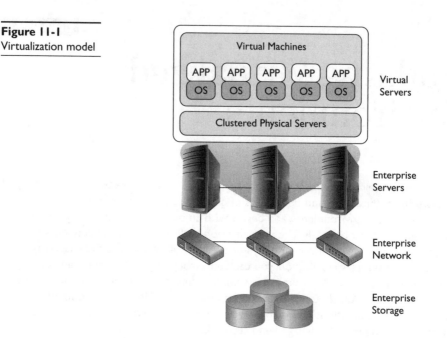

Virtualization software can be installed onto a bare metal server or as an application on top of another operating system. Many vendors allow the hypervisor to be installed either way, on top of the OS or by itself, without the hassle and overhead of the OS. The software is designed to utilize embedded processor instructions specifically designed to support multiple operating systems. Processor manufacturers led this charge a few years ago, and the highly customized hardware packages by Cisco Systems, VMware, and other global players foretell the intent to package as much power, security, and management as possible into the hardware to support virtual infrastructures. Gartner believes—and the readers of this book will know—that by the time this book is published and distributed, more than 50 percent of the world's servers will be virtualized.

Commercial and Open Source Projects

Several commercial players are in this market, including VMware, Microsoft, Citrix, Oracle, Parallels, Red Hat, and Novell. Some of these players maintain open source projects, including Xen by Citrix and VirtualBox by Oracle-Sun Microsystems. KVM is a popular open source virtualization project for Linux. Links to each of these projects are located in "Knowledge Base" at the end of the chapter.

Virtualization Auditing Essentials

To understand the material in this chapter, you need a basic understanding of the components that make up the virtualization environment. Your role as an auditor and advisor will significantly improve if you understand major technology trends challenging virtualization models.

Security models, business alignment, capacity planning, and performance management are more important than ever before in virtual environments. Smaller environments may have a few virtually hosted servers running on a single powerful physical server, whereas larger environments support hundreds or thousands of virtually hosted servers and desktops running on a complex infrastructure of clustered servers connected to a massive Storage Area Network (SAN). The scale may change the scope or approach to the audit, but the same business requirements and controls exist. Resource management and monitoring of each of the components separately and collectively enable the virtual environment to function.

Figure 11-2 illustrates an example collective environment and several audit considerations. Notice that these considerations also apply to a normal server or storage audit. What's different? What are the security concerns that keep administrators awake? What should auditors explore? The hypervisor has control requirements similar to those found in a server, but it also has unique requirements to ensure that the hosted environment doesn't present additional control weaknesses to the guest operating systems. The guest operating systems have unique control requirements because of the necessity to keep appropriate segregation controls in place between servers. Mildly complicating this mix are different conceptual approaches to creating the virtual environment.

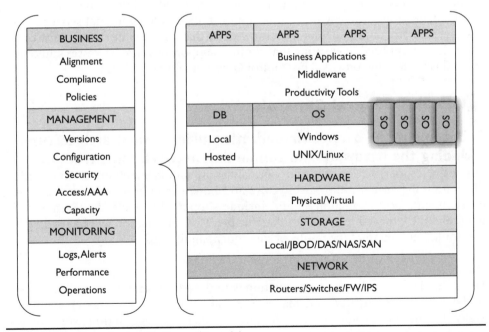

Figure 11-2 Example virtualization audit model

Test Steps for Auditing Virtualization

The virtualization audit covered here is designed to review critical controls that protect the confidentiality, integrity, or availability of the environment for the supported operating systems and users that rely on the environment. Each of the following steps applies to some extent; however, use your judgment to determine the depth to which you decide to take any one step. For example, an auditor reviewing high-performance environments supporting a business-critical application might spend more time asking questions and reviewing vendor-specific analysis output that verifies that the virtualized environment has the capacity and performance necessary to handle peak loads.

NOTE This audit focuses on the hypervisor and management of the virtual environment, regardless of where the hypervisor is installed. If the hypervisor is installed as an application on another operating system, audit the underlying operating system separately using the appropriate test steps in Chapter 6, "Auditing Windows Operating Systems," or Chapter 7, "Auditing UNIX and Linux Operating Systems."

Note that there are several excellent hardening guides and configuration checking utilities, and we encourage the use of these tools to help provide consistency across the environment. Vendors have different approaches for shipping products. Some vendors include unnecessary services and product features enabled. Others ship their products in a hardened state whereby the administrator must enable additional services. Note many of the hardening guides have a narrow scope that focus on the compromise of the hypervisor as opposed to ensuring that controls support business processes and objectives. This is the value provided by Control Objectives for IT (COBIT).

Setup and General Controls

1. Document the overall virtualization management architecture, including the hardware and supporting network infrastructure.

The team responsible for managing virtualization should maintain documentation illustrating the virtualization architecture and how it interfaces with the rest of the environment. Documentation should include supported systems, management systems, and the connecting network infrastructure. This information will be used by the auditor to help interpret the results of subsequent audit steps.

How

Discuss and review existing documentation with the administrator. As applicable, verify that document structure and management are aligned with corporate standards. Verify the entire environment, including management, storage, and network components, are properly documented.

2. Obtain the software version of the hypervisor and compare with policy requirements.

Review the software version to ensure that the hypervisor is in compliance with policy. Older software may have reliability, performance, or security issues that can increase the difficulty in managing the virtualization platform(s). Additionally, disparate software versions may increase the scope of administrator's responsibilities as he or she attempts to maintain control over the different hypervisors and their feature, control, and administration differences.

How

Work with the administrator to obtain this information from the system and review vendor documentation. Ensure that the software is a version the vendor continues to support and does not contain widely known and patchable vulnerabilities that would bypass existing controls. Also verify that the current running version does not contain performance or reliability issues that would affect your environment. Review any mitigating factors with the administrator, such as issues that have not been fixed but are not applicable to the environment.

3. Verify that policies and procedures are in place to identify when patches are available and to evaluate and apply applicable patches. Ensure that all approved patches are installed per your policy requirements.

Most virtualization vendors have regularly scheduled patch releases. You should be prepared for the scheduled releases so that you can plan appropriately for testing and installation of the patches. If all the patches are not installed, widely known security vulnerabilities or critical performance issues could exist.

How

Interview the administrator to determine who reviews advisories from vendors, including timely notifications about new vulnerabilities and zero-day attacks, what steps are taken to prepare for the patches, and how the patches are tested before being applied to the production systems. Ask to review notes from the previous patching cycle.

Obtain as much information as possible about the latest patches through conversations with the administrator and review of vendor documentation, and determine the scope of the vulnerabilities addressed by the patches. Compare the available patches with the patches applied to the hypervisor. Talk with the administrator about steps taken to mitigate potential risk if the patches are not applied in a timely manner.

4. Determine what services and features are enabled on the system and validate their necessity with the system administrator.

Unnecessary services and features increase risk exposure to misconfigurations, vulnerabilities, and performance issues and complicate troubleshooting efforts.

How

Today's virtualization systems range from the very simple to the extremely complex. Work closely with the virtualization administrator to discuss enabled services and their applicability to the environment. Review and evaluate procedures for assessing vulnerabilities associated with necessary services and features and keeping them properly configured and patched.

Account and Resource Provisioning and Deprovisioning

Administrative accounts in the virtual environment must be managed appropriately, as should the provisioning and deprovisioning of virtual machines.

5. Review and evaluate procedures for creating administrative accounts and ensuring that accounts are created only when a legitimate business need has been identified. Also review and evaluate processes for ensuring that accounts are removed or disabled in a timely fashion in the event of termination or job change.

Effective controls should govern account creation and deletion. Inappropriate or lacking controls could result in unnecessary access to system resources, placing the integrity and availability of sensitive data at risk.

How

Interview the system administrator, and review account-creation procedures. This process should include some form of verification that the user has a legitimate need for access. Take a sample of accounts and review evidence that they were approved properly prior to being created. Alternatively, take a sample of accounts and validate their legitimacy by investigating and understanding the job function of the account owners.

Review the process for removing accounts when access is no longer needed. This process could include a component driven by the company's human resources (HR) department providing information on terminations and job changes. Or the process could include a periodic review and validation of active accounts by the system administrator and/or other knowledgeable managers. Obtain a sample of accounts and verify that they are owned by active employees and that each employee has a legitimate business requirement for administrative access.

6. Verify the appropriate management of provisioning and deprovisioning new virtual machines, including appropriate operating system and application licenses.

Written policies should govern the process used to create new virtual machines, manage users, and allocate software licenses. The ease of spinning up new servers for development and testing has created a new challenge for managing hardware and license resources.

Policies or procedures should also exist for "cleaning up" or removing virtual machines, rights, and licenses that are no longer needed when a project is completed.

Failure to manage virtual host allocation could unnecessarily expend virtualization capacity and software licenses.

Virtual machines should be accountable to specific groups or users. Failure to govern rights management may allow users that should no longer have access to hosts to maintain inappropriate levels of access.

How

Discuss policies and procedures for provisioning and deprovisioning new hosts and accounts with the virtualization administrator, including license allocation, user management, and host ownership. Several tools help manage this process, particularly in development environments where server sprawl tends to become a problem. For example, VMware's Lab Manager allows the provisioning administrator to set time limits for how long a virtual machine can be active. Lab Manager provides a control that protects the virtualization resources from becoming overrun with virtual machines that consume resources from the virtual hosts that really need those resources.

Virtual Environment Management

The virtual environment must be managed appropriately to support existing and future business objectives. Resources must be monitored and evaluated for capacity and performance. Resources must also support the organization's Business Continuity/Disaster Recovery objectives.

7. Evaluate how hardware capacity is managed for the virtualized environment to support existing and future business requirements.

Business and technical requirements for virtualization can change quickly and frequently, driven by changes in infrastructure, business relationships, customer needs, and regulatory requirements. The virtualization hardware and infrastructure must be managed to support existing business needs and immediate anticipated growth. Inadequate infrastructure places the business at risk and may impede critical business functions that need more hardware capacity.

How

Virtual machine capacity is managed by the hypervisor to allocate a specific amount of storage, processor, and memory to each host. Verify that capacity requirements have been documented and that customers have agreed to abide by them. Capacity allocation may directly affect performance. Review processes for monitoring capacity usage for storage, memory, and processing, noting when they exceed defined thresholds. Evaluate processes in place for responding and taking action when capacity usage exceeds customer-approved thresholds. For example, some organizations utilize cloud bursting to offload increases in demand for internal computing capacity, whereby a service provider makes additional capacity available as needed. Discuss the methods used to determine present virtualization requirements and anticipated growth. Review growth plans with the administrator to verify that the hardware can meet the performance requirements, capacity requirements, and feature requirements to support infrastructure and business growth.

8. Evaluate how performance is managed and monitored for the virtualization environment to support existing and anticipated business requirements.

Virtualization performance of the infrastructure as a whole and for each virtual machine is driven by several factors, including the physical virtualization media, communication protocols, network, data size, CPU, memory, storage architecture, and a host of other factors. Inadequate virtualization infrastructure places the business at risk of losing access to critical business applications. It's possible to have adequate capacity but incorrectly configured and underperforming virtual machines that fail to deliver on the Service Level Agreement (SLA).

How

Verify that regular periodic performance reviews of the processor, memory, and bandwidth loads on the virtualization architecture are performed to identify growing stresses on the architecture. A common performance measurement for virtual environments is based on Input/Output Operations Per Second (IOPS). Verify that performance requirements have been documented and that customers have agreed to abide by them. Review processes for monitoring performance and noting when performance falls below defined thresholds. Evaluate processes in place for responding and taking action when performance falls below customer-agreed thresholds. Discuss the methods used to determine present performance requirements and anticipated changes.

 NOTE A review of capacity management and performance planning is essential to this audit. Be careful to ensure that the administrator has a capacity management plan in place and verifies that performance needs are appropriate for the organization.

9. Evaluate the policies, processes, and controls for data backup frequency, handling, and offsite management.

Processes and controls should meet policy requirements, support Business Continuity/Disaster Recovery (BC/DR) objectives, and protect sensitive information. Data backups present monumental challenges for organizations, particularly when it comes to the central data repositories in the organization, namely the databases and virtualization platforms. Vendors offer several solutions to manage the frequency, handling, and offsite delivery of data and system backups. The implemented solution should be appropriate to meeting the stated goals of the BC/DR plans.

How

Review policy requirements for meeting Recovery Point Objectives (RPOs), which affect how much data might be lost from a disaster, and Recovery Time Objectives (RTOs), which affect how long it will take to restore data after a disaster occurs. The RPOs and RTOs, shown in Figure 11-3, for virtualized hosts should be aligned with the BC/DR programs. Discuss the relative priority to other systems based on business criticality and dependencies. Verify that an appropriate Service Level Agreement (SLA) is in place

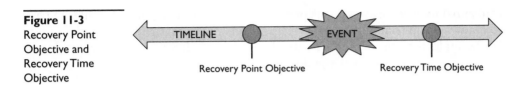

Figure 11-3
Recovery Point
Objective and
Recovery Time
Objective

TIMELINE   EVENT

Recovery Point Objective   Recovery Time Objective

that supports your stated RPO/RTO objectives if part of this process is outsourced or handled by another party. You should also ensure that sensitive data is encrypted prior to offsite storage.

10. Review and evaluate the security of your remote hypervisor management.

Secure remote hypervisor management protects the hypervisor from remote attacks that might otherwise disrupt the hypervisor or hosted virtual machines. Each of the hypervisors has its own management tools designed to allow remote administration of the hypervisor and virtual machines. Many of these commercial tools can manage other commercial hypervisors in an effort to manage heterogeneous virtual environments seamlessly. Despite their obvious differences, the areas that should be reviewed have some commonalities.

Unused services, accessible APIs, and installed applications may subject the hypervisor to additional attack vectors if a security flaw is discovered. In addition, remote users should be forced to access the system using accounts that can be tied to a specific user for logging and tracking. The difference between this step and step 4 is the careful analysis of network-accessible components for the hypervisor with regard to remote management. Unless specifically required and appropriately controlled, network-accessible features should not be enabled. Enable only those components that are necessary and appropriately configured for remote management.

How

Each vendor provides specific security guides for enabling remote management. These security guides are generally easy to read and should be reviewed in detail prior to beginning the audit. The execution of this step consists of a policy review, account permissions review, and a configuration review.

Review remote access policies and access methods with the administrator. Verify that all remote access is logged to a system separate from the environment. Question the need for any clear-text communications used for remote access. Identify and validate the appropriateness of administrative accounts that have remote access.

NOTE The use of secure protocols is particularly important in a DMZ and other high-risk environments. It is also advisable to use secure protocols for management on internal networks to minimize internal attack vectors. Attackers will use a single compromised beachhead system to learn about the environment, pivot, and attack other systems from within.

Obtain vendor appropriate guidance for configuring secure remote hypervisor access. These should be used to identify and verify that the environment is securely configured for remote access. This process can be conducted manually, but we highly recommend using one of the several available versions of configuration checking tools. For example, the Tripwire-VMware developed tool verifies the following which may also assist you with other parts of this audit:

- Virtual network labeling
- Port Group settings
- Network isolation for VMotion and iSCSI
- NIC Mode settings / Layer 2 Security settings
- MAC address parameters
- VMware ESX Service Console security settings
- SAN resource masking and zoning
- Disk partitioning for Root File System
- VirtualCenter database configuration
- Configuration changes

Additional Security Controls

11. Review and evaluate the security around the storage of virtual machines.

Virtual machines are stored and manipulated as files that are easily transported, copied, and viewed. Shared storage for virtual machines should have controls in place to isolate sensitive virtual machines and content from the rest of the environment.

Some environments might encrypt data-at-rest. Encryption of data-at-rest involves encrypting data as it is stored on disk. Encryption of data-at-rest is more important than other forms of encryption because the lifetime of data on disk is much longer than the lifetime of data on the network. If you look at where data is most likely to be stolen, you'll find it is most likely to be taken directly from the storage while at rest and not while traversing the network.

This step isn't appropriate for all environments and may be covered by other controls or applications.

How

Ensure virtual machines are stored in such a manner that sensitive virtual machines are isolated from the rest of the network and that only appropriate administrators have access. Consideration must also be given to managing and auditing administrative access to a storage environment containing sensitive virtual machines.

Verify that encrypted data is encrypted properly. Additionally, review the location where the encryption keys are stored because the strength of encryption relies on the strength of protection of the encryption keys. If the encryption keys are stored with the encrypted data, an attacker can subvert the security simply by extracting the encryption keys.

If encryption is used, then verify the disaster recovery plan contains encryption key management. A mistake you do not want your administrator to make is to implement encryption features but fail to include key management in the backup procedures. Failing to back up encryption keys properly may result in the inability to recover a backup.

12. Verify that network encryption of data-in-motion is implemented where appropriate.

Policy requirements may require that traffic be encrypted for applications that contain sensitive information or for backing up some virtualized hosts to another location. Network encryption serves two main purposes: to protect authentication credentials as they move across the network, and to protect the actual data as it moves over the network. The network is not a secure environment—IP addresses can be spoofed, and network traffic can be redirected and sniffed.

How

Work with the administrator to verify that encrypted protocols are used for remote administration of the virtual environment. Review policy requirements with the administrator and determine if any of the virtualization data is required to be encrypted in transit. If the virtual hosts contain sensitive data, verify that network traffic used to backup or replicate the hosts is encrypted.

Given the additional potential complexity derived from dedicated networks for storage, backup, management, failover, and so on, an auditor might want to document the data flow between these components for the virtual environments. This may have been accomplished in step 1.

13. Evaluate the low-level and technical controls in place to segregate or firewall highly sensitive data on critical virtual machines from the rest of the virtualization environment.

Controls should exist that restrict access between virtual machines to protect sensitive information such as cardholder data (CHD), personally identifiable information (PII), source code, and other types of proprietary data, including administrative rights to the host. Each of the hypervisors has specific settings and controls that can be implemented to assist with the segregation of data between hosts. Commonly discussed threats specifically include the use of shared folders and the ability to copy and paste between a host operating system and the hosted virtual machine. If encryption is used, describe it here and evaluate the handling of keys, including the granting and revocation of rights, keys, and certificates.

How

Review with the virtualization administrator the controls in place to isolate virtual machines that have different classification levels. Identify technical and administrative controls that force separation between sets of data. Strong controls will prevent comingling of disparate data types, and create actionable, nonrepudiated logs when these controls are bypassed. Sensitive virtual machines should not be directly accessible by the rest of the environment.

Review auditing and log management procedures governing administrative access to the virtualization environment that could bypass intended controls. Consider compensating controls such as data encryption.

The detail of configuration options between the variant hypervisors to protect virtual machines from each other and the host (when installed on a hosted OS) requires that the auditor gather additional knowledge to identify vendor-recommended best practices. Discuss specific options with the administrator in the business context of environmental risk and compensating controls.

There are several resources available. One particularly well-written resource readily found online is from McAfee/Foundstone titled *How Virtualization Affects PCI DSS: Part 2: A Review of the Top 5 Issues*. Figure 11-4 illustrates the use of firewalls to segment virtualized components. This particular example was created for the PCI-SSC Virtualization Information Supplement for a discussion around segmenting sensitive credit card data from other virtual machines in a multitenant environment. Note that firewalls and switches may be virtualized as well and appropriate controls must be verified for these components.

14. Review and evaluate system administrator procedures for security monitoring.

The virtualization administrator should regularly monitor the environment for changes and periodically review the environment for security vulnerabilities. A poor monitoring program could allow security incidents to occur without the administrator's knowl-

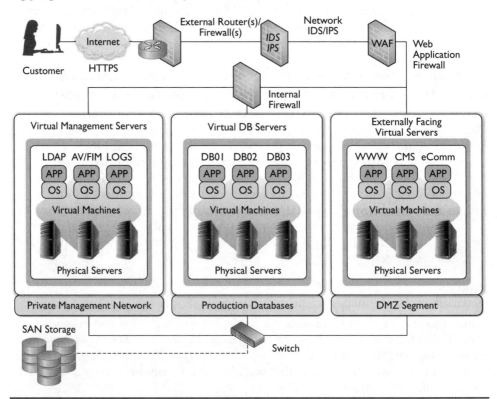

Figure 11-4 Segmenting virtual machines with firewalls

edge. *Monitoring* in this case means actively watching for issues (detection) and actively searching them out (identifying and mitigating vulnerabilities).

How

Interview the system administrator and review relevant documentation to gain an understanding of log monitoring practices. Several methods of log monitoring may be performed. The level of monitoring should be consistent with the criticality of the system and the inherent risk of the environment (for example, a virtualization environment supporting critical financial data should have robust security monitoring). The system administrator is responsible for monitoring the environment to identify activity and trends that might allow the prevention of critical issues. Several robust and excellent tools are available for monitoring virtual environments.

If security event monitoring is performed using an Intrusion Prevention System (IPS) or similar system to identify malicious events, assess the frequency of the monitoring and the quality with which it is performed. Look for evidence that the security monitoring tools are actively used. It may be possible to review recent events and determine whether the events were investigated. Leverage the results of the rest of the audit in performing this assessment. For example, if you found significant issues in an area the administrator was supposedly monitoring, you might question the effectiveness of that monitoring.

15. Evaluate the use of baseline templates and the security of hosted virtual machines as appropriate to the scope of the audit.

Baseline templates allow you to provision configured virtual machines quickly. One of the best ways to propagate security throughout an environment is to ensure that new systems are built correctly before moving into testing or production. In addition, if the scope of the audit includes evaluating hosted virtual machines, refer to Chapters 6 and 7.

How

Through interviews with the system administrator, determine the methodology used for building and deploying new systems. If a standard build is used, consider auditing a newly created system using the steps in Chapters 6 and 7. It's a good practice to include your baseline configurations as part of your normal audit routines.

16. Perform the steps from Chapter 4, "Auditing Data Centers and Disaster Recovery," and Chapter 10, "Auditing Storage," as they pertain to the environment you are auditing.

In addition to auditing the logical controls of the system, you must ensure that appropriate environmental controls are in place to provide for system protection and availability. Also consider a deep review of the storage environment to ensure that data is protected and that capacity and performance are managed.

How

Reference the steps from Chapter 4, and perform those that are relevant to the system being audited. For example, the following topics are likely to be pertinent:

- Asset inventory
- Physical security

- Environmental controls
- Capacity planning
- Change management
- System monitoring
- Backup processes
- Disaster recovery planning

Reference the steps from Chapter 10 and perform those that are relevant to the system being audited. For example, the following topics are likely to be pertinent:

- Capacity management
- Performance management
- Data protection

Knowledge Base

Following are additional resources that can offer information about virtual environments and related controls. Vendors include a tremendous amount of information on their websites for general consumption. In addition, the community of helpful enthusiasts, open source projects, and forums continues to grow daily.

Hypervisors

Hypervisor	Website
VMware	www.vmware.com
Microsoft Hyper-V	www.microsoft.com/virtualization
Open Source (XenServer) (Citrix is a major contributor)	www.xen.org www.citrix.com/xenserver/overview
Open Source by Oracle (OracleVM)	www.oracle.com/technologies/virtualization
Open Source by Sun Microsystems (VirtualBox) (Owned by Oracle)	www.virtualbox.org
Open Source Linux (KVM)	www.linux-kvm.org

Tools

Tool	Website
VMware's Open Source Tools	http://open-vm-tools.sourceforge.net/faq.php
VMware Security Utilities	www.vmware.com/technical-resources/security/utilities.html
CIS Benchmarks	www.cisecurity.org/tools2/vm/CIS_VM_Benchmark_v1.0.pdf
DISA ESX STIG Guidelines	http://iase.disa.mil/stigs/stig/esx_server_stig_v1r1_final.pdf
VMware Security Advisories	www.vmware.com/security/advisories/

Tool	Website
VMware Security Guidelines	www.vmware.com/resources/techresources/726 www.vminformer.com/ www.vkernel.com/download/free-vm-tools
RSA enVision	www.rsa.com

Master Checklists

The following checklist summarizes the steps for auditing virtualization.

Checklist for Auditing Virtualization

☐ 1. Document the overall virtualization management architecture, including the hardware supporting network infrastructure.

☐ 2. Obtain the software version of the hypervisor and compare with policy requirements.

☐ 3. Verify that policies and procedures are in place to identify when patches are available and to evaluate and apply applicable patches. Ensure that all approved patches are installed per your policy requirements.

☐ 4. Determine what services and features are enabled on the system and validate their necessity with the system administrator.

☐ 5. Review and evaluate procedures for creating administrative accounts and ensuring that accounts are created only when a legitimate business need has been identified. Also review and evaluate processes for ensuring that accounts are removed or disabled in a timely fashion in the event of termination or job change.

☐ 6. Verify the appropriate management of provisioning and deprovisioning new virtual machines, including appropriate operating system and application licenses.

☐ 7. Evaluate how hardware capacity is managed for the virtualized environment to support existing and future business requirements.

☐ 8. Evaluate how performance is managed and monitored for the virtualization environment to support existing and anticipated business requirements.

☐ 9. Evaluate the policies, processes, and controls for data backup frequency, handling, and offsite management.

☐ 10. Review and evaluate the security of your remote hypervisor management.

☐ 11. Review and evaluate the security around the storage of the virtual machines.

☐ 12. Verify that network encryption of data-in-motion is implemented where appropriate.

☐ 13. Evaluate the low-level and technical controls in place to segregate or firewall highly sensitive data on critical virtual machines from the rest of the virtualization environment.

☐ 14. Review and evaluate system administrator procedures for security monitoring.

☐ 15. Evaluate the use of secure baseline templates and the security of hosted virtual machines as appropriate to the scope of the audit.

☐ 16. Perform the steps from Chapter 4, "Auditing Data Centers and Disaster Recovery," and Chapter 10, "Auditing Storage," as they pertain to the environment you are auditing.

Auditing WLAN and Mobile Devices

This chapter discusses two separate audits, beginning with wireless local area networks (WLAN) and then covering data-enabled mobile devices. WLAN audits include the clients, communications, access points, and operational factors that enable a WLAN on your network. Data-enabled mobile device audits include Blackberry, iPhone, Droid, and similar data-enabled devices and the infrastructure that supports them. The following topics are discussed:

- The background of WLAN and mobile device technologies
- Essential auditing issues for these technologies
- Key technical steps and suggestions regarding how to approach the technologies
- Operational steps necessary to keep these technologies operating efficiently on your network

Background

Mention *wireless* inside a corporate environment and people immediately think of either their data-enabled mobile phones or the nearest WLAN access point. For different reasons, both of these growing and generally accepted technologies present challenges to corporate security.

Conceptually, WLAN and mobile devices both communicate using electromagnetic radio waves from the device to a local base station. User *stations* (STAs) wirelessly connect to the network through *access points* (APs) set up by your company. Data-enabled mobile devices communicate to cell towers set up by mobile operators such as AT&T, Verizon, Orange, and NTT DOCOMO before reaching your network. Both technologies are capable of carrying sensitive company data over the network and out over the airwaves. Both technologies also have issues that necessitate forethought. This chapter covers the expanding open access to your protected and sacred network.

WLAN Background

WLAN lets you to roam past your cube into the conference room and still get your e-mail. However, WLAN traditionally presents problems to information technology (IT) administrators because of the low cost of the APs and the willingness of corporate citizens to compromise the security of the network in favor of getting more work completed. The good news is that WLAN is improving in both the underlying standards and administrator education to keep the network secure. Enough bad press and stories of compromised networks have forced even home users to start paying attention to wireless security.

In 1990, the Institute of Electrical and Electronic Engineers (IEEE) formed a group to develop a standard for wireless equipment. The 802.11 standard was born on June 26, 1997, built on the physical and data-link layers of the OSI model to allow mobile devices to communicate wirelessly with wired networks.

You might hear *Wi-Fi* used in the place of WLAN. Wi-Fi is a brand originally licensed by the Wi-Fi Alliance to describe the underlying technology based on IEEE 802.11 specifications. The term *Wi-Fi* is used widely, and the brand is no longer protected. The Wi-Fi Alliance originally began as an initiative to help bring interoperability to the growing number of devices using different implementations of the 802.11 technologies. Table 11-1 references the most common wireless technologies used in corporate environments. Be aware that several other standards in the 802.11 family exist, and those listed here are the most commonly referenced for commercial use.

 NOTE Technically, every component in a wireless network is called a *station* (STA) because each contains IEEE 802.11-compliant medium access control and physical layers. However, it's much more common to refer to access points as APs and the clients that connect to the APs as stations or STAs. To keep this simple and structured, remember that you have a device that wants to connect (STA) and a gateway component to the jewels of your network (AP).

Wireless clients include software called *supplicants.* APs connect the wireless network to the wired network, and the supplicants connect the mobile device to the wireless access point (WAP). Mobile devices could be a laptop, a wireless enabled personal digital assistant (PDA), or another device configured to communicate with the AP. The set of stations communicating with each other or a single AP is the *basic service set* (BSS). The *Service Set Identifier* (SSID) is the logical name for the area covered by the BSS. All devices in the BSS must share the same SSID to communicate with each other.

An *Extended Service Set* (ESS) may have multiple radios (APs) sharing an SSID. Clients use the SSID to connect to the wireless network. However, clients need a reliable

Protocol	Frequency	Bandwidth	Comment
IEEE 802.11	2.4 GHz	2 Mbps	Original specification; not widely used
IEEE 802.11a	5 GHz	54 Mbps	Not compatible with 802.11b/g
IEEE 802.11b	2.4 GHz	11 Mbps	Popular standard for many years but 802.11a/g/n are faster
IEEE 802.11g	2.4 GHz	54 Mbps	Backward-compatible with 802.11b (note same band)
IEEE 802.11n	2.4 & 5 GHz	300 Mbps	Backward-compatible with 802.11a/b/g (note same bands)

Table 12-1 Common 802.11 Technologies

method for communicating with a single AP from the several that might be part of an ESS sharing the same SSID. The client communicates with the same AP using the *BSS Identifier* (BSSID). The BSSID is the *Media Access Control* (MAC) address of a specific AP and acts as a unique identifier to clients. Bringing these ideas together, the BSSID allows clients to communicate with a specific radio within an ESS that contains multiple APs using the same SSID.

There are two types of BSSs: independent and infrastructure. Independent BSSs are ad hoc networks that work without an AP. For example, you could use an ad hoc network to share files with a friend's laptop. Infrastructure BSSs have an AP that serves as a bridge to a wired network. Some APs can also communicate with each other, allowing stations in one BSS to communicate with other stations in a different BSS. This is called a *Wireless Distribution System* (WDS). An ESS is a set of connected BSSs (Figure 12-1).

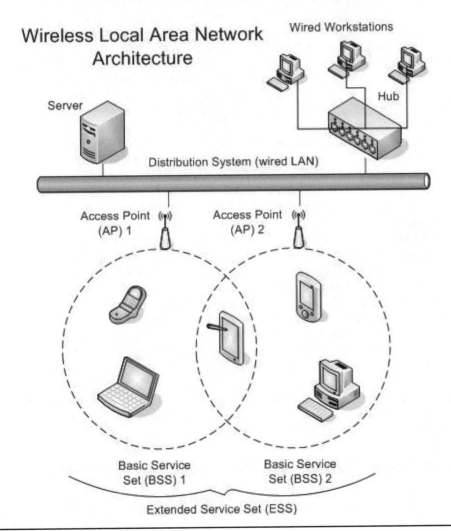

Figure 12-1 Example WLAN architecture

If you're new to WLANs, this probably sounds like a lot, and you may think that it's overly difficult to audit. We are going to stick to the basics during the audit process and suggest that you do the same. It's easy to let the scope of a WLAN audit get out of hand, but you can audit for most of the risk by concentrating your efforts on the items listed in the test steps section that follows. We'll discuss how to go about this process in easily digestible sections.

Data-Enabled Mobile Devices Background

Blackberry devices were by far the most widely used mobile devices in the corporate world at the turn of the twenty-first century. Since then, other providers have developed similar personal information management (PIM) services and software clients to run on data-enabled mobile devices, or "smartphones." Development is in process and continues such that smartphones such as your everyday Blackberry, Droid, and iPhone support clients from many different mobile device management providers such as Blackberry, GoodLink, and Sybase. Although these devices are also capable of connecting to the corporate network without any such middleware or client, using Wi-Fi or VPN technologies, the focus of the mobile device audit is on managed devices connecting remotely, such as devices used by sales or another type of mobile team. Rogue devices are certainly important and are addressed here.

Smartphones enable the workforce to take data outside the walls of their companies with the help of providers such as Blackberry, Good Technologies, and several others, which interface your users with your network and the rest of the world through the mobile operator's wireless framework. The components we want to understand as part of the audit are those that interface directly with your network and end users, such as the gateway into your network and the mobile device the user carries.

Again, there is no doubt you need to determine what access controls you do or do not have in place to prevent wireless devices from connecting to your network. A perfect world might suggest that you have access controls in place to prevent such connections, but this is certainly not always the case. We have experience with Network Access Controls (NAC) with entities as diverse as the United Nations, DoD, high-tech, health care, and manufacturing. The chosen objectives and implementation of access controls are incredibly diverse, as are their effectiveness. If you allow wireless devices to access your network in an ad hoc fashion, the risk to the network increases exponentially.

Finally, remember that not all devices necessarily need a separate client to communicate with the infrastructure as a managed device. The software, for example, to communicate with RIM's Blackberry server is built into the Blackberry handset. The challenge comes from the hundreds of diverse devices on the half-dozen prevalent mobile operating systems used on the half-dozen major mobile networks that need to communicate with your *one* data infrastructure. Securely. Without failure.

WLAN and Mobile Device Auditing Essentials

WLAN and data-enabled mobile device auditing requires an understanding of how the technology is implemented in your organization. WLAN is typically managed by networking teams, whereas data-enabled mobile devices can be jostled back and forth between networking, helpdesk, e-mail, productivity, and other teams in the organization.

Both WLAN and data-enabled mobile devices require the following at a conceptual level:

- Wired network gateways
- Clients
- Management software
- Some approved method of communicating wirelessly between the wired network gateway and the wireless clients.

For the purpose of our discussion, wired network gateways include those items physically touching your network and acting as the interface or gateway between the wireless world and your organization's physical network. An audit of your wired network components includes verifying the security of the underlying platform and the settings on that platform. The clients in our case present unique risks to data theft, and we'll explore some easy and common methods for mitigating the risk.

Management software for our purposes includes software that manages the process enabling your mobile clients to communicate with the network. This may be Cisco's software that manages your access points or Blackberry Enterprise Server's software that manages client access. The management software may or may not run on the gateway component that isolates clients from your physical network.

Finally, the method used to transmit your data wirelessly may be of concern if you are using older protocols or insecure methods to transmit data. An audit of wireless authentication and communication protocols may include something as simple as researching and verifying the use of secure protocols, or it may include more complex hacking attempts.

These four components describe how we will approach the technical portion of the two audits conceptually, reviewing the gateway, client, management, and communications. Specific tools and methods are discussed in line with the audit steps.

In addition to the technical component of the audit, a number of critical intangibles also affect the ongoing operations for mobile users. These include such processes as problem tracking for end user issues, security policies, wireless system monitoring, and general continuity of operations. Collectively, we'll address these as *operational components*. Too often ignored, any one of these can undermine the best intentions of your organization to roll out robust, secure, and effective mobile solutions.

Test Steps for Auditing Wireless LANs

We divided the WLAN audit into technical and operational sections. Depending on your goals and needs, you might require more or less than these audit steps.

Part I: WLAN Technical Audit

I. Ensure that access points are running the latest approved software.

Running old firmware on the AP may leave it open to known attacks or prevent the organization from taking advantage of more robust security features.

How

Evaluate a representative sample of APs with an administrator, and verify that the code running on the AP is the latest version. Verify that the latest version is correct using the manufacturer's website or some other similar updated source of information from the manufacturer. Examine the change-management processes used to evaluate and maintain current code releases for the APs. Note whether this process is automated and coordinated and whether it scales operationally across regional offices.

2. Evaluate the controls around centralized WLAN management.

Verify that management software is used to the fullest extent possible and that it's kept under tight control with sound policies and procedures. Centrally managed WLAN tool suites are a powerful way to control the many APs likely under the network team's supervision, especially across different geographic locations. Often management software is available from the same company that manufactured the APs. The access controls surrounding the tool suite must also be managed to prevent someone from purposefully or inadvertently wreaking havoc on your network and user population by changing AP settings.

How

Discuss the capabilities of the management software with your administrator, and ask for a demonstration of the management suite and its capabilities. Ask for procedures discussing access to the management suite, including who has access and how that access is controlled. If passwords are used, ensure that passwords match company policy and are rotated according to appropriate policies. In some organizations, every 90 days may be fine; others may want their passwords rotated every 180 days or as quickly as 30 days. This is driven in large part by the perceived value of the information accessed wirelessly and the use of mitigating factors such as second-factor authentication. Passwords do not have to be changed as often for systems that support robust or second-factor authentication because the password is only one of two components needed for a successful authentication. For example, the second authentication factor might come from a SecurID token.

3. Verify that your mobile clients are running protective software.

This broad step ensures that your clients have basic protections in place to mitigate the risk of compromise from an external source. You also want to make sure that a connecting client that has been off the network for a long period of time isn't going to harm your network.

How

Ensure that your clients have basic protection mechanisms in place if they are going to connect wirelessly to your network. At a minimum, your clients should have firewall and antivirus software, and if you have the capabilities to check for these prior to connection, you should probably verify that your access controls are working correctly. Other mitigating protections in place might include ensuring that all laptops are managed by a patch-management suite and members of your active directory. In this way, you can keep your systems patched and push down policies as appropriate for your network. You may also use standard known images for the laptops to minimize the complexity of the systems, the costs to your helpdesk, and the likelihood that your laptops have malware installed on them that could hurt your network.

4. Evaluate the security of the chosen authentication method.

Inappropriate authentication methods place the integrity of your network at risk of compromise. The tools and methods used to compromise WEP/WPA/WPA2 using a Pre-Shared Key (PSK) are readily available and easy to use.

How

Consider the following for the chosen authentication method in your environment: Do you want users to authenticate or just the mobile device? What systems do you want clients to use on the backend for authentication? How is your infrastructure set up? Does your network support all or some of the 802.11i standard?

Choosing the correct authentication method is beyond the scope of this short section, but you should have an understanding of the most common methods nicely outlined and discussed in special publications *Establishing Wireless Robust Security Networks: A Guide to IEEE 802.11i*, SP800-97.pdf. A detailed discussion here is beyond the scope of the chapter. The bare minimum you need to know is that the use of a PSK with authentication mechanisms such as WEP and WPA/WPA2 are no longer secure. At the time of this writing, NIST provides a special publication, *Guide to Securing Legacy IEEE 802.11 Wireless Networks*, SP800-48r1.pdf, which may lead some to believe that legacy wireless systems can be secured. This is a dangerous assumption, however. You may be able to minimize your risk exposure, but not by any useful measure. This said, also remember that controls should be commensurate with the data at risk. For example, you may not care as much about your guest wireless devices as you do your wireless Point of Sale (POS) devices.

Cracking Pre-Shared Keys

Cracking can be as simple as finding the right wireless card, downloading BackTrack, and surfing YouTube for tutorials. WEP networks can be cracked in less than a minute in most cases. WPA-PSK networks can be cracked using services such as www.wpacracker.com, which conveniently offer a massive farm of computers for a modest fee that allows the keys to be cracked in an average of 20 minutes.

Example Setup

- Laptop with VMWare loaded (server or desktop editions).
- Alfa wireless USB card (search Amazon for Alfa wireless).
- BackTrack Virtual Machine (download from www.backtrack-linux.org).
- Several Windows tools are available for viewing network information, but they lack the flexibility of working with BackTrack and the dozens of wireless tools installed. Check out metageek, Xirrus, and AirMagnet. The Xirrus WiFi Inspector and metageek inSSIDertool tools are free and can be useful for viewing network information.

5. Evaluate the security of the chosen communications method.

After clients authenticate to the network, they send data using the approved communications channel. If the frames are passed in clear-text or an easily broken format, the contents are subject to eavesdropping.

How

More than likely, you are passing data over an encrypted link if you have implemented wireless in the last couple of years. This step is a reminder that your data is passing wirelessly and is subject to another party intercepting and recording the conversation. Well-designed yagi antennas can detect and read traffic hundreds of yards or even miles away in a clear line of sight. Work with your network administrator to understand how the traffic is encrypted between the clients and the APs.

6. Evaluate the use of security monitoring software and processes.

Security monitoring software and regular log reviews can reveal potential issues before a serious event occurs.

How

Speak with the WLAN administrator to understand what is being logged and whether the logs are reviewed. It's preferable that an automated review process be used with one of the many Security Event Information Managers (SEIMs) on the market or through a process supported by the provider of the WLAN management software. The monitoring devices or software ideally help you identify issues, record authentication events, and locate potential rogue APs. Work with the administrator to understand whether these logs are useful; if not, determine what barriers exist to prevent them from being reviewed or from delivering actionable data.

7. Verify that rogue access points are not used on the network.

This is the step that most people think about when someone brings up a wireless audit. We hope that you do more than just locate rogue APs (unauthorized APs) and realize that the scope of an effective WLAN audit is much greater than just this step. This said, we don't want to take away from the importance of finding rogue APs that are violating your policies and bypassing intended authentication and communication security measures designed to protect your network from outside sources.

How

You can approach a search for rogue APs in a number of ways, including specialized wireless monitoring appliances, war-driving tools, and searching through your network traffic.

Commercial WLAN Security Monitoring Tools   If commercial WLAN monitoring tools are available, use them to corroborate other evidence you may find. Examples include Aruba's AirWave RAPIDS or Cisco's Adaptive Wireless IPS. Centrally managed wireless detection and prevention systems are a key component for enterprise control of wireless operations and compliance with policies. Proactive wireless monitoring is really the best way to identify wireless intrusions and rogue APs, because war-driving shows you what happens only at a particular moment in time.

War-driving   One common method for identifying rogue APs is to use war-driving software and tools and manually search for them. This is similar to what an attacker might use and fun for most auditors. War-driving can be effective in some scenarios, but here several challenges must be addressed:

- WLAN signal density or noise may make this prohibitive.
- The results are only for that snapshot in time.
- A wide choice of software and hardware is available.
- The work scope needs to be carefully defined.

If you are considering war-driving or war-walking around a high rise in a densely populated area, you may find it nearly impossible to detect rogue APs among the noise on your network. However, if you are located outside an urban area, detecting them may be easy. A variety of hardware and software is available, but for most purposes, we recommend sticking to the basics. Commercial versions of war-driving software are available, but most people will find free tools more than adequate for their purposes. If you are comfortable with Linux or Mac and have a laptop available for use, you may prefer using kismet because of its rich feature set.

Built-in wireless tools come with most security-focused and self-booting Linux distributions. These free applications are a great way to get your feet wet with Linux-based tools. Perhaps the most popular is BackTrack (www.backtrack-linux.org), although a few Google searches will turn up dozens of others.

> **NOTE**   Use these tools carefully and only with permission. Never break into another person's network "just because you can." Remember that, as an auditor, you're held to a code of ethics and generally very high standards.

If you want to extend the range of the default antenna you use for daily wireless connectivity, consider buying a high-powered card and a wireless antenna. We have used Alfa cards with great success. Speak with an old-hat shortwave radio enthusiast, and you'll quickly get bogged down in the complexities of antenna design and function. This is well beyond the scope of what you need to know to use them. You basically need to be aware of two types of antennas:

- **Directional antennas**   One example is a yagi antenna, which is a cannon-shaped antenna. Yagi antennas have a directional beam that can help you to triangulate and pinpoint where rogue APs may be hiding. You may find this useful for locating a source while driving or walking around a building. The range of a yagi antenna generally is very good because all its sensitivity is focused in one direction.

- **Omnidirectional antennas**   An example is a blade antenna. These antennas are capable of communicating with sources in all directions, which is great if you just want to add an antenna booster to your laptop. If you tried this with a yagi antenna and pointed the yagi in the wrong direction, you would be sorely disappointed, because you would never get a signal. The range of a blade antenna typically is much less than that of a yagi antenna.

Carefully consider the scope of the work to be done. It's one thing to use these tools to locate rogue APs and another to use tools similar to these to compromise your network. Scope the finding of rogue APs separately from determining the level of risk associated with weak protocols and weak authentication schemes.

Searching Through MAC OUIs   Finally, you theoretically could search through your network for MAC addresses belonging to wireless APs. Each network card has a MAC address uniquely assigned to it by the manufacturer. Each MAC address contains as part of the address an OUI, or company_id, a 24-bit globally unique assigned number. The OUI usually is concatenated with another 24 bits that are assigned by the company to make a 48-bit number that is unique to a particular piece of hardware. The 48-bit number is the MAC address. Each network card has a MAC address assigned to the card used to route packets from the network card to the next hop on the network. The idea is to address a piece of hardware uniquely. In the past, some have attempted to search for equipment on their network using the OUI, or company_id, which works in some cases, but not all.

As a real-world example, we have worked with access control products on global networks that periodically query network routers for their Address Resolution Protocol (ARP) tables. The software would then identify the switchport into which each device was attached and could alert an administrator when a possible AP was plugged into the network based on the MAC OUI.

Your ability to do this depends on your network topology, network administrator, monitoring tools, and the amount of work you want to do. MAC addresses are kept by IEEE and located in their entirety at http://standards.ieee.org/regauth/oui/oui.txt. The challenges you will encounter if you choose to do this are false positives and false negatives. Some MAC addresses have been reassigned or bought by others, and one company may use another manufacture's chipset. And MAC addresses are easily spoofed! It's an elegant solution on the surface, but you may face challenges and find that one of the other methods is an easier solution.

Part 2: WLAN Operational Audit

8. Evaluate procedures in place for tracking end user trouble tickets.

Failure to establish ownership and tracking of end user issues could result in users being unable to resolve connectivity problems.

How

End user issues should be tracked through a trouble ticketing system. An owner for these issues should be assigned and a group should be made responsible for tracking the progress toward closure of any tickets opened because of WLAN issues. Discuss these processes with the administrator.

9. Ensure appropriate security policies are in place for your WLAN.

Policies help to ensure compliance with a standard, help with repeatable processes, and allow the company to act against documented company violations.

How

Determine whether WLAN policies exist and whether the administrator responsible for the WLAN knows and understands the content of the policies. Determine whether the policies are being followed or what barriers might exist that prevent them from being followed. Finally, ensure that relevant portions of the WLAN policies are communicated to employees that use the wireless network. A few common policy items might include the following:

- All wireless transmissions must be encrypted to prevent eavesdropping.
- All APs must have updated firmware.
- Only authorized people on the [insert name here] team may have direct administrative controls of the APs.
- Only authorized people on the [insert name here] team may install APs.
- Passwords to APs must adhere to company policy.
- All efforts will be made to reduce propagation of radio waves outside the facility.
- Devices accessing the network must use personal firewalls and antivirus programs.
- Client devices must use IPSec-based virtual private network (VPN) technology (if appropriate).
- The [insert name here] team must monitor for rogue APs on a [insert time frame here] basis.
- Only authorized systems owned by the company may access the network and only for appropriate business use.

10. Evaluate disaster-recovery processes in place to restore wireless access should a disaster occur.

Failure to have appropriate recovery processes in place prevents a timely restoration of wireless access for users who must have it to conduct company business. In addition, it would be extremely easy without a plan and during the recovery process to deploy an insecure WLAN, leaving the organization's network open to unwanted guests. Depending on the disaster, WLAN may be the fastest method for restoring network access for critical employees and processes.

How

Restoring a WLAN may not be at the top of most people's list following a critical disaster, but some forethought should be given and procedures should be in place to facilitate this process. Discuss this with the administrator, and ensure that the recovery processes are in line with the expectations and standards of other recovery processes in the company. Depending on the use of wireless, this may be a critical component, such as a large warehouse that depends on wireless mobile scanners. Other environments, such as one that uses wireless to supplement existing and working wired infrastructures, may not view this as very important. This is a business risk that should be evaluated and measured appropriately when reviewing the WLAN security policies and the WLAN *Business-Continuity/Disaster-Recovery* (BC/DR) processes.

11. Evaluate whether effective change-management processes exist.

Change-management processes help to track and provide controlled changes to the environment. Controlled environments are more secure and have less impact on user productivity.

How

Discuss change-management practices with the administrator. Consider asking for evidence of a recent change, and follow through how the change was handled from start to finish, verifying that appropriate approvals were obtained and documentation created.

Test Steps for Auditing Mobile Devices

Several *mobile device management* (MDM) vendors hope to offer solutions to customers struggling to handle the explosive demand for smartphones. (Note that the MDM vendors are not the same as the handset manufacturers.) MDM solutions are designed to handle the management of smartphones created by the handset manufacturers, such as the Blackberry, iPhone, and Droid.

Established providers include Good Technology, Research in Motion (RIM), Microsoft, Motorola, and Sybase. We will cover some of the supporting company infrastructure required for their implementations, but we don't go beyond this here. We don't such components as e-mail servers or network equipment, which may or may not be in the scope of your audit. Consider other sections of this book as necessary if you want to expand the scope of the audit beyond the following steps, which conceptually follow closely to the steps in the WLAN audit with some slight changes.

Part I: Mobile Device Technical Audit

I. Ensure that mobile device management software is running the latest approved software and patches.

Running old software on the mobile device gateways may leave the gateways or remote mobile devices open to known attacks or prevent the organization from taking advantage of more robust security features.

How

Evaluate the gateway with an administrator, and verify that the code running on the gateway is the latest version. Verify that the latest version is correct using the manufacturer's website or other similar updated source of information from the manufacturer. Examine the change-management processes around evaluating and maintaining current code releases for the APs. Note whether this process is automated and coordinated and whether it scales operationally across regional sites.

2. Verify that mobile clients have protective features enabled if they are required by your mobile device security policy.

Many MDM solutions, including GoodLink and RIM (maker of Blackberry), both provide several client features such as password controls and remote or local wiping that can bolster your security should a device become lost or stolen.

How

Requisition a mobile device with an administrator's help, and verify that it has the protective features enabled as determined by your mobile security policy or other agreed-on standard. If you don't have a policy, we'll suggest some components for a mobile security policy in step 7.

Some common features available with MDM solutions include enforced passwords, password settings, remote lock, remote wipe, and local wipe. Passwords can be set up to meet several different requirements in terms of length and complexity. Emergency calls to 911 should be allowed when configured to enforce passwords. Remote lock allows administrators to lock a lost or stolen mobile device until it is either found or a decision is made to wipe the device remotely. Wiping the device prevents an attacker from retrieving any data. The local wipe feature is designed to wipe the device if a user exceeds the maximum number of tries to log into it.

If you have the capability, you should evaluate the process a user would follow if his or her PDA phone were lost or stolen. Test these features to verify that your company processes work as designed and that all parties understand how to carry out the process.

3. Determine the effectiveness of device security controls around protecting data when a hacker has physical access to the device.

This is an advanced step and would be performed with the help of your company's computer forensic or security team. The subtle reason for performing this step is to help shed light on the need for security on mobile devices. The company's e-mail server and global address book are accessible remotely on lost or stolen devices until the device account tied into the company network is deactivated.

How

In one large company, it was estimated by the administrator that wiping a device succeeds only about 20 percent of the time. One of the reasons for this is because users tend to wait too long before reporting that their devices have been lost or stolen. If users are not aware of what to do when they lose a device, a window of opportunity opens for someone with malicious intent to attempt to record data from the device. Waiting to raise a potential issue renders the remote lock and erase controls ineffective.

If you determine that you need to use forensic tools to test your controls, you need to state your assumptions clearly. You could, for example, give yourself a timeframe to pull data from a device before remotely attempting to kill the device. Assume that you have the ability to kill devices remotely, and assume that Faraday bags are not used by the attacker. Faraday bags prevent radio signals from reaching a device and lend an unfair advantage to an attacker. These bags might be used by a skilled, intentioned attacker, but they are not common. You can review the Guidelines on Cell Phone Forensics (SP800-101) located at http://csrc.nist.gov/publications/nistpubs/800-101/SP800-101.pdf.

The following additional controls may help to prevent physical access hacks. These must be turned on manually and should be in line with your policies.

- Managed devices must be password-protected and erase themselves automatically after, for example, 15 incorrect password attempts.
- Devices can be locked or erased remotely.
- A password is required to read data on a mobile device.

4. Evaluate the use of security monitoring software and processes.

Security monitoring and regular log reviews can reveal potential issues before a serious event occurs.

How

Speak with the mobile device administrator in an attempt to understand what's being logged and how those logs are reviewed. It's best to have an automated review process. Work with the administrator to understand whether these logs are useful; if they are not, determine what barriers exist to prevent them from being reviewed and delivering actionable data.

5. Verify that unmanaged devices are not used on the network. Evaluate controls over unmanaged devices.

Unmanaged devices often contain sensitive personal and corporate data without the benefit of the security controls enforced on managed devices. This makes them easy targets for compromise when they are lost or stolen.

How

One method for discovering the number of potential unmanaged devices on your network is to look for the existence of the supporting desktop software on your systems. This doesn't prove that an employee is actively using the device but suggests that at one point he or she tried to do so. You could use your endpoint management software, for example, to search for the existence of the executables associated with the desktop software used with the mobile devices. The reality is that this can be a very difficult step; however, it's important to manage mobile devices on the corporate network.

Advanced controls might include a preventative control such as Network Access Controls that can prevent these devices from connecting to the network. Discuss detective and preventative controls with your administrator.

Part 2: Mobile Device Operational Audit

6. Evaluate procedures in place for tracking end user trouble tickets.

Failure to establish ownership and tracking of end user issues could result in end users being unable to resolve connectivity problems.

How

End user issues should be tracked through a trouble ticketing system. An owner for these issues should be assigned and a group should be held responsible for tracking the progress to closure for any tickets opened because of mobile device issues. Discuss these processes with the administrator.

7. Ensure that appropriate security policies are in place for your mobile devices.

Policies help to ensure compliance with a standard, help with repeatable processes, and allow the company to act against documented company violations.

How

Determine whether mobile device policies exist and whether the administrator responsible for the mobile devices knows and understands the content of those policies. Determine whether the policies are being followed or what barriers might exist to prevent them from being followed. Finally, ensure that relevant portions of the WLAN policies are communicated to employees that use the wireless network. A few common policy items might include the following:

- You must use one of the defined and supported devices.
- Synchronizing to your local workstation is allowed only with approved managed devices.

- When available, antivirus and encryption tools should be used on your handheld device.
- The password policy for handhelds that access the company's Internet and/or e-mail systems is [defined policy].
- After 15 failed password tries, the handheld must be erased automatically.
- The device must time out after 30 minutes of inactivity.

8. Evaluate disaster recovery processes in place to restore mobile device access should a disaster happen.

Failure to have appropriate recovery processes in place prevents a timely restoration of mobile e-mail access for users who must have it to conduct company business.

How

Restoring mobile device access may not be at the top of most people's list following a critical disaster, but at least some thought should occur around and procedures in place to facilitate this process. Discuss this with the administrator, and ensure that the recovery processes are in line with the expectations and standards of other recovery processes in the company. Depending on the use of mobile e-mail, this may be a critical component, such as with a large mobile sales force that depends on wireless mobile e-mail to conduct business and close deals efficiently. Other environments, such as those that use wireless e-mail to supplement existing and working wired infrastructures, may not view this as very important. This is a business risk that should be evaluated and measured appropriately when you review the mobile device security policies and BC/DR processes.

9. Evaluate whether effective change management processes exist.

Change management processes help track and provide controlled changes to the environment. Controlled environments are more secure and have less impact on user productivity.

How

Discuss change management practices with the administrator as they relate to changing components in the environment that affect the infrastructure and *especially changes that might affect the end user*. Consider asking for evidence of a recent change and following through how the change was handled from start to finish, verifying that appropriate approvals were obtained and documentation created.

10. Evaluate controls in place to manage the service life cycle of personally owned and company-owned devices and any associated accounts used for the gateway.

The service life cycle of devices is defined as the provisioning, servicing, and deprovisioning of devices over the period of time such devices are used at the company. The risk of not tracking a device through the service life cycle includes losing track of the device to an employee who leaves the company with sensitive information still on the mobile device.

How

Measures should exist to manage the service life cycle of the mobile devices managed by your company and the accounts associated with those devices. Discuss this with the administrator, and look for records supporting his or her statements. Walk through a recent provisioning and deprovisioning process with the administrator.

Additional Considerations

Additional considerations might exist for your environment depending on your size, your geographic reach, and what kind of data exists on your network. Additional considerations might include the following:

- Ensure that license management for software is tracked by the number of users.
- Verify that processes exist for international support for diverse or geographically scattered organizations.
- Categorize the types of data typically stored on corporately managed mobile devices and the level of protection typically required in accordance with your information classification policy.
- Evaluate the switching and routing infrastructure as it relates to these components.

Tools and Technology

Here is a list of tools discussed in this chapter and others you might find useful:

Tools	Website
NetStumbler	www.netstumbler.com
kismet	www.kismetwireless.net
Wi-Fi Planet	www.wi-fiplanet.com
WirelessDefence.org	www.wirelessdefence.org
Aircrack-ng	www.aircrack-ng.org
TamoSoft	www.tamos.com
BackTrack Virtual Machine	www.backtrack-linux.org
Xirrus WiFi Inspector	www.xirrus.com/library/wifitools.php
AirMagnet	www.airmagnet.com
metageek and inSSIDertool	www.metageek.net
Wardriving tools	www.wardrive.net/wardriving/tools
Sybase Mobile Enterprise	www.sybase.com/products/mobileenterprise
GoodLink	www.good.com
Research in Motion (RIM)	www.blackberry.com
Mobile Device Manager	www.microsoft.com/systemcenter/mobile/default.mspx
Paraben	www.paraben-forensics.com

Knowledge Base

Following are URLs where you can find more information:

Resource	Website
NIST Special Publications	csrc.nist.gov/publications/PubsSPs.html
MAC OUIs	standards.ieee.org/regauth/oui/oui.txt
Wireless tutorials	www.wi-fiplanet.com/tutorials

Master Checklists

The following tables summarize the steps listed for WLAN and mobile devices.

Auditing Wireless LANs

Checklist for Auditing Wireless LANs
❑   1. Ensure that access points are running the latest approved software.
❑   2. Evaluate the use and controls around centralized WLAN management.
❑   3. Verify that your mobile clients are running protective software.
❑   4. Evaluate the security of the chosen authentication method.
❑   5. Evaluate the security of the chosen communications method.
❑   6. Evaluate the use of security monitoring software and processes.
❑   7. Verify that rogue access points are not used on the network.
❑   8. Evaluate procedures in place for tracking end-user trouble tickets.
❑   9. Ensure that appropriate security policies are in place for your WLAN.
❑   10. Evaluate disaster-recovery processes in place to restore wireless access should a disaster occur.
❑   11. Evaluate whether effective change-management processes exist.

Auditing Mobile Devices

Checklist for Auditing Mobile Devices
❑   1. Ensure that mobile device gateways are running the latest approved software and patches.
❑   2. Verify that mobile clients have protective features enabled if they are required by your mobile device security policy.
❑   3. Determine the effectiveness of device security controls around protecting data when a hacker has physical access to a device.
❑   4. Evaluate the use of security monitoring software and processes.

Checklist for Auditing Mobile Devices *(continued)*

❏   5. Verify that unmanaged devices are not used on the network. Evaluate controls over unmanaged devices.

❏   6. Evaluate procedures in place for tracking end-user trouble tickets.

❏   7. Ensure that appropriate security policies are in place for your mobile devices.

❏   8. Evaluate disaster recovery processes in place to restore mobile device access should a disaster happen.

❏   9. Evaluate whether effective change management processes exist.

❏   10. Evaluate controls in place to manage the service life cycle of personally owned and company-owned devices and any associated accounts used for the gateway.

PART II

Auditing Applications

Each application is unique, whether it supports financial or operational functions, and therefore each has its own unique set of control requirements. It is impossible to document specific control requirements that will be applicable to every application. However, in this chapter, we will describe some general control guidelines that should be pertinent to any application regardless of its function, programming language, and technology platform. The following topics are discussed in this chapter:

- Essential components of application audits
- How to drill down into possible issues with frameworks and key concepts
- Detailed steps for auditing applications, including the following:
  - Input controls
  - Interface controls
  - Audit trails
  - Access controls
  - Software change controls
  - Backup and recovery
  - Data retention and classification and user involvement

Background

Business applications systems, or applications for short, are computer systems that are used to perform and support specific business processes. Your company likely has dozens of applications, each used to perform a particular business function, such as accounts receivable, purchasing, manufacturing, customer and contact management, and so on. Most of these applications have interfaces that allow end users to interact with and enter data into the systems, although some may consist purely of offline (batch) processing.

These applications may be systems that were purchased from an external vendor (for example, many companies use an enterprise resource planning [ERP] system such as SAP R3 to perform their core financial functions) or they may be home grown (that is, applications developed specifically by your company for use within your company). Applications can range in size, from an enterprise system that is accessed by every employee, to a small client application accessed by one employee. Obviously, your audits will tend to focus on those larger applications that support critical business processes, but each application will need to be considered individually when you perform risk ranking and determine what to audit.

Each application has its own control nuances, depending on the business process it supports, the programming language that was used to develop it, and the technology platform(s) on which it resides (for examples, the database management system, middleware, and operating system used). Although it is not realistic to provide detailed test steps and checklists for every possible permutation of an application, this chapter provides guidance on control concepts that are common to almost all applications and that can be used to generate thoughts and ideas regarding audit test steps more specific to the application being audited.

Staying on top of every new technology that attaches itself to your environment is tough. It's our job as auditors to drill down quickly into new or existing applications to find potential control weaknesses. We will therefore discuss how to examine applications conceptually using big-picture and abstract frameworks. We also will suggest a comprehensive set of checklists that will greatly assist you in covering the vast majority of common control weaknesses.

 NOTE Chapter 8 contains test steps specific to auditing web-based applications, which can be used in conjunction with the standard application auditing test steps in this chapter.

Application Auditing Essentials

In a perfect scenario, you have a perfect audit program that you can apply quickly to your perfect application. However, although the test steps in this chapter will serve as a great starting point, in reality you're often faced with new ideas and approaches for solving business problems with new technology, all of which get bundled together to create a unique application that requires a unique audit program. As you struggle with the questions to ask, you will find the following frameworks and best practices helpful.

Generalized Frameworks

Generalized frameworks are useful in meetings when you've been put on the spot to come up with questions and possible risks associated with an application. You might even find yourself walking into a meeting, taking out a blank sheet of paper, and writing "PPTM," "STRIDE," and "PDIO" (as explained in the following sections) at the top before the meeting starts. Then, as you discuss the application or project under review, you can ask questions regarding and make note of how each element of each framework is being addressed. At the end of the meeting, if you find "blanks" by any of the framework elements, it's possible that you've discovered a gap in the controls. This sort of quick-and-dirty thought process should never take the place of detailed and thorough testing, of course, but it can be very useful when you're participating in initial discussions and consulting on controls.

PPTM

People, processes, tools, and measures (PPTM) is a great brainstorming framework for examining an application from the macro level. Detailed specific technical review steps dominate this chapter. PPTM helps you to come up with your own steps quickly and efficiently as they apply to your unique situation.

People   *People* in PPTM describes every aspect of the application that deals with a human. For example, if you have the opportunity to provide input during application development, ensure that the right people are involved in the planning, design, implementation, or operations for the project and that the right stakeholders are involved. If the application involves end users, ensure that the application has controls around provisioning and deprovisioning access and that the end users have been involved in the components with which they will ultimately interface. Little is more embarrassing than spending time and money rolling out an application, just to find out that upper management doesn't approve it or that the end users find that the interface is too complicated to use.

Process   *Process* in PPTM describes every aspect of the application that is involved in a policy, procedure, method, or course of action. Review the interaction of the application with interfacing systems and verify compliance in security models (For example, ensure that firewalls are in place to protect the application from external applications, users, business partners, and the like.) Procedures and policies should be written to support how the application is intended to be used. Adequate documentation also should exist to support technicians who need to maintain the application.

Tools   *Tools* in PPTM describe every aspect of the application that deals with a concrete technology or product. Ensure that the appropriate hardware and environment exist to support the application and that the application interfaces with recommended technologies appropriate to your intended policies and procedures. Verify that the application and infrastructure are tested and audited appropriately.

Measures   *Measures* in PPTM describe every aspect of the application that is quantifiable conceptually, such as the business purpose or application performance. For example, you can verify that the application meets well-documented and well-thought-out acceptance criteria. If the application is intended to solve a quantifiable business problem, verify that it does indeed solve that problem. Verify that logs are meaningful and that you can measure the performance of the application.

STRIDE

The STRIDE acronym stands for the following: *s*poofing identity, *t*ampering with data, *r*epudiation, *i*nformation disclosure, *d*enial of service, and *e*levation of privilege. STRIDE is a methodology used for identifying known threats. It is an example of a simplified threat-risk model that is easy to remember and apply. When assessing an application, you can use the acronym to develop steps that address how each of the following risks are mitigated.

Spoofing Identity   Identity spoofing is a key risk for applications that have many users but provide a single execution context at the application and database levels. In particular, users should not be able to become any other user or assume the attributes of another user.

Tampering with Data   Data should be stored in a secure location, with access appropriately controlled. The application should carefully check data received from the user and validate that it is sane and applicable before storing or using it. For web and other applications with a client component, you should perform your validation checks on the server and not the client, where the validation checks might be tampered with. This is particularly important for web applications, where users can potentially change data delivered to them, return it, and thereby potentially manipulate client-side validation. The application should not send data to the user, such as interest rates or periods, that are obtainable only from within the application itself and allow the user potentially to manipulate that data.

Repudiation   Users may dispute transactions if there is insufficient auditing or re-cord-keeping of their activity. For example, if a user says, "But I didn't transfer any money to this external account!" and you cannot track his or her activities through the application, then it is extremely likely that the transaction will have to be written off as a loss. Therefore, you should consider whether the application requires nonrepudiation controls, such as web access logs, audit trails at each tier, or the same user context from top to bottom. Preferably, the application should run with the user's privileges, not more, but this may not be possible with many commercial off-the-shelf applications.

Information Disclosure   Users are rightfully wary of submitting private details to a system. If it is possible for an attacker to reveal data publicly, especially user data, whether anonymously or as an authorized user, there will be an immediate loss of confidence and a substantial period of reputation loss. Therefore, applications must include strong controls to prevent user ID tampering and abuse and to secure system data stored in databases and data files.

Also consider whether the user's web browser may leak information. Some web browsers may ignore the no-caching directives in HTTP headers or handle them incorrectly. In a corresponding fashion, every secure application has a responsibility to minimize the amount of information stored by the web browser in case it leaks or leaves information behind, which can be used by an attacker to learn details about the application or the user, possibly using that information to assume the role of an authorized privileged user.

Finally, in implementing persistent values, you should keep in mind that the use of hidden fields is insecure by nature. Such storage should never be trusted to secure especially sensitive information or to provide adequate personal privacy safeguards.

Denial of Service   Application designers should be aware that their applications may be subject to a denial-of-service attack. Therefore, the use of expensive resources such as large files, complex calculations, heavy-duty searches, or long queries should be reserved for authenticated and authorized users and should not be available to anonymous users.

For applications that don't have this luxury, every facet of the application should be engineered to perform as little work as possible, to use fast and few database queries, and to avoid exposing large files or unique links per user to prevent simple denial-of-service attacks.

Elevation of Privilege   If an application provides distinct user and administrative roles, ensure that the user cannot elevate his or her role to a more highly privileged one. In particular, it is not sufficient simply to not display privileged-role links. Instead, all actions should be gated through an authorization matrix to ensure that only the permitted roles can access privileged functionality.

PDIO

PDIO comes from Cisco Systems and stands for *p*lanning, *d*esign, *i*mplementation, and *o*perations. Sometimes you need to consider the potential challenges at each stage of a project. You might find this framework useful as you look at a new application and think ahead to the upcoming challenges. A problem might occur, for example, if system administrators are tossing around ideas in a planning or design session for a network solution and the senior networking engineer isn't in the room. If you, as an auditor, are asked to look at the implementation of a new solution, you should immediately ask questions about the ongoing operations of the solution. Refer to Chapter 15 for more details on auditing company projects.

Best Practices

These best practices can help you quickly spot common weaknesses and poor controls.

Apply Defense-in-Depth

Layered approaches provide more security over the long term than one complicated mass of security architecture. You might, for example, use Access Control Lists (ACLs) on the networking and firewall equipment to allow only necessary traffic to reach the application. This approach significantly lowers the overall risk of compromise to the system on which the application is running, because you quickly eliminate access to services, ports, and protocols that otherwise would be accessible to compromise.

Use a Positive Security Model

Positive (whitelist) security models allow only what is on the list, excluding everything else by default. However, negative (blacklist) security models allow everything by default, eliminating only the items you know are bad. This is the challenge for antivirus programs, which you must update constantly to keep up with the number of new possible attacks (viruses) that could affect your system. The problem with this model, if you are forced to use it, is that you absolutely must keep the model updated. Even with the model updated, a vulnerability could exist that you don't know about, and your attack surface is much larger than if you used a positive security model. The preferred practice is to deny by default and allow only those things that you consciously permit.

Fail Safely

When an application fails, it can be dealt with in three ways: allow, block, or error. In general, application errors should fail in the same manner as a disallow operation, as viewed from the end user. This is important, because it means the end user doesn't have additional information to use that may help him or her to compromise the system. Log what you want, and keep any messages that you want elsewhere, but don't give the user additional information he or she might use to compromise your system.

Run with Least Privilege

The principle of least privilege mandates that accounts have the least amount of privilege possible to perform their activity. This encompasses user rights and resource permissions such as CPU limits, memory capacity, network bandwidth, and file system permissions.

Avoid Security by Obscurity

Obfuscating data, or hiding it instead of encrypting it, is a very weak security mechanism, especially for an application. If a human could figure out how to hide the data, what's to keep another person from learning how to recover the data? Consider, for example, how some people hide a key to their house under the doormat. A criminal wants the easiest possible way into the house and will check common places such as under the doormat, the rock closest to the door, and above the door frame for a key. Never obfuscate critical data that can be encrypted (or better yet never stored in the first place).

Keep Security Simple

Simple security mechanisms are easy to verify and easy to implement correctly. Cryptographer Bruce Schneier is famous for suggesting that the quickest method to break a cryptographic algorithm is to go around it. Avoid overly complex security mechanisms, if possible. Developers should avoid the use of double negatives and complex architectures when a simple approach would be faster and easier. Don't confuse complexity with layers. Layers are good; complexity isn't.

Detect Intrusions and Keep Logs

Applications should have built-in logging that's protected and easily read. Logs help you troubleshoot issues and, just as important, help you to track down when or how an application might have been compromised.

Never Trust External Infrastructure and Services

Many organizations use the processing capabilities of third-party partners that more than likely have differing security policies and postures than yours. It is unlikely that you can influence or control any external third party, be they home users or major suppliers or partners. Therefore, implicitly trusting externally run systems is dangerous.

Establish Secure Defaults

Your applications should arrive to you or be presented to the users with the most secure default settings possible that still allow business to function. This may require training end users or communications messages, but the end result is a significantly reduced attack surface, especially when an application is pushed out across a large population.

Use Open Standards

Where possible, base security on open standards for increased portability and interoperability. Since your infrastructure is likely a heterogeneous mix of platforms, the use of open standards helps to ensure compatibility between systems as you continue to grow. Additionally, open standards are often well known and scrutinized by peers in the security industry to ensure that they remain secure.

Test Steps for Auditing Applications

The following steps generally refer to controls specific to the application and do not address controls, for example, at the level of the network, operating system, and database management system. Refer to other chapters of this book for test steps for those topics and also consider the frameworks and concepts described earlier in this chapter as you approach developing the audit program for your application.

 NOTE The audit steps in this chapter are written from the standpoint of auditing an application that has already been developed and implemented. See Chapter 15 for additional steps to be performed when auditing an application during the development process.

Input Controls

1. Review and evaluate controls built into system transactions over the input of data.

As much as possible, online transactions should perform upfront validation and editing to ensure the integrity of data before it is entered into the system's files and databases. Invalid data in the system can result in costly errors. It is preferable and much more cost-effective to catch a data entry error prior to that data being entered into and processed by the application. Otherwise, the error may not be caught at all, may only be caught after it results in system disruption, or after time-consuming manual reconciliation procedures, and so on.

How

Verify that invalid data is rejected or edited on entry. You will need to understand the business function being supported by the system and the purpose and use of its various data elements. This likely will require discussion not only with the developers but also with the end users. Once you understand the purpose of the system and its data, you can think through the various data-integrity risks associated with the application. In some cases, a code review may be appropriate if the developers are available and the auditor is a knowledgeable coder. Poorly written, commented, or formatted code is often a red flag that suggests that a deeper review is needed. If possible, obtain access to a test version of the system that mirrors the production environment and attempt to "break" the system by entering invalid data to see whether it is accepted by the application.

Following are some basic examples of good data input controls:

- Fields that are intended to contain only numbers should not allow entry of alphanumeric characters.

- Fields that are used to report such things as dates and hours should be set up either to require input in the correct format (such as *MMDDYY* or *HHMM*) or transform input into the correct format.

- Where applicable, transactions should perform "reasonableness" and "logic" checks on inputs. An example would be preventing users from reporting labor of more than 24 hours in a day or more than 60 minutes in an hour. Another example would be disallowing entry for time, costs, and so on, for an employee who has been terminated or who is on leave. Or consider a transaction used by ticket agents to record how many seats were sold on a flight and the number of no-shows. The transaction should not allow the agent to input numbers indicating that there were more no-shows than seats sold.

- When a finite number of valid entries are available for a field, entries that are invalid should not be allowed. In other words, input screens should validate such things as cost centers, account numbers, product codes, employee numbers, and so on, against the appropriate database(s) or file(s).

- Duplicate entries should not be allowed for data that is intended to be unique. For example, the transaction should not allow a product code to be added to the product database if that code already exists on the database.

- Each input screen generally has certain fields that are required for the transaction to be processed accurately. Execution of a transaction should not be allowed until valid data is entered into each of those fields.

- Where applicable, transactions should perform "calculation" checks on inputs. For example, the system should ensure that journal-entry credits and debits balance to zero before processing a transaction. Another example would be a labor-entry system where hours charged for the week need to add up to at least 40.

- Programmed cutoff controls should be in place to help prevent users from recording transactions in the wrong period. For example, the screen should not allow users to record transactions in prior accounting periods.

- A user should be prevented from updating his or her own personal data in some systems. For example, a user, regardless of his or her access level, should not be allowed to change his or her own pay rate or vacation accrual rate.

- Database operatives (such as `*`, `=`, `or`, `select`) should be disallowed as valid input, as they can be used to disrupt or retrieve information from the database.

2. Determine the need for error/exception reports related to data integrity and evaluate whether this need has been filled.

Error or exception reports allow any potential data-integrity problems to be reviewed and corrected when it's not feasible or practical to use input controls to perform upfront validation of data entered into the system. For example, although it may not be inherently wrong for an employee to enter 80 hours of overtime for one week into a labor system, this sort of unusual event should be captured on a report for review by the appropriate level of management.

How

Discuss the application's error and exception handling with the developer or administrator. Based on the results of the analysis from step 1, look for opportunities for additional data integrity checks (which may not have been feasible to perform with "hard" upfront input requirements). Again, discussions with the end users can be very helpful here. Ask them what sorts of reporting would be helpful for them in catching anomalies and errors. For any error and exception reports that do exist, look for evidence that those reports are being regularly reviewed and appropriately handled.

Interface Controls

3. Review and evaluate the controls in place over data feeds to and from interfacing systems.

When an application passes and/or receives data to or from other applications, controls need to be employed to ensure that the data is transmitted completely and accurately. Failure to do so can result in costly errors and system disruption.

How

Determine what interfaces exist with the system you are auditing, including data flowing into and out of the system. These interfaces could be in the form of real-time data transmission or periodic transmission of data files via batch processes. Review system flow diagrams, review system code, and interview the application developer or administrator to obtain this information. Once you have a feel for the interfaces that exist, determine which controls are in place regarding those interfaces through code review and interviews with the application developer or administrator. Expect to see basic controls such as those discussed in the following paragraphs.

Control totals from interface transmissions should be generated and used by the system to determine whether the transmission completed accurately. If a problem is found, reports should be issued that notify the proper people of the problem. Some examples of control totals that may be applicable are hash totals (totals that have no inherent meaning, such as summing all account numbers or employee numbers in a file being transmitted), record counts, and total amounts (totals that do have inherent meaning, such as summing the total sales entered or salary paid in a file being transmitted). For example, prior to transmission, the sending system might generate a count of all records being sent. After transmission, the receiving system could generate a count of all records received. Those two numbers would then be compared. If they don't match, it would generate an error report, as this would indicate that some records were not received accurately. Another type of control total could flag missing record numbers when records are transmitted in a sequential fashion. All such methods are intended to detect instances when data from the sending system is not correctly received. If these controls do exist, review evidence that applicable error reports are being regularly reviewed and acted upon.

The system should handle items that did not transmit successfully in such a manner that reports and/or processes enable these items to be resolved quickly and appropriately, such as by placing them in a suspense file and generating reports of all items in the suspense file. Verify that any such suspense files and error reports are being reviewed and acted upon.

Data files that contain interface source or target information should be secured from unauthorized modifications. This may mean appropriate authentication controls, authorization controls, or encryption where necessary. Review the file security for any applicable files.

When it is not feasible to use control totals to verify accurate transmission of data, reconciliation reports should be generated that allow users to compare what was on one system with what was received on another system. If applicable, review evidence that reconciliation reports are regularly reviewed and acted upon.

Where applicable, data validation and editing, as described in the "Input Controls" section of this checklist, should be performed on data received from outside systems. Error/exception reports should be generated that allow any data-integrity problems to be corrected, and those reports should be regularly reviewed.

4. If the same data is kept in multiple databases and/or systems, ensure that periodic sync processes are executed to detect any inconsistencies in the data.

Storing the same data in multiple places can lead to out-of-sync conditions that result in system errors. It can also have a negative impact on business decisions, as erroneous conclusions can be reached using inaccurate data.

How

Determine, with the help of the application developer or application administrator, where this sort of control is applicable and review for its existence and effectiveness. Ideally, one database or data file should be designated as the "master" for each data element, and other systems will reference the master location as opposed to keeping a separate copy of the data. Even if multiple copies of the data are kept, the location that represents the master copy should be designated so that the system can easily determine "who wins" in out-of-sync situations and perform automated corrections.

Audit Trails

5. Review and evaluate the audit trails present in the system and the controls over those audit trails.

Audit trails are useful for troubleshooting and helping to track down possible breaches of your application.

How

Review the application with the developer or administrator to ensure that information is captured when key data elements are changed. This information should include in most cases the original and new values of the data, who made the change, and when the change was made. This information should be kept in a secured log to prevent unauthorized updates. The logs should be retained for a reasonable period of time, such as three or six months, to aid investigations into errors or inappropriate activities.

6. Ensure that the system provides a means of tracing a transaction or piece of data from the beginning to the end of the process enabled by the system.

This is important to verify that the transaction was fully processed and to pinpoint any errors or irregularities in the processing of that data.

How

Review the application with the developer or administrator and evaluate the existence of this ability. Identify a sample of recent transactions and attempt to trace them through the system's various processing steps.

Access Controls

7. Ensure that the application provides a mechanism that authenticates users based, at a minimum, on a unique identifier for each user and a confidential password.

Failure to authenticate users or just having a poor authentication scheme presents an open opportunity for curious users and malicious attackers to access your system.

How

Review the application with the developer or administrator and verify that appropriate authentication measures exist commensurate with the type of data on the application. For example, two-factor authentication might be required in some cases to authenticate users to sensitive applications or for end users accessing your applications from the Internet.

8. Review and evaluate the application's authorization mechanism to ensure that users are not allowed to access any sensitive transactions or data without first being authorized by the system's security mechanism.

The system's security mechanism should allow for each system user to be given a specific level of access to the application's data and transactions. Without the ability to provide granular access based on user need, users will likely be granted unnecessary levels of access.

How

Employees should be given only the amount of access to the system necessary to perform their jobs. Review the application with the developer or administrator, and verify this functionality in the application. In other words, it should be possible to specify which specific transactions and datasets or files a system user will be able to access. In general, it also should be possible to specify what level of access (such as display, update, and delete) the user will receive to application resources.

9. Ensure that the system's security/authorization mechanism has an administrator function with appropriate controls and functionality.

The administrator user function should exist to help administer users, data, and processes. This account or functionality should be tightly controlled in the application to prevent compromise and disruption of services to other users.

How

Evaluate the use of the administrator function with the developer or application administrator. The user of this function should have the ability to add, delete, or modify user access to the application system and its resources. The security mechanism should also provide the ability to control who has access to this administrator function. Obtain a list of all employees who have been granted the administrator access level and review each for appropriateness. Also ensure that the system's security mechanism provides the system's security administrator with the ability to view who has access to the system and what level of access they have.

10. Determine whether the security mechanism enables any applicable approval processes.

The application's security mechanism should support granular controls over who can perform what approval processes and then lock data that has been formally approved from modification by a lower authority. Otherwise, a lower authority or malicious user could modify or corrupt data in the system.

How

Verify with the developer or application administrator that appropriate controls are in place. For example, if someone needs to approve journal entries before they can be passed on to the general ledger, the system's security mechanism should provide a means for defining who is authorized to perform this approval. Any data that has been through the approval process should be locked in order to prevent any further modifications.

Interviews with system users are a good way to help the auditor determine the need for this sort of ability. It is critical that the auditor understand not only the technical aspects of the application being reviewed but also the business purpose.

11. Review and evaluate processes for granting access to users. Ensure that access is granted only when there is a legitimate business need.

Users should have intentional access granted and governed by the application administrator(s) to prevent unauthorized access to areas outside the user's intended scope. The application should have controls in place and the administrator(s) should have processes in place to prevent users from having more access than is required for their roles. This step embodies the concept of least-privileged access.

How

Review processes for requesting and approving access to the application. Ensure that these processes are documented and that they require approval from a knowledgeable administrator before application access is granted to a user. Select a sample of users, and ensure that user access was approved appropriately. Verify that the authorization mechanism is working appropriately.

12. Review processes for removing user access when it is no longer needed. Ensure that a mechanism or process is in place that suspends user access on termination from the company or on a change of jobs within the company.

Poor deprovisioning processes may leave a user with inappropriate access to your application long after the access or authority should have been removed.

How

Verify that appropriate deprovisioning processes are in place with the developer and application administrator. Review the administrator(s) processes for periodically reviewing user access lists and validating that the access is still appropriate. Be sure to look at both the application and the procedures around the application to ensure that they are being followed and are capable of being followed as written. Automated suspension of accounts in the event of termination or job change is preferable to processes that require manual intervention.

For applications that have been in "production" for some time, select a sample of system users and validate that their access is still appropriate. Alternatively, if possible, select a sample of system users who have changed jobs or left the company, and ensure that their access has been removed.

13. Verify that the application has appropriate password controls. Also, determine whether default application account passwords have been changed.

The appropriateness of the password controls depends on the sensitivity of the data used within the application. Overly weak passwords make the application sensitive to compromise, and overly strong passwords often force users to write them down in plain sight or to never change their password.

Many applications, particularly those that are purchased, have default accounts with well-known default passwords. Many of these default accounts are used for system administration and therefore have elevated privileges. If those default passwords are not changed, it is easy for an unauthorized user to access the application.

How

Verify appropriate password controls with the help of the developer or the application administrator and by reviewing your company policy. For example, three-digit PIN numbers probably are inappropriate for applications that store credit-card data, and a 20-character password probably is overly paranoid for someone trying to access his or her voicemail. Ensure that the security mechanism requires users to change their passwords periodically (such as every 30 to 90 days). When appropriate, the security mechanism also should enforce password composition standards such as the length and required characters. Additionally, the security mechanism should suspend user accounts after a certain number of consecutive unsuccessful log-in attempts. This is typically as low as 3 and can be as high as 25 depending on the application, other forms of authentication required, and the sensitivity of the data.

Determine whether default accounts and passwords exist with the help of the developer or application administrator and by review of system documentation and Internet research. If they do exist, one of the easiest ways to determine whether they have been changed is to attempt to log on using the default accounts and passwords (or by asking the application administrator to attempt to do so).

14. Ensure that users are automatically logged off from the application after a certain period of inactivity.

Without timeout controls, an unauthorized user could obtain access to the application by accessing a logged-in workstation where the legitimate user didn't log off and the application is still active.

How

Review the application with the developer or administrator to evaluate the existence of this ability.

15. Evaluate the use of encryption techniques to protect application data.

The need for encryption is determined most often by either policy, regulation, the sensitivity of the network, or the sensitivity of the data in the application. Where possible, encryption techniques should be used for passwords and other confidential data that is sent across the network. This prevents other people on the network from "sniffing" and capturing this information. For sensitive data, such as passwords, encryption should also be used when the data is at rest (in storage).

How

Review the application with the developer or administrator to evaluate the existence of encryption where appropriate.

16. Evaluate application developer access to alter production data.

In general, system developers should not be given access to alter production data, in order to establish appropriate segregation of duties. Data entry and alteration should generally be performed by business users.

How

Discuss with the developer or administrator and evaluate the separation of duties between developers and business users.

Software Change Controls

Software change management (SCM), used by a trained software development team, generally improves the quality of code written, reduces problems, and makes maintenance easier.

17. Ensure that the application software cannot be changed without going through a standard checkout/staging/testing/ approval process after it is placed into production.

It should not be possible for developers to update production code directly. Your production code is your application and it should be strictly controlled. Segregation of duties must be in place to ensure that all changes to the code are thoroughly reviewed and tested. Without these checks and balances, untested or unintended changes could be made to your production application, severely damaging the system's integrity and availability. Should a failure in the application occur without enforced software change controls, it might be difficult or impossible to track down the cause of the problem.

How

Evaluate this capability with the developers and application administrator. Determine the location of the production code and who has access to update that code. Preferably, the code will be controlled by some sort of librarian mechanism that provides granular control over how access to the code is managed.

Proper software change controls will require that the code first be checked out into a development environment, then checked into a testing or staging environment, and only then checked back into the production environment. Determine whether this is the case.

In addition, ensure that the software-change mechanism requires sign-off before code will be moved into production. The system should require that this sign-off be performed by someone other than the person who developed or modified the code. In addition, the software-change mechanism should allow for specific people to be authorized to perform sign-off on the system's programs. Review the people with this authorization and ensure that the privilege is kept to a minimum.

Evaluate controls in place to prevent code from being modified after it has been signed-off but before it has been moved to production. Otherwise, developers will be able to bypass approval processes.

18. Evaluate controls regarding code checkout and versioning.

Strong software controls regarding code checkout and versioning provide accountability, protect the integrity of the code, and have been shown to improve maintenance and reliability.

How

Verify with the developers that the software-change mechanism requires developers to check out code that they want to modify. If another developer wants to modify the same code while it is still checked out, he or she should be prevented from doing so. Alternatively, the second developer could be warned of the conflict but allowed to perform the checkout. In such a case, a notification of the duplicate checkout should be sent automatically to the original developer.

Ensure that the software-change mechanism "versions" software so that past versions of the code can be retrieved, if necessary. This allows an easy mechanism for backing out changes, should issues be encountered.

19. Evaluate controls regarding the testing of application code before it is placed into a production environment.

Improperly tested code may have serious performance or vulnerability issues when placed into production with live data.

How

Determine whether the software change process requires evidence of testing (including security testing), code walk-throughs, and adherence to software-development guidelines (including guidelines for secure coding). These should occur before the approver signs-off on the code. Testing of any software development or modifications should take place in a test environment that mirrors the production environment, using test data. Ensure that these requirements are in place and documented. Pull a sample of recent software changes and look for evidence that these processes have been followed.

20. Evaluate controls regarding batch scheduling.

Many applications execute programs (often called "jobs") in batch (offline) mode. For example, an accounts receivable application may have jobs scheduled to run every night, and the application may acquire a feed of invoices and automatically apply payments to them. These functions are often performed by a series of jobs scheduled to run in sequence. If proper controls are not in place over the scheduling and monitoring of these jobs, it could result in inaccurate or failed processing.

How

Work with the application developers and administrators to understand what sort of batch processing is occurring and review applicable controls. Following are examples of common controls:

- Ensure that the batch scheduling tool can establish predecessor/successor relationships and that this ability is used where needed. Predecessor/successor relationships allow you to establish a sequence of jobs, where one job cannot kick-off until another predetermined job completes. This allows proper sequencing of processing.

- Determine whether the tool allows for jobs to be monitored for successful completion and has an alert mechanism in the event of unsuccessful completion. This alert mechanism should be used to alert some sort of central monitoring group who in turn should have a contact and escalation list.

- The tool should provide the ability to control who can sign-off on and implement changes to job scheduling and to job definitions (such as where the job is located, the name of the job, the user ID that runs the job, how often the job is scheduled, and so on). Review and evaluate who has the ability to sign-off on and implement changes to job scheduling and job definitions. This ability should be limited.

- For changes to job scheduling and to job definitions, the tool should track who made the change, who signed-off on the change, when the change was made, what was changed, and why the change was made. The tool should also allow you to retrieve previous versions of the schedule and of job definitions in the event of a problem with any changes. Determine whether this is the case.

- Ensure that the tool allows you to perform exception date processing. In other words, it should be able to accommodate changes in the schedule due to holidays, leap years, and so on.

- Ensure that recovery procedures have been developed that will allow for jobs that have ended abnormally to be restarted and reprocessed.

Backup and Recovery

21. Determine whether a Business Impact Analysis (BIA) has been performed on the application to establish backup and recovery needs.

A BIA is performed to obtain input from the application's business users regarding the impact to the business in the event of an extended outage of the application. This drives the engineering of the application's backup and recovery mechanisms.

How

Through interviews with the application support personnel and end users, determine what sort of BIA, if any, has been performed and review associated documentation. At a minimum, look for documented requirements regarding the application's RTO (Recovery Time Objective, which dictates how quickly the system needs to be back up after a disaster) and RPO (Recovery Point Objective, which dictates how much data the business can afford to lose in the event of a disaster).

22. Ensure that appropriate backup controls are in place.

Failure to back up critical application data may severely disrupt business operations in the event of a disaster. A disaster could result in total loss of the application and its data with no ability to recover it.

How

Determine whether critical data and software are backed up periodically (generally weekly full backups with daily incremental backups for the data) and stored offsite in a secured location. If cost beneficial and appropriate, duplicate transaction records should be created and stored to allow recovery of data files to the point of the last processed transaction. Ensure that the backup schedule is in alignment with the RPO and RTO established by the application's users.

Also ensure that the application code is backed up and stored offsite in a secured location, along with any tools necessary for compiling and using the code.

23. Ensure that appropriate recovery controls are in place.

Recovery procedures and testing are necessary to ensure that the recovery process is understood and that it functions operationally as intended.

How

Discuss with the application administrator and appropriate personnel to ensure that detailed recovery procedures are documented that define what tasks are to be performed, who is to perform those tasks, and the sequence in which they are to be performed. Testing of the recovery from backup tapes using the documented recovery procedures should be performed periodically. Ensure that the recovery processes are in alignment with the RTO established by the application's users.

 NOTE To minimize redundancy, only the basics of auditing disaster recovery are included in this chapter. See Chapter 4 for additional details and ideas for auditing your application's disaster recovery capabilities.

Data Retention and Classification and User Involvement

24. Evaluate controls regarding the application's data retention.

Data should be archived and retained in accordance with business, tax, and legal requirements. Failure to do so could result in penalties and operational issues caused by the inability to obtain needed data.

How

Evaluate the appropriateness of the controls with the developers and application administrator. These requirements will vary based on the type of data and should be acquired from the appropriate departments within your company.

25. Evaluate the controls regarding data classification within the application.

All application data should be assigned a business owner, and this owner should classify the data (for example, public, internal use only, or confidential). This provides assurance that the data is being protected in alignment with its sensitivity.

How

Determine the business owner of the data contained within the application and ask for evidence that the data has been classified according to your company's data classification system. This classification should appear on any reports or transactions that display system data. Also, determine whether the application's access control mechanisms are appropriate based on the classification.

26. Evaluate overall user involvement and support for the application.

Without appropriate user involvement and support, the application may not adequately provide for user needs or appropriately support the business.

How

Interview the application's users and support personnel to determine what user involvement and support mechanisms have been put in place. Following are examples:

- Review and evaluate the existence of a formal steering team for the system. Generally, a steering team or some other form of user committee should exist to approve and prioritize system development and modifications.

- Ensure that changes to the functionality of the system are not made without user testing and approval.

- A mechanism should be in place that allows system users and developers to report and track system problems and to request system changes.

- For significant applications, some form of help desk functionality should exist to provide real-time help for user questions and problems.

- Ensure that system documentation and training exists that provides system users with adequate information to use the application effectively in performing their jobs.

Operating System, Database, and Other Infrastructure Controls

Detailed guidelines for controlling the operating system, database, and other related infrastructure components are beyond the scope of this chapter. However, security of the infrastructure on which the application resides is a critical part of application security. The applicable audit programs from this book's other chapters should be executed in addition to the application-specific steps provided in this chapter.

Master Checklists

The following tables summerize the best practices and steps discussed in this chapter for auditing applications.

Application Best Practices

Checklist for Best Practices
❑ Apply defense-in-depth.
❑ Use a positive security model.
❑ Fail safely.
❑ Run with least privilege.
❑ Avoid security by obscurity.
❑ Keep security simple.
❑ Detect intrusions and keep logs.
❑ Never trust external infrastructure and services.
❑ Establish secure defaults.
❑ Use open standards.

Auditing Applications

Checklist for Auditing Applications
❑ 1. Review and evaluate controls built into system transactions over the input of data.
❑ 2. Determine the need for error/exception reports related to data integrity and evaluate whether this need has been filled.
❑ 3. Review and evaluate the controls in place over data feeds to and from interfacing systems.
❑ 4. If the same data is kept in multiple databases and/or systems, ensure that periodic sync processes are executed to detect any inconsistencies in the data.
❑ 5. Review and evaluate the audit trails present in the system and the controls over those audit trails.
❑ 6. Ensure that the system provides a means of tracing a transaction or piece of data from the beginning to the end of the process enabled by the system.
❑ 7. Ensure that the application provides a mechanism that authenticates users, based, at a minimum, on a unique identifier for each user and a confidential password.
❑ 8. Review and evaluate the application's authorization mechanism to ensure users are not allowed to access any sensitive transactions or data without first being authorized by the system's security mechanism.
❑ 9. Ensure that the system's security/authorization mechanism has an administrator function with appropriate controls and functionality.
❑ 10. Determine whether the security mechanism enables any applicable approval processes.

Checklist for Auditing Applications

☐ 11. Review and evaluate processes for granting access to users. Ensure that access is granted only when there is a legitimate business need.

☐ 12. Review processes for removing user access when it is no longer needed. Ensure that a mechanism or process is in place that suspends user access on termination from the company or on a change of jobs within the company.

☐ 13. Verify that the application has appropriate password controls. Also, determine whether default application account passwords have been changed.

☐ 14. Ensure that users are automatically logged off from the application after a certain period of inactivity.

☐ 15. Evaluate the use of encryption techniques to protect application data.

☐ 16. Evaluate application developer access to alter production data.

☐ 17. Ensure that the application software cannot be changed without going through a standard checkout/ staging/testing/approval process after it is placed into production.

☐ 18. Evaluate controls regarding code checkout and versioning.

☐ 19. Evaluate controls regarding the testing of application code before it is placed into a production environment.

☐ 20. Evaluate controls regarding batch scheduling.

☐ 21. Determine whether a Business Impact Analysis (BIA) has been performed on the application to establish backup and recovery needs.

☐ 22. Ensure that appropriate backup controls are in place.

☐ 23. Ensure that appropriate recovery controls are in place.

☐ 24. Evaluate controls regarding the application's data retention.

☐ 25. Evaluate controls regarding data classification within the application.

☐ 26. Evaluate overall user involvement and support for the application.

CHAPTER 14

Auditing Cloud Computing and Outsourced Operations

In this chapter, we will discuss key controls to look for when you are auditing IT operations that have been outsourced to external companies, including the following:

- Definitions of cloud computing and other forms of IT outsourcing
- SAS 70 reports
- Vendor selection controls
- Items to include in vendor contracts
- Data security requirements
- Operational concerns
- Legal concerns and regulatory compliance

Background

The concept of outsourcing IT operations to external service providers is not a new one. Companies have been implementing this concept for years, from hosting their applications via an application service provider (ASP), to storing their computer equipment in a co-location data center (also called a *colo*), to hiring an external company to run their IT operations. The decision to outsource operations is usually based on a desire to reduce costs and to allow a company to focus on its core competencies. In other words, if I own a company that makes hockey sticks and my core competency is designing and building those hockey sticks, I might not want to invest the time and money required to run a data center to support my operations. It's expensive and it's not what I'm good at. Instead, I can pay someone who runs data centers for a living to do that for me. They can probably do it better than I could and at a lower cost, and it allows me to focus on those hockey sticks.

Recently, a new concept has been introduced into the outsourced operations world called *cloud computing*, where IT services are provided through the Internet (that is, the cloud) using shared infrastructure. This has resulted in a new trend of companies moving their IT services to external providers.

Although outsourced operations can provide benefits to a company in terms of cost and resource efficiency, they also introduce additional risks, as the company gives up control over its data and IT environment.

The methods used for outsourcing IT operations can be defined, separated, and categorized in multiple ways. None of those methods will be perfect or all-encompassing, but for the purposes of this chapter, they are divided into two major categories:

- IT systems and infrastructure outsourcing
- IT service outsourcing

IT Systems and Infrastructure Outsourcing

IT systems and infrastructure outsourcing is the practice of hiring another company to provide some or all of your IT environment, such as data center, servers, operating systems, business applications, and so on. This service can be provided using either cloud computing or dedicated hosting.

Cloud Computing

As a relatively recent trend, the industry is still settling on the definitions of cloud computing. Gartner defines it as "a style of computing that provides scalable and elastic, IT-enabled capabilities 'as a service' to external customers via Internet technologies." The National Institute of Standards and Technology (NIST) defines cloud computing as "a model for enabling convenient, on-demand network access to a shared pool of configurable computing resources (e.g., networks, servers, storage, applications, and services) that can be rapidly provisioned and released with minimal management effort or service provider interaction."

Basically, cloud computing provides IT services over the Internet in such a way that the end user doesn't have to worry about where the data is being stored, where the infrastructure is located, and so on. The user receives the service without worrying about any of the details of how it's provided. Also, as a consumer of cloud computing, you are sharing the backend infrastructure that provides the service with other users; it is not dedicated to you and your company. This is analogous to the utilities you use at home. You don't know or necessarily care how you get your electricity; but you do care that it works. You let the electric company worry about what it takes to provide the service. And you don't have your own dedicated infrastructure at the electric company; you share it with all of your neighbors. Also, just like with your electricity at home, you pay for only what you use with cloud computing.

On a personal level, you've likely experienced cloud computing at home. If you have a personal e-mail address with a provider such as Yahoo! or Gmail, you are receiving your e-mail in the cloud. You don't know and don't care where your data is stored and what sort of infrastructure is being used to provide the service to you. All you care about is that you can send and receive e-mail and manage your contacts. Also, you do not have a dedicated e-mail server on the backend; many other e-mail accounts are on the same server as yours. As to how many there are and who they are, you don't know and don't care. All you know and care about is that your e-mail is available and secure.

Cloud computing at the corporate level expands on this concept, resulting in enterprise business applications, client (PC) applications, and other aspects of the IT environment being provided over the Internet using a shared infrastructure.

A number of attempts have been made to determine what truly defines something as cloud computing, but we'll use the NIST definition here. According to NIST, for something to qualify as cloud computing, it must exhibit five characteristics:

On-Demand Self-Service This means that you can provision computing capabilities, such as storage, as needed automatically without requiring human interaction with each service's provider. It also implies that the implementation details are hidden from (and irrelevant to) the consumer. For example, the customer need not worry about what storage technology is used, but simply needs to define their business requirements and let the service provider determine how those requirements will be met.

Broad Network Access This means that capabilities should be accessible from anywhere and from any device (such as laptops and mobile devices) as long as Internet connectivity is available.

Resource Pooling This means that the provider's computing resources are pooled to serve multiple consumers using a multi-tenant model, with different physical and virtual resources dynamically assigned and reassigned according to consumer demand. It provides a sense of location independence in that the customer generally has no control over or knowledge of the exact location of the provided resources. Examples of resources in this context include storage, processing, memory, network bandwidth, and virtual machines.

Rapid Elasticity This means that capabilities can be rapidly and elastically provisioned (often automatically) to scale out quickly, and rapidly released to scale in quickly. To the consumer, the capabilities available for provisioning often appear to be unlimited and can be purchased in any quantity at any time.

Measured Service This means that cloud systems automatically control and optimize resource usage by leveraging metering capabilities appropriate to the type of service (such as storage, processing, bandwidth, and active user accounts). Resource usage can be monitored, controlled, and reported, providing transparency for both the provider and consumer of the service. This also implies transparency in cost, allowing the consumer to know that he is paying for only what he is using.

If a service your company is procuring does not meet those five criteria, it is likely not truly using cloud computing, but is instead using some form of dedicated hosting (discussed later in this chapter).

Cloud computing appeals to companies because it allows them to avoid the investment in physical infrastructure (and the operations for managing that infrastructure) and instead rent infrastructure (hardware and software) from another company, paying for only the resources they use.

The next important concept to understand is the three primary models of cloud computing. The classifications of these three models have been relatively broadly accepted, but once again we'll lean on the NIST definitions.

Software as a Service (SaaS)   In this model, you will access the cloud provider's applications, which are running on a cloud infrastructure. The applications are accessible from client devices through a thin client interface such as a web browser (for example, web-based e-mail). As the consumer, you don't manage or control the data center, network, servers, operating systems, middleware, database management system (DBMS), or even individual application capabilities (with the possible exception of limited user-specific application configuration settings), but you do have control over your data. Common examples of this form of cloud computing include salesforce.com, Google Apps, and Microsoft's Business Productivity Online Suite. Figure 14-1 shows a representation as to what layers of the infrastructure are dedicated to your company and what layers are shared with other customers in the SaaS model.

Platform as a Service (PaaS)   In this model, you will deploy applications you created or acquired onto the provider's cloud infrastructure, using programming languages and tools supported by the cloud provider. As the consumer, you don't manage or control the data center, network, servers, operating systems, middleware, or DBMS, but you do have control over your data and the deployed applications and possibly application hosting environment configurations. Figure 14-2 shows a representation as to what layers of the infrastructure are dedicated to your company and what layers are shared with other customers in the PaaS model.

Infrastructure as a Service (IaaS)   In this model, processing, storage, networks, and other fundamental computing resources are rented from the cloud provider. This allows you to deploy and run arbitrary software, which can include operating systems and applications. As the consumer, you don't manage or control the data center or network, but you do have control over your data and the operating systems, middleware, DBMS, and deployed applications. Figure 14-3 shows a representation as to what layers of the infrastructure are dedicated to your company and what layers are shared with other customers in the IaaS model.

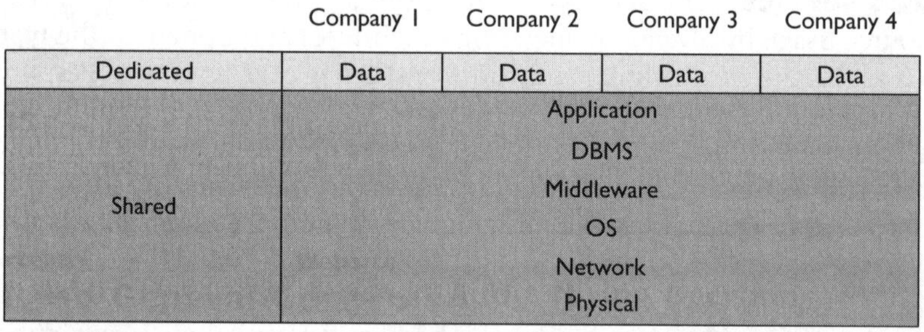

	Company 1	Company 2	Company 3	Company 4
Dedicated	Data	Data	Data	Data
Shared	Application			
	DBMS			
	Middleware			
	OS			
	Network			
	Physical			

Figure 14-1   SaaS model

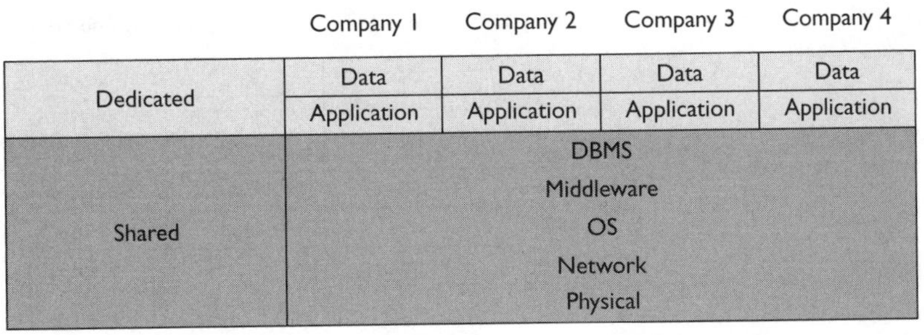

	Company 1	Company 2	Company 3	Company 4
Dedicated	Data	Data	Data	Data
	Application	Application	Application	Application
Shared	DBMS			
	Middleware			
	OS			
	Network			
	Physical			

Figure 14-2   PaaS model

Dedicated Hosting

Dedicated hosting is conceptually similar to cloud computing, in that you're hiring someone else to provide (and probably manage) your infrastructure. The key difference is that, with dedicated hosting, your company will have dedicated infrastructure, potentially sharing no more than the physical layer with the vendor's other customers. An example of this would be a co-location (colo) data center, where you place your infrastructure (such as servers) in another company's data center, saving you the cost of building out and operating your own data center. Another example of this would be an application service provider (ASP) that hosts a business application for you, differentiated from SaaS only by the fact that you're on dedicated server(s) not shared with the vendor's other customers. In contrast, with cloud computing, your data will be segregated but you may be sharing the rest of the infrastructure (such as network, servers, middleware, and so on) with the vendor's other customers. Figure 14-4 shows a representation as to what layers of the infrastructure are dedicated to your company and what layers are shared with other customers in the dedicated hosting model.

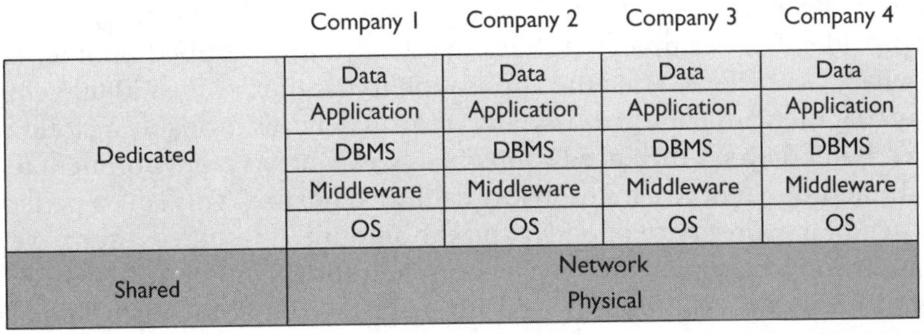

	Company 1	Company 2	Company 3	Company 4
Dedicated	Data	Data	Data	Data
	Application	Application	Application	Application
	DBMS	DBMS	DBMS	DBMS
	Middleware	Middleware	Middleware	Middleware
	OS	OS	OS	OS
Shared	Network			
	Physical			

Figure 14-3   IaaS model

	Company 1	Company 2	Company 3	Company 4
Dedicated	Data	Data	Data	Data
	Application	Application	Application	Application
	DBMS	DBMS	DBMS	DBMS
	Middleware	Middleware	Middleware	Middleware
	OS	OS	OS	OS
	Network	Network	Network	Network
Shared	Physical			

Figure 14-4   Dedicated hosting model

Although the concepts of what you need to protect may be the same between dedicated hosting and cloud computing, implementation will be vastly different. With dedicated hosting, you will look at how your network is isolated from other customers' (such as via firewalls). With cloud computing, you will look at how your data is segregated since you're sharing the infrastructure. With dedicated hosting, encryption within your isolated network area may not be important. With cloud computing, you will want to see your data encrypted end-to-end since it is comingled on the same infrastructure as other customers' data.

Because you're operating on dedicated infrastructure, dedicated hosting may not have the characteristics of cloud computing regarding on-demand self-service (the ability to provision additional capacity or other capabilities may not be automatic), broad network access (access may not be available via general Internet connections), resource pooling (you're on your own dedicated infrastructure), rapid elasticity (the ability to provision additional capacity or other capabilities may not be rapid, as procurement and setup time may need to be encompassed), or measured service (resource usage may not be automatically controlled and optimized).

There is often a fine line between whether you're using cloud computing or dedicated hosting. If you're not sure whether something is cloud or hosting, run a scenario by your provider. For example, tell them that you've just acquired another company and ask what it will take to scale the application to handle another 30,000 employees. If they say that they can handle it basically immediately, it's probably a cloud computing model. But if they say they need some time to expand your environment to accommodate the additional needs, it's probably dedicated hosting. This isn't a perfect test, as it will depend on your service provider and the amount of resources they have "on the bench" at the time, but it will give you a good indication.

Figure 14-5 shows a comparison of dedicated hosting and the three cloud computing models.

	Hosting	IaaS	PaaS	SaaS
Data	Dedicated	Dedicated	Dedicated	Dedicated
Application	Dedicated	Dedicated	Dedicated	Shared
DBMS	Dedicated	Dedicated	Shared	Shared
Middleware	Dedicated	Dedicated	Shared	Shared
OS	Dedicated	Dedicated	Shared	Shared
Network / Servers	Dedicated	Shared	Shared	Shared
Physical-Data Center	Shared	Shared	Shared	Shared

Figure 14-5 IT systems and infrastructure outsourcing model comparisons

NOTE Be aware that the definitions and distinctions among the various types of cloud computing and hosting are not always clear and are still maturing. Overlap can occur between these models and customizations (based on specific data protection requirements, cost constraints, and so on) can lead to hybrid models. Also, people do not always use the terminology consistently or accurately. You will often find people who, for example, say they are using SaaS when they actually have dedicated hosting of their application (or vice versa). The auditor needs to be familiar with the concepts and standard models but should also realize that real-world scenarios will not always be as neat and tidy as what is reflected here. Not everyone will agree on the same terminology and definitions, so don't get too caught up in semantics.

IT Service Outsourcing

IT service outsourcing is the practice of hiring another company to perform some or all of your IT operations functions (that is, hiring the company to provide the people and processes necessary to perform the function). Commonly outsourced operations include help desk operations and PC support. This can obviously go hand-in-hand with the outsourcing of IT systems and infrastructure. For example, if you have placed your IT equipment in another company's data center, you are also likely to hire that company to perform data center operation activities (such as tape operations, hardware support, and so on). Similarly, if you deploy cloud computing, it is a given that the cloud provider will perform the operations over the cloud infrastructure.

Two types of IT service outsourcing are available, on-site and off-site, though there are obviously hybrids of these models, where portions of the function are performed onsite and portions are performed offsite.

On-site

This model is used when a company outsources an operation but wants or needs for that function to be performed on company property. The external company is responsible for providing and training the people and establishing and monitoring the operational processes necessary for performing the function, managing all day-to-day aspects of the operation. However, the employees performing the function physically sit on the company's premises, using the company's network and IT environment.

Off-site

This model is used when a company outsources an operation without any on-site activity. Not only is the external company responsible for providing the personnel and processes necessary for performing the function, but they are also responsible for providing the facilities and infrastructure necessary for performing the function (often with connectivity back to the hiring company).

Other Considerations for IT Service Outsourcing

Additional topics related to IT service outsourcing are supplemental labor and offshoring.

Supplemental Labor

Many companies hire supplemental (contract) labor to assist in their day-to-day operations. This is often done to assist with short-term needs or to perform jobs that require workers with skills that are easy to find and replace. This sort of activity should not be confused with truly outsourced operations. Supplemental labor workers perform activities under the day-to-day guidance and direction of your company's staff and therefore are subject to the controls and security already established for the functions your employees are performing. This is vastly different from a function where day-to-day operations have truly been outsourced.

Offshoring

Many companies have moved IT functions to locations in the world that provide lower-cost resources. This can occur both with operations that have been outsourced as well as by hiring employees to work for your company in those lower-cost regions. Although sourcing operations from remote locations can provide significant cost benefits, it also presents unique internal control challenges and additional complexities into the environment, especially in the areas of coordination and communication.

IT Service Outsourcing Models

In summary, when it comes to staffing IT services, the following basic models are used:

- Internal employees only
- Internal employees plus supplemental labor
- Outsourced: on-site

- Outsourced: off-site
- Outsourced: on-site/off-site mix

For each of these provisioning models, the following deployment options are used:

- Onshore
- Offshore
- Onshore/offshore mix

SAS 70 Reports

When auditing vendors, you need to understand SAS (Statement on Auditing Standards) 70 reports. SAS 70 is an auditing standard developed by the American Institute of Certified Public Accountants (AICPA) to deal with service organizations. It essentially provides a standard by which service organizations (such as those that provide IT services) can demonstrate the effectiveness of their internal controls without having to allow each of their customers to come in and perform their own audit. Without this standard, service organizations would expend a prohibitive volume of resources responding to audit requests from each customer. With this standard, service organizations can hire a certified independent service auditor (such as Ernst & Young) to perform a SAS 70 audit and issue a report. This report can in turn be presented to any customers requiring evidence of the effectiveness of the service organization's internal controls.

SAS 70 reports have become particularly important since the implementation of Section 404 of the Sarbanes-Oxley Act in 2002, as companies can use them as evidence of the effectiveness of internal controls over any aspects of financial processing and reporting that have been outsourced. Without them, any company providing financial services would be bombarded with Sarbanes-Oxley audits from all of their customers, as opposed to being able to hand each customer the same SAS 70 report.

SAS 70 service auditor reports are of two types: Type 1 and Type 2. Both types include a description of and opinion on the design of the service organization's internal controls at a point in time. However, only a Type 2 report contains the results of testing by the service auditor regarding whether the controls were operating effectively during the period under review to provide assurance that the control objectives were achieved. As an auditor, you will want your service providers to provide a Type 2 report, as Type 1 reports do not provide evidence that the controls are operating effectively.

For Sarbanes-Oxley purposes, it is also recommended that you influence your vendors to have their SAS 70 Type 2 audits performed with an end date of the examination period that falls within three months of the end of your fiscal year. Type 2 examinations are usually performed with an examination period of six to twelve months. So if the review period ends 6/30 and your fiscal year ends 12/31, the results will be six months' old by the time you use it for your certification. This is not ideal, but Sarbanes-Oxley guidance does provide directions for how to deal with it, so the report still has value.

Test Steps for Auditing Cloud Computing and Outsourced Operations

Here are a few notes on the test steps in this chapter.

First and foremost, whatever audit steps you would want to perform if the service were being performed by your company (that is, if it were not outsourced) should be considered when you're auditing an outsourced function. The same risks likely exist and will need to be mitigated. For example, if a business application is hosted in the cloud via SaaS, you will need to review for the sorts of application controls that are documented in Chapter 13. Those risks don't go away just because the application has been outsourced, and they are all still relevant to an audit program. However, the way you audit for them may be vastly different if the function has been outsourced.

Second, you need to determine whether you will be auditing the vendor and evaluating its controls or whether you will be auditing your own company and asking how it ensures that the vendor is providing the necessary controls. Both approaches are valid, and it may depend on what sort of right to audit and influence you have with the vendor. However, in general, it is preferable that you ask the questions of the vendor directly as opposed to using a middleman. You're more likely to get thorough and accurate answers. It's also sometimes interesting to ask the same question of both the vendor and your own internal IT team and compare their answers. This can tell you how well your company understands and reviews the controls over the outsourced operations.

Finally, for each step in this section, we will note which types of outsourcing (such as cloud computing, dedicated hosting, service outsourcing) are most applicable to that step. These are not intended to be absolute, because the scope of each outsourcing engagement is unique, but instead are intended to be guidelines.

Preliminary and Overview

1. Review the audit steps in the other chapters in this part of the book and determine which risks and audit steps are applicable to the audit being performed over outsourced operations. Perform those audit steps that are applicable.

The risks present for an insourced function are also present for an outsourced function. Remember that the components and functions of what you've outsourced are similar in many cases to what you would have internally. They are simply being handled by a different entity. Regardless of who is responsible for your data and applications, you still have controls that must be put in place. Although additional risks are present when a function is outsourced, you still must review for the basic controls that you would expect of an internally sourced function. For example, if you outsource a business application, you will still be interested in access controls, data input controls, and software change controls over those applications. Those controls are still critical to the confidentiality, integrity, and availability of that application. And if you outsource your data center, you will still be concerned as to how the people running that data center ensure physical security and continuity of operations.

This step is applicable to all forms of outsourcing.

How

Although you could argue that you would perform all of the same steps for an outsourced function as you would for an insourced one (again, because the risks are all still present), in reality, you probably won't have the same level of access with an outsourced process that you would get for an internal process, so you need to pick your battles. For example, if you want to review operating system security, the vendor may not give you access to accounts on its operating systems so that you can review system configuration. Maybe it will, and it's certainly worth asking, but you will often be limited by contractual rights. Perhaps instead, you will focus on their processes for keeping their systems patched and for regularly monitoring the security of the systems themselves (that is, review their processes regarding ensuring system security rather than reviewing the configuration of specific servers), and you ask the vendor to run a set of read-only scripts that pull key system configuration information from their environment and send you the output. After developing your wish list of steps you would like to perform during the audit, you might go ahead and determine which ones are the most critical to you so that you'll know which ones to fight for should you encounter resistance from the vendor.

Significant variability will be the norm with regard to how you perform these steps—it all depends on the rights, influence, and relationship you have with your supplier. Some may allow you to come in and audit their processes and infrastructure just as if you were their own internal auditors. Others will hand you a SAS 70 report and be done with you, informing you that they have fulfilled their obligation. You will have to negotiate each instance separately and enlist the aid of your procurement, legal, and operations groups to see how far you can push for transparency from your supplier. This is why it is critical to establish robust "right to audit" clauses in your contracts to deal with these situations up-front, while you still have leverage.

NOTE This is a critical step. For efficiency's sake, we are not duplicating the audit steps from other chapters here. However, if, for example, you are performing an audit of data center operations that have been outsourced to a co-location facility, it is critical that you perform not only the steps in this chapter but also the steps in Chapter 4. Likewise, if you are performing an audit of a business application that uses the SaaS model, you must perform not only the steps in this chapter but also the steps in Chapter 13 (at a minimum). In fact, just as when you're auditing an internal application, you might also want to perform steps from Chapters 6 to 9 on auditing the pertinent operating system, the database, and so on.

2. Request your service provider to produce independent assurance from reputable third parties regarding the effectiveness of their internal controls and compliance with applicable regulations. Review the documentation for issues that have been noted. Also, determine how closely these certifications match your own company's control objectives and identify gaps.

Although you are attempting to perform your own audit of your service provider's controls, experienced service providers will already be engaging third parties for regular assessments. These assessments can be used to reduce your need to audit the service provider's functions, thereby reducing the scope of your audit. In fact, many service providers, especially the larger ones, will insist that you use these assessments in lieu of performing your own audit.

This step is most applicable to cloud computing, dedicated hosting, and offsite service outsourcing.

How

Request this information from your vendor. The type of independent assurance you ask for will vary depending on your industry, but the most common assessment you should look for will be a SAS 70 report. Make sure you request a Type 2 SAS 70 assessment. Another common assessment you may see is ISO 27001, which is a standard dealing with information security that is intended to form a basis for a third-party audit of security. You will need to determine what assessment(s) should be expected based on your industry, the type of outsourcing being performed, and the type of auditing you're performing. For example, if you're performing an audit of an outsourced website, you should expect to see some form of web security certification. As part of this exercise, you will need to determine whether your vendor subcontracts any relevant functions to additional third parties (for example, if you're using a SaaS vendor and it uses another vendor's data center facilities to host its systems). If so, request that your vendor obtain applicable independent assessments from those subcontract vendors and provide them to you.

Once you receive whatever assessments are available, you must review them in a number of areas. First, obviously, you must review the results of the assessment to understand any issues noted and the vendor's remediation plans. You will want to track these items to ensure that they have been remediated satisfactorily (which again you may need to determine via a third-party assessment). It is also important to ensure that the assessment was performed by a qualified independent third party and to determine the time period covered by the assessment to be sure it is still relevant.

You will also need to review the scope of the assessment performed and determine how many of your control objectives were addressed by the assessment. You will likely see some gaps between your company's control objectives and the control objectives addressed by the independent assessment. Once you identify these gaps, you can attempt to perform your own assessments of those items not covered by the third-party assessment. You will have to negotiate each instance separately and enlist the aid of your procurement, legal, and operations groups to see how far you can push for the ability to perform your own audit. This again emphasizes the importance of placing a "right to audit" clause in your contracts.

If you find that your vendor does not have appropriate third-party assessments, you will have to attempt to perform all pertinent audit steps yourself (which may be limited by your right to audit). If this is the case, you should push your vendor to obtain a SAS 70 Type 2 and/or other pertinent independent assessments, possibly making this a negotiating point at contract renewal time. You should expect to see this type of assessment for any form of IT systems and infrastructure outsourcing (such as cloud computing). It may not be reasonable to expect it for IT service outsourcing models where you are providing significant guidance on day-to-day activities (such as when you outsource a function but leave it onsite using your own systems).

Vendor Selection and Contracts

3. Review applicable contracts to ensure that they adequately identify all deliverables, requirements, and responsibilities pertinent to your company's engagement.

The contract is your only true fallback mechanism should you have issues with the vendor. If it's not spelled out in the contract, it becomes very difficult, if not impossible, to enforce requirements and/or seek restitution should there be issues.

This step is applicable to all forms of outsourcing.

How

The best time to perform this step is before the contract is finalized and signed, because that's when you can make changes and influence the contents of the contract relatively easily. However, if you are performing the audit after the contract has been signed, it is still relevant for two reasons: First, it will give you an idea as to what you're working with and what sort of leverage you will have during the audit. Second, it will allow you to provide input as to what changes need to be made in the contract when it's time to renegotiate.

Regardless of whether you're reviewing a signed contract or providing input before the fact, you should make sure the following areas are addressed in the contract:

- Specify how performance will be measured, including Service Level Agreements (SLAs) that specify requirements for availability (such as expected uptime), performance (such as speed of transaction response after the ENTER key is pressed), response time (such as whether the vendor will respond to problems 24/7 or only during normal business hours), and issue resolution time (such as how quickly you should expect issues to be fixed).

- SLAs for security (that is, requirements for controls to protect the confidentiality, integrity, and availability of data) can include requiring specific control frameworks (such as COBIT) to be followed and requirements for third-party assessments. It should also include requirements for how data should be stored (such as encryption, including requirements for the algorithm and key length), who may be granted access to it, how business continuity and disaster recovery will be ensured, how investigations will be supported, what security training and background checks are required for personnel who will access your systems and data, how data retention and destruction should occur, and so on. Overall, you want to make sure your vendor takes contractual responsibility for security.

- Other key metrics and performance indicators should be included, which can be used by your company to measure the quality of the service. For example, if you have outsourced your helpdesk function, you might want to set an expectation as to tickets closed per analyst and customer satisfaction rating.

- Outline requirements for compliance with applicable laws and regulations (such as PCI, HIPAA), including requirements for independent assessments certifying compliance.

- Provide provisions for penalties upon nonperformance or delayed performance of SLAs and conditions for terminating the agreement if performance goals are not met.

- Add a right to audit clause, specifying what your company is allowed to audit and when. You obviously will want to push for a broad right to audit, allowing you to audit whatever you want, whenever you want (including the ability to perform surprise audits). You can negotiate from there. The broader you make this clause, the more freedom you will have.

- Include provisions for your right to audit and review independent assessments (such as SAS 70) for functions that your vendor subcontracts out to other vendors (for example, if your SaaS vendor is hosting its systems with another third party). If possible, dictate in the contract what functions (if any) your vendor is allowed to subcontract and/or obtain the right of approval for any subcontracting relationships.

- Gain assurance that you can retrieve your data when you need it and in the format you desire.

- Add language prohibiting the vendor from using your data for its own purposes (that is, for any purposes not specified by you).

- Include nondisclosure clauses to prevent the vendor from disclosing your company's information.

- Include evidence that the contract was reviewed by your procurement and legal organizations, as well as applicable operations groups.

- Basically, include anything you expect from the service provider that needs to be specifically outlined in the contract. Consider the other steps in this chapter for ideas as well.

4. Review and evaluate the process used for selecting the outsourcing vendor.

If the process for selecting the vendor is inadequate, it can lead to the purchase of services that do not meet the requirements of the business and/or poor financial decisions.

This step is applicable to all forms of outsourcing.

How

Obviously, your goal should be to perform this step prior to vendor selection, when you can influence the decision. However, if your audit is being performed after the fact, there is still value in understanding the vendor selection process. It can identify gaps that must be addressed and provide information that can be used when it's time to renew the contract or enter into other contracts.

Review the vendor selection process for elements such as these:

- Ensure that multiple vendors are evaluated and involved in the bid process. This provides for competitive bidding and lower prices.

- Determine whether the vendors' financial stability was investigated as part of the evaluation process. Failure to do so may result in your company signing up with a vendor that goes out of business, causing significant disruption to your operations as you attempt to bring them back in-house or move them to another vendor.

- Determine whether the vendors' experience with providing support for companies of similar size to yours and/or in a similar industry was evaluated. This can include obtaining and interviewing references from companies that currently use the vendor's services. You generally want to use vendors who have already demonstrated that they can perform the types of services you're looking for at a similar scale.

- Ensure that the vendors' technical support capabilities were considered and evaluated.

- Ensure each vendor was compared against predefined criteria, providing for objective evaluations.

- Determine whether there was appropriate involvement of procurement personnel to help negotiate the contract, of operations personnel to provide expert evaluations as to the vendor's ability to meet requirements, and of legal personnel to provide guidance on potential regulatory and other legal ramifications of the outsourcing arrangement.

- Ensure that a thorough cost analysis was performed. The total cost of performing the operation in-house should be developed as well as the total cost for using each vendor. This analysis should include all relevant costs, including costs for one-time startup activities, hardware and related power and cooling, software, hardware maintenance, software maintenance, storage, support (labor), and so on. Too often, companies make decisions without considering all relevant costs. For example, some of the cost savings from cloud computing may be offset by increased monitoring to ensure that requirements are met. These costs need to be included in the analysis to ensure that the company is making an informed decision.

Data Security

For all of the steps in this section (except step 8), your first option should be to determine whether an evaluation of the area is available via a third-party assessment (such as SAS 70). If it is not, you'll need to work with your operations, procurement, and legal departments to determine your rights to audit the vendor in this area. Hopefully, those rights are spelled out in the contract. If they are not, your company will need to attempt to press for that right, possibly using the next contract renewal as negotiating leverage.

If the area is not covered by an assessment such as a SAS 70 and if you have the right to audit it, you will need to interview the vendor and review their documentation regarding their technical controls and processes, testing those controls as you're able.

You will also want to see your company's requirements for these controls spelled out in your contract and look for evidence that those specific requirements are being met.

5. Determine how your data is segregated from the data of other customers.

If your company chooses a form of outsourcing in which your data is being stored on the vendors' systems at their site (such as in cloud computing and dedicated hosting), you no longer have full control over your data. Your data may be comingled with other customers' data (a likely scenario with cloud computing). This creates a number of risks. For example, if data is not properly segregated, another customer (including one of your competitors) on the same shared infrastructure may be able to access your data. Likewise, if one customer's system is breached, the confidentiality, integrity, and availability of other customers in the same environment may be at risk. For example, viruses might be transmitted from one customer to another or an attacker might be able to download data from all customers in the environment.

This step is most applicable to cloud computing and dedicated hosting.

How

Review the technical controls and processes for assuring segregation and protection of your systems and data. There's no single way to do this, and the implementation will differ depending on the technologies being used by your vendor, but the vendor needs to demonstrate how they have segregated and compartmentalized systems, storage, network, and so on. For example, in a dedicated hosting environment, you'll be looking for network devices (such as firewalls) to segregate the network hosting your systems from the networks hosting other customers. In a SaaS environment, you'll be looking for segregation of databases containing customer data. Ideally, you would like to perform your own tests to validate that their controls are working as designed. Again, the nature of these tests will depend on the technology and the implementation.

6. Review and evaluate the usage of encryption to protect company data stored at and transmitted to the vendor's site.

If your data is no longer fully under your control (that is, it is being stored at a third-party site and possibly being comingled with data from other customers), it is critical that the data be encrypted to protect against possible compromise. This reduces the risk of a breach impacting the confidentiality or integrity of your data. If you have unencrypted data in a shared environment (such as cloud computing), you can assume that it is no longer confidential.

This step is most applicable to cloud computing, dedicated hosting, and offsite service outsourcing.

How

Look for encryption of data both in transit (for example, via SSL for browser-enabled transactions) and at rest (that is, in storage), because both are outside of your control if your data is stored at a third-party site. Evaluate the strength of the encryption. Hopefully, you will have contractually-dictated requirements for encryption (such as algorithm and key length) against which you can compare the system.

Determine how key management is performed and how your keys are separated from those of other customers in your environment. Ideally, this function should be performed either by your company or by a separate vendor from your standard outsourcing vendor, providing for segregation of duties.

7. Determine how vendor employees access your systems and how data is controlled and limited.

If your data is being stored or processed by employees outside of your company and you do not maintain ownership regarding who has access to that data, you're putting its confidentiality, integrity, and availability at risk.

This step is applicable to all forms of outsourcing.

How

Determine who has access to your data and systems and review for appropriateness. Determine how appropriate segregation of duties is maintained. Ensure that the concept of "minimum necessary access" is followed.

Review the approval process for determining who will have access to your systems and data. Ideally, the data owner at your company will be the gatekeeper for approval. Your company should maintain the right (hopefully spelled out in the contract) to deny access to your data from vendor personnel.

Review your vendor's processes for hiring and screening employees, ensuring that appropriate background checks are performed and rules regarding security and management of your environment are communicated to the employees. These requirements should be dictated in the contract.

Ask for a listing of any third-party relationships that your vendor has and any interfaces those additional parties have to your systems. Each of these represents additional exposure of your data.

8. Review and evaluate processes for controlling non-employee logical access to your internal network and internal systems.

If you're using service outsourcing and/or supplemental (contract) labor, you are likely allowing a third-party vendor's personnel to have a degree of logical access to your network and systems. Because these personnel are not employees of your company, they are less likely to have a personal investment in the company's success or an awareness of its policies and culture. If their access to company information assets is not governed and if expectations regarding their usage of that access are not communicated, it is more likely that company information assets will be unnecessarily exposed or misused.

This step is most applicable to onsite and offsite service outsourcing plus supplemental labor.

How

Ensure that policies require approval and sponsorship from an employee prior to a non-employee obtaining logical access to company systems. If feasible, obtain a sample of non-employee accounts and validate that they have appropriate approval and sponsorship.

Review and evaluate processes for communicating company policies (including IT security policies) to non-employees prior to granting them system access. Look for evidence that this communication has occurred. For example, if all non-employees are required to sign a statement that they have read and agree to the policies, pull a sample of non-employees and obtain copies of these agreements.

Review and evaluate processes for removing logical access from non-employees when they have ceased to work with your company or otherwise no longer need access. Consider obtaining a sample of current non-employee accounts and validating that those non-employees are still working with your company and still have a need for their current level of access.

Ensure that nondisclosure agreements (NDAs) are signed by non-employees to legally protect your company from inappropriate use of company data. Pull a sample of non-employee accounts and obtain a copy of the NDA for those accounts.

Ensure that consideration has been given to identifying data that should not be accessed by non-employees and activities that should not be performed by non-employees. For example, your company may decide that access to certain levels of financial data should never be granted to non-employees. Or it may decide that non-employees should never be granted system administration duties. The answer will depend on your company's industry and philosophies; however, an evaluation process should take place and the results of that evaluation should be documented in company policy and enforced.

9. Ensure that data stored at vendor locations is being protected in accordance with your internal policies.

No matter where you store your data, it is still subject to your internal policies. Outsourcing storage to a third party does not absolve your company of responsibility to comply with policies and ensure proper security of the data.

This step is most applicable to cloud computing and dedicated hosting.

How

Ensure that data stored at third-party sites has been classified in accordance with your company's data classification policy and is being protected in accordance with that policy. Data with certain levels of classification might be inappropriate to store outside the company (such as employee and customer personal information). Review your company's policies on data security and ensure that off-site data is being protected in accordance with those policies. Encrypting data that is stored with the vendor will greatly benefit you in this area.

10. Review and evaluate controls to prevent, detect, and react to attacks.

Without appropriate intrusion detection and prevention techniques, your systems and data are at an increased risk of compromise. This risk is increased in an outsourced model, specifically when outsourcing systems and infrastructure, because of the shared infrastructure,—an attack and compromise on one customer could result in compromise of your systems.

This step is most applicable to cloud computing and dedicated hosting. Also, consider whether this risk is applicable if you're using offsite service outsourcing, as the service provider may store your data on their systems and/or have connectivity to your internal systems.

How

This step might be divided into separate substeps. For infrastructure and systems located at third-party sites, determine the effectiveness of processes such as those listed next.

Intrusion Detection   Look for the usage and monitoring of Intrusion Detection Systems (IDSs) to detect potential attacks on your systems and integrity checking tools to detect potential unauthorized changes to system baselines.

Intrusion Prevention   Look for the usage and monitoring of Intrusion Prevention Systems (IPSs) to proactively detect and cut off potential attacks on your systems.

Incident Response   Look for clearly defined processes for responding to potential security incidents, including notification and escalation procedures.

Discovering and Remediating Vulnerabilities   Look for the usage and monitoring of vulnerability scanning tools to detect and mitigate potential vulnerabilities that might allow an intruder to access and/or disrupt your systems.

Logging   Look for the logging of significant activities (successes and failures) on your systems, for the monitoring of these logs, and for the storage of these logs in a secure location for an adequate period of time.

Patching   Look for procedures to receive and apply the latest security patches so that known security holes are closed.

Protection from Viruses and Other Malware   Look for the usage of antivirus software and the application of new signature files as they are released.

PART II

11. Determine how identity management is performed for cloud-based and hosted systems.

Proper identity management practices are critical for controlling access to your systems and data. Distributed computing became popular in the 1990s. When each user was required to track IDs and passwords on multiple systems, it led to problems such as employees sharing accounts, inconsistent password controls (for example, password strength, aging), accounts not being removed when no longer needed, employees with more access than they needed, and other issues. Without some form of central control, no real governance was possible. To resolve these issues, many companies deployed enterprise IDs, giving users one account name for all systems, as well as strong enterprise passwords, which can be used to authenticate to multiple systems.

As your company begins adopting cloud computing, you run the risk of seeing the same issues arise again. Users may end up with accounts with multiple cloud providers, each with a different ID and password. If you're not careful, you'll encounter the same issues that companies encountered in the '90s with distributed computing.

This step is most applicable to cloud computing, particularly SaaS, and dedicated hosting, particularly of purchased applications.

How

Although it's possible to review the identity management controls over each outsourced system (checking each for appropriate password controls, account management controls, and so on), you should prefer to have a federated identity management capability. This will allow your users to authenticate to your internal systems with their enterprise ID and password and then for your vendor to trust your assertion that each user has been properly authenticated. This offers the benefits of centralized identity management and allows you to avoid storing user credentials with your vendor.

If you implement this form of federated identity management, be sure that your internal credential data (such as IDs and passwords) are not being made directly available to your vendor (that is, they should not be able to make direct calls against your internal identity management systems) and that they are not being transmitted in the clear or stored in the clear at your vendor's site. These requirements will preferably be dictated in your contract. If you are unable to implement federated identities, you will need to review the identity management controls over your outsourced systems to ensure that they meet the requirements of your policies. An alternative solution is to use an identity management service as a "middle man" between your company and your vendor, but of course that solution introduces another third party that you must audit into your environment.

12. Ensure that data retention and destruction practices for data stored offsite comply with internal policy.

If the lifecycle of data is not defined, data might be retained longer than necessary (resulting in additional storage costs and possible legal liabilities) or may be destroyed prematurely (leading to potential operational, legal, or tax issues).

This step is most applicable to cloud computing, dedicated hosting, and offsite service outsourcing (if the supplier is storing your data).

How

Determine whether lifecycle requirements have been defined for data stored with vendors. For a sample, review the documentation of the data's lifecycle requirements, including retention, archive, and destruction requirements. Ideally, requirements will be identified for how long the data should be active (online, easily accessible, modifiable if appropriate, and backed up periodically), when and for how long it should be archived (possibly offline, not necessarily easy to access, no longer modifiable, and no longer backed up periodically), and when it should be destroyed. Ensure that these requirements appropriately reflect the nature of the data (for example, external public content on your website should be treated differently than customer data). The contract should dictate that the vendor manage data per your lifecycle requirements. Review evidence that lifecycle requirements have been implemented, concentrating especially on evidence that your vendor has destroyed data per your requirements. Note that data destruction can often be very difficult to prove in the cloud, increasing the importance of using strong encryption for your data, as described earlier.

13. Review and evaluate the vendor's physical security.

Physical security impacts logical security, because physical access can override some logical access controls. You can have excellent logical security, but if someone can walk in off the street and walk off with the computer (or perhaps just the disk drive or tape cartridges) containing your systems and data, you will at a minimum experience a disruption of service, and if the data is not adequately encrypted, you may also be looking at a security breach.

This step is most applicable to cloud computing, dedicated hosting, and offsite service outsourcing.

How

Review the vendor's physical security for controls such as these:

- Badge readers and/or biometric scanners
- Security cameras
- Security guards
- Fences
- Lighting
- Locks and sensors
- Processes for determining who will be granted physical access

See Chapter 4 for additional information on auditing physical security controls.

Operations

14. Review and evaluate your company's processes for monitoring the quality of outsourced operations. Determine how compliance with SLAs and other contractual requirements are monitored.

Although you have hopefully dictated expectations in your contract, unless you monitor for compliance with those expectations, you will have no way of knowing whether they're being met. If those expectations are not met, the availability, efficiency, and effectiveness of your operations and the security of your systems and data can be impacted.

This step is applicable to all forms of outsourcing.

How

Review the contract to understand requirements. Interview your company's internal management to determine their processes for monitoring that each of those requirements is being met. Obtain and review metrics, slides from operations reviews, and other materials, and compare the results to the requirements stipulated in the contract. Where deviances have occurred, review for corrective action plans and evidence that those plans have been implemented and were effective.

If requirements have not been dictated in the contract, determine how the quality of services is monitored and how the vendor is held accountable. The inclusion of SLAs should be a requirement when the contract is renewed.

Ensure you cover the following basic topics in performing this step:

- Availability (such as expected uptime)
- Performance (such as speed of transaction response after the ENTER key is pressed)
- Response time (such as whether the vendor will respond to problems 24/7 or only during normal business hours)
- Issue resolution time (such as how quickly you should expect issues to be fixed)
- Security and compliance requirements
- Other key metrics and performance indicators that can be used by your company to measure the quality of the service

15. Ensure that adequate disaster recovery processes are in place to provide for business continuity in the event of a disaster at your service provider.

Just as with internally-hosted systems, you must to prepare for recovery from a disaster when outsourcing operations. Failure to do so will likely result in extended outages and business disruptions if a disaster occurs with your vendor.

This step is most applicable to cloud computing, dedicated hosting, and offsite service outsourcing.

How

You should expect that your vendor will follow sound disaster recovery disciplines, such as those you would look for when auditing your internal operations. This includes steps outlined elsewhere in this book, such as reviewing for offsite backups, up-to-date documented recovery procedures, periodic testing, hardware redundancy, and so on. Your first option should be to determine whether an evaluation of this area is available via a third-party assessment (such as SAS 70). If not, you'll need to work with your operations, procurement, and legal departments to determine your rights to audit the vendor in this area. Ideally, that right is spelled out in the contract. If not, your company will need to attempt to press for that right, possibly using the next contract renewal as negotiating leverage.

If the area is not covered by an assessment such as a SAS 70 and if you have the right to audit it, you will need to interview the vendor and review their documentation regarding their controls and processes, testing those controls as you're able. You will also want to see the requirements for disaster recovery controls, including recovery time objectives (how quickly your systems should be back up after a disaster) and recovery point objectives (how many days' worth of data you're willing to lose), spelled out in your contract. Determine how the vendor ensures compliance with the requirements in the contract.

While it is important that you understand your vendor's disaster recovery procedures, you should also expect that your company will have documented procedures regarding how they would recover in the event of a disaster at your vendor. This should include notification and escalation procedures, any necessary hand-offs between your company and the vendor during the recovery, and potential manual workarounds while waiting for recovery. It should also include contingency plans should the vendor be unable to recover for an extended period of time (or ever). Request information regarding the location of your data and regarding any replication in the architecture. If the data and infrastructure are replicated across multiple sites, your vulnerability and need for contingency plans decrease. If your systems are at a single location, it becomes more critical for your company to document contingency plans, which need to include a method for obtaining your data and bringing it back in-house if necessary.

16. Determine whether appropriate governance processes are in place over the engagement of new cloud services by your company's employees.

Cloud computing makes it easy for business unit personnel to meet their needs without ever engaging corporate IT. Because most cloud services can be accessed via an Internet-connected browser, a business unit can engage a cloud vendor and outsource the systems and data related to one of their business processes without really having to tell anyone else. This has the potential to bypass all of the governance processes normally in place to ensure proper security of company data, interoperability of systems, appropriate support capabilities, and so on.

This step is most applicable to cloud computing.

How

Review company policies to determine whether this topic has been addressed. Policies should be in place requiring company personnel to follow specific procedures when engaging vendors for this sort of service. If this policy exists, review it for adequacy. It should require that IT be engaged and that specific security and operational needs be addressed. Determine how employees are made aware of the policy. Also, determine how the policy is enforced. For example, if your company has a centralized procurement organization that must be engaged to sign contracts and pay invoices, you can use them as the gatekeeper for ensuring that proper procedures are followed for new engagements.

17. Review and evaluate your company's plans in the event of expected or unexpected termination of the outsourcing relationship.

Your company might terminate the outsourcing relationship in the future for many reasons. The provider could go out of business or discontinue the service you're using. You could be unhappy with the provider's cost or performance. You might engage in a new competitive bid at the end of your contract and another vendor may win the business.

If you can't bring the service back in-house or switch it to another vendor, you'll find yourself locked in with your vendor, which greatly damages your leverage to influence price and service quality. And if that company goes out of business, you'll experience significant business disruption.

This step is applicable to all forms of outsourcing.

How

Determine whether your company has a documented plan indicating how they would bring the functions back in-house (or move them to another vendor) if necessary. If bringing the function in-house is unrealistic, you should see evidence that alternative service providers have been identified. Ensure that an analysis has been performed regarding how long it would take to transition the services and determine whether appropriate contingency plans are in place to keep the business running in the interim.

Look for contractual requirements for your vendor to return your data and assets upon request. If this has not been indicated in the contract, the vendor can hold your data hostage or can comingle it with other customers' data in such a way that it's nearly impossible to extract your data. Your company should require that your vendor deliver copies of your data to you periodically in an agreed-upon format (one that can easily be ported to a new application). Where applicable, ensure that code is put in escrow to protect against the vendor going out of business.

For IaaS and PaaS, your systems should be developed and deployed so that they are easily portable to new environments. Review your company's processes for ensuring that portability is a key goal in any development for cloud-based services.

18. If IT services have been outsourced, review the service provider's processes for ensuring quality of staff and minimizing the impact of turnover. If those services are being performed offshore, look for additional controls to ensure employee attendance and effective communication and hand-offs with the home office.

If service provider employees aren't qualified to perform their jobs or the provider experiences high levels of turnover, the quality of IT services will obviously be poor. This risk generally increases with outsourced operations, where turnover tends to be higher.

Outsourced operations that are performed offshore contribute to the risks of communication breakdowns and absenteeism that can impact the quality of service received.

This step is most applicable to IT service outsourcing (onsite and offsite).

How

Review the contract to ensure job descriptions and minimum qualifications for each position are documented (such as education level, skills, experience). Pull a sample of supplier employees and verify that these minimums have been met. Review the provider's employee screening process to verify that appropriate background checks and qualification reviews take place prior to employment offers.

Determine how continuity of services is ensured in the event of turnover of service provider employees. Review staffing assignments and determine whether any single points of failure exist. Review cross-training processes.

Review the vendor's processes for providing training to update skills and knowledge. Request evidence that the training policy is being followed for a sample of employees.

Review the vendor's processes for monitoring attendance. This is particularly important if the services are being performed offshore, where absenteeism tends to be high. This should include reviews of physical security logs and system access logs. Request copies of these logs and verify the attendance of a sample of employees.

For offshore outsourcing, determine how appropriate language skills are ensured. This could include a language test with minimum test score requirements defined, conducting spoken and written interviews in the required language, and so on. You should also determine how the inherent complexity of communication and hand-offs is mitigated. Look for the existence of periodic hand-off and status meetings between countries. SLAs should be documented and monitored. An employee of your company at the offshore site (or at least in the same city with easy access to the site) should be available to act as your liaison and perform monitoring and oversight of the operations.

Requirements for all of these items should be dictated in the contract. Review the contract to verify this.

Legal Concerns and Regulatory Compliance

19. Review and evaluate your company's right and ability to obtain information from the vendor that may be necessary to support investigations.

Your company may be required to perform e-discovery (electronic discovery) in support of litigation. Inability to produce applicable data may result in legal ramifications, as your company will be held legally responsible for your information, even if it's being stored and processed by a third-party provider. Your company may also need to perform investigations for its own reasons (for example, to investigate inappropriate activities such as fraud or hacking attempts). An inability to access appropriate logging and other data will prevent you from performing your investigations, leaving you with no real recourse when those inappropriate activities occur.

This step is most applicable to cloud computing.

How

Because cloud providers often comingle their customers' data, especially logging data, it is critical that you receive a contractual commitment from your vendors to support investigations. Review the contract and ensure this is documented as a requirement, including details as to the kind of investigative support you may need (such as specific log information, data format requirements) and the required response time for requests. It is also important that the contract define the responsibilities of both the cloud provider and your company related to e-discovery (for example, who is responsible for conducting the searches, for freezing data, for providing expert testimony, and so on). Review the vendor's processes to ensure that a formal process is in place to cooperate with customer investigations and to handle subpoenas for information.

If you find that the cloud provider is incapable of (or unwilling to) providing adequate support of investigations, your company may need to maintain copies of its data in-house. If this is the case, the costs of doing so will affect the benefits of the cloud relationship.

20. Review requirements for security breach notification. Ensure that requirements are clearly defined regarding when and how the vendor should notify your company in the event of a security breach and that your company has clearly defined response procedures when they receive such notification.

A security breach at your service provider not only puts your data and operations in jeopardy but may also have legal implications. For example, if you're hosting personal information and a security incident occurs, you may be legally required to notify all users who may have been impacted. It's therefore critical that the service provider notify you in a timely fashion as to what has happened so that you can put together any necessary response.

This step is most applicable to cloud computing and dedicated hosting.

How

Review the contract for existence of requirements and evaluate those requirements for adequacy. Look for requirements regarding what constitutes a breach, how quickly a breach needs to be communicated to your company, and the method by which it should be communicated. Determine whether penalties have been built into the contract so that your company can be compensated for the costs incurred because of a breach.

Obtain a copy of your company's response procedures and ensure that they cover the basic information regarding what processes should be followed, who should be notified, when they should be notified, and how any compensating processes should be enacted.

If a breach has been reported, review for evidence that the correct processes were followed.

21. Determine how compliance with applicable privacy laws and other regulations is ensured.

Regardless of where your data is stored and who manages it, you are still responsible for making sure that your company is complying with all applicable laws and regulations. If your company is found to be in violation of applicable laws and regulations, it can lead to stiff penalties and fines, a damaged reputation, lawsuits, and possibly the cessation of the company. The fact that it was being managed by a cloud provider will not be an acceptable defense.

This step is most applicable to cloud computing and dedicated hosting.

How

Review the contract, and look for language requiring that the vendor obtain third-party certification regarding compliance with applicable regulations (such as PCI and HIPAA) as well as requiring SAS 70 assessments. If you find such language, review evidence that your company is requesting these reports from the vendor and reviewing the results. Review the most recent reports for any issues that have been noted and determine how your company is tracking those issues.

The contract should require that the vendor disclose where your data is located and provide assurance that they are complying with local privacy requirements related to your data. The contract should also contain language specifying who is liable in the event of noncompliance.

If the contract does not require these certifications and/or the vendor will not undergo these assessments, determine how your company is certifying compliance with applicable regulations. If this is the case, your company should seriously consider a withdrawal strategy.

22. Review and evaluate processes for ensuring that the company is in compliance with applicable software licenses for any software hosted offsite or used by non-employees.

Using software illegally can lead to penalties, fines, and lawsuits. If companies do not develop processes for tracking the legal usage of software and licenses, they may be subject to software vendor audits and will not be able to account properly for the company's use of the vendor's software. This becomes more complex when dealing with outsourced operations, as purchased software may be hosted on third-party infra-structure and/or used by outsourced service provider employees. You must ensure that copies of the software continue to be tracked and that the usage is in compliance with the terms of agreement.

This step is applicable to all forms of outsourcing.

How

Look for evidence that the company maintains a list of enterprise software licenses (such as Microsoft Office, ERP application accounts, and so on) and that it has devel-oped a process for monitoring usage of those licenses and complying with the terms of agreement. Ensure that this process incorporates copies of your software that are hosted by a third party and copies of the software used by non-employees.

Knowledge Base

The knowledge base for cloud computing security and audit techniques is still develop-ing. However, a few organizations have begun to focus on this area and have produced some useful results:

- The National Institute of Standards and Technology (NIST) has developed definitions and standards related to cloud computing, as well as guidance for secure usage. See http://csrc.nist.gov/groups/SNS/cloud-computing/.

- The Cloud Security Alliance (CSA) promotes best practices for security with cloud computing. CSA developed one of the most comprehensive security guides for cloud computing in 2009. This document, along with other useful information on the topic, can be viewed at www.cloudsecurityalliance.org.

- ISACA has produced some research on the topic, including an excellent white paper on cloud computing security in 2009, which can be accessed at http://isaca.org/.

- The cloud security blog at http://cloudsecurity.org/ also provides an array of useful research and viewpoints on the topic.

Regarding materials on auditing general (non-cloud–specific) IT outsourcing, your best bets are to search for relevant materials on the ISACA website (http://isaca.org/), specifically within the COBIT framework.

Master Checklist

The following table summarizes the steps listed herein for auditing cloud computing and outsourced operations.

Auditing Cloud Computing and Outsourced Operations

	Checklist for Auditing Cloud Computing and Outsourced Operations
❑	1. Review the audit steps in the other chapters in this part of the book and determine which risks and audit steps are applicable to the audit being performed over outsourced operations. Perform those audit steps that are applicable.
❑	2. Request your service provider to produce independent assurance from reputable third parties regarding the effectiveness of their internal controls and compliance with applicable regulations. Review the documentation for issues that have been noted. Also, determine how closely these certifications match your own company's control objectives and identify gaps.
❑	3. Review applicable contracts to ensure that they adequately identify all deliverables, requirements, and responsibilities pertinent to your company's engagement.
❑	4. Review and evaluate the process used for selecting the outsourcing vendor.
❑	5. Determine how your data is segregated from the data of other customers.
❑	6. Review and evaluate the usage of encryption to protect company data stored at and transmitted to the vendor's site.
❑	7. Determine how vendor employees access your systems and how data is controlled and limited.
❑	8. Review and evaluate processes for controlling non-employee logical access to your internal network and internal systems.
❑	9. Ensure that data stored at vendor locations is being protected in accordance with your internal policies.
❑	10. Review and evaluate controls to prevent, detect, and react to attacks.
❑	11. Determine how identity management is performed for cloud-based and hosted systems.
❑	12. Ensure that data retention and destruction practices for data stored offsite comply with internal policy.
❑	13. Review and evaluate the vendor's physical security.
❑	14. Review and evaluate your company's processes for monitoring the quality of outsourced operations. Determine how compliance with SLAs is monitored.
❑	15. Ensure that adequate disaster recovery processes are in place to provide for business continuity in the event of a disaster at your service provider.
❑	16. Determine whether appropriate governance processes are in place over the engagement of new cloud services by your company's employees.

Checklist for Auditing Cloud Computing and Outsourced Operations *(continued)*

❑ 17. Review and evaluate your company's plans in the event of expected or unexpected termination of the outsourcing relationship.

❑ 18. If IT services have been outsourced, review the service provider's processes for ensuring quality of staff and minimizing the impact of turnover. If those services are being performed offshore, look for additional controls to ensure employee attendance and effective communication and hand-offs with the home office.

❑ 19. Review and evaluate your company's right and ability to obtain information from the vendor that may be necessary to support investigations.

❑ 20. Review requirements for security breach notification. Ensure that requirements are clearly defined regarding when and how the vendor should notify your company in the event of a security breach and that your company has clearly defined response procedures when they receive such notification.

❑ 21. Determine how compliance with applicable privacy laws and other regulations is ensured.

❑ 22. Review and evaluate processes for ensuring that the company is in compliance with applicable software licenses for any software hosted offsite or used by non-employees.

Auditing Company Projects

In this chapter we will discuss key controls to look for when auditing the processes used for managing company projects, including understanding the following as it relates to information technology (IT) audit project management:

- Keys to successful project management
- Requirements gathering and initial design
- System design and development
- Testing
- Implementation
- Training
- Wrapping up project

All the other chapters in this part of the book have dealt with how to audit specific technologies and processes that are already in place and operating in a production environment (such as operating systems, data centers, applications, and so on). However, before any system or process can be implemented, a project must be funded and staffed to develop or procure that system or process. If proper disciplines are not followed throughout the project, the chances of failure in meeting requirements and/or of inefficient use of company assets are greatly increased.

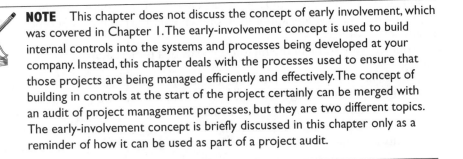

NOTE This chapter does not discuss the concept of early involvement, which was covered in Chapter 1. The early-involvement concept is used to build internal controls into the systems and processes being developed at your company. Instead, this chapter deals with the processes used to ensure that those projects are being managed efficiently and effectively. The concept of building in controls at the start of the project certainly can be merged with an audit of project management processes, but they are two different topics. The early-involvement concept is briefly discussed in this chapter only as a reminder of how it can be used as part of a project audit.

Background

Proper project management techniques are essential elements in the success of any company endeavor. These techniques help to ensure that pertinent requirements are gathered and tested, project resources are used efficiently, and all elements of the system are tested properly. Without such techniques, it is likely that the system being developed won't work or won't perform as expected by key stakeholders. This leads to rework and extra costs to the company (and can sometimes lead to people losing their jobs).

Good project management does not ensure success, but it improves the chances of success. The intent of this chapter is not to provide a training course on the basics of project management or the software development life cycle (SDLC), but is instead intended to provide a list of basic risks you should review when auditing a systems project to ensure that the most essential project management disciplines are being followed.

NOTE The words *software, system,* and *process* are used interchangeably in the following test steps and in conjunction with one another. They are intended to represent "the thing that is being developed by the project team." The use of one word versus another in a given test step is not intended to convey any specific meaning.

Project Auditing Essentials

In this section, we will define the goals of a project audit and define the basic approaches to and elements of auditing projects.

High-Level Goals of a Project Audit

Project audits are performed to identify risks to the success of company projects. This chapter deals specifically with IT projects (such as software development, infrastructure deployment, and business application implementation), but the concepts could apply to any sort of project.

Following are some of the high-level goals of a project audit:

- Ensure that all appropriate stakeholders are involved in the development of requirements and testing of the system and that frequent and effective communication occurs with all stakeholders. Failure to gather customer requirements and to obtain ongoing customer involvement and buy-in lead to software, systems, and processes being developed or procured that do not align with business needs.

- Ensure that project issues, budgets, milestones, and so on, are recorded, baselined, and tracked. Without these mechanisms, projects are more likely to go over budget and over schedule with unresolved issues.

- Ensure that effective testing encompasses all system requirements. Inadequate testing leads to unstable, low-quality systems that fail to meet customer requirements.

- Ensure that appropriate documentation is developed and maintained. Incomplete or out-of-date technical and user documentation could increase cost and cycle time to maintain the software, increase support and training costs, and limit the system's usefulness to the customer.

- Ensure that adequate training is provided to end users upon implementation. Inadequate training leads to systems, processes, and software that go unused or that are used improperly.

Basic Approaches to Project Auditing

Two basic approaches can be taken with project auditing. The first approach is quick and short term—the in-and-out approach. The second approach takes a long-term view of the project and is a more consistent approach.

The short-term approach can be challenging; auditors choose a point in the project to perform their audit, and then they review the project as of that point in time and make a judgment based on what has happened and what is planned. This approach suffers from two major downfalls.

First, it is difficult for the auditors to impact the phases that have already been completed. For example, the user acceptance testing phase is a bad time to learn that poorly controlled processes were used during the project definition phase. The project team either has to revisit and rework to improve earlier tasks or move forward, knowing that problems exist and hoping for the best. Either way, the auditors' input is not very timely and may even be seen as counter-productive, damaging relationships between the auditor and his or her customers.

Second, fully evaluating phases that have not yet begun is difficult. Auditors might be able to review plans for user acceptance testing at the beginning of the project, for example, but until those plans are fully developed and being executed, auditors will find it difficult to evaluate their true effectiveness.

The longer term, or consistent involvement, approach allows auditors to perform some assessment activities during each major phase of the project. Each audit evaluates the processes within the current phase while simultaneously assessing and providing input on plans for future phases. This is an effective means of auditing projects and leads to a more collaborative approach with audit customers. On the negative side, this approach stretches out the audit over a long period of time and can be difficult to schedule. However, the positives far outweigh the negatives.

If the project spans an exceptionally long period of time, the auditors might consider one of two approaches:

- Release interim audit reports after each major project phase so that the information in the report doesn't become too stale.

- Meet with the project manager to discuss issues on a regular basis (such as every two weeks). At this meeting, the auditors can communicate new risks to the project discovered since the last meeting and also follow-up on the status of previous issues to determine whether remediation is complete. If, in the auditors' opinion, the project risk is increasing to an unsatisfactory level, or if issues are not being mitigated, the auditors can escalate to a higher level of management at their discretion. The auditors should reserve the right to issue a full-scale audit report at any time, but by trying to work with the project manager first, issues will more likely be resolved without escalation and without the issuance of interim audit reports.

Seven Major Parts of a Project Audit

Projects can be separated into seven major parts (Figure 15-1), each of which require disciplines and controls that we will evaluate during the project audit:

1. *Overall project management*   Mechanisms that should be used throughout the project, such as issue tracking, project documentation, and change management.

2. *Project startup, requirements gathering, and initial design*   Covers the birth of a project: where the need for the project is established, requirements are gathered, and the initial design and feasibility studies are performed.

3. *Detailed design and system development*   Covers the "meat" of the project: where the code is written, the product is procured or implemented, the processes are developed, and so on.

4. *Testing*   The system, software, or process is tested to ensure that it meets requirements.

5. *Implementation*   The system, software, or process is implemented or installed into a production environment.

6. *Training*   Covers the activities for training end users on using the system, software, or process that has been developed and implemented.

7. *Project wrap-up*   Covers post-implementation activities.

NOTE   These project elements will not necessarily be performed in this precise order, nor will they necessarily be performed sequentially. Multiple iterations of each phase may exist, and some may be performed in parallel with each other (for example, user training is often performed in parallel with testing and implementation). However, just about every project should have some of each of these elements.

The rest of this chapter will focus on key audit steps and tests to perform with regard to these seven categories.

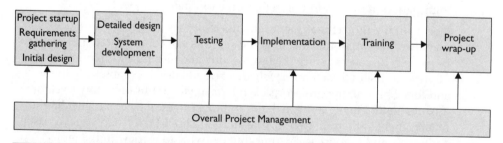

Figure 15-1   Major elements of projects

Test Steps for Auditing Company Projects

To provide some context and structure, the test steps in this section are provided according to project phase. However, the steps don't always work out as neatly as what has been laid out; each process has unique situations and requirements to consider. For example, the time to address a step from the testing section may occur during the requirements-gathering phase.

You should perform each step at the point in the project at which it makes the most sense, based on how the project is run. It is critical for the auditor to understand the methodology of the project and adjust his or her approach accordingly. For example, if the project is using incremental development, where each project phase is executed multiple times, you may need to audit each phase concurrently or possibly even multiple times. The controls required for a project generally will be the same regardless of the project methodology, but matching the audit phase to the project and coordinating the timing will be more difficult for some types of projects than for others. Part of the planning process should involve obtaining an understanding of the project methodology used and determining the appropriate timing and method for accomplishing the steps in this program.

When planning the audit, you should determine what project management tool is used by the project team and become familiar with the tool and its terminology. This will allow you to "speak the same language" as the people you are auditing and further enhance credibility.

In addition, some of these steps may be overkill for smaller projects. You should use judgment in determining which of these risks are material enough to address for each specific project.

Finally, these steps are written so that they can be used for any sort of IT project, whether it involves acquiring or developing software, procuring new technology, or developing a process. Use your judgment to determine which steps are most applicable based on the kind of project being audited.

Overall Project Management

The steps in this section should usually be performed thoroughly at the beginning of the project and then again lightly during each phase of the project to ensure that the disciplines are still being followed. Project management may start out strong, but it often wanes as people become busy and are scrambling to meet deadlines.

1. Ensure that sufficient project documentation and software development process documentation (if applicable) have been created. Ensure that the company's project methodology standards are being followed.

This sort of documentation will increase the likelihood that the project is being implemented in a disciplined manner and is following your company's established standards and methodologies. This, in turn, greatly increases the chances that the project will be executed successfully and will produce the business value desired. This documentation can also benefit future projects, allowing the company to leverage past efforts. Finally, your company may have specific standards for executing projects based on either internal or regulatory requirements.

How

Review copies of existing project documentation and compare it with your company's standards and requirements. The documents required will vary by company, but look for documents covering areas such as milestones, work breakdown structure (WBS), project approach, statement of work (SOW), requirements, test plans, and design documents. Obtain a copy of your company's project methodology standards and compare them with the methodology being executed on the project being reviewed. When reviewing this documentation, look for evidence of adequate project and resource planning. Performing this step is not an exact science; you are trying to develop a feel for the overall level of documentation and processes established for the project. Some of this documentation will be examined in more detail during later steps. In this step, the auditor should obtain the document(s) that constitute the basic project plan and determine whether customer needs, deliverables, objectives, and scope are clearly defined.

2. Review procedures for ensuring that project documentation is kept up-to-date.

For reasons mentioned in the preceding step, this documentation enhances the quality of current and future projects. However, if it is allowed to become outdated, it quickly becomes useless.

How

Through interviews with the project team, understand the processes in place for updating these documents when necessary. Look for evidence that updates have been made.

3. Evaluate security and change-management processes for critical project documentation.

If proper security and change controls are not in place, unauthorized, inaccurate, and /or unnecessary changes may be made to the project documentation.

How

Ensure that files containing project documentation are locked down and can be modified only by an appropriate subset of project personnel (using techniques described in Chapter 6 for Windows files and Chapter 7 for Unix or Linux files). Interview project personnel to understand processes for changing critical project documents. Ensure that an approval process is required before changes are made to significant project documents and that the approval process cannot be circumvented. The documents that constitute the basic project plan (such as customer needs, deliverables, objectives, scope, budget, risks, and communication strategies) should be baselined early in the project so that they cannot be changed without agreement from all key stakeholders.

4. Evaluate procedures for backing up critical project software and documentation. Ensure that backups are stored offsite and documented procedures exist for recovery.

If these processes are not in place, a system crash or data center disaster could result in the permanent loss of project software and documentation.

How

Review processes or scripts indicating that project data is backed up and stored offsite. Review written recovery procedures, ensuring that they specify what steps are to be performed for recovery, the order of those steps, and who is to perform each step. Note that these written recovery procedures may not be created for and unique to a particular project. They may instead be part of the IT team's standard recovery procedures for lost files. Consider requesting a test recovery of the critical project material.

5. Ensure that an effective process exists for capturing project issues, escalating those issues as appropriate, and tracking them to resolution.

During the course of any project, issues inevitably will arise regarding the project itself or the system, process, or software being developed. Without a robust method of capturing and resolving those issues, some issues will likely "slip through the cracks" and not be resolved, resulting in failures in the product or failures in execution of the project.

How

Review the issues database, spreadsheet, or other method established for recording and tracking issues. Ensure that the issue-tracking tool records adequate information regarding each issue, including description of the issue, priority level, due date, latest status, and resolution information. Ensure that controls exist over the tool used to track issues, such as backups and security to prevent unauthorized updates. Review processes for escalating issues and for ensuring that issues are tracked to resolution. Review the issues list for evidence that issues are being closed. Interview customers to ensure that the process is working.

6. Ensure that an effective process exists for capturing project change requests, prioritizing them, and dispositioning them.

During most projects, requests for additional functionality will arise after the project has commenced and the requirements have been established and approved. Without a method for ensuring that these requests are prioritized and dispositioned, these requests may get lost, and/or the scope of the project will shift continually, making it impossible to execute the project effectively. A change request process will help prevent *scope creep* and provide for ongoing discussions with the project's customers regarding how change requests will impact the project's budget and schedule.

How

Review the change management process and ensure that it provides allowance for entering, ranking, and approving change requests. Verify that it covers changes to scope, schedule, budget, requirements, design, and so on (that is, all major elements of the project). Ensure that it records adequate information regarding each change request, including description of the request, priority level, latest status, approval, and resolution information. Select a sample of change requests, and walk them through the process, ensuring that proper approvals were received prior to final resolution.

7. Verify that a project schedule has been created and that it contains sufficient detail based on the size of the project. Ensure that a process is in place for monitoring progress and reporting significant delays.

Project schedules are used to ensure that the project is on track, resources are being used effectively, and all tasks have been accounted for and scheduled.

How

Review the project schedule, and look for items such as a work breakdown, milestone dates, task dependencies, and the critical path. Look for evidence that the schedule is followed and kept up-to-date. Seek explanations for any significant deltas. Ensure that an escalation procedure exists for any significant schedule or resource overruns, and review evidence that the process has been used. One potential way for the project to ensure schedule compliance is to create strategic points in the life cycle in which the project passes through a "tollgate process." At these points, the project team reports to a review panel to convey the status of the project, successes and issues, and progress versus the schedule and budget. This helps identify struggles and failures quickly as they occur.

8. Ensure that a method is in place for tracking project costs and reporting overruns. Ensure that all project costs, including labor, are considered and tracked.

Without these mechanisms, project budgets can often be exceeded, and often the appropriate levels of management are not made aware of these issues. Management presumably has placed a cap on the funding for a specific project. If all relevant expenses are not tracked, management will be unaware if that cap has been exceeded and will, therefore, be unable to make an informed decision regarding how to proceed.

How

Obtain a copy of the budget, and compare it with expenses to date. Seek explanations for any significant deltas. Ensure that the budget includes all costs associated with the project, including labor, software, and hardware. Ensure that an escalation procedure exists for any significant cost overruns, and review evidence that the process has been used. See the tollgate description from step 7 for a potential review methodology.

9. Evaluate the project leadership structure to ensure that both the business and IT are represented adequately.

Except for some pure infrastructure projects, most projects are undertaken at the request of the business to meet a business need. If the key business stakeholders are not part of the overall leadership and approval structure for the project, the odds of the project getting off track from the business needs increase, because information and decisions about the project will be handled by IT people, who may not have the perspective necessary to make all decisions. Remember that IT exists to support the business, and therefore the IT organization should not be making decisions regarding the business's IT needs in a vacuum.

Conversely, IT personnel also should be part of the structure, because they generally bring important knowledge and perspective regarding the elements of success for IT-related projects. They can help ensure that the system is being designed in a cost-effective way that enables long-term support. Systems that are developed without IT involvement are far more likely to have issues with scalability, interoperability, and supportability. They are also more likely to experience deployment issues, resulting in negative impacts to the project schedule.

How
Obtain a copy of the project's leadership structure, and look for evidence that both business and IT leaders and stakeholders are represented.

Project Start-up: Requirements Gathering and Initial Design

10. Ensure that appropriate project approval processes were followed prior to project initiation.

Projects should not be initiated without approval from the appropriate members of management who are authorized to allocate resources and funds to new projects.

How
Review evidence that the project passed through the company's standard approval process. If no such process exists, review evidence that the appropriate manager(s) approved the project prior to startup. Look for evidence that alternative and cost-benefit analyses were performed. Ensure that cost-benefit analyses considered not only the project start-up costs but also ongoing costs, such as software maintenance, hardware maintenance, support (labor) costs, power and cooling requirements for system hardware, and other factors. This element is often omitted erroneously, leading to misinformed decisions. Start-up costs are only a fraction of the total ongoing costs for implementing a new system. A multiyear (five years is often a good target) total cost model should be developed as part of the initial project analysis.

11. Ensure that a technical feasibility analysis has been performed along with, if applicable, a feasibility analysis by the company's legal department.

Prior to the start-up of an IT project, qualified technical architects, network personnel, database administrators, and other applicable IT experts should agree that the proposed concept will work within the company's environment. If these experts are brought in early, it is likely that the technical professionals can find a way to make the concept work. However, if they are brought in after key elements of the system have been developed or procured, it may be determined that the solution is not technically feasible, leading to costly rework or discontinuation of the project. Likewise, it is important to engage the legal team to ensure that regulatory requirements are considered in the project.

How

Review evidence that appropriate technical and legal personnel were involved in the initial project proposal and that they agreed to the feasibility of the project.

12. Review and evaluate the requirements document. Determine whether and how customer requirements for the project are obtained and documented before development takes place. Ensure that the customers sign off on the requirements and that the requirements encompass standard IT elements.

Systems, software, and processes should be built based on the requirements of the end users. If end user requirements are not captured and approved by the customers, the product likely will not meet the customers' needs, requiring rework and changes. In addition, certain standard IT elements should be included in the requirements definition of any system. Customers may not be aware of these elements and therefore require guidance from the IT team. Establishing clearly defined requirements will also assist in discussions down the road regarding what is a bug fix (that is, when the system is not functioning as designed) and what is an enhancement request (that is, when the system is functioning as designed but the customer wants to make a change), which can be an important distinction depending on your IT organization's support and funding models.

How

Review project documentation for evidence that customer requirements were gathered. Ensure that all key stakeholders, including the project sponsors, were involved in this process. Look for evidence that the key stakeholders agreed to the final list of requirements.

Review customer requirements to ensure that they are documenting business requirements and are not dictating a solution. Often, business leaders will speak to a vendor or read an article and decide to create a project for the purpose of implementing a specific product or technology. However, that particular product may not be the most effective fit for your particular company's situation. For example, it may not fully meet the business's needs, it may be redundant with other products currently used in the environment, or it may not interface well with existing company technologies. It is critical that the customer focus on determining and documenting the business requirements and allow the IT organization the flexibility to determine what tool(s) best meet those requirements.

Ensure that the requirements encompass standard IT elements such as the following:

Distributed and centralized processing requirements (for example, the location of the storage and processing in a multitier architecture)	Service level agreements (for example, system availability, speed of response to problems)
Response time (for online transactions)	Interface requirements
Security	Backup/recovery/restart requirements
Execution frequency	Hardware requirements
Data retention requirements	Capacity, including needs for future anticipated growth
Requirements for output distribution	Fault tolerance and redundancy
Screen definitions	

If this project is intended to replace an existing system, look for evidence that an analysis of the current system was performed to determine what is working well and what is not. Also, look for evidence that the existing system has been carefully analyzed and all the existing use cases (functions) that it fulfills are met with the new system. The results of this analysis should be reflected in the requirements documentation. (The requirements should call for the new system to do the things that work well in the old system and to improve on the things that don't.) Error logs and backlog requests from the old system can aid in the effort to determine what is not working well.

13. Evaluate the process for ensuring that all affected groups that will be helping to support the system, software, or process are involved in the project and will be part of the sign-off process, indicating their readiness to support it.

Multiple organizations in the IT environment are usually involved in supporting any new system, including network support, operating system support, database support, data center personnel, IT security, and the help desk. If these organizations are not involved in the project early on, they may not be prepared to support the system after it is ready, and/or the system may not be in compliance with applicable standards and policies.

How

Review evidence that other affected IT organizations have been notified of the project and are part of the approval process (as it relates to their readiness to support it).

14. Review the process for establishing the priority of requirements.

Often, more system requirements exist than can be encompassed in the project (or at least in the initial phase of the project). The most critical requirements must be identified, prioritized, and implemented.

How

Look for evidence that the requirements were prioritized and that the key stakeholders approved the prioritization.

15. Determine whether the system requirements and preliminary design ensure that appropriate internal control and security elements will be designed into the system, process, or software.

Internal controls are necessary to protect company systems and to ensure their integrity. It is much easier to build controls into new systems up front than to attempt to add them post-implementation.

How

This step is referring to the execution of the early-involvement concepts discussed in Chapter 1. The auditor will need to determine what sorts of controls he or she would audit the system for post-implementation and ensure that those controls are being designed into the system. Appropriate application controls and infrastructure controls should be considered. The other chapters in Part II of this book provide most of the detail needed to perform this step. Although those chapters discuss the techniques for auditing systems, processes, and software post-implementation, the same information can be used for providing input as to what controls need to be built in during design. In addition, it might be appropriate to assign a financial/operational auditor to the project to ensure that the proper business controls are built into the system logic and workflows.

16. If the project involves the purchase of software, technology, or other external services, review and evaluate the vendor selection process and related contracts.

Purchasing a product from an outside vendor is usually a significant investment and represents a commitment to that vendor's product. If the process for selecting the vendor is inadequate or the contract does not provide the company with adequate protection, it can lead to the purchase of products that do not meet the requirements of the project and a lack of legal recourse.

How

Review the vendor selection process for elements such as these:

- Ensure that products from multiple vendors are evaluated as to their ability to meet all project requirements and their compatibility with the company's IT environment. This not only helps you select the best product for your requirements, but it provides for competitive bidding and lower prices.

- Ensure that a cost analysis has been performed on the products being evaluated. This analysis should include all relevant costs, including product costs, one-time startup costs, hardware costs, licensing fees, and maintenance costs.

- Determine whether the vendors' financial stability was investigated as part of the evaluation process. Failure to do so may result in your company signing up with a vendor that goes out of business, causing significant disruption to your operations as you attempt to move them to another vendor.

- Determine whether the vendors' experience with providing support for the product for similar companies in the industry was evaluated. This may include obtaining and interviewing references from companies that currently use the product. You generally want to use vendors that have already demonstrated that they can perform the types of services you require at a scale similar to yours.

- Ensure that the vendors' technical support capabilities were considered and evaluated.

- Ensure that each vendor was compared against predefined criteria, providing for objective evaluations.

- Determine whether there was appropriate involvement of procurement personnel to help negotiate the contract, of operations personnel to provide expert evaluations as to the vendor's ability to meet requirements, and of legal personnel to provide guidance on potential regulatory and other legal ramifications.

- After a vendor is chosen, ensure that the contract clearly identifies deliverables, requirements, and responsibilities. The contract should specify how performance will be measured and penalties for nonperformance or delayed performance. It also should provide conditions for terminating the agreement. Basically, anything you expect from the vendor needs to be specifically outlined in the contract.

- Ensure that the contract contains a nondisclosure clause preventing the vendor from disclosing company information.

- Ensure that the contract contains a "right to audit" clause that allows you to audit vendor activities that are critical to your company.

- Where applicable, ensure that code is put in escrow to protect against unavailability should the vendor go out of business and that an appropriate exit strategy is in place should the relationship between your company and the vendor be discontinued for any reason.

Detailed Design and System Development

17. Ensure that all requirements can be mapped to a design element.

A defined process for tracing requirements to the system design will provide assurance that all requirements are addressed, including such standard IT elements as interfaces, response time, and capacity.

How

If a requirements trace map exists, review it and verify that all requirements are represented and mapped to a design element. If a trace map doesn't exist, review the process for ensuring that all requirements are encompassed.

18. Verify that the key stakeholders have signed off on the detailed design document or "use case" catalog.

The detailed design document is used for the design of the system, software, or process. A "use case" catalog may be created for the project customers as a less technical document that details the system design from a more functional standpoint (that is, detailing exactly how each required system function will be implemented). This document will specify the success and failure criteria for each scenario within the application. For example, customer check-out for an e-commerce application would be a use case that would lead to multiple steps (such as verifying that the user logged in, validating the shipping address, and so on), all of which would be documented in detail.

If key stakeholders have not signed off on these appropriate documents, the chances are greater that the output of the project may not meet their needs.

How

Look for the equivalent of a detailed design document and for evidence of customer approval. Note that nontechnical personnel may not be in a position to understand the detailed design document, depending on how it is written. If this is the case, ensure that compensating design reviews or "use case" catalogs have been developed that allow the stakeholders to understand the planned design elements.

19. Review processes for ensuring ongoing customer involvement with the prioritization of tasks on the project.

Most projects experience fluidity, with the initial set of requirements rarely ending up as the final set of requirements. If key stakeholders are not involved throughout the project, the project runs the risk of straying away from customer requirements, and decisions can be made that are not in alignment with customer wishes.

How

Determine whether a direction-setting group has been established and contains key customers and whether they are involved in project decisions on a regular basis. Consider interviewing a small sample of customers to obtain their opinions on customer involvement. Look for evidence of periodic project review meetings and periodic communication with key stakeholders.

20. Look for evidence of peer reviews in design and development.

This quality-control discipline, which involves a review of code and configuration by the developer's peers, can help to increase the odds that the system will be designed with sound logic and a minimum of errors.

How

Determine whether peer reviews are required by the process, and look for evidence that they are actually occurring.

21. Verify that appropriate internal controls and security have been designed into the system.

See step 15 for further information.

How

Validate (either through interviews or design reviews) that the input you provided in step 15 has been encompassed in the design of the system.

Testing

22. Verify that design and testing are occurring in a development/ test environment and not in a production environment.

Failure to perform design and test work in dedicated environments could result in disruption of normal business activities.

How

View evidence that the environments being used during development and testing are separate from the environment being used for production. View a layout of the architecture, and validate segregation of the environments. View project member logins to the various environments, and confirm that the servers being used for design, testing, and production match the architecture layout. Also, ensure that the test environment closely mirrors the production environment. Otherwise, a successful test of code in the testing environment may not be an indicator that the code will work in the production environment or that it will be scalable with the production load.

23. Review and evaluate the testing process. Ensure that the project has an adequate test plan and that it follows this test plan.

Testing the system, software, or process will provide assurance that it works as intended.

How

Review the test plan for several elements. First, determine whether the test plan includes the following:

- **Unit testing**   Testing of individual system modules or units or groups of related units

- **Integration testing**   Testing of multiple modules or units to ensure that they work together correctly

- **System testing**   Testing of the overall system by the development team

- **Acceptance testing**   Testing performed by the end users to validate that the system meets requirements and is acceptable

- **Regression testing**   Retesting select areas to ensure that changes made to one part of the system did not cause problems in other parts of the system

Then review the plan for the following:

- Ensure that the test plan and related procedures and test cases are repeatable so that they can be used for regression testing and for future releases.

- Ensure that test plans and cases go through a peer review to ensure quality.

- Determine whether the test plan includes testing of bad/erroneous data, system error handling, and system recovery.

- Determine whether the test plan includes testing of security and internal controls.

- Ensure that results of testing are fully documented.

- Ensure that gaps identified during testing are documented, tracked, resolved, and retested. Ensure that the gap/bug-tracking process is approved up front. This process needs to be baselined and a system of controlled change established quickly, or it can become a mess, with code being pulled in and out of production haphazardly.

- Ensure that the project team has agreed to metrics to be captured and reported during testing and that these metrics are reported in a timely fashion to the appropriate members of the project leadership.

- Ensure that the test plan includes the testing of performance requirements and thresholds.

- Ensure that each test case identifies the product, component, or module that it is testing.

- Evaluate the process for ensuring that all major functionality is tested and that all key logic paths are identified and tested. If a use case catalog is used, evaluate the process for ensuring all elements of all use cases are tested.

- Ensure that test data has been created and that the customers agree that test data is valid.

- Determine whether test steps define expected results and customer acceptance criteria.

- Ensure that all test tasks are identified and assigned an owner and that the "who, what, where, and when" of testing have been clearly identified for all parties involved.

- Ensure that appropriate sign-offs have been obtained for the plan.

- Determine whether the test plan lists the sequence in which test steps should be performed.

- Ensure that test planning includes the identification of and plans for obtaining hardware and software needed for testing.

- If using a combination of vendor software and internally developed code, determine whether a process has been defined for ensuring that both parties' code will be merged in a well-coordinated fashion.

 NOTE This list should not be used as a mechanical checklist. The absence of one of these items should not automatically result in an audit issue. Instead, look at the testing process as a whole, and determine whether enough of the key elements are present to provide reasonable assurance that adequate and controlled testing is occurring.

24. Ensure that all requirements can be mapped to a test case.

A defined process for tracing requirements to the test plan will provide assurance that all requirements are addressed and tested.

How

If a requirements trace map exists, review it and verify that all requirements are represented and mapped to a test case. If a trace map doesn't exist, review the process for ensuring that all requirements are tested.

25. Ensure that users are involved in testing and agree that the system meets requirements. This should include IT personnel who will be supporting the system and IT personnel who were involved in performing initial technical feasibility studies for the project.

The system, software, or process is being developed to meet a specific business need. The project cannot be a success if the key stakeholders are not satisfied. Therefore, they must be involved in testing and must sign off on the system prior to implementation. Also, as mentioned in step 13, multiple organizations in the IT environment usually will be involved in supporting any new system, including network support, operating system support, database support, data center personnel, IT security, and the help desk. If these organizations are not involved in system testing and sign-off, they may not be prepared to support it, and/or the system may not be in compliance with applicable standards and policies.

How

Look for evidence of user acceptance testing. Ensure that key stakeholders who were involved in requesting and approving the project and in defining system requirements (including affected IT organizations) are also involved in project testing and sign-off.

26. Consider participating in user acceptance testing and validating that system security and internal controls are functioning as intended.

This is necessary for the same reasons outlined in step 15. By participating in testing, you will be able to validate these controls independently.

How

During earlier steps, you should have worked with the project team to identify the internal controls that should be built into the system, software, or process. Review the test plan to ensure that it encompasses testing of those internal controls. Participate as an acceptance tester of those test cases.

Implementation

27. Ensure that an effective process exists for recording, tracking, escalating, and resolving problems that arise after implementation.

Unforeseen problems arise after the implementation of almost any new system. Without a robust method for capturing and resolving those issues, issues can "slip through the cracks" and not be resolved in a timely fashion. Also, an issue-tracking system is needed to ensure that issues are being prioritized and fixed according to their importance.

How

Review the issues database, issues spreadsheet, or whatever other method has been established for recording and tracking post-implementation issues. Ensure that the issue-tracking tool records adequate information regarding each issue, including description of the issue, priority level, due date, latest status, and resolution information. Ensure that controls exist over the tool used to track issues, such as backups and security to prevent unauthorized updates. Review processes for escalating issues and for ensuring that issues are tracked to resolution. Review the issues list for evidence that issues are being closed. Interview customers to ensure that the process is working.

28. Review and evaluate the project's conversion plan. Ensure that the project has an adequate conversion plan and follows this plan.

If the project being reviewed involves replacing an existing system, at some point, users will switch over to the new system. It is critical that existing data be converted successfully to the new system prior to this time to ensure a smooth transition.

How

Review the conversion plan, and look for elements such as the following:

- Ensure that all critical data is identified and considered for conversion.

- Review controls for ensuring that all data is converted completely and accurately. Examples of such control mechanisms could be control totals on key fields, record counts, and user reconciliation procedures.

- Determine whether all conversion programs are fully tested with user involvement and that the test results are documented.

- If historical data is not converted, ensure that a method is developed for accessing the data if needed. For example, if financial data is involved, historical financial data may be needed in the future for tax reporting.

- Review and evaluate plans for parallel processing or other fallback methods in case difficulties are experienced during transition to the new system.

- Ensure that the conversion process includes establishing data that was not used in the legacy systems. For example, a record in the new system may contain fields that were not contained in a similar record on the legacy systems. Consideration should be given to populating these new fields.

- Review and evaluate the plan for a "conversion weekend." A detailed plan should contain criteria and checkpoints for making "go/no-go" decisions.

 NOTE This list should not be used as a mechanical checklist. The absence of one of these items should not automatically result in an audit issue. Instead, look at the conversion process as a whole, and determine whether enough of the key elements are present to provide a reasonable assurance that adequate and controlled conversion is taking place.

29. Review plans for converting the support of the new system or software from the project team to an operational support team.

After the project has been completed, it is likely that project personnel will be redeployed to other projects. It is therefore critical that run/maintain support personnel be trained properly in the functionality of the system so that they will be prepared to support it when users identify issues or request enhancements. This is one of the most commonly overlooked elements of projects.

How

Through interviews or review of documentation, look for evidence that support personnel have been identified, adequately involved in the project, and appropriately trained on the system and its functionality.

30. Ensure that sufficient documentation has been created for use of the system or process being developed and maintenance of the system or software. Evaluate processes for keeping the documentation up-to-date. Evaluate change controls and security over that documentation.

Incomplete or outdated technical and user documentation could increase costs and cycle time to maintain the software, increase support and training costs, and limit the system, process, or software's usefulness to the customer.

How

Obtain copies of existing documentation, and evaluate its adequacy. Look for evidence that would indicate that documentation has been updated when the system has changed, and review processes for ensuring ongoing maintenance of the documentation. Ensure that files containing documentation are locked down and can be modified only by appropriate personnel (using techniques described in Chapters 6 and 7). Interview appropriate personnel to understand processes for changing critical documents. Ensure that an approval process is required before changes are made to significant documents and that the approval process cannot be circumvented.

Training

31. Review plans for ensuring that all affected users are trained in the use of the new system, software, or process.

Training is an essential element for preparing end users on the functionality and nuances of a newly developed system. If training is not provided or is inadequate, the new system, software, or process likely will be misused, used ineffectively, or avoided.

How

Review the training plans and interview users to develop an opinion on its adequacy. Compare a list of planned training recipients with the population of end users to ensure that no significant gaps exist.

32. Ensure that processes are in place for keeping training materials up-to-date. Evaluate change controls and security over the training materials.

As new employees and new users need to use the system, they will want to take advantage of the training materials. If these training materials have become outdated (for example, because of system changes), the training materials' effectiveness will be limited.

How

Look for evidence that would indicate that training has been updated when the system has changed, and review processes for ensuring ongoing maintenance of the documentation. Ensure that files containing documentation are locked down and that they can be modified only by appropriate personnel (using techniques described in Chapters 6 and 7). Interview appropriate personnel to understand processes for changing critical documents. Ensure that an approval process is required before changes are made to significant documents and that the approval process cannot be circumvented.

Project Wrap-up

33. Ensure that a process exists for closing out the project and recording lessons learned and that the process is followed.

Finalized project documentation and recorded lessons learned can be used to aid in the effectiveness and efficiency of future company projects. This step is often missed, as the project team quickly moves on to other tasks after successful implementation.

How

Review the project documentation, and ensure that all relevant documents have been finalized and baselined. Look for evidence that a final list of lessons learned from the project has been documented.

Knowledge Base

The Project Management Institute (PMI) is responsible for publishing the well-known Project Management Professional (PMP) certification. For more information about PMI or the PMP, visit www.pmi.org.

The Software Engineering Institute (SEI) and its Capability Maturity Model Integration (CMMI) are useful tools for gathering best practices for software-development methodology. The SEI's mission is to advance software engineering and related disciplines to ensure the development and operation of systems with predictable and improved cost, schedule, and quality. The CMMI is a process-improvement approach that provides organizations with the essential elements of effective processes. For more information on SEI, visit www.sei.cmu.edu.

Master Checklists

The following tables summarize the steps listed herein for auditing company projects.

Auditing Overall Project Management

Checklist for Auditing Overall Project Management

❏   1. Ensure that sufficient project documentation and software development process documentation (if applicable) have been created. Ensure that the company's project methodology standards are being followed.

❏   2. Review procedures for ensuring that project documentation is kept up-to-date.

❏   3. Evaluate security and change-management processes for critical project documentation.

❏   4. Evaluate procedures for backing up critical project software and documentation. Ensure that backups are stored offsite and that documented procedures exist for recovery.

❏   5. Ensure that an effective process exists for capturing project issues, escalating those issues as appropriate, and tracking them to resolution.

❏   6. Ensure that an effective process exists for capturing project change requests, prioritizing them, and dispositioning them.

❏   7. Verify that a project schedule has been created and that it contains sufficient detail based on the size of the project. Ensure that a process is in place for monitoring progress and reporting significant delays.

❏   8. Ensure that a method is in place for tracking project costs and reporting overruns. Ensure that all project costs, including labor, are considered and tracked.

❏   9. Evaluate the project leadership structure to ensure that both the business and IT are represented adequately.

Auditing Project Startup

Checklist for Auditing Project Startup

❏   10. Ensure that appropriate project approval processes were followed prior to project initiation.

❏   11. Ensure that a technical feasibility analysis has been performed along with, if applicable, a feasibility analysis by the company's legal department.

❏   12. Review and evaluate the requirements document. Determine whether and how customer requirements for the project are obtained and documented before development takes place. Ensure that the customers sign off on the requirements and that the requirements encompass standard IT elements.

❏   13. Evaluate the process for ensuring that all affected groups who will be helping to support the system, software, or process are involved in the project and will be part of the sign-off process, indicating their readiness to support it.

❏   14. Review the process for establishing the priority of requirements.

❏   15. Determine whether the system requirements and preliminary design ensure that appropriate internal control and security elements will be designed into the system, process, or software.

❏   16. If the project involves the purchase of software, technology, or other external services, review and evaluate the vendor selection process and related contracts.

Auditing Detailed Design and System Development

Checklist for Auditing Detailed Design and System Development

☐ 17. Ensure that all requirements can be mapped to a design element.

☐ 18. Verify that the key stakeholders have signed off on the detailed design document or "use case" catalog.

☐ 19. Review processes for ensuring ongoing customer involvement with the prioritization of tasks on the project.

☐ 20. Look for evidence of peer reviews in design and development.

☐ 21. Verify that appropriate internal controls and security have been designed into the system.

Auditing Testing

Checklist for Auditing Testing

☐ 22. Verify that design and testing are occurring in a development/test environment and not in a production environment.

☐ 23. Review and evaluate the testing process. Ensure that the project has an adequate test plan and that it follows this test plan.

☐ 24. Ensure that all requirements can be mapped to a test case.

☐ 25. Ensure that users are involved in testing and agree that the system meets requirements. This should include IT personnel who will be supporting the system and IT personnel who were involved in performing initial technical feasibility studies for the project.

☐ 26. Consider participating in user acceptance testing and validating that system security and internal controls are functioning as intended.

Auditing Implementation

Checklist for Auditing Implementation

☐ 27. Ensure that an effective process exists for recording, tracking, escalating, and resolving problems that arise after implementation.

☐ 28. Review and evaluate the project's conversion plan. Ensure that the project has an adequate conversion plan and follows this plan.

☐ 29. Review plans for converting the support of the new system or software from the project team to an operational support team.

☐ 30. Ensure that sufficient documentation has been created for use of the system or process being developed and maintenance of the system or software. Evaluate processes for keeping the documentation up-to-date. Evaluate change controls and security over that documentation.

Auditing Training

Checklist for Auditing Training

❑   31. Review plans for ensuring that all affected users are trained in the use of the new system, software, or process.

❑   32. Ensure that processes are in place for keeping training materials up-to-date. Evaluate change controls and security over the training materials.

Auditing Project Wrap-up

Checklist for Auditing Project Wrap-up

❑   33. Ensure that a process exists for closing out the project and recording lessons learned and that the process is followed.

PART III

Frameworks, Standards, and Regulations

16

Frameworks and Standards

As *information technology* (IT) matured during the late twentieth century, the IT department within each organization typically developed its own methods for managing operations. Eventually, frameworks and standards emerged to provide guidelines for the management and evaluation of IT processes. In this chapter we will look at some of today's most prominent frameworks and standards related to the use of technology. Our discussion will cover the following:

- Introduction to internal IT controls, frameworks, and standards
- Committee of Sponsoring Organizations (COSO)
- Control Objectives for Information and Related Technology (COBIT)
- IT Infrastructure Library (ITIL)
- ISO 27001
- National Security Agency (NSA) INFOSEC Assessment Methodology
- Frameworks and standards trends

Introduction to Internal IT Controls, Frameworks, and Standards

In the 1970s, concern over the rise in corporate bankruptcies and financial collapses began to heighten a demand for more accountability and transparency among publicly held companies. The *Foreign Corrupt Practices Act of 1977* (FCPA) criminalized bribery in foreign countries and was the first regulation that required companies to implement internal control programs to keep extensive records of transactions for disclosure purposes.

When the savings and loan industry collapsed in the mid-1980s, there was a cry for governmental oversight of accounting standards and the auditing profession. In an effort to deter governmental intervention, an independent private-sector initiative, later called Committee of Sponsoring Organizations (COSO), was initiated in 1985 to assess how best to improve the quality of financial reporting. COSO formalized the concepts of *internal control* and *framework* in 1992 when it issued the landmark publication *Internal Control–Integrated Framework*.

Since that time, other professional associations have continued to develop additional frameworks and standards to provide guidance and best practices to their constituents and the IT community at large. The following sections highlight COSO and some of the other most prominent IT frameworks and standards in use today.

COSO

In the mid-1980s, the National Commission on Fraudulent Financial Reporting was formed in response to growing U.S. financial crises and the cry for governmental oversight of accounting and audit practices. This independent private-sector consortium was more commonly referred to as the *Treadway Commission* because it was headed by James C. Treadway, Jr., executive vice president and general counsel at Paine Webber Incorporated and a former commissioner of the U.S. Securities and Exchange Commission. In its initial 1987 report, the group recommended that the organizations sponsoring the commission work together to develop comprehensive guidelines for internal control. Hence COSO was formed by the five major professional associations in the United States:

- American Institute of Certified Public Accountants (AICPA)
- American Accounting Association (AAA)
- Financial Executives Institute (FEI)
- Institute of Internal Auditors (IIA)
- Institute of Management Accountants (IMA)

The commission is wholly independent of each of the sponsoring organizations and includes representatives from industry, public accounting, investment firms, and the New York Stock Exchange.

COSO published the first formalized guidelines for internal controls, *Internal Control–Integrated Framework*, in 1992. This publication established a common definition for *internal control* and a framework against which organizations can assess and improve their control systems. In 1994, COSO's work was endorsed by the head of the General Accounting Office (GAO) of the U.S. Congress. These voluntary industry guidelines were intended to help public companies become self-regulating and thus avoid the need for governmental regulation of the accounting and auditing industries.

In 2001, COSO began its second major initiative aimed at expanding previous work on internal controls to address the growing emphasis on risk management. At about the same time, the United States was barraged with the sensational failures of Enron, Tyco, Global Crossing, Kmart, Adelphia, WorldCom, HealthSouth, and many others. The U.S. government quickly enacted the Sarbanes-Oxley Act of 2002 to mandate the requirement for internal controls to be audited along with financial statements (as discussed in more detail in Chapter 17). On the heels of all this high-profile activity, COSO published *Enterprise Risk Management–Integrated Framework* in 2004. This second document provided a more comprehensive framework for identifying, assessing, and managing risk.

The COSO works are commonly accepted today in the United States as the corner-stones of modern internal control and enterprise risk-management practices. COSO revolutionized the accounting and auditing professions by establishing a common definition for internal control, enterprise risk management, and other fundamental concepts.

COSO Definition of Internal Control

Internal control is a process, affected by an entity's board of directors, management, and other personnel, designed to provide reasonable assurance regarding the achievement of objectives in the following categories:

- Effectiveness and efficiency of operations
- Reliability of financial reporting
- Compliance with applicable laws and regulations

Key Concepts of Internal Control

The following are key concepts of internal control according to COSO:

- Internal control is a process. It is a means to an end, not an end in itself.
- Internal control is affected by people. It's not merely policy manuals and forms, but people at every level of an organization.
- Internal control can be expected to provide only reasonable assurance, not absolute assurance, to an entity's management and board.
- Internal control is geared to the achievement of objectives in one or more separate but overlapping categories.

Internal Control–Integrated Framework

The *Internal Control–Integrated Framework* publication introduced what is now a well-known graphic: the *COSO cube* (Figure 16-1).

Figure 16-1
COSO cube

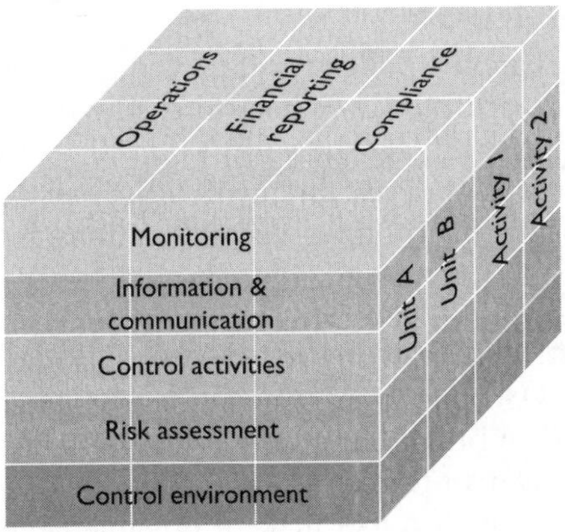

As explained by COSO, internal control consists of five interrelated *components*:

- Control environment
- Risk assessment
- Control activities
- Information and communication
- Monitoring

These are derived from the way management runs a business and are integrated with the company's management process. Although the components apply to all entities, small and midsize companies may implement them differently than large ones. Its controls may be less formal and less structured, yet a small company still can have effective internal control.

Control Environment

The *control environment* sets the tone of an organization, influencing the control consciousness of its people. It is the foundation for all other components of internal control, providing discipline and structure. Control-environment factors include the integrity, ethical values, and competence of the entity's people; management's philosophy and operating style; the way management assigns authority and responsibility and organizes and develops its people; and the attention and direction provided by the board of directors.

Risk Assessment

Every entity faces a variety of risks from external and internal sources that must be assessed. A precondition to risk assessment is establishment of objectives that should be linked at different levels and internally consistent. *Risk assessment* is the identification and analysis of relevant risks to achievement of the objectives forming a basis for determining how the risks should be managed. Because economic, industry, regulatory, and operating conditions will continue to change, mechanisms are needed to identify and deal with the special risks associated with change.

Control Activities

Control activities are the policies and procedures that help to ensure that management directives are carried out. They help to ensure that necessary actions are taken to address risks and thus achieve the entity's objectives. Control activities occur throughout the organization, at all levels and in all functions. They include a range of activities as diverse as approvals, authorizations, verifications, reconciliations, reviews of operating performance, security of assets, and segregation of duties.

Information and Communication

According to COSO, pertinent *information* must be identified, captured, and *communicated* in a form and time frame that enable people to carry out their responsibilities. Information systems produce reports containing operational, financial, and compliance-related information that make it possible to run and control the business. They deal not only with internally generated data but also with information about external events, activities, and conditions necessary to informed business decision-making and external reporting.

Effective communication also must occur in a broader sense, flowing down, across, and up the organization. All personnel must receive a clear message from top management that control responsibilities must be taken seriously. Each must understand his or her own role in the internal control system, as well as how individual activities relate to the work of others. They must have a means of communicating significant information upstream. There also needs to be effective communication with external parties, such as customers, suppliers, regulators, and shareholders.

Monitoring

Internal control systems need to be *monitored*—a process that assesses the quality of the system's performance over time. This is accomplished through ongoing monitoring activities, separate evaluations, or a combination of the two. Ongoing monitoring occurs in the course of operations. It includes regular management and supervisory activities and other actions personnel undertake in performing their duties. The scope and frequency of separate evaluations will depend primarily on an assessment of risks and the effectiveness of ongoing monitoring procedures. Internal control deficiencies should be reported upstream, with serious matters reported to top management and the board.

Component Relationships

There is synergy and linkage among these components, forming an integrated system that reacts dynamically to changing conditions. The internal control system is intertwined with the entity's operating activities and exists for fundamental business reasons. Internal control is most effective when controls are built into the entity's infrastructure and are a part of the essence of the enterprise. "Built-in" controls support quality and empowerment initiatives, avoiding unnecessary costs and enabling quick response to changing conditions.

A direct relationship exists between the three categories of *objectives* (described in the COSO definition of internal control) that an entity strives to achieve and the *components* that represent what is needed to achieve the objectives. All components are relevant to each objective's category. When looking at any one category—the effectiveness and efficiency of operations, for instance—all five components must be present and functioning effectively to conclude that internal control over operations is effective.

The internal control definition—with its underlying fundamental concepts of a process, affected by people, providing reasonable assurance—together with the categorization of objectives and the components and criteria for effectiveness and the associated discussions, constitutes this internal control framework.

Enterprise Risk Management—Integrated Framework

COSO published *Enterprise Risk Management—Integrated Framework* in 2004 to provide companies with a benchmark for managing risk within their organizations.

COSO Definition of Enterprise Risk Management

Enterprise risk management is a process, affected by an entity's board of directors, management, and other personnel, applied in strategy setting and across the enterprise and designed to identify potential events that may affect the entity, and manage risk to be within its risk appetite, to provide reasonable assurance regarding the achievement of entity objectives.

This definition reflects certain fundamental concepts. Enterprise risk management is

- A process, ongoing and flowing through an entity;
- Affected by people at every level of an organization;
- Applied in strategy setting;
- Applied across the enterprise, at every level and unit, and includes taking an entity-level portfolio view of risk;
- Designed to identify potential events that, if they occur, will affect the entity and to manage risk within its risk appetite;
- Able to provide reasonable assurance to an entity's management and board of directors;
- Geared toward achievement of objectives in one or more separate but overlapping categories.

Enterprise Risk Management–Integrated Framework Concepts

In the publication *Enterprise Risk Management–Integrated Framework,* the original COSO cube was expanded, as illustrated in Figure 16-2.

Figure 16-2
Expanded
COSO cube

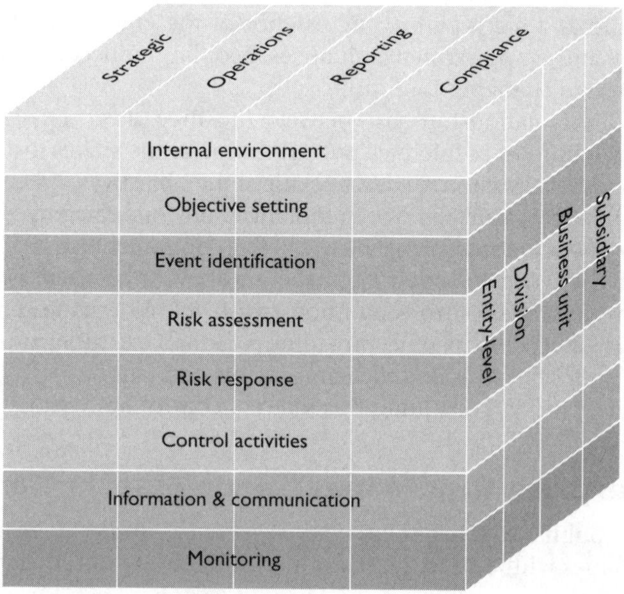

This enterprise risk-management framework is geared toward achieving an entity's objectives, set forth in four categories:

- **Strategic**   High-level goals, aligned with and supporting its mission
- **Operations**   Effective and efficient use of its resources
- **Reporting**   Reliability of reporting
- **Compliance**   Compliance with applicable laws and regulations

Enterprise risk management consists of eight interrelated components. These are derived from the way management runs an enterprise and are integrated with the management process.

- Internal environment
- Objective setting
- Event identification
- Risk assessment
- Risk response
- Control activities
- Information and communication
- Monitoring

Internal Environment   The internal environment encompasses the tone of an organization and provides the basis for how risk is viewed and addressed by an entity's people. It includes risk-management philosophy and the entity's risk appetite, integrity, and ethical values.

Objective Setting   Objectives must exist before management can identify potential events affecting their achievement. Enterprise risk management ensures that management has in place a process to set objectives and that the chosen objectives support and align with the entity's mission and are consistent with its appetite for risk.

Event Identification   Internal and external events affecting achievement of an entity's objectives must be identified, distinguishing between risks and opportunities. Opportunities are channeled back to management's strategy or objective-setting processes.

Risk Assessment   Risks are analyzed, considering likelihood and impact, as a basis for determining how they should be managed. Risks are assessed on an inherent and a residual basis.

Risk Response   Management selects risk responses—avoiding, accepting, reducing, or sharing—and develops a set of actions to align risks with the entity's risk tolerances and risk appetite.

Control Activities   Policies and procedures are established and implemented to help ensure that the risk responses are carried out effectively.

Information and Communication   Relevant information is identified, captured, and communicated in a form and time frame that enables people to carry out their responsibilities. Effective communication also occurs in a broader sense, flowing down, across, and up the entity.

Monitoring   The entirety of enterprise risk management is monitored and modifications are made as necessary. Monitoring is accomplished through ongoing management activities, separate evaluations, or both.

Relationship Between Internal Control and Enterprise Risk-Management Publications

Because the *Internal Control–Integrated Framework* has stood the test of time and is the basis for existing rules, regulations, and laws, the document remains in place as the definition of and framework for internal control. At the same time, internal control is an integral part of enterprise risk management. The entirety of the *Internal Control–Integrated Framework* is incorporated by reference into the publication *Enterprise Risk Management–Integrated Framework*. The enterprise risk-management framework incorporates internal control, forming an additional conceptualization and tool for management.

The Impact of COSO

The far-reaching principles outlined in the landmark COSO documents are gradually being implemented across the United States in publicly held corporations. COSO is the only framework for internal control mentioned by the *U.S. Securities and Exchange Commission (SEC) and the Public Company Accounting Oversight Board* (PCAOB) as a framework for internal control.*

NOTE   COSO is specifically referenced by the SEC in its guidance to companies for implementing the provisions of the Sarbanes-Oxley Act.

The PCAOB is the agency within the SEC that was created by the Sarbanes-Oxley Act of 2002 to oversee the accounting processes used by publicly held corporations. This is discussed in more detail in Chapter 17. In Auditing Standard No. 2, "An Audit of Internal Control over Financial Reporting Performed in Conjunction with an Audit of Financial Statements," the PCAOB specifically references COSO.

In providing guidance related to the Sarbanes-Oxley Act, Audit Standard No. 2 states, "Management is required to base its assessment of the effectiveness of the company's internal control over financial reporting on a suitable, recognized control framework. The COSO report known as *Internal Control–Integrated Framework* provides a suitable and available framework for purposes of management's assessment. For that reason, the performance and reporting directions in this standard are based on the COSO framework."

Further, COSO principles are also making their way into governmental agencies, private companies, non-profit organizations, and additional entities around the globe. Stakeholders are recognizing that good practices for public companies are often good practices for them as well.

COSO's Effect on IT Controls

COSO introduces the concept of controls over information systems. In *Internal Control–Integrated Framework*, COSO states that due to widespread reliance on information systems, controls are needed over significant systems. It classifies information systems control activities into two broad groupings. The first is *general computer controls*, which include controls over IT management, IT infrastructure, security management, and software acquisition, development, and maintenance. These controls apply to all systems—from mainframe to client-server to desktop computer environments.

The second grouping is *application controls*, which include computerized steps within application software to control the technology application. Combined with other manual process controls where necessary, these controls ensure completeness, accuracy, and validity of information.

COBIT

COBIT, *Control Objectives for Information and Related Technology*, was first published in April 1996. It is the foremost internationally recognized framework for IT governance and control. The most recent version, COBIT 4.1, was released in 2007.

COBIT was developed by the IT Governance Institute (ITGI) using a worldwide panel of experts from industry, academia, government, and the IT security and control profession. In-depth research was conducted across a wide variety of global sources to pull together the best ideas from all germane technical and professional standards.

COBIT Concepts

COBIT divides its primary *control objectives* into four domains: plan and organize, acquire and implement, deliver and support, and monitor and evaluate. Each of the domains shows the key IT control activities associated with that area.

The framework highlights seven qualities of information:

- Effectiveness
- Efficiency
- Confidentiality
- Integrity
- Availability
- Compliance
- Reliability

The COBIT framework outlines 34 high-level *control objectives* and 215 lower level *control activities*. IT resources are defined as people, applications, infrastructure, and information.

The model shows how all IT activities need to support the governance objectives that, in turn, support the business objectives. The control activities of the four domains work together in a cyclic manner to produce a well-governed IT support organization that produces optimal results based on the priorities and resources of the organization.

The COBIT framework goes on to elaborate on each of the control activities by providing detailed auditing guidelines (Figure 16-3).

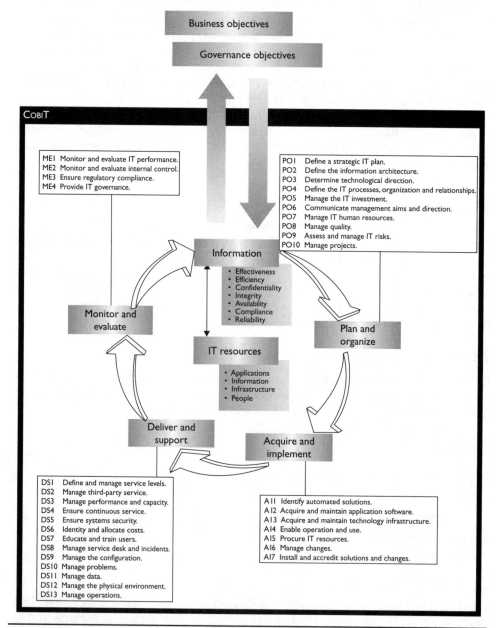

Figure 16-3 COBIT framework

COBIT Features

Following are some are some additional features that COBIT provides:

- COBIT represents a generally applicable and internationally accepted standard of good practice for IT controls.
- COBIT is independent of technical platform.
- COBIT is management and business process owner-oriented.
- COBIT has become the international de facto standard for IT governance.

The nonprofit, independent ITGI (www.itgi.org) is a research entity affiliated with ISACA. ITGI was established in 1998 to advance international thinking and standards in directing and controlling an enterprise's IT. In addition, ITGI offers original research and case studies to assist organizations and boards of directors in managing their IT resources.

ISACA (www.iscaca.org) is a recognized worldwide leader in IT governance, control, security, and assurance, with more than 86,000 members in more than 160 countries. Founded in 1969, ISACA sponsors international conferences, publishes the *Information Systems Control Journal*, and develops international information systems auditing and control standards. Additionally, ISACA administers the globally respected *Certified Information Systems Auditor* (CISA) designation as well as the *Certified Information Security Manager* (CISM), *Certified in Governance of Enterprise IT* (CGEIT), and *Certified in Risk and Information Systems Control* (CRISC) designations.

IT Governance

ISACA was an early promoter of the IT governance concept. It created the ITGI to assist enterprise leaders in their responsibility to ensure that IT goals align with those of the business by ensuring that IT delivers value, performance is measured, resources are allocated properly, and risks are mitigated.

ITGI provides the following definition: "IT governance is the responsibility of the board of directors and executive management. It is an integral part of enterprise governance and consists of the leadership and organizational structures and processes that ensure that the organization's IT sustains and extends the organization's strategies and objectives."

The growing need for IT governance tools and techniques was fueled by the following factors:

- Growing complexity of IT environments
- Fragmented or poorly performing IT infrastructures
- User frustration leading to ad hoc solutions
- IT costs perceived to be out of control
- IT managers operating in a reactive, rather than proactive, manner
- Communication gaps between business and IT managers
- Increasing pressure to leverage technology in business strategies

- Need to comply with increasing laws, standards, and regulations
- Scarcity of skilled staff
- Lack of application ownership
- Resource conflicts/shifting priorities
- Impaired organizational flexibility and nimbleness to change
- Concern for risk exposures
- Volatile organizational, political, or economic environment

IT Governance Maturity Model

ITGI developed a maturity model for the internal control of IT that provides to organizations a pragmatic and structured approach to measuring how well developed their processes are against a consistent and easy-to-understand scale. The maturity model was fashioned after the one originated by the *Software Engineering Institute* (SEI) for software development. SEI is a federally funded research and development center sponsored by the U.S. Department of Defense and operated by Carnegie Mellon University.

ITGI expanded the basic concept of the maturity model by applying it to the management of IT processes and controls. The principles were used to define a set of levels that allow an organization to assess where it is relative to the control and governance over IT. As shown in Figure 16-4, these levels are presented on a scale that moves from nonexistent on the left to optimized on the right. By using such a scale, an organization can determine where it is and define where it wants to go, and if it identifies a gap, it can perform an analysis to translate the findings into projects. Reference points can be added to the scale. Comparisons with what others are doing can be performed if that data is available, and the organization can determine where emerging international standards and industry best practices are pointing for the effective management of security and control. A description of the ITGI rating is provided in Figure 16-5.

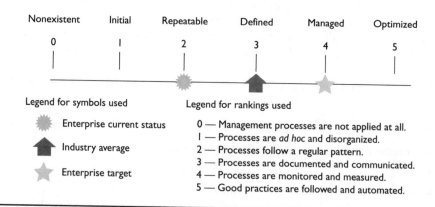

Figure 16-4 ITGI maturity scale

Maturity Model for Internal Control

Maturity Level	Status of the Internal Control Environment	Establishment of Internal Controls
0 Nonexistent	There is no recognition of the need for internal control. Control is not part of the organization's culture or mission. There is a high risk of control deficiencies and incidents.	There is no intent to assess the need for internal control. Incidents are dealt with as they arise.
1 Initial/ad hoc	There is some recognition of the need for internal control. The approach to risk and control requirements is *ad hoc* and disorganized, without communication or monitoring. Deficiencies are not identified. Employees are not aware of their responsibilities.	There is no awareness of the need for assessment of what is needed in terms of IT controls. When performed, it is only on an *ad hoc* basis, at a high level and in reaction to significant incidents. Assessment addresses only the actual incident.
2 Repeatable but Intuitive	Controls are in place but are not documented. Their operation is dependent on knowledge and motivation of individuals. Effectiveness is not adequately evaluated. Many control weaknesses exit and are not adequately addressed; the impact can be severe. Management actions to resolve control issues are not prioritized or consistent. Employees may not be aware of their responsibilities.	Assessment of control needs occurs only when needed for selected IT processes to determine the current level of control maturity, the target level that should be reached and the gaps that exist. An informal workshop approach, involving IT managers and the team involved in the process, is used to define an adequate approach to controls for the process and to motivate an agreed action plan.
3 Defined Process	Controls are in place and are adequately documented. Operating effectiveness is evaluated on a periodic basis and there are an average number of issues. However, the evaluation process is not documented. While management is able to deal predictably with most control issues, some control weaknesses persist and impacts could still be severe. Employees are aware of their responsibilities for control.	Critical IT processes are identified based on value and risk drivers. A detailed analysis is performed to identify control requirements and the root cause of gaps and to develop improvement opportunities. In addition to facilitated workshops, tools are used and interviews are performed to support the analysis and ensure that an IT process owner owns and drives the assessment and improvement process.
4 Managed and Measurable	There is an effective internal control and risk management environment. A formal, documented evaluation of controls occurs frequently. Many controls are automated and regularly reviewed. Management is likely to detect most control issues but not all issues are routinely identified. There is consistent follow-up to address identified control weaknesses. A limited, tactical use of technology is applied to automate controls.	IT process criticality is regularly defined with full support and agreement from the relevant business process owners. Assessment of control requirements is based on policy and the actual maturity of these processes, following a thorough and measured analysis involving key stakeholders. Accountability for these assessments is clear and enforced. Improvement strategies are supported by business cases. Performance in achieving the desired outcomes is consistently monitored. External control reviews are organized occasionally.
5 Optimized	An enterprisewide risk and control program provides continuous and effective control and risk issues resolution. Internal control and risk management are integrated with enterprise practices, supported with automated real-time monitoring with full accountability for control monitoring, risk management and compliance enforcement. Control evaluation is continuous, based on self-assessments and gap and root cause analyses. Employees are proactively involved in control improvements.	Business changes consider the criticality of IT processes, and cover any need to reassess process control capability. IT process owners regularly perform self-assessments to confirm that controls are at the right level of maturity to meet business needs and they consider maturity attributes to find ways to make controls more efficient and effective. The organisation benchmarks to external best practices and seeks external advice on internal control effectiveness. For critical processes, independent reviews take place to provide assurance that the controls are at the desired level of maturity and working as planned.

Figure 16-5 ITGI maturity model for internal control

The COSO-COBIT Connection

Figure 16-6 illustrates how COBIT carries forward the COSO concepts by providing the domains, processes, and control activities for the IT world that guide an enterprise toward meeting the internal control requirements it deems appropriate for its own environment. For more information on COBIT, visit www.isaca.org.

COBIT 5.0

As of this writing, COBIT 5.0 is still being developed, but based on the initial exposure draft it will be revolutionary. While COBIT 4.1 is a powerful IT controls framework that includes IT process related goals, metrics, maturity, and other valuable features,

	IMPORTANCE	COSO				
		Control Environment	Risk Assessment	Control Activities	Information and Communication	Monitoring
Plan and Organise						
PO1 Define a strategic IT plan.	H		P		S	S
PO2 Define the information architecture.	L			P	P	
PO3 Determine technological direction.	M		S	P	S	
PO4 Define the IT processes, organisation and relationships.	L	P			S	S
PO5 Manage the IT investment.	M		S	P		
PO6 Communicate management aims and direction.	M	P			P	
PO7 Manage IT human resources.	L	P			S	
PO8 Manage quality.	M	P		P	S	P
PO9 Assess and manage IT risks.	H		P			
PO10 Manage projects.	H	S	S	P		S
Acquire and Implement						
AI1 Identify automated solutions.	M			P		
AI2 Acquire and maintain application software.	M			P		
AI3 Acquire and maintain technology infrastructure.	L			P		
AI4 Enable operation and use.	L			P	S	
AI5 Procure IT resources.	M			P		
AI6 Manage changes.	H		S	P		S
AI7 Install and accredit solutions and changes.	M			P	S	S
Deliver and Support						
DS1 Define and manage service levels.	M	S		P	S	S
DS2 Manage third-party services.	L	P	S	P		S
DS3 Manage performance and capacity.	L			P		S
DS4 Ensure continuous service.	M	S		P	S	
DS5 Ensure systems security.	H			P	S	S
DS6 Identify and allocate costs.	L			P		
DS7 Educate and train users.	L	P			S	
DS8 Manage service desk and incidents.	L	S			P	P
DS9 Manage the configuration.	M			P		
DS10 Manage problems.	M			P	S	S
DS11 Manage data.	H			P		
DS12 Manage the physical environment.	L		S	P		
DS13 Manage operations.	L			P	S	
Monitor and Evaluate						
ME1 Monitor and evaluate IT performance.	H				S	P
ME2 Monitor and evaluate internal control.	M					P
ME3 Ensure regulatory compliance.	H			P	S	S
ME4 Provide IT governance.	H	P	S		S	P

Legend:
H = High
M = Medium
L = Low
P = Primary
S = Secondary

Note: The COSO mapping is based on the original COSO framework. The mapping also applies generally to the later COSO *Enterprise Risk Management—Integrated Framework*, which expands on internal control, providing a more robust and extensive focus on the broader subject of enterprise risk management. While it is not intended to and does not replace the original COSO internal control framework, but rather incorporates the internal control framework within it, users of CoBIT may choose to refer to this enterprise risk management framework both to satisfy their internal control needs and to move toward a fuller risk management process.

Figure 16-6 COBIT-COSO relationships

COBIT 5.0 will incorporate value delivery, risk management, information security, and IT audit features as well. In fact, the 5.0 release of COBIT will combine the following three frameworks:

- COBIT 4.1 (IT governance and control)
- Val IT 2.0 (value delivery)
- Risk IT (risk management)

COBIT 5.0 will also incorporate many features of the BMIS (Information Security) and ITAF (IT Audit Assurance) frameworks.

Val IT 2.0

The ITGI released the 2.0 version of the Val IT framework in 2008 with the goal of providing a tool for executives to use in optimizing the value of IT investments. Val IT 2.0 was originally designed to complement COBIT. Where COBIT provides the "means" for IT value creation, Val IT provides the "ends" though measurement, monitoring, and optimizing IT investments. Key Val IT processes and management practices are presented in three domains:

- Value governance
- Investment management
- Portfolio management

Risk IT

The Risk IT framework was developed in 2009 to provide a comprehensive view of business-related IT risks. It addresses not only security, but also project, value, compliance, and service delivery related risks. The key features of the Risk IT framework include the following:

- Executive guidance for risk-based decision-making
- Tools for addressing business risk
- IT risk management integration into overall enterprise risk management
- Guidance to determine risk tolerance

The Risk IT process model is divided into three domains:

- Governance
- Response
- Evaluation

Each domain addresses aspects of the risk management lifecycle including, but not limited to, alignment with the enterprise risk management process, risk analysis, and reaction to events.

ITIL

The IT Infrastructure Library (ITIL) was developed by the U.K. government in the mid-1980s and has become a de facto standard for best practices in the provision of IT infrastructure management and service delivery. ITIL is a registered trademark of the U.K. Office of Government Commerce (OGC), which owns and develops the ITIL best-practices framework.*

---

* ITIL is a registered trademark and a registered community trademark of the Office of Government Commerce and is registered in the U.S. Patent and Trademark Office.

PART III

The ITIL evolved as a result of businesses' growing dependence on IT and has enjoyed a growing global recognition and adoption from organizations of all sizes. Previously, the definition of best practices in IT services had relied on individual and subjective judgments of what IT managers thought best.

Unlike many standards and frameworks, the widespread adoption of the ITIL has caused a variety of commercial and not-for-profit product vendors to develop products directly supporting the ITIL. In addition, major infrastructure service management products have been refined and organized around the ITIL approaches, which, in turn, has fostered wider acceptance.

In addition, the growth of ITIL has been supplemented by the proliferation of ITIL professional consulting and manager certifications that provide ready access to the expertise needed to plan, configure, and implement the standards.

ITIL Concepts

The ITIL provides a series of practical references and specific standards for infrastructure and services management adaptable virtually to any organization. The service-support functions address such issues as problem management, incident management, service desk, change management, release management, and configuration management. The service-delivery functions address capacity management, availability management, financial management, continuity management, and service levels.

To keep the ITIL current and to foster continued growth of the standard, the OGC has continued to work closely with the *British Standards Institute* (BSI) and the *Information Technology Service Management Foundation* (itSMF). In 2000, BSI and OGC undertook to work together to align the *BSI Management Overview* (PD0005), the *Specification for Service Management* (BS 15000-1), the *Code of Practice for Service Management* (BS 15000-2), and ITIL guidance into a consolidated framework. The management overview provides the introduction to ITIL and leads users into supplemental and increasingly expanded information regarding the standards.

ISO 27001

Since its inception in 1947, the *International Organization for Standardization* (ISO) has created a number of standards for network security management, software development, and quality control, in addition to a number of other standards for various business and government functions.

ISO 27001, ISO 17799, and BS 7799 are, essentially, the same core set of standards dealing with several aspects of information security practices, information security management, and information security risk management.

The precursor to BS 7799 was first promulgated as an information security standard in 1993 by the U.K. Department of Trade and Industry. Two years after the information security standard was published by the Department of Trade and Industry, it became formalized into the British Standard 7799. Subsequent to that initial publication, BS 7799 has gone through three distinct iterations as the British Standard 7799, adding information security management standards and the most recent version (2005), which added guidelines for information security risk management.

In December 2000, the BS 7799 morphed into ISO Standard 17799. Participation from the international standards community updated the original British standard, but the core of the BS 7799 remained largely intact despite the fact that BS 7799 itself has been discontinued.

Continuing the thread, ISO 27001 was published in October 2005. This standard dealt largely with the topic of BS 7799-2—that is, management of information security systems. This ISO standard was created to provide guidelines for effective information management systems. One of the underlying principles in this incarnation of the information security standard is use of the *Organization for Economic Cooperation and Development* (OECD) principles governing security of information and network systems. ISO 27001 is the first in a series of information security management and practices standards. This series of standards (27000) was created to "harmonize" with other widely recognized international operations standards, namely, ISO 9001 (quality management) and ISO 14001 (environmental management).

Confusing as the standards names are, adoption and compliance can be equally challenging. Some organizations use one or more versions of the standards as implementation frameworks to guide development of internal information security practices, procedures, and controls. Compliance with certain of the standards may be "certified" by being audited by a qualified "assessor" working for a "certification body" duly recognized by the local (country-specific) "certifying authority."

Fully adopting these standards is not a trivial undertaking and should be done with a significant amount of preplanning and analysis. Consulting, training, and products supporting various aspects of these standards are widely available.

Despite the evolving names and scope, this series of standards has become one of the most recognized and internationally accepted sets of information security practices, frameworks, and guidelines available.

ISO 27001 Concepts

Also referred to as the *Code of Practice for Information Security Management*, ISO 27001:2005 addresses 11 major areas within the information security discipline. The standard outlines 133 security controls in the following 11 areas:

- Security policy
- Organization of information security
- Asset management
- Human resources security
- Physical and environmental security
- Communications and operations management
- Access control
- Information systems acquisition, development, and maintenance
- Information security incident management
- Business continuity management
- Compliance

NSA INFOSEC Assessment Methodology

The *National Security Agency INFOSEC Assessment Methodology* (NSA IAM) was developed by the U.S. National Security Agency and incorporated into its *INFOSEC Training and Rating Program* (IATRP) in early 2002. Though the IATRP program and support for the NSA IAM was discontinued by the NSA in 2009, it is still widely used and is now being maintained by Security Horizon, which is one of the companies that provided NSA IAM and IEM training for the NSA.

NSA INFOSEC Assessment Methodology Concepts

The NSA IAM is an information security assessment methodology that baselines assessment activities. It breaks information security assessments into three phases: pre-assessment, on-site activities, and post-assessment. Each of these phases contains mandatory activities to ensure information security assessment consistency. It is important to note, however, that NSA IAM assessments consist of only documentation review, interviews, and observation. No testing occurs during an NSA IAM assessment. The NSA released the INFOSEC Evaluation Methodology to baseline testing activities.

Pre-assessment Phase

The purpose of the pre-assessment phase is to define customer requirements, set the assessment scope and determine assessment boundaries, gain an understanding of the criticality of the customer's information, and create the assessment plan. The NSA IAM measures both organizational information criticality and system information criticality. Organizational information consists of the information required to perform major business functions. System information is then identified by analyzing the information that is processed by the systems that support the major business functions.

The NSA IAM provides matrices that are used to analyze information criticality. A matrix is created for each organization/business function and each system that supports the organization. The vertical axis consists of the information types, whereas the horizontal axis includes columns for confidentiality, integrity, and availability. Information criticality impact values are assigned for each cell. Table 16-1 is an example of a human resources' organization information criticality matrix.

Information Type	Confidentiality	Integrity	Availability
Payroll	H	H	M
Benefits	L	M	L
Employee performance appraisals	H	H	L

Table 16-1 Organizational Information Criticality Matrix

On-Site Activities Phase

The on-site activities phase consists of validating pre-assessment–phase conclusions, gathering assessment data, and providing initial feedback to customer stakeholders. Eighteen baseline areas are evaluated during an IAM assessment:

- Information security documentation such as policies, procedures, and baselines
- Roles and responsibilities
- Contingency planning
- Configuration management
- Identification and authentication
- Account management
- Session controls
- Auditing
- Malicious code protection
- System maintenance
- System assurance
- Networking/connectivity
- Communications security
- Media controls
- Information classification and labeling
- Physical environment
- Personnel security
- Education, training, and awareness

Post-assessment Phase

Once the assessment information is gathered, it is analyzed and consolidated into a report in the final post-assessment phase. The final report includes an executive summary, recognition of good security practices, and a statement regarding the overall information security posture of the organization.

Frameworks and Standards Trends

Business requirements and practices vary significantly around the world, as do the political interests of many of the organizations creating standards. It's not likely that a single set of frameworks and standards will appear in the near future to cover everyone's needs. The complexity of mapping hundreds of authority documents from regulations (international, national, local/state, and so on) and standards (ISO, industry-specific, vendor, and so on) created an opportunity and market niche. Technology vendors rightfully identified this important market niche, or differentiator, to boost product sales by identifying how to get their products to address authority requirements. Vendors jumped at the opportunity to map their capabilities to address specific controls from multiple regulations and standards.

Network Frontiers is perhaps the best known company that attempted the impossible: to create a common mapping of IT controls across every known regulation, standard, and best practice available. The result is called the IT Unified Compliance Framework, and can be found at www.unifiedcompliance.com. Subsequently, these mappings were adopted by Archer Technologies, Microsoft, Computer Associates, McAfee, and several other vendors to help bridge the alignment of the controls managed or tracked by the vendors with the requirements of individual authority documents.

One viewpoint suggests a single adopted framework would simplify technology product development, organizational structures, and control objectives. The other viewpoint suggests that the complexity of disparate regional, political, business, cultural, and other interests ensures a universally accepted control framework will never be created. The truth probably rests somewhere in the middle. Although a single set of international standards isn't imminent, the tools described in this chapter are nonetheless serving to create reliable, secure, and sustainable technology infrastructures that ultimately benefit the participants.

References

Reference	Website
Auditing Standard No. 2: "An Audit of Internal Control Over Financial Reporting Performed in Conjunction with an Audit of Financial Statements" (Effective June 17, 2004)	www.pcaobus.org
Committee of Sponsoring Organizations of the Treadway Commission	www.coso.org
Wikipedia COSO information	http://en.wikipedia.org/wiki/COSO
Wikipedia ITIL information	http://en.wikipedia.org/wiki/ITIL_v3
International Organization for Standardization, "ISO—Overview", February 2004	www.iso.org
ISACA (prior to January 1, 2006 was known as Information Systems Audit and Control Association)	www.isaca.org
IT Infrastructure Library	http://www.itil.co.uk
IT Governance Institute	www.itgi.org
IT Governance Institute, *Board Briefing on IT Governance*, 2nd ed. Rolling Meadows, IL, 2003. Copyright 2003 by the IT Governance Institute	www.itgi.org
IT Governance Institute, *COBIT 4.0*, Rolling Meadows, IL, 2005. Copyright 2005 by the IT Governance Institute	www.itgi.org

Reference	Website
"NSA INFOSEC Assessment and Evaluation Methodologies"	www.iatrp.com
Soleil, Darcy, "Sarbanes Oxley Section 404 Compliance Tips for IT Managers," 2004	ISACA SOX Forum listserv
Sarbanes Oxley Section 404 Compliance for IT Managers"	Auditnet.org
Software Engineering Institute	www.sei.cmu.edu
IT Unified Controls Framework	www.unifiedcompliance.com

Regulations

The global business community continues to usher in new regulations and laws that affect and increase corporate responsibility for internal controls. This chapter reviews the development of regulations related to internal controls with respect to the use of information and technology. In particular, this chapter addresses the following:

- An introduction to legislation related to internal controls
- The Sarbanes-Oxley Act of 2002
- The Gramm-Leach-Bliley Act
- Privacy regulations such as California SB1386
- The Health Insurance Portability and Accountability Act of 1996
- EU Commission and Basel II
- Payment Card Industry (PCI) Data Security Standard
- Other regulatory trends

An Introduction to Legislation Related to Internal Controls

The global nature of business and technology drove the need for standards and regulations that govern how companies work together and how information is shared. Strategic and collaborative partnerships have evolved with bodies like the International Organization of Standardization (ISO), the International Electrotechnical Commission (IEC), the International Telecommunication Union (ITU), and the World Trade Organization (WTO). Participation in these standards bodies has been voluntary, with a common goal of promoting global trading for all countries. Individual countries have gone further to establish governmental controls over the business activities of corporations operating within their boundaries.

The motivation for the creation and adoption of legislation is much more complex than it might seem. National interests, industry concerns, and corporate jockeying create strong political drivers. Politics can have a negative connotation, but in this context, "political" simply refers to the understanding that regulations generally benefit or protect a representative group of people. Nations, industries, and companies have concerns about the confidentiality, integrity, and availability of their information. Standards and legislation are two methods that ensure these concerns are met.

Regulatory Impact on IT Audits

The impact regulations have on IT audit is evolving as businesses adapt to the complexity of complying with multiple authorities. Over the past decade, the U.S. government has passed numerous industry-specific privacy acts and other regulations. Each has been passed with the intent of protecting the business consumer. Consequently, internal and external audit groups are tasked with reviewing business processes and procedures to ensure appropriate controls exist that protect business and consumer interests.

Consider the Porter Value Chain shown in Figure 17-1. Each of the functional components of today's business continues to draw higher partnership demands on IT organizations to support business processes. The interlocking connection between IT controls and their supporting business functions has created a massive undertaking to tie specific IT controls to existing and new business processes. The effort is comprised of lawmakers trying to protect consumers, financial services trying to protect their assets, helpful vendors trying to sell more products, and businesses trying to comply with seemingly evolving and inconsistent requirements.

The International Association of Internal Auditors (IIA) and the International Information Systems Audit and Control Association (ISACA) publish guidelines to assist members of these internal and external audit groups in establishing common controls and audit processes. Technology can affect every part of the business. Purposed, controlled, and efficient, at its best, technology offers a competitive advantage. At its worst, technology is your competitor's advantage when you don't have the appropriate activities and processes in place to ensure the governance, risk management, or compliance management of technologies and the organization.

History of Corporate Financial Regulation

In the 1970s, the concern over internal controls related to financial reporting began to take shape as a result of the growth in bankruptcies and financial collapses such as Penn Central Railroad in 1970, the largest bankruptcy in U.S. history at that point in time. In 1976, a congressional investigation by the Moss and Metcalf committees rec-

Figure 17-1
Porter Value Chain (Source: http://www.netmba.com/strategy/value-chain. Illustration Source: CSLLC Original Work)

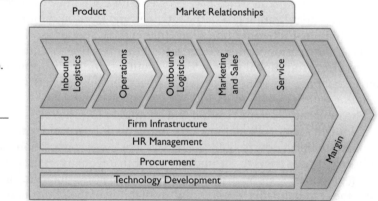

ommended increased federal regulation in the areas of accounting and auditing. In 1977, the Foreign Corrupt Practices Act made bribes illegal and required corporations to keep extensive records of transactions for disclosure purposes.

By the mid-1980s, the savings and loan industry had collapsed. Congress looked at whether the government should take over the issuance of accounting standards and oversight of auditors. In 1986, the Committee of Sponsoring Organizations (COSO) examined how fraudulent financial management could be curtailed and how auditors could reduce the recognized gap between what auditors do and what the public expects. COSO published the first formalized guidelines for internal controls known as *Internal Controls–Integrated Framework*, described in more detail in Chapter 16. These voluntary industry guidelines were intended to help public companies become self-regulating and thus avoid the need for governmental regulation.

In 1991, the Federal Deposit Insurance Corporation Improvement Act (FDICIA) was enacted for the banking industry as a response to the savings and loan collapse. It introduced upper-management accountability using sign-offs.

 NOTE Despite numerous voluntary standards and guidelines in addition to regulatory mandates, several corporations operating in the United States have been involved in notorious scandals in the early years of the 21st century. These scandals rocked global confidence in the U.S. public markets.

However, when Enron and other major corporations failed in 2001 and 2002, the U.S. government moved swiftly to enact the most extensive corporate reforms of all in an effort to restore public confidence in U.S. business operations. The Sarbanes-Oxley Act of 2002 and its subsequent revisions have far-reaching impact on all corporations (foreign and domestic) doing business with the United States and on the technology groups supporting those businesses. This chapter will summarize the impact of Sarbanes-Oxley and other government- and industry-imposed regulations on information services departments.

The Sarbanes-Oxley Act of 2002

The Sarbanes-Oxley (SOX) Act of 2002 (formally known as the Public Company Accounting Reform and Investor Protection Act) was a response from the U.S. government to a rash of notorious corporate scandals that began with Enron and Arthur Andersen, followed closely by Tyco, Adelphia Communications, WorldCom, HealthSouth, and many others.

The Sarbanes-Oxley Act and the Public Company Accounting Oversight Board (PCAOB) were created to restore investor confidence in U.S. public markets. The primary goal was to enhance corporate responsibility, enhance financial disclosures, and deter corporate and accounting fraud. As such, the required controls for compliance to SOX focus on key controls essential to ensuring the confidentiality, integrity, and availability of financial data.

SOX's Impact on Public Corporations

The monetary impact on corporations of complying with this legislation has brought much dissent and lobbying for less strict guidelines. Small companies are seeking exemption from the extensive documentation and reporting. Adjustments during 2005–2006 clarified the extent to which technology controls must be tested and which companies must assert adequate internal controls for all areas with any impact on financial transactions and reporting.

SOX requires company executives to attest to the adequacy and effectiveness of their internal controls related to financial transactions and reporting, including IT controls. These controls must be audited externally, and a statement of control must be included in the annual corporate report filed with the Security and Exchange Commission (SEC). Consequently, corporate CEOs and CFOs are now being held accountable for the quality and integrity of information generated by their company's applications and communications, as well as the infrastructure that supports those applications.

As a result, information services (IS) managers who may not be keenly aware of the internal control measures necessary when dealing with SOX requirements are being asked to examine the technology risks and thoroughly test all controls. This means that many IS managers request guidelines or consulting assistance to ensure that they are in compliance with the new laws. Because of the different business cultures involved in global corporations and the number of international investors in U.S.-based corporations, the global IT community must be aware of the impact that financial audits have on the way IS departments operate.

Core Points of the SOX Act

SOX has many provisions. Sections 101, 302, 404, 409, and 906 are the key sections with relevance and impact on information services departments.

Section 101

In Section 101, the PCAOB is established as the governing agency to create auditing standards and rules for public companies. In addition, the PCAOB is given the authority to regulate the accounting firms that audit public companies. The rules issued by the PCAOB and approved by the SEC are referred to as *Auditing Standards*.

The primary guidance from the PCAOB in regard to auditing internal controls is provided in Auditing Standard No. 2, effective June 17, 2004, entitled, "An Audit of Internal Control Over Financial Reporting Performed in Conjunction with an Audit of Financial Statements." We will explore Auditing Standard No. 2 later in this chapter.

Section 302

Section 302 specifies the legal responsibilities of the company's CEO and CFO. According to SOX, the CEO and CFO are responsible for all internal controls and for reporting quarterly on any significant changes to internal controls that could affect the company's financial statement. Basically, these two officers must personally certify that they are responsible for and knowledgeable about all financial statements submitted quarterly and annually. They also must certify that they have knowledge of the design and have evaluated the effectiveness of all internal controls and that these controls ensure that complete and accurate information is reported to them. Significant changes to disclosure controls and any deficiencies, weaknesses, or fraudulent acts that may compromise the accuracy of reporting must be disclosed.

Section 302 also defines the external auditor's role over financial reporting. The external auditor evaluates internal controls to determine whether modifications need to be made for accuracy and compliance. The external auditor must attest that he or she has reviewed management's assessment of internal controls and has approved the process and evaluation of that assessment.

This section also requires that management particularly address any changes to internal controls over financial reporting that has occurred during the last quarter.

Section 404

Under Section 404, the CEO and CFO attest that internal controls are in place, documented, and effective. Management assessment contains four parts. The first three parts cover the following:

- Responsibility of management for the existence and rigidity of internal controls
- Evaluation of the effectiveness of internal controls
- Statement of the framework used to evaluate the effectiveness of controls

Management is prohibited from stating that internal controls are effective if one or more material weaknesses exist in the controls.

The fourth part concerns the external auditor. The company's external auditor must separately attest that management's statement concerning the effectiveness of internal controls is accurate.

NOTE   Many organizations find it difficult to furnish the formal documentation regarding the existence and rigidity of internal controls and the evidence of the effectiveness of internal controls.

PCAOB Auditing Standard No. 2   On March 9, 2004, the PCAOB approved Auditing Standard No. 2, entitled, "An Audit of Internal Control over Financial Reporting Performed in Conjunction with an Audit of Financial Statements." This audit standard establishes the requirements for performing an audit of internal control over financial reporting and provides some important directions on the scope and approach required of corporation management and external auditors. It also provides guidance on the controls that should be considered, including program development, program changes, computer operations, and access to programs and data. PCAOB Auditing Standard No. 2 specifically addresses the financial reporting controls that should be in place for a period before the attestation date and the controls that may operate after the attestation date.

Section 409

Section 409 states that the CEO and CFO will ensure "rapid and current public disclosure" of any material event that could affect the company's financial or operational performance. Material events could include any type of company restructuring, changes in personage or duties of key personnel, budget overruns on IT projects, and stock sales by corporate officers. It may even be necessary to disclose a major new financial or operational application that is determined to "not work." "Rapid and current disclosure" essentially requires near-real-time reporting. This can be a nightmare for companies with a dependence on batch-oriented processing methods that tend to take longer to complete.

Section 906

Section 906 consists of three parts. First is that every periodic report with financial information must be accompanied by a written statement by the CEO and CFO. The second part specifies that the content of this report fairly represents the financial condition of the company. The last section lays out the fines and imprisonment penalties for either knowingly or unknowingly submitting a false statement. It also sets criminal penalties for failure of corporate officers to certify the financial reports in a timely manner.

SOX's Impact on IT Departments

For most organizations, IT services are now a vital part of the financial reporting process. The applications and services support creation, storage, processing, and reporting of financial transactions. Therefore, SOX compliance also must include controls for the use of technology in data handling, processing, and reporting. General computing controls thus are critical to the overall financial reporting process in ensuring data integrity and secure operations. IT departments now must formally address the design, documentation, implementation, testing, monitoring, and maintenance of IT internal controls.

The CEOs and CFOs look to the IS department to ensure that the general and specific internal controls for all applications, data, networking, contracts, licenses, telecommunications, and physical environment are documented and effective. Overall risk and control considerations are assessed at the departmental level of information services and then at the entity level. Entity-level review may vary depending on the following questions:

- How large is the organization?
- Are key functions outsourced?
- What is the division of process and responsibilities for geographically dispersed locations?
- How are the control responsibilities split among user groups, IS functions, and third-party providers?
- How is the strategy for IS—both application and infrastructure—developed, documented, and managed?

To date, audits have found that the primary weaknesses among corporations are consistency, documentation, and communication. A given group within IS might believe that its strategy, tactical procedures, and applications are well controlled. However, communication with other groups can be lacking to the point that no one group knows what the other is doing. One of the most common deficiencies in organizations is the lack of a comprehensive strategic plan concerning how IT can best serve the overall business objectives. Together, these omissions lead to weak security and an uncontrolled or inconsistent architecture.

SOX Considerations for Companies with Multiple Locations

Global organizations and non–U.S.-based companies should examine their business-unit technology operations to determine their significance to the organization as a whole. The assessment of an IS business unit depends on the materiality of transactions processed by that unit, the potential impact on financial reporting if the IS business unit fails, and other qualitative risk factors.

Impact of Third-Party Services on SOX Compliance

Controls surrounding third-party services should ensure that roles and responsibilities of third parties are clearly defined, adhered to, and continue to satisfy requirements. Control measures are aimed at reviewing and monitoring existing contracts and procedures for their effectiveness and compliance with organization policy. The dissolution of a major contract could have significant impact on financial reporting. Thus it would fall within the guidelines for disclosure by the company officers.

During an audit, company organizations often will contend that they are not responsible for a given control because either the function is outsourced or the software was purchased from and maintained by a third party. According to legislative guidelines, a company can outsource a service but not the responsibility for control of that service. It is next to impossible for a company to outsource problems and expect them to go away.

Documentation of the third-party controls is required for attestation by the independent auditor, so an assessment must determine the effectiveness and completeness of the service organization's internal controls. If SAS 70/SSAE 16 or similar audit opinions do not include controls testing, results of the testing, and the third-party service auditor's opinion on control effectiveness, the reports are insufficient for SOX compliance. Companies should be sure to note whether the specific environment, platforms, and applications used in fulfillment of the outsourced services are covered by the SAS 70/SSAE 16 (or similar audit) reports.

Four functional objectives for auditing third-party services and outsourcing major portions of company activities that are relevant to companies, corporation subsidiaries, and multinationals are summarized as follows:

- Policy statements regarding data integrity, availability, and confidentiality are determined by senior management and must be maintained and contractually supported by any outsource arrangement.

- Asset-protection requirements should be clearly defined and understood by the principals in any outsourcing agreement.

- Data and information custodial responsibilities should be well defined and complied with.

- Service levels should be defined, measurable, and acceptable to both parties. Failure to meet service-level agreements should have some compensatory action. Billing and invoices should be accurate and costs within budgeted amounts.

NOTE   See Chapter 14 for additional information on SAS 70/SSAE 16 reports and auditing outsourced operations. SSAE 16 has replaced SAS 70 for reporting on controls at services organizations effective June 15, 2011.

Specific IT Controls Required for SOX Compliance

To date, the PCAOB and external auditors reviewing compliance with SOX have been attentive primarily to security, change management, and problem management. A key focus for the audit is integrity of the technology infrastructure for processing, storage, and communication of financial data. This is especially true when financial reports are generated from a data warehouse fed by multiple accounting and business operation systems.

Ownership of IT controls may be unclear, especially for application controls. Therefore, the audit in each area must integrate automated and manual controls at the business-process level.

In general, the following IT controls must be documented and evaluated as effective to be in compliance with SOX requirements:

- Access control
- Change control
- Data management
- IT operations
- Network operations
- Asset management

Access Control

Security administration must have an effective, documented process for monitoring and enforcing the security policies dictated by management. These policies and processes must be communicated to all user groups. If "user group stewards" are used to distribute the security administration workload, those stewards must follow the same policies and procedures used by the IS support staff. They, too, must communicate thoroughly and effectively with the user community.

Ask the following questions: Who has access to the application and data? Who authorizes access? How often is access level reviewed? What is the authorization process? What happens when an authorized person leaves or changes jobs? Is data security enforced at the element level? Are passwords enforced and changed regularly?

Execution of financial transactions or transactions that lead to financial transactions must be limited to those individuals who have an authorized business reason to do so. Access to financial and "protected personal" data likewise must be limited to those individuals who have an authorized business reason for access.

Change Control

To ensure accuracy, completeness, and integrity of financial reporting, companies must have a documented, effective change-control process that includes changes to financial applications, all interface applications, operating systems that control the desktop and host server, productivity tools used to create summary analysis, database management systems, and networks. The change process must provide the following:

- Points for management review
- Authorization
- Migration of changed components
- Change scheduling
- Management reporting
- Communication of changes to the user community

Ask the following questions: Who can initiate a change? Who authorizes changes? Who can make changes? What testing should be done prior to making a change to production components? Who does the testing and validates the changes? How is testing documented? What process is used to promote development components into production?

Change control applies to applications, productivity tools, and operating system software. Communication of infrastructure changes traditionally has been weak. IS department personnel have long felt that users do not care what is changed, or when, as long as it works. But what if it doesn't work? What if a seemingly unrelated change to an application or operating system causes a category of transactions to be unreported?

Financial application change control is an obvious concern when reviewing controls over financial reporting. Frequently, compliance auditors have not assessed the risks of inadequate change control for interface systems, database infrastructure, operating systems, network systems, or hardware configurations. Even internal IS groups may not realize the relevance of documented and enforced controls in these areas related to financial reporting activities. Recent analysis by risk-assessment experts has shown that inadequate change-control methods can lead to a loss of information integrity in financial applications and data systems. The potential risks include inaccurate reporting or incomplete reporting.

Data Management

Data management encompasses both logical and physical data management as well as identification and protection of critical data, especially data related to financial processing and reporting.

Data Transfer Between Systems   Timing and frequency of downloads from interface systems to a financial data warehouse or enterprise resource planning (ERP) system are audit review items. The response performance of data warehouse queries and reporting is not an issue for SOX but is critical for data warehouse functionality. The relevant issue is whether downloads are consistent, timely, and complete with validation routines. Errors found in the extract, transform, and download process should be segregated, reported, and cleared within a reasonable time frame to ensure accurate financial reporting.

Database Structures   Compatibility of database management systems used to store financial data is important. If the transactional data used for financial reporting are stored in different data structures, the integrity of summation, interpretation, and analysis can be jeopardized. If different data structures are necessary, then compensating controls must be in place to validate the final compilation of data.

Data-Element Consistency   Many companies run multiple accounting systems that use different terminology to represent the same information or the same terminology to represent different information. Therefore, metadata files and data dictionaries should be used to ensure consistent interpretation of key data elements.

Physical Control of Data   The physical control of data is crucial to the integrity of financial reporting as well. If the facilities where servers, workstations, and hard-copy reports are located are not secured, then unauthorized viewing or change may compromise transactions and/or data.

Data Backup   Timing and frequency of the backup process should be determined by the business need for short-term recovery of data in problem situations. Disaster recovery and business continuity plans are not an inherent part of the latest requirements for SOX compliance but are critical to business resiliency. See Chapter 4 for additional information about disaster recovery.

IT Operations

The PCAOB stated that ineffective IT control environments are a significant indication that material weaknesses in internal control over financial reporting exist. IT operations controls extend well beyond the obvious management of hardware and the data center. With respect to acquiring an IT environment, there are controls over the definition, acquisition, installation, configuration, integration, and maintenance of the IT infrastructure. Ongoing daily controls over operations include the following:

- Day-to-day service-level management
- Management of third-party services

- System availability
- Client services
- Configuration and systems management
- Problem management and resolution
- Operations management scheduling
- Facilities management

The system software component of operations includes controls over acquisition, implementation, configuration, and maintenance of operating system software, database management systems, middleware software, network communications software, security software, and utilities. System software also includes the incident tracking, logging, and monitoring functions. Finally, another example of an IT operations control would relate to detail reporting on the use of utilities that alert management to unauthorized access to powerful data-altering functions.

Network Operations

Audit of the network operations and problem management includes a review of entry points to the wide area network (WAN) or local area network (LAN). Proper configuration of externally facing firewalls, routers, and modems is essential to avoid unauthorized access to and potential modification of the company financial applications and data. The network configuration diagram, including critical servers, routers, and firewalls as it relates to financial reporting, must be included in the documentation provided to the auditors. Inbound modem and virtual private network (VPN) connections pose a particularly high risk of unauthorized access. All outside telecommunication connections (Internet or point-to-point) must be forced to go through the company network routers and firewalls. See Chapter 5 for more information about auditing network devices.

The current threat of hackers, viruses, worms, and other malicious behavior dictates that each server and workstation (especially portable computers) install antivirus software and the latest antivirus definitions. Potential risk for loss of critical financial data is high should companies not keep antivirus software up-to-date.

Any virus or worm problems encountered on a workstation or server in the company network should be fully documented. Such documentation should include the determined impact and resolution steps taken.

Asset Management

Audit of asset management deals mostly with authorization, financial expenditure, and appropriate depreciation and reporting. Have key assets (such as software, data, hardware, middleware, and facilities) been inventoried and their "company owners" identified? Examples of asset-management-related items that may be reviewed during a SOX audit include inventory, asset disposal, change management of asset inventory, and an overall understanding of asset procedures. Records management is an indispensable part of the asset-management plan.

Within asset management, companies should consider facilities controls. Are data center facilities equipped with adequate environmental controls to maintain systems and data? For example, fire suppression, uninterruptable power supply, air conditioning, elevated floors, and documented emergency procedures may be appropriate to review. See Chapter 4 for more information pertaining to auditing facilities controls.

The Financial Impact of SOX Compliance on Companies

Costs for reviewing internal controls and complying with SOX were initially a critical concern—both in internal resources and external services. Many internal auditors lacked the background, knowledge, or experience with evaluating controls to assess adequately whether the current environment meets SOX requirements. Employees also often lacked motivation for thorough documentation or communication. As a result, external services companies capitalized on the opportunity to provide a gap analysis to help determine control deficiencies between their interpretation of SOX requirements and the present state of controls in the company. These projects in many cases resulted in the need for new infrastructure, services, software, headcount, and related requirements.

Despite the perceived high cost of compliance, ineffective controls or noncompliance will result in a much higher cost. These controls, once adopted by the business, should become part of everyday business operations. SOX is not about becoming compliant once a year to pass an audit. Should a company's external auditor find material weaknesses in controls, the competency and credibility of the company may be questioned—thus causing a drop in share price and capital availability. Investors' views of the risks associated with management structure and controls affect their interest in investing in a company.

In multinational corporations, auditors may be pressed to question more closely any suspicious payments that have the earmarks of bribes. In the past, corporate executives were not required to disclose questionable payments that were paid to receive offshore services. This may no longer be an option.

For more specific points to consider, illustrative controls, or tests of those controls, see www.isaca.org/sox for the *IT Control Objectives for Sarbanes-Oxley 2nd Edition*.

Gramm-Leach-Bliley Act

The formal title of this law is the Financial Services Modernization Act. The act, more commonly known as the Gramm-Leach-Bliley Act (GLBA), was directed primarily at allowing expanded functions and relationships among financial institutions. The law covers how and under what circumstances bank holding companies can undertake new affiliations and engage in previously restricted activities.

GLBA Requirements

From the perspective of an impact on internal controls, the GLBA Title V section provides a series of specific regulations governing how individual information for customers of financial institutions may be shared. GLBA requires that financial firms disclose to customers the institutions' privacy policies and practices. The law provides some limited control to customers about how the information retained by a financial institution may be retained via an "opt-out" option. On an annualized basis, the financial institution is required to reinform clients of the institution's privacy policies.

Enforcement of the act's provisions is assigned to the Federal Trade Commission, the federal banking agencies, the National Credit Union Administration, and the SEC.

Customer Privacy Provisions

GLBA requires financial institutions to review and, in many cases, overhaul how they deal with maintaining the privacy of customer information. Further, the act requires an ongoing review of who has access to what information, under what circumstances the information could be shared, and with whom. The most pervasive impact of the act is an ongoing requirement to control access to and use of client information on an individual-by-individual basis. The legislated "opt-out" requirement made operational and marketing activities much more complicated.

Internal Control Requirements

Section 501B of GLBA essentially mandates three high-level control objectives:

- Ensuring the confidentiality of customer financial information
- Protecting against anticipated threats to customer records
- Protecting against unauthorized access to customer information that could result in substantial impact to the customer

Section 501B also gives the following governing agencies the authority to establish appropriate standards within their jurisdiction:

- Federal Trade Commission (FTC)
- Federal Deposit Insurance Corporation (FDIC)
- Office of the Comptroller of the Currency (OCC)
- Office of Thrift Supervision (OTS)
- Security and Exchange Commission (SEC)
- Federal Reserve Board (FRB)
- National Credit Union Administration (NCUA)
- Commodity Futures Trading Commission (CFTC)

Two prevalent standards outline internal control requirements: the "FTC Safeguard Rule" and "Interagency Guidelines Establishing Standards for Safeguarding Customer Information," which was released by the OCC, OTS, FDIC, and FRB. Generally, the interagency guidelines document, which affects banks, requires the following:

- A written information security program/strategy
- Risk assessment and management
- Access controls for customer information systems
- Physical access control for areas containing customer information

PART III

- Encryption of customer information either stored or transmitted electronically
- Change-control procedures
- Dual control procedures, segregation of duties, employee background checks
- Security monitoring systems to detect unauthorized access to customer information
- Incident-response program to address security incidents effectively
- Methods to provide protection from physical destruction of customer information

It is important to note, however, that different agencies govern different types of entities. Other rules and guidelines differ to some extent.

Federal Financial Institutions Examination Council

The Federal Financial Institutions Examination Council (FFIEC) comprises the FRB, FDIC, OCC, OTC, and NCUA. The FFIEC provides IT examination handbooks that can be used by auditors to identify required controls in specific areas such as business continuity, e-banking, and information security. These FFIEC handbooks can be found at www.ffiec.gov.

Privacy Regulations

Summarizing the excellent work done by Thomas Karol in *A Guide to Cross-Border Privacy Impact Assessments*, personal information was once viewed as proprietary business content with little regard to the personal rights of the individual whose information the company owned. Government organizations and privacy activist groups have served to create a slew of legislation protecting personal information. National and state requirements govern how health, financial, and personally identifiable information may be used and stored. Unfortunately, the varying interests and comfort thresholds (political interests) has created disparate requirements, and the lack of uniformity delivers a challenge to the appropriate handling of personal information.

 TIP   You can find the online sources for many authority documents by navigating to www.unifiedcompliance.com/matrices/ucf_ad_list.html. The list of authorities on the left side of the page are links that take you to the source for the authority document.

Visit the website in the accompanying tip for finding sources for authority documents. Perform a search for the word "privacy" and start looking through the dozens of results. This doesn't conclusively illustrate every authority related to privacy, but it does demonstrate the large number of privacy specific documents and legislation. If you want awe-inspiring, overwhelming lists of authority documents, find the spreadsheets on unifiedcompliance.com, search each spreadsheet for specific controls related to privacy, and then visit the control ID. This exercise will make much more sense when you find the spreadsheets and start walking through it.

TIP   If you are struggling with multiple privacy laws, consider spending time with the ITUCF Spreadsheets from www.unifiedcompliance.com. The time you spend here, particularly if you are working with large organizations, will help you find each of the controls mapped to the authority documents. Next, download Thomas Karol's *A Guide to Cross-Border Privacy Impact Assessments*, referenced at the end of this chapter. Alternatively, consider one of the many software packages designed to assist with this effort, such as Archer Technologies or RSAM.

California SB 1386

California SB 1386 was one of the first and certainly the most visible state laws dealing with breaches of security that cause private information to be disclosed. Several states have adopted or are considering similar legislation. The law requires an agency, person, or business that conducts business in California and owns or licenses computerized personal information to disclose any breach of security to any resident whose unencrypted data is "believed to have been" disclosed. The law applies not only to companies with direct operations but also those who operate out of state and have California resident data on file.

Included in the law are definitions of what is considered private information, methods of evaluating whether or not information has been unlawfully disclosed, and requirements for notifications of California citizens.

International Privacy Laws

Although U.S. privacy laws, including SB 1386, are becoming more prevalent, some international privacy legislation is more stringent. Two such laws include the European Directive on the Protection of Personal Data and the Canadian Personal Information Protection and Electronic Documentation Act (PIPEDA).

European Directive on the Protection of Personal Data

In October 1995, the European Union passed the European Directive on the Protection of Personal Data. The directive governs personal information within all member countries of the EU and places minimum protection requirements on it. The directive also prohibits the transmission of information to entities in nonmember states with lesser information privacy protection requirements, including the United States. As with many laws that govern information privacy, the European directive requires entities that collect, transmit, process, or disclose personal information to use appropriate measures to protect such information. Some of the other directive requirements include these:

- Notification of individuals about the purposes for which their information is collected
- Opt-out provisions regarding third-party disclosure or use beyond the original purpose

- The right of individuals to correct, alter, or delete information pertaining to them that is inaccurate

- Confinement of stored information to that which is relevant to the stated purpose

Canadian PIPEDA

Canada enacted this national privacy law in 2004. It sets forth the following provisions to govern the collection, use, and disclosure of personal information:

- Parties engaged in the collection of information must show accountability.

- Information collectors must identify the purposes for the collection of personal information.

- Information collectors must obtain consent from consumers.

- The collection of personal information must be limited.

- The use of personal information must be limited.

- Disclosure and retention of personal information must be limited.

- Information collectors must ensure the accuracy of personal information.

- Information collectors must provide adequate security for the protection of personal information.

- Information collectors must make information management policies readily available.

- Information collectors must provide individuals with access to information about themselves.

- Individuals are given the right to challenge an organization's compliance with these principles.

Privacy Law Trends

One of the consequences of California SB 1386 is the adoption of identical or nearly identical versions of the bill by other states within the United States. Keeping up with the multiple varieties of similar laws is a significant task. For example, the Michigan Social Security Number Privacy Act, MCL 445.81, became effective January 1, 2006. This statute prohibits all entities from displaying or mailing an individual's Social Security number in a public manner. Further complicating matters, exemptions listed within the act allow some public organizations to continue operations in the same way they were operating before the act became law. The Workers' Compensation Agency is one such organization that qualifies for exceptions listed within the act.

Many countries have or are in the process of adopting privacy laws as well, such as Argentina, Japan, Australia, Canada, and of course, all the EU member states. A number of countries, including the United States, are considering privacy legislation at a national level.

Health Insurance Portability and Accountability Act of 1996

In 1996, the U.S. Congress passed the Health Insurance Portability and Accountability Act (HIPAA). The act includes two sections. Title I provides health insurance coverage after employees have lost or changed jobs. Title II deals with administrative actions intended to simplify and standardize health information. The IT component of Title II deals with security and handling of health information in an electronic age. When the topic of HIPAA arises, particularly among IT staff, the implications of this section are most prevalent.

The IT components of the act prescribe a standard methodology for security. Further, HIPAA standardizes formats for health-related information. The standards encompass methods that ensure patient confidentiality and data integrity for any information that can be associated with an individual patient.

The most commonly identified component of the act is a body of data collectively known as protected health information (PHI) or Electronic Protected Health Information (EPHI) which encompasses Individually Identifiable Health Information (IIHI). IIHI relates to an individual's medical condition, treatment, or payment for treatment. Any entity that maintains and uses individually identifiable PHI is subject to the act. The effective scope of HIPAA encompasses entities from hospitals, to insurers, to doctors (of all types), to laboratories, and to companies that operate or participate in health plans. Organizations affected by HIPAA are referred to by the act as *covered entities*.

 NOTE HIPAA is a very large, complex piece of legislation. Two great places for information are the government website, www.hhs.gov/ocr/privacy, and the "HIPAA Survival Guide" located at www.hipaasurvivalguide.com. The latest edition of the "HIPAA Survival Guide" is sold for a nominal fee as a PDF. This guide will save you from aging 30 years while digesting all-things-HIPAA.

HIPAA Privacy and Security Rules

Two rules were published in the *Federal Register* by the Department of Health and Human Services after HIPAA was passed. The HIPAA Privacy Rule was published in December 2000, and the HIPAA Security Rule was published in February 2003.

The HIPAA Privacy Rule is focused mostly on administrative controls designed to protect patient privacy, such as securing or masking medical charts, locking file cabinets, and establishing privacy policies. The HIPAA Privacy Rule was enforced beginning in April 2003.

The HIPAA Security Rule is focused on technical controls such as network perimeter protection, encryption, and workstation security. The primary objective of the Security Rule is to protect EPHI when it is stored, maintained, or transmitted. The HIPAA Security Rule is divided into high-level standards and implementation specifications that support each standard. Implementation specifications are either required (mandatory)

PART III

or addressable (required unless justified otherwise). Table 14-1 outlines the implementation specifications required by the HIPAA Security Rule. The implementation specifications with (R) next to them are required; those with (A) are addressable. Organizations were given until April 2005 to comply with the HIPAA Security Rule.

Standard	Security Rule Reference	Implementation Specification
Administrative Safeguards		
Security management process	164.308(a)(1)	Risk Analysis (R)
		Risk Management (R)
		Sanction Policy (R)
		Information System Activity Review (R)
Assigned security responsibility	164.308(a)(2)	Assigned Security Responsibility (R)
Workforce security	164.308(a)(3)	Authorization and/or Supervision (A)
		Workforce Clearance Procedure
		Termination Procedures (A)
Information access management	164.308(a)(4)	Isolating Health Care Clearinghouse
		Function (R)
		Access Authorization (A)
		Access Establishment and Modification (A)
Security awareness and training	164.308(a)(5)	Security Reminders (A)
		Protection from Malicious Software (A)
		Log-in Monitoring (A)
		Password Management (A)
Security incident procedures	164.308(a)(6)	Response and Reporting (R)
Contingency plan	164.308(a)(7)	Data Backup Plan (R)
		Disaster Recovery Plan (R)
		Emergency Mode Operation Plan (R)
		Testing and Revision Procedure (A)
		Applications and Data Criticality Analysis (A)
Evaluation	164.308(a)(8)	Evaluation (R)
Business associate contracts and other arrangements	164.308(b)(1)	Written Contract or Other Arrangement (R)

Table 17-1   HIPAA Security Rule Requirements

Standard	Security Rule Reference	Implementation Specification
Physical Safeguards		
Facility access controls	164.310(a)(1)	Contingency Operations (A)
		Facility Security Plan (A)
		Access Control and Validation Procedures (A)
		Maintenance Records (A)
Workstation use	164.310(b)	Workstation Use (R)
Workstation security	164.310(c)	Workstation Security (R)
Device and media controls	164.310(d)(1)	Disposal (R)
		Media Reuse (R)
		Accountability (A)
		Data Backup and Storage (A)
Technical Safeguards		
Access control	164.312(a)(1)	Unique User Identification (R)
		Emergency Access Procedure (R)
		Automatic Logoff (A)
		Encryption and Decryption (A)
Audit controls	164.312(b)	Audit Controls (R)
Integrity	164.312(c)(1)	Mechanism to Authenticate Electronic Protected Health Information (A)
Person or entity authentication	164.312(d)	Person or Entity Authentication (R)
Transmission security	164.312(e)(1)	Integrity Controls (A)
		Encryption (A)

Table 17-1 HIPAA Security Rule Requirements *(continued)*

The HITECH Act

The Health Information Technology for Economic and Clinical Health Act (HITECH Act) is part of the American Recovery and Reinvestment Act of 2009 (ARRA). The ARRA incentivizes the adoption of technologies that support a national health care infrastructure. A key component of the infrastructure are the electronic health record (EHR) systems used by providers, and these are expected to expand in size and scope massively in the coming years, housing sensitive personal information about each of the patients.

Anticipating massive growth from the accelerated adoption, the HITECH Act provides for additional protections by expanding the scope of privacy and security requirements. Additionally, noncompliance penalties have increased, penalties for "willful neglect" are mandatory, and notification requirements exist for data breaches.

The HITECT Act introduces new teeth into the enforcement of controls protecting health information.

HIPAA's Impact on Covered Entities

Successfully complying with HIPAA provisions requires cultural and organizational alignment with the requirements of the act. Education and compliance activities, along with associated identified compliance roles, are required. A privacy officer and, in most cases, a security officer are also required. Reporting relationships regarding visibility and accessibility to senior management often mean that key security and compliance individuals charged with HIPAA compliance have an unambiguous solid or dotted reporting line to the CEO.

Compliance with HIPAA is certainly far more than technical controls. Policies, procedures, and controls should precede the application of IT. Many HIPAA compliance experts caution against letting technology overshadow the underlying requirements for strong and ongoing policy development/administration. For those organizations where HIPAA compliance required the most changes, a visible and engaged senior management endorsement of the policies, procedures, and privacy/security investments has been the key to success.

EU Commission and Basel II

Because of European corporate scandals comparable with those in the United States, the EU Commission imposed similar requirements for improvement in auditing standards, oversight, and responsibilities by creating directives related to corporate governance, transparency, audit, accounting standards, and information services. A major difference is that the U.S. SOX Act carries fines and criminal sanctions, whereas the EU Commission does not recommend that level of enforcement.

Although the SOX legislation originated in the United States, it has ramifications for companies headquartered in other countries. Emerging European professional standards such as those established by the International Accounting Standards Board and the Basel II Capital Accord also will continue affecting many multinational companies.

Basel II Capital Accord

Basel II is a consortium of international banks mostly in Europe but also in the United States and Canada. Initiated in 1974, the group publishes *accords* that cover a variety of banking topics and are intended to provide increased supervision and oversight of international banks. The advisory committee intended to promulgate a variety of technical and financial standards. The focus of the group is to provide a risk-management framework around capitalization standards for international banks. The Basel II accords are entirely voluntary, and any adoption is governed by the central bank of each country.

The Basel II Capital Accord is the most recent and most visible of the recommendations. The intention of this accord is to implement increased risk-management and capital-supervisory regulations governing the capital adequacy of internationally active banks.

In general, the Basel II Capital Accord provides for IT controls revolving around risk management in relation to loans. Therefore, as with SOX, the IT auditor should be concerned primarily with controls that protect the integrity of financial information.

Payment Card Industry (PCI) Data Security Standard

Visa USA created the Cardholder Information Security Program (CISP) in mid-2001. The standard became a requirement for Visa member banks. The CISP program was intended to ensure high levels of information security for Visa cardholder data. The security standard applies to all Visa member banks, merchants accepting Visa cards, and all service providers processing Visa cardholder transactions. In 2004, the data security standards were cosponsored by Visa and MasterCard into an industry standard now known as the *Payment Card Industry Data Security Standard*. Other card issuers began adopting the standard and on September 7, 2006, American Express, Discover Financial Services, JCB, MasterCard Worldwide, and Visa International created the Payment Card Industry Security Standards Council. Their website is located online at www.pcisecuritystandards.org. An international version of the VISA CISP program called the Visa Account Information Security (AIS) applies to non–U.S.-based entities.

The PCI standard is not a law per se, but it is a mandatory compliance requirement for participants in the card payment-processing industry. Generally speaking, any entity, system, or component that stores, processes, or transmits cardholder information anywhere in the value chain is subject to the standard. Merchants must be compliant with the standard if they want to continue processing credit cards.

Participants in the payment-processing system must not only adopt PCI but must also validate compliance with the standard. Specific standards apply to various sections of the payment-processing environment. Specific compliance standards and auditing requirements are published for merchants, service providers, and shared hosting providers. The auditing standards and compliance requirements are identical for merchants regardless of their size, but the reporting requirements for compliance vary according to what the acquirer demands from the merchant. Although there are guidelines for merchant levels based on the number of credit card transactions, ultimately it's up to the acquirer to make the determination about the level of effort your organization will exert to demonstrate compliance.

Merchants with the highest risk are classified as Level 1 Merchants and are required to have quarterly internal and external scans. Level 1 Merchants also are required to have independent validation of compliance whereby a Qualified Security Assessor (QSA) reviews controls with the organization and delivers a Report of Compliance (ROC). Other merchants, depending on the acquirer's requirements, may simply be required to fill out a much shorter self-evaluation, called a Self-Assessment Questionnaire (SAQ). The Merchant Level equates to the amount of risk the merchant is to the loss of cardholder information. The merchant's acquirer has the authority to determine the Merchant Level for the merchant independent of the rules set forth by the PCI Council.

To facilitate the program, Visa and other card issuers have published lists of organizations authorized to conduct validation inspections (audits), as well as conduct incident-response investigations. The publication of the auditing standards, approved service providers, and the various approved auditing organizations has served to raise awareness for information security in the payment-processing industry.

PCI Impact on the Payment Card Industry

Conformance to the PCI data security standard represented by PCI has become a "cost of doing business." To participate in the card payment-processing industry, conformance is not negotiable. The only *enforcement* necessary to ensure adoption of the standard is exclusion from participation in the industry. Visa, MasterCard, and other card issuers have "decertified" service providers for nonconformance with the standard. The most notable of these events have occurred after disclosure of security breaches, resulting in loss of cardholder private data.

From a data security standpoint, the PCI standard represents commonly accepted data security standards and practices. There is nothing extraordinary in the standard. It is a set of standard best practices already well accepted in the IT security field. Although the PCI standard represents basic security practices, the imposition of the PCI standard on the card payment-processing industry has had a dramatic impact on the technical infrastructure of the industry.

PCI has changed the focus of every software developer of card payment-processing software in any form to shift from adding feature functionality and reducing cost to restructuring their software to accommodate the standard. The impact has been felt across the spectrum of commercial software and system providers to individual retailers who develop and maintain their own systems. Similar to the general impact of SOX, the PCI standard has added vocabulary regarding standards, controls, and audits to an entire industry from smallest to largest and across the spectrum of industries.

A specialized cottage industry has arisen from the introduction of the standard around evaluating conformance to the PCI standard, testing for conformance, and training companies on how to assess and comply with the standard. Although the standard does not represent cutting-edge security technology, the introduction and enforced compliance with the standard changed the entire card payment-processing industry in less than four years.

Other Regulatory Trends

As computers proliferated in the heyday of the 1980s and 1990s, internal controls over IT failed to keep pace with the rapidly changing infrastructure architectures. However, the crackdown on internal controls initiated over financial reporting has expanded to include IT, and rightfully so.

Now, in addition to SOX, GLBA, California SB 1386, HIPAA, and other regulations, further requirements are coming. With identity theft nearing crisis proportions, data protection and privacy are very pressing topics for legislators.

The increased regulatory requirements are raising awareness among senior corporate management. Information security is gaining increasingly serious visibility. Most companies are now realizing that they previously had little understanding of their exposures and are admitting that they need to make a conscious effort to identify their risks and take increasingly definitive measures to address them.

References

- Auditing Standard No. 2: "An Audit of Internal Control Over Financial Reporting Performed in Conjunction with an Audit of Financial Statements" (effective June 17, 2004), www.pcaobus.org.
- California State Senate, http://info.sen.ca.gov/pub/01-02/bill/sen/ sb_1351-1400/ sb_1386_bill_20020926_chaptered.html.
- cisp_PCI_Data_Security_Standard.pdf.
- Federal Reserve Board, *Basel II Capital Accord*, www.federalreserve.gov/ generalinfo/ basel2.
- Federal Trade Commission, www.ftc.gov/privacy/privacyinitiatives/glbact.html.
- *FFIEC Information Technology Handbook*, www.ffiec.gov.
- Ford, Paul. "Sarbanes-Oxley and the Global Capital Market," Simpson Thacher & Bartlett: New York, 2004.
- "Implications of Proposed Auditing Standard on Internal Control," KPMG's Defining Issues, KPMG, No. 03-22, October 2003, http://www.us.kpmg.com/ RutUS_prod/Documents/12/1921810Alert0322.pdf.
- "Implications of Sarbanes-Oxley on IT Departments," Seminar and Panel Discussion, Baylor University, Waco, TX: April 15, 2004.
- International Accounting Standards Board, www.iasb.org.
- International Organization for Standardization. *ISO—Overview*, February 2004, www.iso.org.
- IT Governance Institute, *CoBIT*, Committee of Sponsoring Organizations of the Treadway Commission (COSO), Rolling Meadows, IL, July 2000, www.coso.org.
- IT Governance Institute, *IT Control Objectives for Sarbanes-Oxley: The Importance of IT in the Design, Implementation and Sustainability of Internal Control Over Disclosure and Financial Reporting*, Rolling Meadows, IL, 2004, www.isaca.org.
- Karol, Thomas. "A Guide to Cross-Border Privacy Impact Assessments," Feb 2010, http://www.isaca.org/Knowledge-Center/Research/ResearchDeliverables/ Pages/A-Guide-To-Cross-Border-Privacy-Impact-Assessments.aspx.
- McDowall, Bob. "U.S. Approach to Corporate Governance Looks Set to be Introduced in Europe," www.it-analysis.com.

- Mishkin, Frederic S. "Evaluating FDICIA," Federal Reserve Bank of New York, Graduate School of Business, Columbia University, and National Bureau of Economic Research, December 1996, www0.gsb.columbia.edu/faculty/ fmishkin/ PDFpapers/FDICIA96.pdf.

- Office of the Privacy Commissioner of Canada. *Personal Information Protection and Electronic Payment Card Industry Data Security Standard*, Version 1.0, December 15, 2004. Visa U.S.A., Inc., usa.visa.com/download/business/ accepting_visa/ops_ risk_management/

- Protiviti, Inc. *Guide to the Sarbanes-Oxley Act: It Risks and Controls—Frequently Asked Questions*, December 2003.

- Public Company Accounting Oversight Board, "An Audit of Internal Control Over Financial Reporting Performed in Conjunction with an Audit of Financial Statements," Final Auditing Standard, Release No. 2004-001, March 9, 2004.

- Sarbanes-Oxley Act 2002, U.S. Securities and Exchange Commission (effective July 30, 2002), www.sec.gov/about/laws/soa2002.pdf.

- "Sarbanes-Oxley: A Focus on IT Controls," ISACA SOX-IT Symposium, Chicago, IL, April 7, 2004.

- "Sarbanes-Oxley Financial Rules Will Challenge IS Organizations," Gartner FirstTake, Gartner Research, May 30, 2003.

- "Sarbanes-Oxley Section 404 Compliance for Information Technology Managers," Auditnet.org.

- "SEC Extends Sarbanes-Oxley Section 404 Deadlines," *E-Compliance Advisor*, March 12, 2004, www.advisor.com.

- "Section 302 Corporate Responsibility for Financial Reports," RSM McGadrey, 2003, www.rsmmcgladrey.com.

- "Section 906—Corporate Responsibility for Financial Reports," University of Cincinnati College of Law, 2002.

- "The Clock Ticks on Sarbanes-Oxley Section 404," *Financial Executives International*, May 15, 2004, www.fei.org.

- Trainor, Ed. "Do the Right Thing! Making Sense of Sarbanes-Oxley," SIM publication, 2003.

- U.S. Department of Health & Human Services, Office of Civil Rights, HIPAA, www.hhs.gov/ocr/hipaa/privacy.html.

- Van Ecke, Patrick, "EMC Centera—Corporate Governance in the European Union: Enhancing Credibility," Belgium, April 2005, www.bitpipe.com/detail/ RES/1118421898_858.html.

CHAPTER 18

Risk Management

Only a few years ago, firewalls and antivirus software were all that most organizations used to mitigate IT risk. In recent years, however, the threat landscape has changed considerably. Today, the insider threat is more pronounced, thousands of variants of malware are being distributed, and governments have enacted legislation requiring the implementation of myriad controls. As a result, a formal risk management process now should be a part of every IT audit program.

Today's million dollar question is this: What is a formal risk management program? In this chapter we'll explore the risk-analysis process, risk management life cycle, and methods for identifying and addressing risk effectively. At the end of this chapter is a summary of the formulas we use in the text.

Benefits of Risk Management

No doubt the potential of IT risk management is still a well-kept secret. Over the past few years, many organizations have increased the effectiveness of their IT controls or reduced their cost by employing sound risk-analysis and risk management practices. When management has a representative view of organizational IT exposures, it can direct appropriate resources to mitigate the areas of highest risk rather than spending scarce resources in areas that provide little or no return on investment (ROI). The net result is a higher degree of risk reduction for every dollar spent.

Risk Management from an Executive Perspective

The truth is, business is all about risk and reward. Executives are required to weigh the benefits of investments with the risks associated with them. As a result, most have become quite adept at measuring risk through ROI analyses, key performance indicators, and myriad other financial and operational analysis tools. To be successful in managing organizational IT risk, you should understand that executives view risk in financial terms. As a result, some kind of financial analysis is normally required to make a business case for an investment in additional controls.

Addressing Risk

Risk can be addressed in three ways: accept it, mitigate it, or transfer it. The appropriate method entirely depends on the financial value of the risk versus the investment required to reduce it to an acceptable level or transfer it to a third party. In addition to prescriptive controls, regulations such as HIPAA/HITECH and PCI require that organizations assess risk to protected information and implement reasonable controls to reduce risk to an acceptable level.

Risk Acceptance

The financial value of a risk is often smaller than the cost of mitigating or transferring it. In this case, the most reasonable option is to accept the risk. However, if the organization opts to accept a risk, it should demonstrate that risk was indeed assessed and document the rationale behind the decision.

Risk Mitigation

When a risk has a significant financial value, it is often more appropriate to mitigate the risk rather than accept it. With few exceptions, the cost of implementing and maintaining a control should be less than the monetary value of the risk being mitigated. We demonstrate how to assign monetary value to risk later in this chapter.

Risk Transfer

The insurance industry is based on risk transference. Organizations often buy insurance to cover the costs of a security breach or catastrophic system outage. It is important to note that insurance companies offering these types of policies often require that policy holders implement certain controls. Failure to comply with the control requirements may nullify the policy.

When the management of IT systems is outsourced to a third party, a certain level of risk may be contractually transferred to the third party as well. In these cases, it is the responsibility of the organization outsourcing its systems to verify that IT risk is reduced to an acceptable level and that the company managing its systems has the financial strength to cover a loss should it occur. See Chapter 14 for information on auditing outsourced operations.

Quantitative vs. Qualitative Risk Analysis

Risk can be analyzed in two ways: quantitatively and qualitatively. Like anything else, each has advantages and disadvantages. Where the quantitative approach is more objective and expresses risk in financial terms that decision-makers can more easily justify, it is also more time-consuming. The qualitative approach is better suited to present a stratified view of risk, but it can be more subjective and therefore difficult to substantiate. The organizations with more successful risk management programs tend to rely more heavily on qualitative risk analysis to identify areas of focus and then use quantitative risk analysis techniques to justify risk mitigation expenditures. We will explore each approach later in this chapter.

Quantitative Risk Analysis

With few exceptions, whether related to financial, physical, or technological resources, different types of risk can be calculated using the same universal formula. Risk can be defined by the following calculation:

Risk = asset value × threat × vulnerability

Elements of Risk

As you can see in the preceding equation, risk comprises three elements: *asset value*, *threat*, and *vulnerability*. Estimating these elements correctly is critical to assessing risk accurately.

Assets

Normally represented as a monetary value, *assets* can be defined as anything of worth to an organization that can be damaged, compromised, or destroyed by an accidental or deliberate action. In reality, an asset's worth is rarely the simple cost of replacement; therefore, to get an accurate measure of risk, an asset should be valued taking into account the bottom-line cost of its compromise. For example, a breach of personal information may not cause a monetary loss at first glance, but if it actually were realized, it likely would result in legal action, damage to the company's reputation, and regulatory penalties. These consequences potentially would cause a significant financial loss. In this case, the asset-value portion of the equation would represent the personal information. The calculated value of the personal information would include an estimate of the cumulative dollar cost of the legal action, reputation damage, and regulatory penalties.

Threats

A *threat* can be defined as a potential event that, if realized, would cause an undesirable impact. The undesirable impact can come in many forms, but it often results in a financial loss. Threats are generalized as a percentage, but two factors play into the severity of a threat: degree of loss and likelihood of occurrence. The *exposure factor* is used to represent the degree of loss. It is simply an estimate of the percentage of asset loss if a threat is realized. For example, if we estimate that a fire will cause a 70 percent loss of asset value if it occurs, the exposure factor is 70 percent, or 0.7. The *annual rate of occurrence*, on the other hand, represents the likelihood that a given threat would be realized in a single year in the event of a complete absence of controls. For example, if we estimate that a fire will occur every 3 years, the annual rate of occurrence would be 33 percent, or 0.33. A threat, therefore, can be calculated as a percentage by multiplying the exposure factor by the annual rate of occurrence. Given the preceding example, the threat of fire would result in a value of 23.1 percent, or 0.231.

Vulnerabilities

Vulnerabilities can be defined as the absence or weakness of cumulative controls protecting a particular asset. Vulnerabilities are estimated as percentages based on the level of control weakness. We can calculate control deficiency (CD) by subtracting the effectiveness of the control by 1 or 100 percent. For example, we may determine that our industrial espionage controls are 70 percent effective, so 100 percent – 70 percent = 30 percent (CD). This vulnerability would be represented as 30 percent, or 0.3.

NOTE Usually, more than one control is employed to protect an asset. For example, we may have identified the threat of an employee stealing trade secrets and selling them to the competition. To counter this threat, we implement an information classification policy, employ a data loss prevention technology to monitor outgoing e-mail, and prohibit the use of portable storage devices. When estimating our vulnerability to industrial espionage, we must consider the cumulative effectiveness of each of these controls.

Practical Application

Now that we've defined how to analyze risk, we can begin to put it into practice. Following are a couple of examples of how this equation is relevant in IT as well as other areas.

Physical Risk Scenario

The U.S. government regards a command and control center at a military installation in the Middle East to be critical to its ability to operate in the region. If this facility is destroyed, it likely will cause loss of life (both in the facility and in the field), damage to the facility itself, and a setback to military objectives.

In this example, the asset is the command and control center. The actual value of the command and control center includes the lives of the soldiers who would be affected, the command and control facility itself, and the military objectives that would go unmet in the event of its loss. The experts estimate that the cumulative cost of a loss of the command and control center would be $500 million (not that you can put a dollar figure on a soldier's life). We have identified a threat of a bomb to the facility and estimate that a successful attack would cause an 85 percent loss. The experts say that this type of attempted attack would occur once per week, or 52 times annually, if no controls were in place to prevent it. The command and control center has several safeguards, such as physical barriers, perimeter alarm systems, military police patrols, and 3500 additional soldiers on base protecting it. As a result, we estimate that the controls are 99.99 percent effective, or 0.01 percent deficient. With this information, we can calculate the monetary value of the risk of a command and control center bomb to be $500 million [asset value] × 0.85 loss (EF) × 52 times per year (ARO) [threat] × 0.001 control deficiency (CD) [vulnerability] = $22,100,000 [risk].

To take this exercise a step further, we can justify a total investment of up to $22.1 million to protect the command and control center. The exact amount that we can justify will depend entirely on the dollars already spent to mitigate this risk and the projected level of risk reduction for the selected control. We are aiming for maximum risk mitigation by reducing the vulnerability part of the risk equation. We will get into more detail on choosing controls later in this chapter.

IT Risk Scenario

The IT audit director at a national retailer has determined that the legal climate is changing in relation to the credit card information with which the company is entrusted. Until now, the company had not considered the risk of a disclosure of its customer's personal or credit-card–specific information.

After interviewing public relations, legal, and finance stakeholders, the IT audit director estimates the cost of a single breach to be approximately $30 million in lost revenues, legal costs, and regulatory consequences. So we now know that the asset is personal credit-card and associated financial information. Furthermore, its value to the company is $30 million. Since several breaches that involved hacking have recently been reported in the news, the audit director decides to explore this threat. In a conversation with the information security director, the audit director learns that the company is under constant attack, although most of the attacks are nothing more than probes for vulnerabilities. He estimates that about one actual attack per week occurs and that a compromise of the credit card–processing system would result in a complete asset loss. The information security director estimates that current controls are 99.99 percent effective, but if the company does not invest in additional controls, a successful breach is imminent. Given this information, we can calculate the risk of an external security breach to be $30 million [asset value] × 100 percent loss (EF) × 52 hacking attempts per year (ARO) [threat] × 0.01 percent or 0.0001 control deficiency (CD) [vulnerability] = $156,000 [risk].

Quantitative Risk Analysis in Practice

Okay, we know what you're thinking: "This is all pie in the sky. In the real world, there is barely enough time to perform essential job duties, let alone spend a lot of time calculating risk. Though these calculations are great theory, I don't have the time to apply them for every threat. In fact, who has time to identify every threat?" Well, the truth is that it is impractical to perform these calculations for every threat, although you should do your best to identify all the threats that your organization faces.

If you haven't begun to identify your organization's current threats, it would be worthwhile to do so. From there, identifying new threats can be a daily mental exercise. As business or technology changes, you should be asking, What new threats does this change introduce? If realized, how would these threats affect your business? When you identify significant threats and want to make a business justification for purchasing additional controls, you can use the preceding calculations to support your case.

Common Causes for Inaccuracies

Most risk analyses attempted today result in bottom-line estimates that are way off the mark. Unfortunately, when organizational management loses faith in the risk information that is presented to it, it tends to dismiss a disproportionate number of requests for risk-mitigation investments. Management is interested in investing limited resources in areas that either will make the organization money or will save the organization money. This is why it is so important that you present a solid analysis of risk whenever approaching management for additional resources. Following are the most common causes of risk analysis inaccuracies.

Failure to Identify Assets, Threats, or Vulnerabilities

The most common cause of inaccuracies in the risk analysis process is the failure to identify assets, threats, and vulnerabilities. This is mostly due to the fact that most organizations do not use a formal risk management process and practitioners have not been trained to analyze risk. As we pointed out earlier, it can be especially difficult to identify threats and vulnerabilities because they are dynamic in nature. For example, we know that new variants of viruses, worms, and other forms of malware are introduced daily. Additionally, new computer-related vulnerabilities are discovered almost daily.

Although identifying threats and vulnerabilities can be difficult, you can access some resources for help, such as information security alerts from CERT, Bugtraq, and other free and subscription-based security vulnerability notification services. IT auditors also can examine security incidents when they are publicized to learn how such violations occur. One Internet web resource that consolidates and chronicles information about security incidents is www.privacyrights.org/ar/ChronDataBreaches.htm. We will discuss proven methods for identifying assets, threats, and vulnerabilities later in this chapter.

NOTE   As the workforce becomes more mobile, information can no longer be contained within an organization's protected boundaries. Every year, tens of thousands of laptops containing sensitive information are stolen from airports, coffee shops, and vehicles. In fact, according to the Ponemon Institute, lost or stolen laptops are the cause of roughly 40 percent of the breaches that become public. Though laptop related breaches have been making news on a weekly basis for at least 5 years, many companies still have little or no control over the sensitive information that resides on laptop computers. As you can see, it is important to monitor the headlines to identify emerging threats and monitor trends.

Inaccurate Estimations

Unfortunately, a fair amount of estimation is involved in analyzing risk, which makes it an inexact science. Many errors can be attributed to this fact.

Assets   The traditional approach to risk analysis does not take into account the costs resulting from a compromise outside of the loss to the asset itself. As you saw in the preceding examples, the cost of a compromise rarely stops at the asset book value. Therefore, it is important to include the consequential losses as well as the actual loss in asset value. Consequential losses may include legal costs, regulatory costs, brand damage, remediation costs, or a reduction in productivity. Including these costs will increase the accuracy of your risk assessment.

Threats   Unlike assets or vulnerabilities, the threat is the only element of the risk analysis equation that is always derived from a single value. In the IT risk scenario discussed earlier, the threat involved hacking attempts. Combining the hacking threat with another threat, such as employees abusing access privileges, or stealing and selling credit card information, would cause an inaccurate calculation of risk.

Another common error is failing to estimate and incorporate the exposure factor into the threat value. This error often inflates the risk value. To calculate an accurate threat value, both exposure factor and annual rate of occurrence must be included.

Vulnerabilities As discussed earlier, vulnerability is the absence of or weaknesses in cumulative controls. Therefore, to identify a vulnerability, we must understand the strength of the controls. Risk analysis errors are often made because the strengths of controls are not evaluated properly or compensating controls are not taken into account.

Qualitative Risk Analysis

Unlike the quantitative approach to risk analysis, qualitative risk analysis techniques can provide a high-level view into enterprise risk. Where quantitative methods focus on formulas, a qualitative risk analysis will focus on values such as high, medium, and low or colors such as red, yellow, and green to evaluate the risk.

As mentioned earlier in the chapter, qualitative and quantitative approaches complement one another. Most organizations base their risk management methodologies on the qualitative method, using quantitative formulas to build business cases for risk mitigation investments. We will spend the rest of the chapter on qualitative risk analysis.

IT Risk Management Life Cycle

As with most methodologies, risk management, when applied properly, takes on the characteristics of a life cycle (Figure 18-1). It can be divided into several phases, beginning with identification of information assets and culminating with management of residual risk. The specific phases are as follows:

- **Phase 1** Identify information assets.
- **Phase 2** Quantify and qualify threats.
- **Phase 3** Assess vulnerabilities.
- **Phase 4** Remediate control gaps.
- **Phase 5** Manage residual risk.

Figure 18-1
Risk management
life cycle

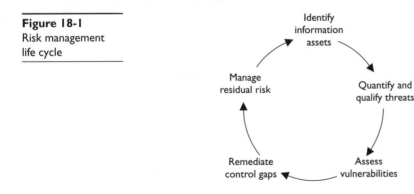

Phase 1: Identify Information Assets

The first phase in the risk management life cycle is to identify the organization's information assets. To be successful, you must complete several tasks:

- Define information criticality values.
- Identify business functions.
- Map information processes.
- Identify information assets.
- Assign criticality values to information assets.

The goal of this phase is to identify all information assets and assign each information asset a criticality value of high, medium, or low for its confidentiality, integrity, and availability requirements. For example, we may identify credit card information as an information asset that is processed by our retail system. This information asset is governed by the Payment Card Industry (PCI) data security standard and is valuable to thieves if disclosed in an unauthorized manner. We also know that if altered, this information is useless to us, but that in most cases a temporary loss of access to this information is tolerable. As a result, we would assign credit card information values of high for both confidentiality and integrity and medium for availability.

The best way to identify information assets is to take a top-down approach beginning with organization functions, identifying the processes that support those business functions, and drilling down to the information assets that are processed by the systems that support each business function. Figure 18-2 represents this approach to information asset identification using business function decomposition.

Defining Information Criticality Values

Before we begin to identify information assets, shouldn't we know what information criticality values of high, medium, and low mean to our business? This is why the first

Figure 18-2
Business function
decomposition

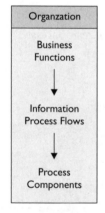

step in the process is to define each value in terms of how severe the impact would be in the event of a breach of an asset with a given value. For example, we may define the high value to mean a potential monetary loss of $500,000 or more in the event of a security violation. This definition would be consistent with the confidentiality, integrity, and availability of any information asset we identify.

To be successful, we need to gain consensus from major organizational stakeholders regarding the definitions and to document those definitions. If a criticality value of high means something different to the CEO, CFO, and vice president of operations, we will want to gain a level set with these individuals to obtain their buy-in on a single definition. We will certainly need this later in the process.

Identifying Business Functions

One of the most difficult aspects of risk management is identifying where information assets reside and then which assets are most critical to the business. Fortunately, most businesses are organized by function. As a result, critical business functions can be identified using the organization chart. Of course, it is still necessary to verify that all the business functions are represented accurately.

Once the business functions are identified, we can assign criticality values to each. For example, we may determine that the retail operations business function requires a high level of confidentiality because of use of credit card information. It may require a high degree of information integrity because transactions are financial in nature, and a medium degree of information availability because a short delay in processing transactions would have only a moderate impact on the organization.

Mapping Information Processes

Since the nature of IT is to process information, IT risk (as opposed to other types of risk) has the added complexity of touching several points in a process. Identifying these process flows is absolutely critical for a few reasons:

- It helps us identify which information assets are used by each process.

- It helps us identity process points (steps) that require manual input (which tend to be more vulnerable than fully automated processes).

- It helps us understand which information systems need protection.

Once we have identified our organization's critical business functions, we can begin to identify the processes that support those business functions and the information assets that flow though the processes. It is important to note that we are not concerned with the technology used to process the information at this point but rather with the process flow itself.

We had identified the retail operations business function earlier. We know that the retail operations business function is responsible for processing credit card transactions that feed the company's cash flow and are regulated by PCI. Thus, we can identify credit card processing as a critical process. From here we will need to determine the

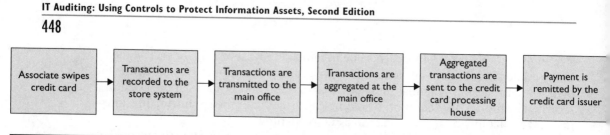

Figure 18-3   Credit card process diagram

steps or systems (process points) that are included in the process. For our example, we may determine that credit cards are processed in the following manner (Figure 18-3):

1. Associate swipes a credit card during a retail sale.

2. Transactions are aggregated to a system within each retail store.

3. Aggregated transactions are transmitted to the main office during the night over the Internet via site-to-site virtual private networks (VPNs).

4. Store transactions are aggregated with transactions from all the other stores into a central database.

5. The transactions from all of the stores are sent to the credit card processing house over a dedicated telecom data link in a batch file the following day.

6. The credit card processing house deposits funds into a corporate bank account 2 days later.

Assigning Information Criticality Values to Information Assets

Once we have mapped out the information process, we can identify the information asset(s) and assign them criticality values. When reviewing a process, we need to consider all the potential assets that traverse the process. For example, it is obvious that credit card data is an information asset, but we may also want to consider system management or monitoring information used for the systems that aggregate the credit card transactions in the preceding illustration. These types of information assets are often overlooked but can be critical.

When assigning criticality values, we need to consider the asset's requirements for confidentiality, integrity, and availability. This relationship is represented well using the information criticality matrix originally developed by the National Security Agency for the NSA INFOSEC Assessment Methodology. An example of this matrix is provided in Table 18-1.

Information Asset	Confidentiality	Integrity	Availability
Credit card data	H	H	M
System configurations	M	H	M
System monitoring information	L	H	H

Table 18-1   Information Criticality Matrix

Phase 2: Quantify and Qualify Threats

Information threats impact organizations through diminished brand loyalty, lost resources, recovery costs, and legal and regulatory actions. When threats are realized, these costs are often unaccounted for because they are not identified properly. For example, let's say that our organization is attacked by a malicious worm that causes a temporary loss of processing capacity and several hundred hours of recovery time. The cost may be calculated by quantifying the hours required for recovery and estimating the losses associated with the processing delays. However, other considerations must be weighed as well: Has the company's reputation been adversely affected because it was not able to service customers? Were there any lost sales? Were some employees unable to work? What is the organization's legal exposure due to the security breach? As you can see, identifying all the areas within an organization that may be affected requires a fair amount of thought. Therefore, we will help break down the process of analyzing of these threats.

The next step in the risk management life cycle is to quantify and qualify threats (Figure 18-4). We'll also take a top-down approach as we identify threats, starting with business threats and moving on to technical threats that may give rise to the identified business threats. We'll explain this in more detail later.

This phase of the risk management life cycle requires the following steps:

- Assess business threats.
- Identify technical, physical, and administrative threats.
- Quantify threat impact and probability.
- Evaluate process flows for weaknesses.
- Identify process-component threats.

NOTE To identify threats to our information effectively, we need to complete the first phase of the risk management process: identifying information assets. Properly identified threats are associated with an information asset or a group of information assets. Threats associated with systems flow through to the information assets that they process.

Assessing Business Threats

Threats can be accounted for in several ways, but at a high level, business threats to information can be divided into three categories: financial threats, legal threats, and regulatory threats. All business threats will fall into one of these categories.

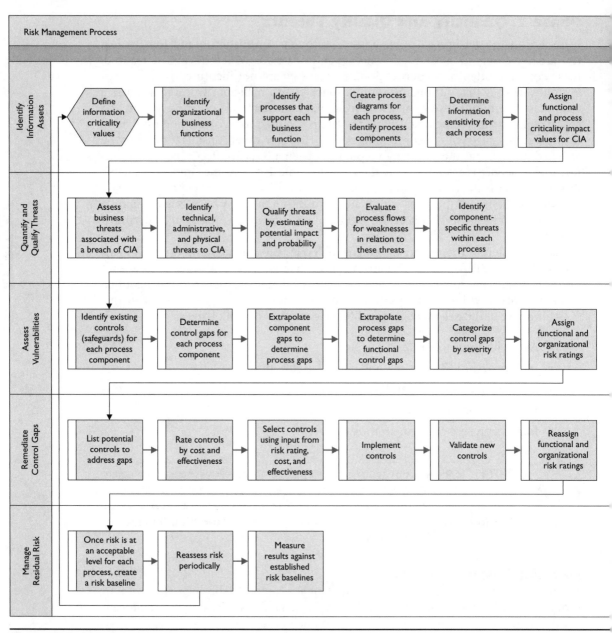

Figure 18-4 Risk management process

Financial Threats   One could argue that all information threats are financial in nature because they all boil down to a monetary loss, if realized. Although this may be true, we also define regulatory and legal threats because of their prevalence. For our purposes, a financial threat is defined as a threat that, if realized, would cause a loss of actual funds, reputation, operational effectiveness, or competitive advantage, ultimately resulting in a monetary impact. Financial threats may include the following:

- Financial fraud
- Loss of proprietary information
- Loss of productivity

Once the information assets are identified, these types of threats become more evident. For example, the credit card information asset we identified earlier has exposure to all three of these threats. The next question becomes, If realized, how would the threat affect operational effectiveness, company reputation, competitive advantage, or the company's cash position?

Legal Threats   After we've identified some of the financial threats, we must consider the potential legal exposure associated with realization of a threat. Given current privacy laws, if an individual's private information such as his or her name and associated address, Social Security number, health information, or credit information is disclosed in an unauthorized manner, you can bet that some legal exposure will result. Additionally, if service levels are affected or another organization's confidential information is disclosed, a breach of contract could occur. Needless to say, legal fees can be very expensive, even if a court finds in your organization's favor.

To get an accurate business threat assessment, we need to identify potential legal exposure in the event of an information security violation.

Regulatory Threats   Along with financial and legal threats, it is important to consider regulatory threats. A regulatory infraction resulting from an information security incident could lead to fines or other penalties (including imprisonment of company officers), as well as temporary or permanent suspension of company operations. Financial institutions generally take the laws governing their operation very seriously because of the severe consequences of noncompliance, but health care entities, merchants, and public companies are also heavily regulated.

The key to identifying regulatory threats is understanding the laws or mandatory industry standards governing the information your organization is processing. Given our earlier example, we know that the PCI data security standard will govern the protection of the credit card information our organization processes. See Chapter 17 for additional information regarding regulations affecting U.S. companies.

PART III

Identifying Technical, Physical, and Administrative Threats

Once all the business threats pertaining to our information assets are identified, we can begin identifying the technical, physical, and administrative threats. These threats, if realized, will give rise to one of the business threats that we have identified. For example, a system malfunction will give rise to a loss of organizational productivity.

Technical Threats   Technical threats are generally system related, affecting electronically stored or transmitted information. Given our previous credit card processing example, one technical threat would be system intrusion. This threat then could give rise to the theft of proprietary information, regulatory or legal business threats. Here are some examples of technical threats:

- System intrusion
- Worms, viruses, spyware, and other malware
- System failure
- Logical access control failure

Physical Threats   Physical threats are normally facility related and often can be tied to natural events or mechanical breakdowns. Here are some examples of physical threats:

- Natural or man-made disasters
- Physical intrusion
- Fire
- Water seepage from burst pipes or weather-related flooding
- Excessive heat or humidity
- Electrical disruptions or black-outs

Although physical in nature, these threats can cause significant information loss. Business continuity/disaster recovery plans and data center controls aim to address these threats. See Chapter 4 for information on auditing data centers and business continuity plans.

Administrative Threats   It is common knowledge in information security circles that the "human factor" is the cause of most security violations. Administrative threats are people related. They may include the following:

- Unintentional disclosure of sensitive information
- Social engineering
- Information theft
- Industrial espionage
- Malicious destruction of information
- Accidental deletion or corruption of information

- System configuration errors
- Inappropriate use of computing resources (such as pornography in the office)

Administrative threats are often overlooked because they tend to be more nebulous and imply an inherent mistrust of employees. Nonetheless, people within an organization introduce quite a few threats to information assets.

NOTE The Great Wall of China was built to defend China from northern armies, but what many people don't realize is that it was rendered useless by a trusting Chinese general who allowed the Manchu army through the gate at the Shanghai Pass. Once China was conquered, the wall was of little strategic value because Manchu-controlled lands extended far north of the wall. Similarly, a single employee could introduce a world of peril to your organization.

Evaluating Process Flows

Now that we understand our business and high-level technical threats, we can examine the processes that we mapped out when we identified our information assets. We will review the process as a whole for weaknesses. For example, processes that are manual in nature are more susceptible to vulnerabilities than highly automated processes. In fact, we can look for several things that might indicate a need for increased controls, such as the following:

- Manual inputs and outputs
- Data transmission over untrusted networks
- Interfaces between applications
- External data inputs and outputs (including cloud providers)
- Nonsegregated data stores

With the increase in utility computing in recent years, information flows have become more decentralized. This obviously increases risk because of the necessity to trust cloud providers with sensitive information that would have remained within the boundaries of internal networks just a few years ago. See Chapter 14 for more information on auditing cloud computing environments.

Identifying Process Component Threats

Since we have now mapped our process flows and examined them for obvious weaknesses, we can analyze the threats to different process components such as systems, manual inputs, or outputs. Refer to Figure 18-3, which outlined the six steps in a credit card payment process.

Our goal is to identify the threats associated with each step in the process. For example, when an employee swipes a card (step 1), we might identify a threat of employees keeping credit cards or credit card numbers of store customers. Or we might identify a risk of system failure or system intrusion when transactions are aggregated to a system within each retail store (step 2). We should be able to identify several threats for each process component. When combined, they represent all the threats associated with the processing of an information asset.

Quantifying Threats

After we've identified our threats, we need to understand their potential impact and the probability that they will occur if not mitigated. As we discussed in the "Quantitative Risk Analysis" section earlier, two factors play into estimating the severity of a threat:

- Degree of asset loss
- Likelihood of occurrence

We can use the exposure factor (EF) to represent the degree of loss and the annual rate of occurrence (ARO) to represent the likelihood of an occurrence. A threat then can be quantified by multiplying EF × ARO. If we look at our credit card processing example, we may estimate that a hard disk failure would cause the loss of one day's worth of a store's sales and would fail in the store-side systems once every 2 years. We would calculate the threat by multiplying 1/365 (0.00274) × 0.5. The result would be approximately 0.00137. We then would multiply this by each store's annual sales to quantify the threat.

Phase 3: Assess Vulnerabilities

We now have identified our information assets and the threats to each asset. In this phase, we will assess vulnerabilities. In examining threats, the common denominator is the information asset, because each threat is tied to an information asset. When assessing vulnerabilities, on the other hand, the common denominator is the information process. We will first identify process-component vulnerabilities and then combine them to determine our process vulnerabilities. Process vulnerabilities then will be combined to determine business function vulnerabilities.

Instead of working from the top down (from business function to process component), we will work from the bottom up in assessing vulnerabilities. We will use the following steps in analyzing vulnerabilities:

1. Identify existing controls in relation to threats.
2. Determine process component control gaps.
3. Combine control gaps into processes and then business functions.
4. Categorize control gaps by severity.
5. Assign risk ratings.

NOTE Prior to World War II, France recognized Germany, its neighbor to the east, as a growing threat. Therefore, the French government built a line of walls, tank defenses, and bunkers called the *Maginot Line* to defend against invasion. French military leadership decided to end the wall on the north side at the Ardennes Forest, which was believed to be impassable as a result of its dense nature. When the Germans invaded in 1940, they bypassed the Maginot Line fortifications in favor of the dense forest. History shows that the French certainly understood the threat but miscalculated their vulnerabilities. In the same way, it is critical that you not only understand the threats to your information assets but also that you accurately assess the related vulnerabilities.

Identifying Existing Controls

The initial step in examining vulnerabilities is to review threats and inventory existing controls that mitigate each threat. In our credit card–processing example, we identified the threat of a hard disk failure. We also may determine that systems back up disk information each night and a RAID level 5 disk array provides hard disk redundancy.

To get an accurate understanding of an organization's risk, we need to identify all the controls that have been applied. Like threats, controls can be technical, physical, or administrative in nature. Table 18-2 provides a partial list of each type of control.

Determining Process Component Control Gaps

Now that we've identified the existing controls that have been employed, we can begin to see areas where controls are ineffective or simply do not exist. In the preceding example, we identified two controls that are mitigating the threat of a hard disk failure:

Types of Control	Examples
Technical	Access control systems, two-factor authentication, firewalls, encryption systems, uninterruptible power supplies, intrusion prevention systems, endpoint protection software, redundant systems or system components, backup systems, audit and logging systems, system hardening
Physical	Security guards, key-card physical access systems, alarm systems, safes, fire suppression systems, HVAC systems, fences, lighting, security cameras
Administrative	Acceptable-use policy, business continuity plan, password policy, incident response plan, system baseline configurations, remote access policy, file recovery procedures, information classification, information security training and awareness, audits, assessments

Table 18-2 Types of Controls

PART III

nightly backups and RAID level 5 disk redundancy. Each store closes at 9:00 P.M., and the store-side system transmits the transactions beginning at midnight. A full system backup occurs at 3:00 A.M. at the main office. A system failure any time during the day would result in loss of the entire day's transactions. The system backup strategy therefore is not as effective as the RAID level 5 disk array that provides real-time redundancy. In this step, it is important not only that we identify control gaps, but we must also measure the effectiveness of existing controls.

Combining Control Gaps

After we've identified all the control gaps for process components, we can combine them to begin to see a risk posture for the information process. We can then combine the processes supporting each business function to begin to see the risk posture for each of the business functions. The combined business function risk postures give us the organizational risk posture.

Categorizing Control Gaps by Severity

With a good view of organizational risk, we'll notice that some of the underlying risks naturally will begin to emerge as more critical than others, because they affect valuable information assets or are unmitigated. At this point, we should be able to assign business functions, information processes, and process components qualitative risk ratings of high, medium, or low. We will want to focus our attention on the risks to which we assigned high risk ratings. The more severe risks can be analyzed further to determine their quantitative value to justify additional investments in controls.

Phase 4: Remediate Control Gaps

At this point, our risks should be categorized as high, medium, or low. Initially, we will focus on mitigating the most severe risks, because we will most likely see the highest return on our investment. In essence, we can mitigate more risk with less money. We will use the following steps in control gap remediation:

1. Choose controls.
2. Implement controls.
3. Validate new controls.
4. Recalculate risk ratings.

Choosing Controls

Too often, organizations implement controls because of their use of advanced technologies or a slick interface. More often than not, the controls that mitigate the most risk do not fit into either of these categories. Choosing controls should be purely a business decision that takes into account the level of risk to be mitigated, the cost, and the ease of use of the controls.

Identifying Potential Controls   Most risks can be mitigated in several ways. The methods used will range from very inexpensive to prohibitively expensive and can be technical, physical, or administrative in nature. Organizations often overlook administrative controls such as security policy, security awareness training, and agreements. These controls, when implemented properly, can be extremely effective and affordable.

Rating Controls by Cost and Effectiveness   After controls are identified, they can be compared in three ways: cost, effectiveness, and ease of use. The cost of a control is very quantifiable and often is the only attribute considered. In choosing controls properly, however, you need to consider the effectiveness of the control. For example, to mitigate the threat of network intrusion, an organization upgrades its existing firewall to a $100,000 firewall appliance that has advanced network inspection technologies. However, since the existing firewall mitigates all but a fraction of the risk, was this the best use of company funds? Equally important is a control's ease of use. Many organizations purchased intrusion detection systems in the late 1990s and early 2000s only to find out that they require a high degree technical of expertise and a large amount of analysis time to operate properly.

One method of choosing controls is to list them in a spreadsheet and rate each of the three attributes in separate columns on a scale of 1 to 10. The attributes can even be weighted to provide more granularity. This tool that can be used to make more informed decisions.

Implementing Controls

After we've selected our controls, we must implement them properly. When companies are subjects of IT audits or assessments, most findings are related to misconfigurations or improperly implemented controls, not the absence of controls. Therefore, it is important that we implement new controls properly.

Validating New Controls

To take it one step further, new controls should be tested by an organization's IT audit department to validate their effectiveness. This will provide assurances to management that its investment was justified. The results of this audit or assessment will also feed calculation of the organization's new risk posture.

Recalculating Risk Ratings

If we've done our job correctly, our overall organizational risk and business function risk should now be reduced from its original level. The information process where we implemented the controls will also be affected. Therefore, it is necessary that we recalculate risk in these areas to reflect the addition of the new controls. Our risk ratings will be based on the *residual risk*, which is the risk that remains after mitigation. Instead of having a high risk rating, our process may be assigned a medium or low risk rating.

Phase 5: Manage Residual Risk

Risk is inherently dynamic in nature, especially the threat component of risk. As a result, we will need to measure risk continually and invest in new controls to respond to emerging threats. This phase comprises two steps:

1. Create a risk baseline
2. Reassess risk

Creating a Risk Baseline

Since we now have the recalculated risk ratings, we can aggregate them to create a risk baseline. We will use this baseline to measure changes in our risk posture and identify trends as we cycle through the risk management process in the future. The risk baseline should include overall organizational, business function and process risk ratings, as well as narratives describing the reasoning used in the decision to implement controls or accept risk.

Reassessing Risk

After the process is complete, we will need to plan on reassessing risk periodically. Because of the ever-changing nature of IT, organizations should complete the risk management life cycle at least once per year. Risk assessments, however, should be triggered by certain events, such as the following:

- Corporate mergers or acquisitions
- New system installations
- Business-function changes
- The enactment of new laws or regulations that mandate the addition of new controls (or require risk analysis)

Summary of Formulas

Use	Description	Formula
Definition of risk	Used to represent risk	Risk = asset value × threat × vulnerability
Threat calculation	Numeric representation of threat	Threat = exposure factor (EF) × annual rate of occurrence (ARO)
Vulnerability calculation	Measures control deficiency	Control deficiency (CD) = 1 − control effectiveness
Risk calculation	Used to quantify risk	Risk = asset value × EF × ARO × CD

INDEX

Stop Hackers in Their Tracks